MARXISM AND DEMOCRACY IN CHILE

MARXISM AND DEMOCRACY IN CHILE

FROM 1932 TO THE FALL OF ALLENDE

Julio Faúndez

1988
YALE UNIVERSITY PRESS
NEW HAVEN & LONDON

To my parents, with affection and gratitude

Set in Linotron Plantin by Best-set Typesetter Ltd., and printed in Great Britain at The Bath Press, Avon

LIBRARY OF CONGRESS
Library of Congress Cataloging-in-Publication Data

Faúndez, Julio.
    Marxism and Democracy in Chile: from 1932 to the fall of Allende./Julio Faúndez.
        p.   cm.
    Bibliography: p.
    Includes index.
    ISBN 0-300-04024-5
    1. Socialism – Chile – History – 20th century.   2. Chile – Politics and government –
1920–1970.   3. Chile – Politics and government – 1970–1973.   I. Title.
HX198.F38   1988
324.283'07'09 – dc 19   88–9646

Printed in Great Britain

Contents

List of Acronyms and Abbreviations

ACHA	Asociación Chilena Anticomunista/Chilean Anti-Communist Association
API	Acción Popular Independiente/Independent Popular Action Party
BIH	Basic Irrigated Hectare/Hectaria de Riego Básico
CDP	Christian Democratic Party/Partido Demócrata Cristiano
CERAS	Centros de la Reforma Agraria/Centres of Agrarian Reform
CIF	Cost Insurance and Freight
CODE	Confederación Democrática/Democratic Confederation
CORFO	Corporación de Fomento de la Producción/State Development Corporation
CPSU	Communist Party of the Soviet Union
CRAC	Confederación Republicana de Acción Civica/Republican Confederation for Civic Action
CTCH	Confederación de Trabajadores de Chile/Chilean Workers' Confederation
CUT	Central Unica de Trabajadores/United Workers' Federation
ECLA	[United Nations] Economic Commission for Latin America
Exim-Bank	[United States] Export-Import Bank
FEUC	Federación de Estudiantes de la Universidad Católica/Catholic University Students' Union
FOCH	Federación Obrera de Chile/Chilean Workers' Federation

FRAP	Frente de Acción Popular/Popular Action Front
IC	Izquierda Cristiana/Christian Left
ITT	International Telephone and Telegraph Corporation
IWW	International Workers of the World (Wobblies)
JAPs	Juntas de Abastecimientos y Precios/Supply and Prices Committees
MAPU	Movimiento de Acción Popular Unitaria/Movement of United Popular Action
MIR	Movimiento de Izquierda Revolucionaria/Left Revolutionary Movement
MNS	Movimiento Nacional Socialista/National Socialist Movement
OLAS	Organización Latinoamericana de Solidaridad/Latin-American Solidarity Organisation
PAL	Partido Agrario Laborista/Agrarian Labour Party
PIR	Partido de Izquierda Radical/Left Radical Party
PL	Patria y Libertad/Fatherland and Freedom
POS	Partido Obrero Socialista/Socialist Workers' Party
PSA	Partido Socialista Auténtico/Authentic Socialist Party
PSP	Partido Socialista Popular/Popular Socialist Party
SDG	Statute of Democratic Guarantees/Estatuto de Garantías Democráticas
SNA	Sociedad Nacional de Agricultura/National Agricultural Society
SOFOFA	Sociedad de Fomento Fabril/Industrial Development Society
SWP	Socialist Workers' Party/Partido Socialista de Trabajadores
USRACH	Unión Social Republicana de Asalariados de Chile/Social Union of Chilean Wage Earners

Acknowledgements

I am grateful to my colleagues at the School of Law, Warwick University, for allowing me time off from my teaching on two occasions to write this book. I owe a special debt to my wife, Anne Faúndez, who without the least trace of impatience read all the earlier drafts of this work. Without her critical comments, professional editorial assistance and general support I would not have completed this project. Alan Angell's gentle encouragement and passionate interest in the topic were a permanent source of strength. He read an earlier draft of this book, and his criticism and suggestions greatly assisted me in preparing the final version. My colleague Sol Picciotto generously took time off from his own research to read the whole manuscript. His penetrating criticism helped me clarify the argument on several crucial points. Several friends and colleagues have, in different ways, helped me during the course of writing this book. I am especially grateful to Caroline Hansen, Ernesto Illanes, Emilio Klein, Jorge Larraín, Sergio Muñoz, Richard Parker, Alan Sorvall, Mario Valenzuela and Ricardo Yocelevsky.

Jolyon Hall and Sue Wallington from the University of Warwick Library made available an exceptionally large number of books and articles on Chile. Ruth Hodges, the librarian at Oxford University's Latin American Centre, was also very helpful. Patricia Bruzzone, senior librarian at the Biblioteca del Congreso in Santiago, helped me locate obscure official publications. Alan Crawford made many stylistic suggestions which have greatly improved the text. Philippa Ross-White and June Green typed several versions of this book with speed and accuracy. I am grateful to them.

I am pleased to acknowledge the generous financial assistance which I have received throughout my research. A grant from the Joint Committee on Latin American Studies of the American Council of Learned Societies and the Social Research Council enabled me, several years ago, to begin work on this topic. An award from the Economic and Social Research Council (ESRC) allowed me to complete my research. The Legal Research Institute of the University of Warwick helped me finance a research trip to Chile and several visits to the newspaper section of the British Library.

Unless otherwise indicated, all information on electoral results is taken from Bernardino Bravo, *Régimen de Gobierno y Partidos Políticos en Chile 1924–1973* (Santiago, 1978), pp. 199–204.

THE SETTING

CHAPTER 1

Introduction

THE participation of marxists in the political process of capitalist democracies is an issue which, for a long time, has been debated by intellectuals and politicians from all sides of the political spectrum. Among marxists the debate has focused mainly on the relationship between the ultimate goal of overthrowing capitalism and the political forms of the capitalist state. Those who see an inseparable link between the economic and political structures of capitalism generally argue that participation in democratic politics is a useful, but limited, tactical device since, ultimately, capitalist democracy will not help conquer state power nor will it be of any use in the building of a socialist society. This view is rejected by some marxists – notably, the ideologues of Eurocommunism – who believe that participation in democratic politics is of fundamental strategic importance since, in their view, the transition to socialism can in fact take place without the prevailing system of political democracy being destroyed. Among non-marxists, the issue elicits two kinds of response: one which accepts marxists as participants in the democratic process provided that they abide by the rules of the game; and the other which rejects them on the ground that marxism is a totalitarian ideology inconsistent with democracy. Under this latter view, marxists will, sooner or later, destroy democracy.

Politics in Chile from 1932 to 1973 offers an ideal case for studying how, in practice, marxist parties reconcile their revolutionary objective with participation in a political system which imposes strict limitations on them. For in Chile the marxist parties – the Communist and Socialist parties – were prominent in the country's political development. From 1932 until Allende's downfall in 1973 they were represented in the Congress, participated in electoral alliances, were members of several coalition governments, and finally, in 1970, took control of the executive branch, after winning the presidential elections with a candidate of their own. Such was their involvement in the political system that, out of the eight governments elected during the period 1932–73, they participated at one time or another in five at cabinet level.

The prominent role of the marxists is all the more remarkable if account is taken of the country's underdeveloped economic and social structures. By 1973, Chile had completed just over forty years of uninterrupted democracy, an impressive record – unusual by third-world standards – which, at the time, was unmatched by some developed capitalist states. During those forty years, the President and members of the two houses of the Congress were democratically elected. Parties representing all major ideologies dominated the political arena. The Congress made laws, it was responsive to the demands of the electorate and acted as the main channel for opposition to the government of the day. Besides, democratic freedoms were respected, and the armed forces obeyed the constitution.

The participation of marxists in Chile's political system could be interpreted in different ways. It could, for example, be regarded as having contributed considerably towards strengthening the country's democratic institutions. Alternatively, it could be seen as evidence of the flexibility and liberal spirit of the dominant classes. From a more explicit, ideological standpoint it could be seen as evidence that Chilean marxists had all along sacrificed their revolutionary objectives to achieve limited electoral goals; or it could be regarded as a disruptive factor, slowly corroding political institutions until the complete collapse of democracy.

There is undoubtedly some truth in each of these interpretations. The marxist parties' contribution to the consolidation of democracy through their work in the Congress and in the trade unions can hardly be denied. The highly competitive and well-structured party system which emerged by the end of the nineteenth century, long before the working-class parties were established, could, to some extent, account for the so-called democratic spirit within the country's political institutions. The excessive concern of the marxist parties with electoral politics could well be regarded as evidence that they had abandoned their revolutionary objectives, while their refusal to compromise during the last stages of the Popular Unity government seems to confirm that their adherence to marxist ideology was inconsistent with their commitment to democracy.

An assessment of the marxist parties' role cannot ignore the overall development of the political system. Accordingly, this book traces the development of politics in Chile from 1932 to 1973, taking the participation of marxist parties as its main focus of analysis. This approach enables me to relate the various phases of the political system to the problems the marxist parties had to face. Thus, their views on class alliances and the immediate tasks before them, their policies on political mobilisation, their conceptions about the role of the trade-union movement, their responses to other parties in the system, especially those advocating social and economic reform, their views on economic development, and the influence of the international communist movement on them are all related to changes within the political system.

Each of the main parts of the book examines a distinct phase in the evolution of the political system during which the marxist parties played a clearly defined role. The first phase, examined in Part I of the book, covers the first twenty years, from 1932 to 1952. This phase marks the return to democracy after nearly a decade of political instability and military intervention. During this period, governments were supported by broad coalitions which, at one time or another, included all the parties in the political spectrum. The party system was limited – the electorate comprising only 10 per cent of the population – and government policy was haunted by the spectre of the world depression, which had devastating effects on the country's economy. In this period the marxist parties were members of several coalition governments and were also the leading force in the trade-union movement.

The second phase – discussed in Part II – runs from 1952 to 1970. During this period several attempts were made to re-structure the economy. First, there were two frustrated efforts to liberalise the economy from what was perceived as excessive state intervention. These were followed, in 1964, by an attempt to introduce major economic reforms, relying on a policy of systematic state intervention. This was accompanied by a massive increase in the size of the electorate, a large increase in unionisation and a realignment of political forces along clearly-defined ideological lines. During this period the marxist parties became the leading opposition force. Because of the peculiar features of the electoral system, they also began seriously to consider the electoral road to socialism. To this effect they formed an alliance and made four bids for the presidency.

The marxist parties' electoral success marks the beginning of the third and final phase in the development of the political system. Their

3

victory did not, however, reflect their political and electoral strength, but was largely a consequence of a three-way split of the vote. When the coalition known as the Popular Unity took office, the influence of the marxists parties among organised workers had declined; new groups, hitherto marginal to the system, were beginning to articulate their demands, and the course of Chilean politics was closely followed by the United States government. Under these inauspicious conditions – greatly different from those during the relatively tranquil years of the Popular Front in the late 1930s – the Popular Unity government attempted to bring about a transition to socialism using the mechanisms and procedures of the prevailing political system. After three eventful years, a violent military coup overthrew the Popular Unity government and brought to an end nearly four decades of uninterrupted democracy.

This work, though not a political history of Chile, contains a complete summary of events and all the basic political and economic data from 1932 to 1973. I hope that this will enable readers to reach their own conclusions·on the materials analysed and interpreted in the text.

CHAPTER 2

Economy and Society 1900–1932

CHILE'S forty years of democracy were preceded by nearly a decade of political instability. This instability was largely a consequence of the rise and fall in the sales of nitrate, the country's main export commodity. Towards the end of the nineteenth century Chile had become the world's only supplier of natural sodium nitrate, for which demand in the international markets seemed inexhaustible. The revenue generated by this natural resource recently acquired by conquest, greatly contributed to the modernisation of the economy. However, it also had negative effects as the economy, overdependent on a single export commodity, became highly vulnerable to changes in the world economy. The ease with which nitrate revenue filled the coffers of the state also had negative political consequences, for it encouraged fiscal irresponsibility and political corruption. Thus, not surprisingly, when nitrate exports began to flounder in the international markets the country entered into a protracted political and economic crisis which began in the early 1920s and was not resolved until the mid-1930s.

From 1924 until the return to democracy in 1932, successive governments attempted to come to terms with the changes taking place in the world's nitrate markets. Their efforts were, however, not altogether successful as evidenced by the instability prevailing during those years. Yet, the apparent chaos of those years belies the fact that during the 1920s some of the governments introduced important economic reforms, which made an important contribution towards shaping the political and economic systems after 1932. This chapter begins with a brief explanation of the main political and economic consequences of the nitrate bonanza. It then outlines some of the reforms introduced in the 1920s. Its final section discusses the impact of the world depression on the economy and suggests the way in which it shaped economic policy during the next two decades.

I THE NITRATE ERA

Nitrate dominated the economy for nearly forty years, from the mid-1880s until the late 1920s. Chile acquired its nitrate deposits in the War of the Pacific (1879–83), when it conquered the provinces of Tarapacá from Perú and Antofagasta from Bolivia. Shortly thereafter, world demand for nitrate increased rapidly as a consequence of Alfred Nobel's discovery of its application in the explosives industry and Justus Liebig's discovery of its properties as a fertilizer.[1] These developments brought about an economic boom, transforming nitrate production into the country's main economic activity. For nitrate generated not only the bulk of foreign exchange resources, but also, from 1890 to 1924, provided nearly half of the government's ordinary revenues and accounted for 25 per cent of GDP.[2] Nitrate mining was also a major source of employment, providing between 40,000 and 60,000 jobs, representing more than 5 per cent of total employment.[3]

The nitrate bonanza was a strong stimulus to the development of certain areas of the economy such as transport, construction and some branches of manufacturing industry. Yet, it also depressed the growth of others, notably agriculture. Indeed, while in 1870 agriculture accounted for 30 per cent of the value of exports, by 1895 this figure had dropped to 13 per cent, and in 1900 it was only 6.5 per cent.[4] Copper mining was another productive sector which declined during this period. In the mid-nineteenth century Chile had been one of the main producers and exporters of copper, but by the 1880s copper production had virtually come to an end. Although its decline is generally attributed to lack of adequate technology, recent research has shown a direct economic link between the rise of nitrate production and the collapse of copper.[5]

The rate of urbanisation markedly increased during the nitrate era. It rose from 23 per cent in 1885 to nearly 40 per cent in 1920. During the same period the population increased from 2.5 million to 3.5 million.[6] The state bureaucracy underwent considerable expansion. Between 1896 and 1920 budget allocation for salaries and wages doubled, reaching 40 per cent of the state budget.[7] Education also expanded. Between 1895 and 1920 the number of pupils in primary school trebled, reaching 346,000.[8] This brought about an increase in the literacy rate from 29 per cent in 1885 to 50 per cent in 1920, thus increasing the number of those eligible to vote from 400,000 to one million.[9] Although the electorate did not grow at the same pace, its expansion was significant. In 1921 more than 10 per cent of the population was registered to vote while at the turn of the century this figure was well below 5 per cent.[10]

Nitrate mining introduced a new factor into the country's economy: direct control by foreign capital over a key sector of the economy. One of the features of Chile's economic development in the nineteenth century had been the fact that its two most important productive sectors – agriculture and mining – were controlled by local interests. Local entrepreneurs had in fact shown a remarkable pioneering spirit in the development of silver, copper and coal mining, and by the 1860s had even begun to develop nitrate mining in Peru and Bolivia. Many observers actually suggest that this emergent mining bourgeoisie could have led a process of rapid industrialisation had government policy been more responsive to its needs.[11] However, by the turn of the century, such a possibility had evaporated, as foreign capital – mainly German and British – were in control of more than 80 per cent of Chile's nitrate deposits.

Circumstances surrounding the acquisition by foreign capital of Chile's nitrate deposits were indeed remarkable. Chile had acquired them as a consequence of the War of the Pacific. Under the rules of international law prevailing then, Chile was not required to recognize property rights of the state previously controlling the territory in which the mines were located. However, the government decided to honour pre-existing property rights. In the case of the deposits in what had been Peruvian territory this decision amounted effectively to de-nationalisation of the mines since they had been nationalised by the Peruvian government. The Chilean government decided to turn over the mines to the holders of bonds issued by Peru in compensation for the nationalisation. The rest of the mines were sold off, without giving any preference to local bidders.[12] The decision to de-nationalise the mines was based on the grounds – familiar enough – that the state is an inefficient administrator.[13] It benefited foreign capitalists and, in particular, a group of British financial speculators who had bought Peruvian bonds at a ridiculously low price while the war was still in progress. The irony of this affair was that the British investors had bought the bonds with money borrowed from a Chilean bank.[14]

In Chilean historiography, the government's decision to renounce its rights over the nitrate deposits is generally attributed to the influence of laissez-faire ideology which, at the time, was popular among the ruling elites.[15] There are, of course, some observers who claim that there is a close link between British support for Chile during the War of the Pacific and the nitrate policy adopted by the government at the end of the conflict.[16] In any event, the fact is that after relinquishing such an important natural resource to foreign capital successive governments adopted a carefree attitude which was alarming. Nitrate mining was left practically unregulated. The role of the state was limited to the collection of export taxes, and since they yielded abundant revenue, other areas of economic activity began to enjoy virtual tax immunity. The contribution of direct taxes to state revenue dropped from 8 per cent in 1880 to less than 1 per cent in 1900.[17] Easy access to foreign exchange reinforced the free-trade spirit among the ruling classes, bringing about a liberalisation of imports. Foreign exchange was thus used recklessly to import goods which could have been produced domestically or, in any case, were destined to satisfy the needs of a tiny minority among the very rich. Indeed, it has been reported that in some years the import bill for French wines greatly exceeded that of machinery needed for industry.[18]

The carefree approach to economic policy during the nitrate era was also reflected in the system of government. For this period was characterised by a weak government and absence of coherent policy-making at all levels of public policy. This state of affairs was in sharp contrast with the political system which had prevailed in the past. Indeed, up to the end of the nineteenth century, the basis of the political system had been a strong executive branch led by a President who had sweeping powers of administration. The Congress, elected by a tiny minority of the population – around 2 per cent – was weak and largely dominated by the executive. In 1891, however, after a brief but bloody civil war, which deposed President Manuel José Balmaceda (1886–91), there emerged a peculiar type of parliamentary regime. It was one in which the Congress had the power to bring down cabinets, but the President was not entitled to dissolve the Congress and call for a general election. Not surprisingly, this political arrangement led to paralysis and stagnation.

The extent to which the civil war of 1891 was the consequence of the impact of nitrate on the economy has been the object of lengthy debate among historians. Some see a direct link between the political conflict which generated the civil war and the incorporation of nitrate mining into the economy[19]; while others – without denying that nitrate introduced an important new element into the political arena – argue that the civil war was largely a consequence of unresolved constitutional conflicts pre-dating the nitrate era.[20]

Leaving aside the issue of whether there is a direct link between nitrate policy and the outbreak of civil war, the fact is that the political regime which emerged after the conflict was ideally suited to the needs of foreign capital in the mining sector. For while governments made no effort to regulate the nitrate industry and the political system became increasingly detached from economic and social issues, an elaborate system of corruption and patronage developed as political parties in the Congress fought over the spoils of office and for a share of the nitrate revenue. A symptom of this political malaise was the chronic instability which prevailed in the Cabinet during the parliamentary republic. Indeed, in the fifty years preceding its establishment there had been only thirty-one cabinet changes, while in the following three decades there were more than 120.[21]

Throughout the parliamentary period three parties dominated the political scene. The Conservative Party, representing the pro-clerical landowners of the central valley; the Liberals, a deeply-divided party standing for the principles of laissez-faire and representing largely urban interests; and the Radical Party, an anti-clerical party representing regionally based capitalist interests in agriculture and mining from the south and north of the country, as well as the emerging middle classes in the growing urban centres. Governments during this period were led either by the Conservative Party, in alliance with the Liberals, or by the Liberals in coalition with the Radicals. As politics were dominated by these three main parties, working-class interests were largely unrepresented. Yet, while the official political system ignored their interests, workers in mining areas of the north and south of the country and in the urban centres of Valparaíso and Santiago were slowly developing their own political organisations. As explained in Chapter 3, a strong, nationally-based trade-union movement was to emerge, which soon came under the control of the Socialist Workers' Party (Partido Oberero Socialista/POS), formed in 1912. In 1922 the POS sought affiliation to the Third International to become the Communist Party of Chile. Working-class organisations, however, had practically no access to official political channels.

Weaknesses in the political system became apparent when nitrate exports began to encounter difficulties in the international markets. The nitrate bonanza had in fact lasted practically without interruption until 1910. Nitrate exports maintained a sustained pace of growth, rising from 1.4 million tons a year in the early 1900s to 2.4 million tons by 1910. Likewise, the price of nitrate rose from twenty-seven to thirty-seven dollars per ton.[22] However, by 1910, Chile started to experience the problems derived from over-dependency on a single export commodity. The instability of demand for nitrate led to periodic

9

falls of between 20 and 40 per cent in the volume of exports. The loss of revenue caused by this sharp fluctuation was covered by foreign borrowing, which, in turn, greatly debilitated the overall financial position of the state. Export fluctuations were also accompanied by massive layoffs, thus causing additional difficulties for the government.

The outbreak of World War I further exposed the vulnerability of Chile's nitrate economy. Firstly, Chile lost the German market. Shortly thereafter, when nitrate exports recovered, it discovered that it had the largest-ever trade surplus because the flow of imports had been reduced as a consequence of the war.[23] Secondly, it began to lose its share of the market as a consequence of the increasingly successful commercialisation of synthetic nitrogen. Thus, while in 1914 Chile controlled 55 per cent of the nitrate market, after the War its share had dropped to 32 per cent, and by 1926 it had plummeted to a mere 16 per cent.[24]

The instability of nitrate revenues created considerable social tension and increased the militancy of working-class organisations. The prevailing dissatisfaction paved the way for the emergence of Arturo Alessandri as leader of a middle-class reformist movement. In 1920, Alessandri won the presidential election on a platform which called for immediate changes to the political system and for substantial social and economic reforms.[25] Alessandri was backed by a coalition made up of the Liberal, Radical and Democratic parties. His personal following, however, went well beyond the narrow constituencies of these parties. Relying on his charismatic appeal, he managed to obtain the support of a heterogeneous social group, consisting mainly of state employees, university students, workers from the nitrate mines in the north and from the coal mines in the south, along with the growing ranks of industrial workers in the large urban centres of Santiago and Valparaíso. Although Alessandri won the election by the narrowest of margins, and his victory was strongly disputed by his opponents, he managed to win over to his side the bulk of the newly-registered voters. Indeed, between 1915 and 1920 there had taken place a major process of electoral mobilisation which doubled the size of the electorate from 184,000 to 330,000.[26]

Alessandri's political programme called for greater state control over banking, insurance and financial matters generally.[27] It promised an amendment to the constitution to give more power to the President, thus replacing the ailing system of parliamentary government. It also called for the establishment of a social security system and a detailed framework to regulate industrial relations. Alessandri was particularly aware of the urgent need to incorporate the emergent labour movement into the political system as the risk involved in excluding it from participation had become only too obvious when the number of workers on strike in 1920 reached a record 50,000.

Despite his good intentions, he was unable to transform his heterogeneous electoral coalition into an effective political movement. His failure stemmed mainly from the very nature of the political system he intended to reform. In fact, although the parties which had backed him during the election also held the majority of seats in the Congress, he was unable to get his reforms approved. The complacency shown by the Congress prompted the military to intervene. Initially, in September 1924, the military stepped in at Alessandri's invitation to put pressure on the Congress to secure the approval of several government bills. But they soon outmanoeuvred him, forcing him into exile. There thus began an eight-year period of intense political instability, lasting until 1932, during which there were nine different governments.

Military intervention was initially supported by many trade unionists, left-wing political leaders – including, notably, Luis Emilio Recabarren, the leader of the Communist Party – and other groups which had previously supported Alessandri. But it proved impossible to form a stable alliance between these progressive groups and the military, partly because of the political differences existing within the armed forces. This situation created a political vacuum, which allowed Carlos Ibáñez, an army colonel, to rise to political prominence. Indeed, by January 1925, Ibáñez had become the undisputed leader of the army.[28] Between 1925 and 1927 Ibáñez took advantage of his cabinet post in two short-lived administrations to enhance his influence within the armed forces. In 1927, after persuading the President to resign from office, he managed to get himself elected President in a mock election in which he was the only candidate. During his four years in office he ruled as a dictator, paying little or no respect to the niceties of the democratic process.

II RESTRUCTURING THE STATE

Alessandri failed to implement his comprehensive programme of reforms, although by the end of his administration he did manage to have a new constitution and a package of labour legislation approved by the Congress. The reformist tasks proposed by Alessandri were, ironically, largely completed by the administration of his arch-rival Ibáñez (1927–31). These reforms, introduced in response to the problems created by the instability of nitrate revenue, greatly contributed to modernising the state apparatus. They also laid the foundations for the launching in the late 1930s of a more centralised and diversified economic policy.

Underlying the reformist process of the 1920s was a significant change in the balance of forces within the Latin-American region. In Chile this change involved the decline of British and German economic influence and a corresponding increase of influence by the United States. By the 1920s American capital controlled an important share of nitrate mines, had the concession to supply the main public utilities, provided the bulk of foreign finance, and was in complete control of the recently-revived copper-mining sector.

The revival of copper mining by American capital was perhaps one of the most important developments during this period. As already explained, in the mid-nineteenth century Chile was a major exporter of copper, but by the turn of the century copper mining had practically ceased. This process was reversed, when, in the early 1900s, American companies began to re-open old copper mines and develop new ones. By the mid-1910s, the share of copper in exports was still insignificant, but by the mid-1920s its share in exports had risen to 30 per cent.[29]

At the time, the re-opening of copper mines appears to have gone largely unnoticed by the ruling political circles, since it was practically free of government regulation. Yet the change that his brought about in the composition of exports, greatly strengthened Chile's international credit-worthiness. The Ibáñez administration, however, took full advantage of this situation as foreign loans enabled it to launch a vast programme of public works, which included the construction of roads, ports, railways and irrigation systems. The increase in public expenditure also enabled the Ibáñez administration to promote investment in manufacturing industry and in mining through the establishment of several development agencies which were to be forerunners of CORFO, the State Development Corporation established by the Popular Front government in 1939. As a complement to these measures, the government raised tariffs and skilfully used the exchange rates to protect local manufacturing industry.[30] This new approach to economic policy gave a significant impetus to the process of import substitution which had in fact already begun in the mid-1910s when, as a consequence of World War I, Chile started to encounter difficulties in obtaining access to imported goods.[31]

The interventionist economic policy of the late 1920s was carried out under the aegis of a new constitution, approved in 1925, which replaced the parliamentary regime by a presidential system. It deprived the Congress of its powers to depose cabinets and made parliamentary seats and cabinet posts incompatible. To strengthen the office of the President, it introduced a system of direct presidential elections, extended the President's terms of office from five to six years and gave the chief executive broad administrative powers. Under this new system, the President had a much greater role in the legislative process, particularly in matters concerning public expenditure. It also established a special tribunal to supervise the electoral process. Finally, it separated church and state, thus paving the way for lay education.[32]

Although the new constitution entered into force in 1925, its clauses were not fully honoured until 1932. Ibáñez in fact established an authoritarian regime in complete disregard of the democratic principles established by the constitution. Yet, in a more fundamental way, the Ibáñez administration fulfilled the constitution's objectives by contributing towards consolidating the predominance of the office of the President over the Congress.

This new constitutional framework was complemented by the introduction of a comprehensive programme of administrative and legal reforms. In 1925, the Kemmerer mission – a private firm of consultants from the United States – made several recommendations to the government on how to improve administrative efficiency. Following these recommendations, the government created the Central Bank and introduced a strict legal structure to regulate banking activities and centralise monetary policy.[33] It also adopted modern methods of accounting and undertook a major reorganisation of local government. The police forces were re-structured under a single militarised organisation attached to the Ministry of the Interior, as counterbalance to the army and navy in the Department of War.

An important component of the re-structuring process was the enactment of eight acts dealing with industrial relations and labour law generally. The acts regulated contracts of employment, collective bargaining and industrial disputes.[34] They also introduced a separate regime to govern conditions of employment and social security benefits for blue- and white-collar workers. The two most important provisions within this legislation were those which recognised the existence of unions and regulated the right to strike. This legislation had been conceived by Alessandri, but he could not get it approved by the Congress. In fact, it was only after the military intervened in 1924 that the Congress finally approved it. It was not fully implemented for another three years, by which time the Ibáñez administration had enacted a complex set of regulations giving effect to it.

The new law established a dual system of unions: plant-based and craft-based.[35] Plant-based unions, or industrial unions, could be formed in establishments employing twenty-five or more workers. The law allowed the existence of only one union per plant and provided that once the union was established, union membership was compulsory. Industrial unions were not allowed to form federations with other unions, nor were they allowed to have full-time union officials. Although the new legislation recognised the right to strike, it prohibited the establishment of strike funds. Craft unions were associations of workers in particular occupations not confined to a single plant. These unions were allowed to form national federations, but only for the purpose of looking after the common interests of their members, not for the purpose of representing them in industrial disputes. Most craft unions were little more than mutual aid societies.

The new legislation granted the right to strike only to industrial unions and only after they had completed an elaborate bureaucratic procedure. Government authorities were given the power to call off a strike whenever they felt that doing so was in the national interest. Also, the law provided that officials from the Ministry of Labour should be actively involved during all stages of an industrial dispute. The elaborate procedure governing the right to strike was designed to limit strike action by introducing a distinction between legal and illegal strikes.

Alessandri's intention had been to use the new framework of labour relations as a means of incorporating the increasingly militant working class into the political system. However, on close analysis, the new legislation appeared to be more concerned with controlling and dividing the labour movement than with integrating it into the political system. It effectively debarred the majority of workers in manufacturing industry from forming plant unions. It outlawed the Federación Obrera de Chile (FOCH), the large and hitherto powerful labour confederation. It did not allow the existence of unions in the public sector and gave state authorities broad powers to break strikes and dictate terms for settling industrial conflicts. In Chapter 3, below, I explain how this new legislative framework was used by Ibáñez to repress and destroy working-class organisations.

III IMPACT OF THE WORLD DEPRESSION

The reforms introduced by successive governments in the 1920s greatly eased the adjustment of the economy to the unstable conditions prevailing in the world nitrate markets. As explained in the preceding sections, by the late 1920s, as the country's export base had been broadened to include copper, the government appeared to have a coherent policy for dealing with the rapid decline of nitrate. It had raised tariffs to protect domestic manufacturing industry, it had rationalised state institutions to improve efficiency and it was attempting to revive economic activity by increasing public expenditure. These measures made it possible for the Ibáñez government to withstand quite well the first effects of the world depression in 1929–30. Indeed, such was the international credit-worthiness of Ibáñez that Chile managed to obtain an abundant supply of loans until 1930.[36] By contrast, foreign loans had dried up throughout the rest of Latin America by 1928. However, despite the relative success of the reforms the impact of the world depression on the economy was such that, by the middle of 1931, the Ibáñez government had collapsed and the country was thrown into a brief but intense political crisis.

The world depression had a devastating effect on the economy; foreign trade collapsed, unemployment reached peak levels, foreign loans dried up and wages were cut by as much as 40 per cent. By 1932, exports had fallen to 20 per cent of their 1929 value, while the contribution of imports to GDP fell from 31 per cent to 7 per cent. Foreign loans, which had helped to finance Ibáñez's massive programme of public works, dropped from 682 million dollars in 1930 to 22 million in 1932 and to nil in 1933.[37] The collapse of trade caused enormous pressure on the balance of payments and eventually forced the government to default on the foreign debt. But since this measure did not prevent the drain of foreign exchange, strict exchange controls soon followed.[38]

Mining was the sector worst hit by the depression. Nitrate exports fell from nearly 3 million metric tons in 1928 to 1.6 million metric tons in 1930 and to a mere 275,000 in 1932.[39] The price of a ton of nitrate dropped from forty dollars in 1929 to twenty-four dollars in 1932.[40] Copper production and prices were also severely hit. Copper production fell from 300,000 tons in 1920 to 97,000 tons in 1932, while the price of a ton of copper dropped from eighteen cents to five cents during the same period.[41] Employment in the nitrate mines fell dramatically from 50,000 in 1929 to only 8,000 in 1932.[42] In the same year, the workforce in copper mining was also reduced to 8,000, which was just over one-third of its size in 1929.[43] The collapse of mining activities had a serious effect on agriculture and on the building industry. However, manufacturing industry suffered less than did the other sectors. Indeed, in August 1931 industrial production reached its lowest point of 75 (1927–9 = 100), which was high by comparison with the spectacular fall of mining exports.

The sudden collapse of mining exports depressed the rest of the economy and brought about an increase in unemployment. According to official estimates, the number of people out of work in 1932 was 129,000. This figure represented roughly 12 per cent of the economically active population.[44] However, because official estimates only take into account urban manual workers actually looking for a job, they offer only a partial picture of the employment situation in the country. Other calculations put the total number of unemployed as well over 200,000.[45] Apart from the serious employment consequences, the fall in nitrate production and the general slow-down of the economy had the effect of drying up government revenues, since fiscal deficit could no longer be financed by foreign loans. The government had to obtain the money from the Central Bank. Loans from the Central Bank to the government rose from 25 million pesos in 1931 to 550 million pesos in 1932.

The world depression had a lasting effect on Chile's foreign trade. Twenty years later, the country's capacity to import was still 40 per cent less than during the 1925–9 period, and by 1953, the availability of goods was only 10 per cent higher than in 1925.[46] Yet, despite its enormous impact on the economy, the depression did not bring about revolutionary change or a long period of political instability. Instead, after brief political turmoil, not only was stability restored, but it took a democratic form which was to last for over 40 years. Moreover, this new form of political rule provided the framework for an economic policy which was to modernise and invigorate the ailing process of capitalist development.

That Chile recovered so quickly from the political if not the economic consequences of the depression owes a great deal to the reforms introduced during the twenties by the Alessandri and Ibáñez administrations. However, the spectre of the depression haunted Chile for many years and largely shaped its economic policy for the next two decades. For between 1932 and 1953 successive governments made a determined effort to diversify the country's economic base through a state-management policy of industrialisation to reduce dependency on the external sector. This new economic policy also marked a significant departure from the laissez-faire policy of the nitrate era.

PART I   RETURN TO DEMOCRACY

CHAPTER 3

Political Forces in the 1930s

AFTER the collapse of the Ibáñez government in June 1931 there followed a period of intense political instability. However, the return of Alessandri to the Presidency in December 1932 marked the beginning of forty years of uninterrupted democratic rule. That Chile returned to democracy so soon after the world depression owes a great deal to the significant re-alignment of forces which took place on both sides of the political spectrum in the late 1920s and early 1930s. While in the 1920s organised labour and marxist political groups were largely excluded from the official political system, by the mid-1930s they were both prominent actors within the system. The incorporation of the marxist parties into the political system was as rapid as it was successful. Indeed, by 1936, five years after the Communist Party was allowed to function legally and only three years after the creation of the Socialist Party, the two parties formed, together with the Radical Party, the Popular Front, an electoral alliance which in 1938 won the presidential elections. Since then and during the whole of the next decade government coalitions would always include at least one of the two marxist parties.

The changing political map also affected the established parties. As politics moved unequivocally to the Left, the Radical Party began to distance itself from the Liberal Party, its political ally during the Parliamentary Republic. This process brought the old Conservative and Liberal parties into closer cooperation; yet, without the Radical Party's support, they were unable to win the Presidency. By the early 1940s, however, they eventually accepted the dominant political role of the Radical Party. Thereafter, and up to 1952, they became actively involved in the coalition politics led by the Radical Party.

This chapter discusses the realignment of political forces which took place in the late 1920s and early 1930s. Section I provides a brief explanation of the origins of the labour movement and its relations with left-wing political groups. Section II discusses the political role played by the Communist Party in the 1920s and the factors which in 1933 led to the creation of the second marxist party. Section III examines how and to what extent the Right was affected by the conditions prevailing during the 1930s. The chapter concludes with a brief discussion of the Alessandri administration (1932–8).

I   THE EMERGENCE OF ORGANISED LABOUR

The beginning of the nitrate era in the late nineteenth century marks the emergence of an organised labour movement. Nitrate mining was labour intensive and was carried out in isolated areas in the Atacama desert under harsh conditions. The demand for labour was satisfied by migrant workers from the southern regions of the country. During the first decade of the nitrate boom, employment in the nitrate mines increased from just under 3,000 to 13,000 workers.[1] The first general strike on record took place in the nitrate-producing province of Iquique in 1890. This was followed by several other strikes by dock and tram workers in Santiago and Valparaíso in 1903 and 1905 and by another Iquique strike in 1907, which resulted in the massacre of nearly 3,000 nitrate miners and their families in the yard of the Santa María School. Because the workers lacked a permanent institutional structure to coordinate their action, it was easy for the state to deal with labour unrest by direct repression. Moreover, the political system prevailing at the time provided the means of legitimising state repression against workers. Indeed, in 1904 a congressional committee of inquiry found that all the judges in the nitrate area were on the pay-roll of the nitrate companies.[2]

By the turn of the century most of the permanent organisations of workers were mutual-aid societies and brotherhoods. They developed mainly in the nitrate areas of the north, in the coal-mining areas of the south and among transport workers in docks and railways. In the urban centres artisans, and some groups of transport workers under the influence of anarchist ideas, began to form resistance societies with a more defined syndicalist orientation. By the end of World War I, these diverse organisations had been transformed into a well-organised union movement with a national political outlook. An important factor in this development was the interest shown by some political parties, mainly the Democratic Party, in the electoral potential of the newly-formed working-class constituencies in the mining areas. The Democratic Party, a progressive liberal party established in 1887, was the first party to make a determined effort to form a coalition comprising white-collar workers and artisans from Santiago and Valparaíso and miners from the north and south of the country. Because the party's overriding objective was to participate in government coalitions, its middle-class leadership soon clashed with the more militant wing of the party representing working-class interests, mainly those of the miners. The conflict within the Democratic Party led to the creation in 1912 of the Socialist Workers' Party (Partido Oberero Socialista/POS). The POS was founded in Iquique, the heartland of nitrate mining, and its objective was to serve as a political channel for working-class interests.

The most important working-class organisation to emerge in the pre-war period was the Gran Federación Obrera de Chile, established by railway workers in 1909. Originally, this organisation had been formed to back the railway workers' demand for back pay withheld from their salaries. During its first six years, it followed a mutualist policy and did not participate or support any type of strike action. Because of the structure of the industry and the size of the labour force it employed, the Gran Federación became the largest working-class organisation of the period and the only one with a nationwide institutional structure.

Initially, the POS was critical of the Gran Federación mainly because of its mutualist orientation. However, the party leadership soon changed their minds after realising that it provided them with a ready-made institutional framework which they themselves had been unable to build. Indeed, despite the POS's success in the mining areas, its political influence at the national level was negligible, partly because of the sheer distance between the mining communities and the two main urban centres of Santiago and Valparaíso. By 1917, under the influence of the POS, the Gran Federación changed its name to the Federación Obrera de Chile (FOCH) and became a nationwide federation of unions open to workers of all political tendencies, claiming to represent nearly 60,000 workers. Two years later the FOCH adopted a clear political position calling for the abolition of capitalism.[3]

The influence of the POS grew within FOCH and caused serious divisions within the labour movement. In 1919 the POS proposed the creation of a single party of the working class comprising the FOCH, the POS and the Democratic Party. The proposed party would pursue an independent, class-based political line and would not enter into alliance with non-workers' parties. Since the Democratic Party was an active participant in the coalition-style of politics prevailing at the time and drew a substantial proportion of its electoral strength from non-working class constituencies, it rejected the POS proposal. Moreover, interpreting the POS proposal as a manoeuvre to isolate it, the leadership of the Democratic Party withdrew from the FOCH. Likewise, the anarcho-syndicalist unions broke away from FOCH because they believed the POS was determined to use FOCH as a means to further their parliamentary political objectives thereby disregarding the real interests of their members. After their withdrawal, they formed a local branch of the IWW (International Workers of the World), with a membership of 9,000.

The withdrawal of the Democratic Party and the anarchists from FOCH gave the POS total control over the organisation. In 1920, under the influence of the POS, FOCH approved a proposal to join the Red International of Labour Unions, and in 1922, the POS itself changed its name to the Communist Party of Chile and made a formal application to join the Third International. By 1923 most of the non-communist members in FOCH had been purged, and FOCH effectively became an organ of the Communist Party. However, at this stage, FOCH membership was only 30,000; that is, about half of its membership in 1917.

The conflicts within the labour movement did not have an immediate impact on the militancy of the unions. Indeed, in 1920, the number of strikes and workers on strike reached the record level of 105 and 50,000 respectively.[4] In the following three years, the political strength of the unions diminished, but this was more a consequence of the international economic crisis than of political divisions within the movement. Indeed, by 1925, the union movement had recovered the level of combativeness it had reached in 1920.

Calculations of union membership in the period 1920 to 1925 vary widely and are not reliable. Union membership in each of the years of this period seems to have been subject to the ups and downs of the economy. Some estimates put FOCH membership during this period at about 80,000.[5] At the time FOCH had a nationwide organisation of 125 regional councils.[6] FOCH membership during this period provides the basis for an estimate of total union membership of at least 130,000. Some observers put the figure at about 204,000.[7] If we take the lower figure of 130,000, the number of workers belonging to unions was about 10 per cent of the workforce. However, to put this figure in proper political perspective it must be noted that, at the time, the size of the electorate was only 300,000. Therefore, the political impact of a miltant union movement, concentrated as it was in key sectors of the economy, was much greater than its numerical size would suggest. This explains why the Alessandri government in 1920 regarded the introduction of a comprehensive framework of labour legislation as a top political priority.

II   THE LABOUR MOVEMENT UNDER IBÁÑEZ

As explained in Chapter 2, a new legal framework for the regulation of industrial relations was enacted in 1924. During the Ibáñez adminis-tration (1927–31), this new legislation was used to repress Communist-and anarchist-controlled unions and to secure their replacement by 'legal' unions controlled by the state. Repression of the labour move-ment was relatively easy to accomplish. For it was carried out when the economy was commencing a slight downward trend, and at a time when the labour movement, though numerically strong, was not prepared to cope with government repression. However, Ibáñez did encounter some obstacles in his efforts to fulfil the objective of establ-ishing a reconstituted labour movement based on a network of legal unions. On the one hand, workers were naturally suspicious of a union structure created under the auspices of a government determined to suppress the most articulate and militant representatives within the labour movement. Moreover, while the government's efforts were strongly resisted by the FOCH, the Communist Party launched a major underground campaign attacking the legal unions and demand-ing free and independent unions. On the other hand, the government did not show any willingness to give the new unions scope for inde-pendent action.[8] Inevitably, the government met all strike action with a show of force and tended to rely mainly on the support of mutualist organisations and labour leaders whose loyalty to the government had been well established or could be easily purchased.

The government's distrust of the labour movement is reflected in the regulations used to implement the new legislation. These regula-tions gave broad power to the officials in the Ministry of Labour so that they could supervise the formation of the new unions. They could exclude from union membership any person who in their view was subversive or harmful to the social order. Union officers were also subject to close scrutiny. They were required to fulfil a one-year resi-dence requirement – a major obstacle for the ever-changing migrant workforce in the nitrate mines – and those convicted of a crime or a misdemeanour were not eligible for office.[9] Given these conditions, it is not surprising that the process of establishing legal unions began slowly. By 1929, two years after Ibáñez took office, only sixty-one unions had been established. However, the government adopted an active policy of encouraging and even subsidising the establishing of unions during its last two years in office. This policy had some success leading, by the end of the Ibáñez administration, to the creation of 300 unions with an estimated membership of around 50,000.[10]

The government's objective of using the new structure of legal unions as its principal base of support was made explicit in December 1928 with the creation of CRAC, the Republican Confederation for Civic Action. CRAC was a national confederation of legal unions which, in their constituent assembly, pledged unreserved loyalty to the Ibáñez government.[11] To underline his objective, Ibáñez assigned nineteen parliamentary seats to CRAC in the new Congress, the composition of which had been entirely controlled by the government.[12] Unfortunately for him, his newly-established links with one section of the labour movement did not prove to be strong enough to overcome the popular discontent which eventually led to his resignation.

When the Ibanez government collapsed in 1931, the labour movement was weak and divided. After four years of repression, FOCH membership had been reduced from around 80,000 in 1925 to only a few thousand in 1931, and its nationwide network of regional councils had been nearly destroyed. In fact, while in 1925 FOCH had 125 councils throughout the country, in 1931 it only had twenty-five such councils.[13] Likewise, the anarcho-syndicalist unions, which were smaller and not as well-organised as the unions operating under the FOCH umbrella, were nearly destroyed by the Ibáñez administration. Alongside the remnants of the free union movement, there stood the 300 legal unions created during the Ibáñez administration. But these unions were weak and lacked a clear sense of direction, since they had been created by the outgoing administration to serve its own political objectives.

III   MARXIST PARTIES

Decline of the Communist Party

The difficult conditions under which the labour movement began the rebuilding of its institutions were further complicated by the political divisions which appeared on the left wing of the political spectrum. In 1931, when the Communist Party emerged from clandestinity, it found not only that its social base had been substantially reduced, but also that it had competition from several socialist and anarchist groups formed during the Ibáñez administration. These groups had developed an independent socialist position and had gained enormous influence among workers, students, intellectuals, white-collar workers and even some members in the armed forces.

By the early 1930s the Communist Party was no longer the dominant political force among the working class. Several factors account for the loss of influence. Firstly, the party had been the main target of the repression launched by the Ibáñez government against working-class organisations. This repression seriously disrupted the party's institutional structure. Secondly, the massive unemployment brought about by the world depression hit mainly the mining areas in the north and south of the country from where the party drew the bulk of support. Thirdly, the Stalin-Trotsky feud generated internal divisions which further weakened the party. Indeed Trotskyism became an issue in the Chilean Communist Party as early as 1924, only two years after the party had applied for membership in the Third International.[14] The fourth, and by far the most important factor, was the Party's pursuit of the ultra-left, 'Third Period' line of the Comintern between 1928 and 1933, which isolated it from other left-wing political groups.

The Communist Party's acceptance of the ultra-left policy of the Comintern was a significant departure from its previous political practice and marked the beginning of an uninterrupted and loyal adherence to the policies of the international communist movement. In the early 1920s, as well as in the immediate post-war period, the Communist Party regarded its participation in the parliamentary process as necessary to increase its influence among working-class constituencies. During this early period, the party also tried to form alliances with other political movements representing working-class interests. We have already mentioned that in 1920 the POS proposed a merger with the Democratic Party on condition that the newly-formed party would not enter into alliances with non-working-class parties. During this early period the Communist Party did not discard the parliamentary system, though the speeches made in the Chamber of Deputies by its leader, Luis Emilio Recabarren, show that it had no illusions about that system.[15]

In the mid-1920s, at the time of the military intervention, the Communist Party moved even closer towards participating in the political system by becoming a member of a heterogeneous political movement called USRACH (Unión Social Republicana de Asalariados de Chile), which comprised FOCH and the Democratic Party. The USRACH parties did in fact surprisingly well in the presidential elections of

October 1925, when their candidate, Dr. José Santos Salas, obtained 29 per cent of the vote.

The Communist Party's flirtation with coalition politics was short-lived. In January 1926 the Communist Party disowned the USRACH, and later on in that same year, the Latin-American Secretariat of the Comintern sent a sharply-worded note to the Chilean Communist Party expressing worries about its weak proletarian base and criticising its excessive concern with electoral politics. The Comintern also demanded that the party should be organised into cells.[16] These events prepared the ground for the party's acceptance in 1928 of the Comintern's 'Third Period' Line.

During this 'Third Period' phase, the Communist Party isolated itself, refusing to participate in any form of alliance with other political movements, whether or not they had a working-class base.[17]

Creation of the Socialist Party

The increasing weakness and isolation of the Communist Party during the Ibáñez administration led to the creation of several political movements inspired by the principles of socialism. These groups shared a deep concern for the plight of the working class and the poor together with a profound distrust of the Communist Party's loyalty to the Comintern. Antagonism within the left-wing camp became evident in 1932, when the Communist Party refused to support the Socialist Republic – a short-lived military government led by members of various socialist groups. Although the Socialist Republic lasted only twelve days, it adopted several measures which greatly enhanced the popularity of the socialist groups. Thus, when in 1932 Marmaduque Grove, one of the leading members of the Socialist Republic, became a presidential candidate, he obtained 18 per cent of the popular vote. Grove's success provided the necessary impetus for the unification of the various socialist groups, leading to the creation of the Socialist Party of Chile in April 1933. Thus, just over a decade after the POS had transformed itself into the Communist Party and joined the Third International, there appeared a new and numerically important Socialist Party, also inspired by marxist principles.

From its inception the Socialist Party sought to adopt an ideological and political identity different from that of the Communist Party. Its Declaration of Principles states that the party adheres to marxism, but also rejects the dogmatic interpretation of marxist theory which at the time, and ever since, the Socialists have attributed to the Communist Party. Accordingly, the Declaration accepts marxism as a method of interpreting society, but provides that theoretical insights derived from other social theories may and should be used to supplement and enrich marxist doctrine. In political terms, the Socialist Party marked its independence by refusing to join any of the existing Socialist Internationals on the grounds that membership in these organisations resulted in the imposition of erroneous formulae drawn from alien political contexts. In contrast to the Euro-centred Socialist Internationals, the party called for greater unity among the Latin-American working class to further the struggle against imperialism and local oligarchies.[18]

With regard to the ultimate objectives of the two parties, the position of the Socialist Party does not greatly differ from that of the Communist Party. Indeed, they both claim that their objective is the transformation of capitalism through the abolition of private ownership of the means of production. To achieve this they both accept that the proletariat must take control of the state apparatus in order to establish a transitional government which they describe as a dictatorship of the proletariat. Despite agreement on such a broad issue the Socialist Party has generally disagreed with the Communist Party on the question of class alliances and on how to make use of the political system. This disagreement has over the years gone through various phases, largely dependent on the vagaries of the domestic and international contexts, rather than on significant or profound changes in the ideological orientation of either party.

The independent marxist position adopted by the Socialist Party and their Latin-Americanist orientation can to some extent be attributed to the fact that most of the founding members belonged to the radical intelligentsia, and consequently were fervent nationalists and profoundly suspicious of imported ideology of any kind.[19] This middle-class radical nationalism has been a permanent feature of the Socialist Party. However, in the early 1930s the Socialist Party's decision to follow an independent marxist line was based on a reasonable assessment and critique of the political consequences of the isolationist and dogmatic line followed by the Communist Party. The Socialists were in fact aware that the Communist Party had made a serious mistake by restricting its membership mainly to manual workers in mining and manufacturing. Accordingly, from the outset, the Socialists set for themselves the task of attracting a broad political and electoral constituency made up of manual and white-collar workers.

Marxist Parties and the Labour Movement

In the early 1930s the Communist Party was weak and was no longer the dominant influence among organised workers. The Socialists therefore regarded themselves, rightly, as the party destined to assume hegemony over the working-class movement. But although they regarded themselves as successors to the Communist Party, rather than their competitors, they were determined to avoid isolating themselves politically and geographically as the Communists had done during the 1920s. More specifically, the Socialists were critical of the trade-union policy of the Communists and of their failure to establish themselves as a national political force.

The successful takeover of FOCH by the Communist Party in the post-war period – an impressive feat from an organisational point of view – had brought about serious divisions within the labour movement, the main issue being the Communist Party's union policy. FOCH became a mere appendix of the Party which led to the isolation from the masses of both the party and the union movement. This was exacerbated by the Communist Party's view that the proletarian vanguard consisted mainly of workers from the mining and manufacturing sectors. In practice, such a conception led the Communist Party to labelling white or yellow any union which did not follow the party line or which was not made up of vanguard proletarians, as defined by the party.[20] The narrow ideological prism of the Communist Party also explains why their influence was restricted to selective areas where there was a large concentration of workers; mainly the nitrate and coal mines and the working-class areas of Santiago and Valparaíso.[21]

In marked contrast to the Communist Party, the Socialists advocated a flexible and pluralistic policy towards the unions. They claimed that the party should not seek total control over the unions and that unions should not be discriminated against because of the nature of their membership or the procedure through which they had been established. In their view, to fulfil its role as vanguard, the party was required to wage the ideological struggle from within the labour movement, without introducing artificial distinctions among different groups of workers.[22] Such a flexible union policy stemmed partly from their ability to adapt to the new political circumstances arising from the collapse of the Ibáñez government. During the Ibáñez administration, the Communist Party had campaigned for free unions to oppose the legal unions established by the government. However, after Ibáñez' departure the distinction between free and legal unions became irrelevant. Because Ibáñez had failed to institutionalise his political movement, the network of legal unions created under his administration had no definite orientation. By 1932 there were over 400 legal unions, with a total membership of 56,000.[23] The Socialists, grasping the political importance of these unions, actively sought their support, and by 1934 they already controlled the majority of them.[24] By 1934 the Socialists had in fact become the leading political force within the labour movement.

The early success of the Socialist Party within the labour movement was largely attributable to the enormous popular appeal of its leaders rather than to patient work by its militants at the grassroots level. The short-lived Socialist Republic had given the Socialists an image of political resolution and courage which yielded substantial electoral benefits. In 1932, Grove, obtaining 18 per cent of the vote, was the runner-up in the presidential election. In 1932 the various socialist groups obtained 6 per cent of the vote while the Communist Party only obtained 1 per cent of the vote. By 1937, the Socialists with 11 per cent of the vote became the fourth largest party and nearly three times as large as the Communist Party. Thus, less than four years after its creation, the Socialist Party had managed to establish itself as a leading political force with an electoral base which included manual and white-collar workers as well as students and intellectuals. It should be borne in mind, however, that the dominant position they achieved within the labour movement during the 1930s was due more to their success in the ballot box than to the fact that they were implementing their views about the relationship between party and unions.

IV   THE RIGHT AND THE PARTY SYSTEM

During the first decades of the century, at the time of the Parliamentary Republic, the official political system was dominated by three main traditional parties; the Conservatives, Liberals and Radicals. While the Conservatives represented the interests of the landed oligarchy from the central region of the country, the Liberals were closely identified with industry, commerce and finance. The Radicals, for their part, represented a mixed constituency of recently-established landowners from the south, small and medium-sized mine owners from the north, plus a growing contingent of white-collar workers from the urban centres. The electoral strength of these parties during the first two decades of this century was roughly as follows; the Conservatives had 20 per cent of the vote; the Liberals had between 40 and 60 per cent and the Radicals between 10 and 30 per cent. The share of the vote of the Conservative Party was the most stable, and that of the Liberals the most unstable. The Radical Party showed a sustained pattern of growth until the 1921 congressional elections. On the whole, the three major parties did not disagree over fundamental political issues. Accordingly, during these two decades governments were formed on the basis of coalitions led either by the Conservative Party in alliance with right-wing nationalists and dissident Liberal groups; or by the Liberals, in alliance with the Radicals.[25] However, the Conservatives, a Catholic party which advocated close unity between church and state, disagreed with the Liberals over government religious policies. They also had some disagreement over monetary and commercial policies as the interests of importers and exporters were not always easy to reconcile. Conservatives and Liberals for their part, rejected the anti-clericalism of the Radical Party and were opposed to its attempts to extend the system of public education.

The coalition governments were plagued by cabinet instability; however, because of the ideological homogeneity of the main political parties, this instability did not threaten the political system which was sustained by the seemingly endless flow of nitrate revenue. But, as nitrate revenue became unreliable and pressure for change intensified, the political system began a slow, but inexorable, decline. The first signs of strain appeared during World War I. Later on, in 1920, the Alessandri administration tried, unsuccessfully, to broaden the scope of the political system so as to satisfy the most pressing demands for social and economic change.

During the 1920s the party system was in disarray. When democracy was restored in 1932, the configuration of political forces had undergone important changes. Whereas in the early 1920s Conservatives and Liberals accounted for nearly 60 per cent of the vote and the Radicals for 30 per cent, by 1932 the share of Conservatives and Liberals had dropped to 30 per cent and that of the Radicals to 20 per cent. The emergent new force was the marxist Left, mainly the Socialists. In 1932 the various socialist groups polled 6 per cent of the vote, and in 1937 the Socialist Party increased its share to 11 per cent, while the Communist Party obtained a further 4 per cent of the vote. The marked swing to the left which these results show is underlined by the fact that during this period, 1921–32, electoral registration and electoral participation remained virtually unchanged.[26]

The radicalisation of the electorate which began in the early 1930s brought about important changes in the pattern of alliances among the main political parties. On the right of the political spectrum, it led to a breakdown of the alliance between Liberals and Radicals and heralded closer cooperation between the Conservative and Liberal parties. On the left, it paved the way in 1936 for the establishment of the Popular Front, an alliance of the two marxist parties, the Radical Party and the

Democratic Party. The two well-defined right- and left-wing blocs thus emerging from the re-alignment of political forces became the main protagonists in the 1938 presidential elections. Although these blocs soon collapsed, giving way in 1942 to a complex pattern of coaltition politics, they did reflect some important ideological changes which were beginning to take place within the main political parties.

Dissension within the Right

The radicalisation of politics in the early 1930s had a profound impact on some right-wing groups. This is reflected in the almost simultaneous appearance of three separate political movements from within the ranks of the right-wing supporters; the Movimiento Nacional Socialista (MNS), inspired by fascist ideology, the Agrarian Party, a nationalist party representing the interests of a group within the landed oligarchy, and the Falange Nacional, a group of progressive Catholic youth inspired by the social doctrines of the Catholic Church. The MNS had some political importance during the 1930s but disintegrated in the early 1940s. The Agrarian Party and the Falange did not make much impact at the time, but did acquire considerable political importance during the 1950s. The Agrarian Party provided the base for the political movement which in 1952 elected Ibáñez as President, while the Falange was the nucleus around which the Christian Democratic Party was formed in 1957.

The MNS was officially founded in April 1932; that is, not long after the collapse of the Ibáñez government and only a few months before the military coup which led to the establishment of the twelve-day Socialist Republic. The ideology of the MNS was largely shaped by the writings and speeches of its leader, Jorge González. González was a council employee who achieved considerable success within local government. In accordance with the basic tenets of fascist ideology, González called for the establishment of a new state, an organic whole in which individual and collective interests would be reconciled.[27]

The growth of the MNS during its first four years was slow. This was largely because the leading representatives of the ruling class, including the Conservative and Liberal parties, as well as the Alessandri government, had decided to give their full backing to the republican militia. Since the republican militia was little less than the military wing of the bourgeoisie committed to defending the right-wing policies of the Alessandri government, the MNS did not effectively have much political or military room in which to manoeuvre. The ruling class had in fact directly assumed the task of preserving the system against the threat from the Left, so they had little use for fascist ideology or for a fascist party. The Alessandri government kept the MNS members under close surveillance and often applied emergency legislation to repress their activities.[28]

The dissolution of the republican militia and the establishment in 1936 of the Popular Front alliance gave a considerable boost to the MNS. In the congressional elections of 1937 they polled 3.5 per cent of the vote, gaining three seats in the Chamber of Deputies, and the following year they supported Ibáñez' bid for Presidency. However, since Ibáñez failed to obtain the support of any other major party, he, together with the MNS tried to provoke a military coup before the elections were due to take place. To achieve this objective the MNS held a violent demonstration in the areas surrounding the government palace. The government met this threat with unusual violence, leading to the death of scores of MNS members and to the imprisonment of Ibáñez. As a consequence, Ibáñez withdrew his name from the presidential contest and after securing a promise of amnesty from the presidential candidate of the Popular Front, he called upon his supporters to vote for the Left. The MNS for their part lost most of their popular support and by the early 1940s had disappeared as a political organisation. Interestingly enough, after the MNS had ceased to exist, their leader, Jorge González, joined the Liberal Party.

The emergence of the MNS was not the only challenge which the traditional right-wing parties had to confront during the 1930s. In the southern region of the country, a group of large landowners, dissatisfied with the policies of the Conservative-dominated National Agricultural Society (Sociedad Nacional de Agricultura/SNA), established their own separate association and in 1931 created their own political party. The new party was called the Agrarian Party and consisted mainly of former Liberals and a few Radicals from the Concepción area. During its first twenty years it was largely regionally-based, with very small influence in national politics. During the 1940s it evolved as a right-wing nationalist party adopting a corporatist ideology. By the end of the decade however, the ubiquitous Ibáñez took over the Agrarian Party to form a heterogeneous populist party, the Agrarian Labour Party. (Partido Agrario Laborista/PAL). In 1952, with the support of the PAL he won an overwhelming victory in the presidential elections. The PAL disintegrated shortly after Ibáñez took office.

The changing political context of the 1930s also created problems within the ranks of the Conservative Party. Indeed, under the influence of the social doctrine of the Catholic church, the youth section of the Conservative Party began to challenge the policy of their elders. They criticised their party's unconditional support of the status quo and advocated substantial social and economic reforms to benefit the poorer sections of the population. In their view, these reforms would not only be consistent with the teachings of Christ, but would also contain the growth of marxist socialism. In 1935, they finally broke away from the Conservative party to form a separate political organisation, the Falange. With the creation of the Falange the Conservative Party's claim to be the only channel through which Catholics could participate in politics was seriously undermined. Nevertheless, in the short-term, the Falange was not a real threat to the hegemony which the Conservative Party, with the aid of the Catholic hierarchy, exercised over the Catholic vote. Between 1935 and 1955, the Falange's share of the vote remained well below 5 per cent and it only controlled three seats in the Chamber of Deputies. In spite of their poor electoral performance, the Falange exercised considerable political influence during this period through their participation in various coalition governments with the Radical Party. However, it was not until the mid-1950s that the Falange, under the new name of Christian Democratic Party, began seriously to undermine the political strength of the Conservative and other right-wing parties.

The emergence of dissident groups from within the ranks of the Right did not pose a threat to the Conservative and Liberal parties as main representatives of the dominant classes. During the thirties Conservatives and Liberals began a period of close cooperation, first rallying around the Alessandri government and, later on, in opposition to the Popular Front. This process was largely a consequence of the fact that by the thirties the differences between Conservatives and Liberals were less marked. On the one hand, in the previous decades, the ruling class had become increasingly more cohesive. While urban-based capitalists in industry and finance had acquired a significant portion of agricultural land, individual members of the landed oligarchy had acquired considerable interests in modern capitalist enterprises.[29] On the other hand, the new constitution, enacted in 1925, which provided for the separation of church and state, had made the religious differences between the two parties largely irrelevant. Yet despite these factors, the two parties maintained their separate political identities well into the sixties. Undoubtedly, ideological short-sightedness may be a factor to explain this phenomenon as the Conservatives, with the support of part of the Catholic hierarchy, continued to claim their party as the only legitimate political channel for Catholics. However, the Conservatives also had good reasons to suspect the Liberals as many members of this party were sympathetic to the ideas of economic modernisation which the Radical Party was beginning to articulate.

Conservatives and Liberals formed a strong political alliance. First, they closed ranks in support of the Alessandri government. Later on, their alliance was further consolidated when the Popular Front won the presidential elections of 1938, since together they controlled enough seats in the Congress to block any government initiative. But the collapse of the Popular Front also brought to an end the alliance between Conservatives and Liberals. The Liberals joined in with Radicals, Communists and Socialists as occasional partners in coalition governments. The Conservatives were initially reluctant to support the Radical Party, but by the end of the forties they gave all their support to President Gabriel González when his government sponsored legislation banning the Communist Party and repressing the labour movement. By the early fifties, as the Radical Party became a spent political force, the alliance between Conservatives and Liberals was revived. Yet the two parties did not merge until 1965, when they formed the National Party.

V IMMEDIATE RESPONSE: THE ALESSANDRI ADMINISTRATION

Alessandri won the presidential elections with the support of a centre-right coalition made up of Liberals, Radicals and a fraction of the old Democratic Party. He obtained 55 per cent of the vote, while his two right-wing opponents, a Conservative and a Liberal, both dissidents from their own parties, each obtained just over 10 per cent, and the Communist candidate 1 per cent. Alessandri's main objective was to resolve the crisis brought about by the world depression. His policy was a mixture of measures involving strict fiscal austerity, indirect economic incentives and special programmes to resolve unemployment. In strictly economic terms, it was quite successful. In less than six years, the huge fiscal deficit created by the world depression had been eliminated, unemployment had virtually disappeared, exports had made a substantial recovery and the index of industrial production showed a consistent upward trend.

The Alessandri administration concentrated most of its energies on balancing the budget. Apart from increasing company and personal taxation, the government introduced a 5 per cent sales tax and raised custom duties by 50 per cent.[30] A major devaluation of the peso was followed by the introduction of a strict and complex system of foreign exchange and trade controls. In 1933, the government sponsored a new building law, which remitted taxes on all construction started before 1935. This measure brought about a boom in the building industry, which soon spread over to other sectors of the economy. Also, in an attempt to assert greater control over the marketing of mining exports, the government transformed nitrate trade into a state monopoly. However, in practice the efficacy of this last measure was frustrated as nitrate sales were in fact entrusted for a period of thirty-five years to a mixed company, the Chilean Nitrates and Iodine Sales Corporation, controlled jointly by the government and foreign mining companies operating in the country. Although by that time copper was rapidly displacing nitrate as the main export commodity, no such initiative was taken with regard to copper trade.

The index of industrial production rose quickly from 106 points in 1933 (1927–9 = 100) to 132 points in 1934 and maintained this rhythm of growth until the end of the decade.[31] The process of economic recovery was led by manufacturing industry, which had suffered less than other sectors during the depression years. It should be noted that between 1927 and 1937 growth in manufacturing industry was concentrated mainly in the traditional industries such as textiles and primary food processing. Indeed, contrary to what is generally believed, the import substitution effect in the industrial sector took place largely between 1927 and 1937. According to one estimate, over two-thirds of import substitution in the sector of traditional manufacturing took place in this period[32]. Alongside the recovery in industrial production, the volume of exports rose from the low point of thirteen in 1932 to sixty-eight in 1933 (1927–9 = 100). The index of mining production also recovered rapidly from thirty-one in 1932 (1927–9 = 100) to sixty-two in 1934, reaching a hundred in 1937. These favourable developments in the industrial and mining sectors brought unemployment down from 129,000 in 1932 to 59,000 a year later and to a mere 8,000 in 1935.[33]

The remarkable economic recovery which took place during the decade of the thirties still did not fully compensate for the impact of the world depression. By 1939, GDP was 66 per cent below the 1929 level, and the value of exports was still only 29 per cent of their peak value in the twenties.[34] Moreover, the burden of pulling the economy out of the depression had not been equally shared by all social classes. In fact, the government's economic success was achieved mainly at the expense of the wage-earning population. In the public sector, for example, real remuneration between 1930 and 1938 fell by as much as 48 per cent.[35] There thus developed a growing militancy among

35

workers, which was reflected by the rapid increase in strike activity during Alessandri's term of office. Indeed, while during Alessandri's first year in office there were only 600 workers involved in strike activity, in his second, third and fourth year in office this figure increased to 4,000, 5,000 and 7,000 workers respectively.[36] To deal with this growing unrest, the government sought and obtained from the Congress broad emergency powers which were used both against the labour movement and against the leaders of the Communist and Socialist parties. Alessandri in fact imprisoned and expelled from the country several of the leading figures of the two marxist parties.

Alessandri's repression of the labour movement was not successful. It failed on two main counts: firstly, because it was not sufficiently strong to reduce the level of unrest; and secondly, because it was strong enough to trigger off the process of unification within the labour movement and between the Communist and Socialist parties. The lack of efficacy of Alessandri's repressive policies may to some extent be attributed to the restraints imposed on government action by the prevailing democratic framework. But perhaps a more important factor was Alessandri's relations with the armed forces. Indeed, one of the main political problems that he confronted when he took office was that of discipline in the armed forces. Although after the collapse of the military government in 1931 the armed forces were weak and divided, there were still several high-ranking officers who were anxious to assume the political role vacated by Ibáñez. Therefore, one of Alessandri's most urgent tasks was to ensure that the military would remain in their barracks and respect the newly established constitutional order. To achieve this he carried out a wide-ranging reorganisation of the armed forces, which included forcing several high-ranking officers into early retirement.[37] In the process, he antagonised several groups within the armed forces, thus creating an atmosphere of distrust between the military and the government. In the event, Alessandri succeeded in restoring army discipline, but only at the cost of making his own task of maintaining law and order more difficult. For he could not afford to rely heavily on the army to maintain public order as this conflicted with the government's objective of reducing their political role. To resolve this dilemma, Alessandri quietly encouraged and supported the activities of a republican militia committed to the defence of democracy; that is, to the survival of the Alessandri government.[38]

The republican militia had actually come into existence in mid-1932 during the hectic months of the Socialist Republic. It was led by prominent members of the right-wing establishment and had a contingent of more than 10,000 civilians, mainly from the middle and lower-middle classes. The republican militia was well equipped, its weapons included tanks, artillery and machine guns.[39] Alessandri openly supported it, describing it as the most solid base of support for the newly established constitutional regime. By mid-term, in July 1936, the leaders of the republican militia disbanded their organisation and handed over their arms to the government, as they believed that they had already fulfilled their tasks of protecting democracy.[40]

The republican militia did not consist, as some of its contemporary critics suggested, of white guards inspired by fascist ideology. Although there were many pro-fascist elements within its ranks, its main objective was to act as a buffer between the government and the armed forces so as to give the President a chance to carry out his conflicting tasks of restructuring the personnel within the armed forces and containing the growing militancy within the labour movement. Alessandri was undoubtedly successful in restoring some discipline within the armed forces, but he did not succeed in containing the militancy of the labour movement. Moreover, because he did not restrict political freedoms, despite his intentions, the process of political radicalisation of the electorate continued unabated throughout his term of office. Thus, by the end of the Alessandri administration there had taken place an important change in the correlation of political forces favouring the Left, culminating with the electoral victory of the Popular Front candidate in 1938.

CHAPTER 4

Popular Front: A New Economic Policy

THE Popular Front was a centre-left coalition. Its principal members were the Radical, Communist and Socialist parties. When it was created in 1936 it was little more than a shaky electoral alliance formed in response to the bloc created by the Conservative and Liberal parties in support of the Alessandri government. However, such was the electoral success of the Popular Front that only two years after its establishment its candidate in the presidential elections, the Radical Pedro Aguirre, obtained a narrow victory over Gustavo Ross, the candidate of the right-wing parties. After Aguirre, the Radical party won two Presidential elections in succession, thus completing a fourteen-year period in control of the Presidency. These fourteen years (1938–52) are often referred to as the Popular Front period. This description is, however, not strictly accurate because the Popular Front coalition actually broke up only two years after its electoral victory, and President Aguirre's term in office was cut short by his death in November 1941. However, the influence of the Popular Front's economic policy did in fact extend well beyond 1941. For the Popular Front actually set the general direction for economic policy until 1952.

This chapter is intended as general background to the discussion of the complex politics of the period, 1938–52, which follows in Chapter 5. Section I examines the immediate factors which led to the creation of the Popular Front coalition. It explains the Radical Party's shift to the left as well as the reasons which prompted the rival marxist parties to become partners in an electoral alliance. Section II describes the main features of the Popular Front's economic policy, especially its impact on the policies of the two administrations which followed after President Aguirre's death. Section III provides a brief assessment of the economic consequences of this policy.

I   THE MAKING OF THE POPULAR FRONT

Transformation of the Radical Party

The left-wing orientation assumed by the Radical Party in the early 1930s was to some extent brought about by changes in its membership. While in the first two decades of the century the Radical Party had mainly represented the interests of recently-established capitalists in mining, agriculture and manufacturing industry, by the early 1920s its social base of support had broadened to include white-collar workers in the public and private sectors and members of the liberal professions. In the 1921 congressional elections the Radical Party obtained 30 per cent of the vote, thus becoming the second largest party in the country. But ten years later, after the collapse of the Ibáñez administration and the political confusion created by the impact of the world depression, it was not easy for the Radical Party to reconstitute the political alliance which had been so successful in the more prosperous nitrate years. While in the early 1930s the Radical Party could still claim the allegiance of capitalists from various sectors of the economy, it was rapidly losing its traditional middle- and lower-middle-class constituency to the various socialist groups which had emerged in the early 1920s. Under these circumstances it is not surprising that, in 1931, the Radical Party made a significant move towards the left when it formally rejected the individualistic principles of liberalism and called for the collective ownership of the means of production.[1] This ideological transformation yielded some immediate electoral dividends when, in 1932, the Radical Party became the largest party in the country, although their actual share of the vote had dropped to 18 per cent, that is, almost half their electoral share of 1921. The party's swing to the left was reaffirmed in its conference of 1933 which approved a resolution declaring that capitalism inevitably breeds class struggle and pledged support to the dispossessed classes.[2]

The ideological transformation of the Radical Party must also be assessed within the political context of the early 1930s. From this perspective, it would seem that the leadership of the Radical Party regarded its continuing partnership with the Right as a serious political liability. Indeed, during the first two decades of the century, the Radicals had consistently played second fiddle to the Liberals. Even in 1932, when the Radicals emerged as the largest political group, the Liberals still regarded them as second-rate partners in the broad alliance which had made Alessandri's victory possible. The new political status acquired by the Radical Party in the early 1930s naturally

39

whetted their appetite to win the presidency with a candidate from their own ranks. But since they were not strong enough to achieve this objective on their own – and it was unlikely that the newly formed Conservative-Liberal bloc would ever support a Radical candidate – they naturally turned to the left. But to do this they had first to establish their left-wing credentials. Hence, the party's left-wing statements of the early 1930s. But this ideological swing was largely determined by electoral calculation as evidenced by the continuing support which the Radicals gave to the Alessandri administration. The marxist Left was at first deeply suspicious of the left-wing overtures made by the Radicals. However, a fundamental change of line by the Communist Party in 1935 transformed the Radicals overnight into acceptable partners in the left-wing Popular Front alliance. Yet, even after the creation of the Popular Front, the Radicals still maintained their close links with the government of Alessandri.[3]

The Marxist Parties

After the creation of the Socialist Party in 1933, there were two main marxists parties in the political arena, each with considerable influence within the labour movement. Although the Socialists were more successful than the Communists in electoral terms, they did not have the organisational skills and discipline of the Communists. During the first two years of the Alessandri government relations between the two marxist parties were bad. The Communist Party, following the 'Third Period' line of the Comintern, rejecting contacts with bourgeois parties, objected to the Socialist Party's parliamentary proclivities which led them to form alliances with dissident groups from bourgeois parties, such as the Radicals and Democrats. The Socialist Party, for its part, rejected the ultra-left line pursued by the Communists on the grounds that it isolated the working class from other equally exploited sections of society, and that their policy had been imposed by the Comintern. Notwithstanding the doctrinaire views adopted by the leadership, the interests of Communist and Socialist supporters began to converge as the Alessandri government began to repress communist and socialist unions and supporters indiscriminately.

The anti-labour policies of the Alessandri administration were undoubtedly important in preparing the ground for closer cooperation between the Communist and Socialist parties within the Popular Front. Indeed, some time before the establishment of the Popular Front, both the Communist Party and the Socialist Party had made some attempts, albeit mild and unconvincing, towards achieving greater unity on the Left.[4] But these gestures were still not strong enough to overcome the fundamental differences between the two parties. Likewise, attempts by the Radical Party to establish itself as a party of the Left were not convincing enough to bring about instant unity. The turning point in this process of convergence of left-wing political interests came about in 1935 when the Comintern abandoned its 'Third Period' line and began advocating the creation of broad alliances with bourgeois parties in order to save democracy from the threat of fascism. The new strategy of the Comintern was rapidly adopted by the Chilean Communist Party although, as noted in chapter 2 above, the Right in Chile had not felt the need to rely on fascism to reconstitute the economic structure after the world depression.

The new line adopted by the Comintern made it possible for the Communist Party to lobby the Radical Party with a view to forming a local version of the European Popular Fronts. The Radical Party welcomed the approach made by the Communist Party, considering it consistent with their objective of forming a left-wing coalition to elect a Radical President in the forthcoming elections. Thus, in February 1936 the Santiago Assembly of the Radical Party called for the creation of a Popular Front to include the Communist Party, the Socialist Party and the Democratic Party, as well as other progressive forces in society in order to fight for national liberation, for democratic liberties, and for the betterment of the working masses.[5] The socialists agreed to joint the Front, partly because they were aware of the need to co-ordinate left-wing opposition to the government and partly because they feared that the establishment of the Communist-Radical alliance would isolate them and seriously undermine their electoral strength.

The creation of the Popular Front alliance in April 1936 was followed shortly afterwards by the establishment of a single labour confederation, (Confederación de Trabajadores de Chile/Chilean Workers' Confederation). It included all the main federations of legal unions controlled by the Socialists as well as those controlled by the Communists through the FOCH. The only section of the labour movement which refused to participate in the CTCH was the Federation of Anarchist Unions, which represented less than 10 per cent of organised labour. The CTCH therefore aimed to represent the bulk of the labour movement, and, in contrast to its predecessor the FOCH, it did not embrace the political objective of replacing capitalism with socialism.[6] Although the CTCH became a voting member of the Popular Front, it did not enjoy a great degree of autonomy from the political parties. Indeed, its two leading posts of president and vice-president were tightly controlled by the Socialist and Communist parties respectively.

41

The success of the Popular Front parties in the general election of 1937, in which they came close to matching the combined 40 per cent vote of the right-wing parties, consolidated the newly formed left-wing alliance, as the Popular Front was now a serious contender for the 1938 presidential elections. But the selection of presidential candidates created some dissension. The Radical Party, which had always conceived the Front as a means to gaining the Presidency, became deeply concerned that the immensely popular Socialist leader Marmaduque Grove would win the nomination with the support of the Communist Party and the CTCH. Indeed, the Radicals were so afraid of not winning the presidential nomination for themselves that, in their party convention of 1937, they passed a resolution which, in effect, made their participation in the Popular Front conditional on the nomination of the Radical candidate to the presidential election.[7] The Socialists, for their part, believed that they had a better claim for winning the presidential nomination since Grove was by far the most popular left-wing political leader in the country. This competition between Radicals and Socialists placed the Communists in the powerful role of political brokers. Since the Communists were not prepared to support the candidacy of Grove, the Socialists withdrew their nomination and the Radical candidate, Pedro Aguirre, was adopted by consensus.

II   THE POPULAR FRONT'S ECONOMIC POLICY

The Popular Front Programme called for several economic and political reforms to modernise the system of production, broaden the size of the national market and achieve a more equitable distribution of income. More specifically, the Programme called for the establishment of a system of national planning, a revision of the tax structure and for the introduction of strict controls on the activities of foreign enterprises. The Programme also made a vague call for agrarian reform by demanding more state aid to medium and small landowners and legislation to improve working conditions among agricultural workers.[8] Although today the programme resembles a Third World manifesto written by precursors of the United Nations Economic Commission for Latin America or by dependency theorists, at the time the right-wing parties saw it as a fundamental threat to private property and to the spiritual values of Western civilisation.[9] In practice, however, the Popular Front not only did not bring about revolutionary change, but actually strengthened the unity of the ruling classes. In any event, the policies of the Popular Front had a lasting impact on Chile's economic development.

To understand both the scope and limitations of the Popular Front's economic policy, it must be borne in mind that by the late thirties Chile had practically completed what is generally described as the 'easy phase' of the import substitution process. During the twenty-year period between World War I and the mid-thirties, manufacturing industry had grown fast, and most of this growth can be attributed to import substitution of traditional consumer goods. According to one estimate, nearly 43 per cent of the growth of manufacturing industry from 1914 to 1927 is attributable to this. The process intensified between 1927 and 1937, at which time import substitution of this type of goods accounted for 73 per cent of growth in manufacturing industry.[10] However, by the end of the thirties further growth was seriously restricted by the availability of foreign exchange. The characteristic problem which had given impetus to the first import substitution effort had now reappeared. To increase domestic production it was necessary to import more capital goods, but given the limited supply of foreign exchange, an increase of capital goods in the import bill would have required a proportional reduction of imported raw materials and fuels which were essential for maintaining existing levels of industrial production.[11] Thus, in order to resolve this problem it became necessary to develop basic and intermediate industries which would take the import substitution process into a new and more difficult phase. Since the private sector was unable to accomplish this on its own, the Popular Front decided to rely on the state.

CORFO: Financing a Good Idea

The basic tool that the Popular Front government used to support its import substitution process of industrialisation was CORFO, a state-development corporation established in 1939 and the first of its kind in Latin America. CORFO is regarded, rightly, as the Popular Front's most important achievement. But CORFO also embodies all the limitations and contradictions of the Popular Front's economic policy. In this sub-section I explain some of the problems of the Popular Front's economic policy, focusing mainly on the circumstances surrounding the establishment of CORFO and on its policies.[12]

CORFO's objective was to increase production in all sectors of the economy so as to reduce the balance of payments deficit and raise living standards. To achieve this it was given broad powers to research, promote, finance and participate in any project which would further economic growth. Some of the ideas underlying the CORFO initiative were not entirely new. During the twenties the government had established several development agencies which provided short- and medium-term credit to the mining, agricultural and industrial sectors. Although the scale of these agencies was small by comparison with CORFO they made an important contribution to domestic investment.[13] The speed with which the opposition-controlled Congress approved the CORFO bill (about four months) contrasted sharply with its usual way of dealing slowly with and eventually rejecting practically all government bills. In fact, the CORFO bill was the only major legislative initiative which the Popular Front government managed to get through the Congress. The immediate reason for this exceptional response by the Congress was the violent earthquake of January 1939, which caused enormous destruction and the death of more than fifty thousand persons. This disaster softened the hostile reaction of the parliamentary majority, making it more receptive to the CORFO bill, which was introduced in conjunction with a comprehensive reconstruction plan. But apart from this conjunctural factor, the opposition found that with the CORFO bill it had a unique opportunity to test the government's commitment to its political programme. Thus, the political bargaining surrounding the approval of the bill decisively contributed to shaping the overall direction of the government's economic policy.

The leading associations representing private capital looked favourably upon accepting greater state participation in the process of economic development. Shortly before the CORFO bill was sent to the Congress, the leading employers' association in the manufacturing industry, SOFOFA (Sociedad de Fomento Fabril/Industrial Development Society), had called for the establishment of a national development council, in which private and public sector representatives would discuss and provide guidelines for modernising the country's productive structure.[14] This favourable disposition towards greater state involvement was shared even by the conservative association of landowners, the Sociedad Nacional de Agricultura.[15] Naturally, the role which the representatives of private capital envisaged for CORFO was limited. They supported the CORFO initiative insofar as it would provide them with a source of cheap credits and would give them greater protection from foreign competition. But they did not believe that CORFO's proper role was to become involved directly or indirectly in production. For them, CORFO's main appeal was that it provided a new and direct channel of communication between the state and private capital, which cir-

cumvented both the Congress and the traditionally inefficient $
bureaucracy.[16]

By approving the CORFO bill the Congress had the opportunity of
making explicit their objections to the CORFO initiative and, more
generally, to the ideas underlying the Programme of the Popular
Front government. The two main issues concerned CORFO's autonomy and its mode of financing. Instead of granting CORFO powers
broad enough to formulate and execute production plans in the different sectors of the economy, the opposition proposed that CORFO
initiatives should always be subject to congressional approval. In this
respect, the views held by the right-wing parties in the Congress differed from those held by the representatives of private capital, who
favoured the idea of creating a new institutional mechanism to provide
a direct link between the state and private capital. The opposition rejected the government's proposal to finance CORFO by increasing
personal and corporate taxes. Instead, they approved a clause which
raised taxes on the copper industry by fifteen per cent.[17] This idea of
financing CORFO by relying on the export sector rather than on taxation of domestic activities was warmly supported by SOFOFA.[18]

The parliamentary manoeuvres which took place during the discussion of the CORFO bill were only part of the opposition's overall
strategy. They took advantage of the fact that the government needed
their votes to get the CORFO bill approved to obtain broader political
concessions. Indeed, while the CORFO bill was going through the
Congress, the SNA, the leading association of landowners, sent a
memorandum to the President expressing its grave concern about the
social unrest prevailing in the countryside. The SNA attributed this to
the process of unionisation of agricultural workers promoted by the
Socialist and Communist parties. Because the landowners were over-
represented in the Congress, the SNA was in a position effectively to
block the approval of the CORFO bill. Thus, in order to secure congressional support the government agreed to suspend for an indefinite
time the creation of new unions in the rural sector. In exchange for
this concession, the opposition dropped its demand to subject CORFO's
policies to the Congress and agreed to allow the executive branch to
play a dominant role in CORFO.[19]

The changes introduced in the CORFO bill at the congressional
stage, combined with the political concession the government had to
make to secure its approval, had the effect of restricting the government's economic policy. In the first place, its failure to persuade the
Congress to finance CORFO by increasing personal and company
taxation also meant that it had to give up its more ambitious objective

of reforming the tax laws to bring about a substantial redistribution of income. In the second place, by linking CORFO'S budget to the taxation of United States-owned copper companies, the government was implicitly offering a guarantee that it would not nationalise the country's main natural resource. In the third place, it was forced to rely on inflationary loans from the Central Bank and on politically controlled loans from the United States Export-Import (Exim) Bank. Indeed, during the first five years of CORFO's operation, a large part of its budget was financed by foreign loans.[20] CORFO's dependency on foreign finance provided the United States Exim-Bank with a leverage powerful enough to control the direction of CORFO's policies. Thus, for example, CORFO's project to develop hydro-electric power in competition with American-owned utility companies met with considerable resistance and long delays from the Exim-Bank.[21] In the fourth place, the government's willingness to suspend the process of unionisation in the countryside in exchange for votes was an explicit acknowledgement of the veto power which the landed oligarchy could impose on government policies. Not surprisingly, CORFO's involvement in the agricultural sector was limited and never challenged the prevailing pattern of land distribution. Thus, while the government's intention had been to establish an agency that would promote the development of all economic sectors CORFO was in fact confined to manufacturing industry and its financing was dependent on the external sector. Despite these limitations, CORFO's achievements were impressive.

CORFO was established in April 1939, less than six months after the Popular Front came into office. Its activities can be divided into two stages. The first stage involved a programme of action to assist enterprises in different sectors of the economy, but concentrating mainly in manufacturing industry. The second stage, which started in the mid-1940s, took the form of sector plans to develop infra-structure and basic industries. Under the programme of immediate action CORFO provided assistance to nearly one hundred industrial enterprises according to a criterion which gave priority to branches of industry with the greatest potential for import substitution. CORFO's sector plans concentrated on a few long-term projects to satisfy the basic requirement of manufacturing industry in fuels, electricity and steel. These basic industries were established directly by CORFO through wholly-owned subsidiaries.

CORFO's assistance to industry took the form of capital investment, rather than credit. This style of operation was strongly criticised by the leading industrialists and opposition politicians. SOFOFA argued that CORFO's investment would bring politics into the internal administration of private enterprises, while Jorge Alessandri, a leading spokesman for private enterprise, who became President in 1958, claimed that this form of assistance through capital investment was illegal under CORFO's basic law.[22] Likewise, CORFO's decision to establish wholly-owned subsidiaries to develop basic industries was strongly criticised. Despite these criticisms, the government did not change the direction of CORFO's activities.

Between 1939 and 1943 CORFO concentrated its activities on the programme of action to assist industry. Altogether, ninety-two manufacturing enterprises received injections of capital from CORFO. Nearly 70 per cent of the programme's resources were allocated to enterprises in one of the three branches of industry identified by CORFO as priority areas in terms of their potential contribution to the import substitution process; mainly, in the chemical, metal and textile branches.[23] From the perspective of the type of product manufactured by the enterprise receiving CORFO's assistance, nearly 50 per cent of the resources of the programme were allocated to industries classified as intermediate (mainly metal products), 30 per cent to those involved in the production of traditional consumer goods and 8 per cent to those manufacturing consumer durables. Although it is true that to some extent CORFO scattered its energies by supporting very small enterprises, of the ninety-two enterprises which it supported in the manufacturing industry, eighteen received 60 per cent of the resources allocated to the entire sector.[24] Therefore, CORFO made a significant contribution towards furthering the process of concentration of capital in manufacturing.

The implementation of CORFO's second stage of activities, the sector plans to develop the infra-structures and basic industries, began slowly in the early 1940s and was completed by the early 1950s. During this period, CORFO established wholly owned subsidiaries to develop hydro-electric power, steel, cement, sugar and fuel. But in the development of this aspect of its activity, it became increasingly dependent on finance and technical assistance from the United States. Thus, between 1940 and 1945 the proportion of CORFO's budget financed by loans from the United States rose from 18 per cent to over 30 per cent.[25] After the war, CORFO continued to rely heavily on foreign loans.[26]

CORFO: An Assessment

After the demise of the Popular Front coalition and the death of President Aguirre, there followed a ten-year period during which the executive branch remained in the hands of the Radical Party. Although the two Presidents that succeeded Pedro Aguirre, Juan Antonio Ríos (1942–6) and Gabriel González (1946–52), continued to proclaim their loyalty to the ideals of the Popular Front, their governments did not have the same political coherence as the former. They were in fact supported by broad parliamentary coalitions which, at one time or another, included all the major parties on the right and left of the political spectrum. This political pragmatism eventually evolved into an open, right-wing position, which culminated in 1948 in the repression of the trade-union movement and the banning of the Communist Party. Yet, despite their right-wing orientation, these two governments continued to implement the economic policy laid down by the Popular Front. To understand how these governments could reconcile their increasingly right-wing policies with the progressive economic policy of the Popular Front, it is necessary to examine the consequences of this policy.

The rapid growth of manufacturing industry is generally regarded as the most significant feature between 1932 and 1952. During this period, the index of industrial production increased by 126 per cent, while the index of total production rose by 59 per cent and the population increased by only 36 per cent.[27] From 1940 to 1945, the average annual growth of manufacturing industry reached an all-time high of 11 per cent. This rate dropped dramatically to an average annual rate of 1.8 per cent in the second half of the decade, but it recovered again in the period 1949–56, when the annual average rate of growth was 4.7 per cent.[28] Credit for this achievement is attributed to CORFO; yet failure to maintain a sustained rhythm of growth must also be attributed to CORFO.

CORFO played a crucial role as the pioneer of basic industries, as well as the main provider of financial assistance to industrial establishments in various branches of industry. Moreover, its style of management surprised even its most fervent critics. For CORFO officials made a determined effort to preserve the technical autonomy of their institution by keeping managerial decisions away from the immediate influence of the government of the day. This attitude was complemented by its reluctance to interfere in the management of those enterprises in which it had made capital investment. In fact, its capital investment in the various enterprises was soon privatised, and the sale of its investment was – and still is today – surrounded by secrecy. However, what remains undisputed is that the transfer of CORFO's capital investment back to the private sector was made at substantially less than its market value.[29] CORFO's style of operation was accurately summed up by its executive Vice-President in a speech made in

1947: 'The Corporation has never interfered with private initiative. It has never gone so far as to control any undertaking in which it participates or to which it gives assistance, the Corporation withdraws from a business as soon as private enterprise is ready to take its place'.[30]

In its early years of operation, CORFO fulfilled its role as pioneer and promoter of new investment. In fact, it brought about a substantial increase in the contribution made by the state to gross investment. Between 1940 and 1950, the state's share in total gross investment rose from 30 per cent to 40 per cent. However, despite this, during this same period the overall rate of investment dropped from 11 per cent to 8.5 per cent.[31] It seems then, that through the agency of CORFO, the state was substituting rather than complementing private investment and, therefore, that maintaining a sustained rate of growth in the economy depended largely on the state's capacity to channel financial resources to productive investment. However, the downward trend of the rate of growth in the manufacturing sector reveals that the state's capacity effectively to substitute and eventually to increase the rate of investment was limited. These limits can be explained by the role of copper and agriculture in CORFO's industrialisation efforts.

One of CORFO's main objectives was to diversify and expand domestic production so as to make the economy less vulnerable to sharp fluctuations in international markets and, in particular, to reduce the proportion of state revenue derived from foreign trade. The Popular Front's proposal to finance CORFO by increasing the level of taxation of domestic activities was therefore consistent with this central objective. Unfortunately, as explained above, the Congress rejected the Popular Front's proposal and instead introduced a 15 per cent surcharge on the profits of copper companies. This decision by the congressional majority became a *de facto* guarantee that the government would not nationalise copper mining and clearly demonstrated that neither government nor opposition was firmly committed to reducing the economy's dependency on mining exports. An important factor which may explain why the Popular Front government agreed to subject the core of its economic policy to the vagaries of the export sector is that, by 1938, the bulk of export revenue was no longer derived from nitrate, but from copper. In fact, copper exports, which had experienced a substantial growth in the 1920s, easily overtook nitrate as the country's main export commodity in the post-depression period. While in 1925–9 copper contributed 30 per cent of the value of export and nitrate nearly 50 per cent, by the end of the 1940s copper exports represented over 50 per cent of the value of all exports, while nitrate exports had been reduced to a mere 17 per cent.[32] But despite some changes in the composition of exports, it must be noted that 70 per cent of their total value was still derived from minerals.[33]

Copper and the United States

The introduction of the special CORFO tax on copper was symptomatic of the fact that the habit of relying on the external sector for the bulk of state revenue still persisted. In fact, by the end of the 1932–52 period, taxes on foreign trade still accounted for 52 per cent of total fiscal revenue.[34] During the same period, while direct taxes as a percentage of all taxes decreased from nearly 40 per cent to just over 30 per cent, the taxation of the two American copper companies operating in Chile as a proportion of total direct taxes increased from 30 per cent to 50 per cent.[35] In this same period, the share of the state in the value of each unit of copper exported increased from 22 per cent to nearly 84 per cent.[36] But this sharp upsurge in the taxation of copper did not bring about a corresponding increase in state revenue since the price and demand for copper were not always high.

The outbreak of World War II increased the strategic importance of copper in the world economy. The war brought about an upsurge in the demand of copper, which was not accompanied by a corresponding price increase because Chile's copper exports were subjected to price controls imposed by the American administration on United States producers. Thus, between 1942 and 1946, while the annual export of copper was 40 per cent higher than in 1940, reaching an annual average of approximately 450,000 metric tons, the price of copper was frozen by the United States government at 12 cents per pound. It has been estimated that, because of this price freeze, Chile's contribution to the allied war effort amounted to over 500 million dollars.[37] Given the size of the Chilean economy, this amount is by all accounts gigantic. Moreover the contribution was not voluntary, even though the cause was praiseworthy. Little wonder then that the Chilean government was so reluctant to break with the Axis powers. Indeed, Chile did not declare war against the Axis until January 1943 and only after considerable pressure from the United States government.[38] In exchange the United States government authorised new Exim-Bank loans, which were meant to compensate for the loss of copper revenue. These were the first United States loans since the Exim-Bank loan to CORFO in 1939.[39]

After the war, the price of copper rose sharply from 11.7 cents per pound to 13.8 cents in 1946 and to 20.9 cents in 1947. However, during this same period copper exports fell dramatically from 482,000 metric tons to 374,000 metric tons.[40] To compensate for the loss of revenue the government resorted, yet again, to foreign loans and to the printing press in the Central Bank. This option had the effect of increasing the state's dependence on the United States government, as well as adding fuel to the inflationary process. In the post-war period, United States loans were openly used to achieve political objectives. In 1946 the cold-war fear of communist infiltration in Chile had a credible ring for the United States Government, since the Communist Party was a member of the government coalition and held three cabinet posts. This made it easier for the United States government to subject the availability of loans to changes in Chilean domestic policies. The historical record shows that the United States State Department was an important factor, albeit not the only one, (see Chapter 5 below) in persuading the Chilean government to repress the trade union movement and to ban the Communist Party.[41] Once again, generous development loans became available soon after the wishes of the State Department had been complied with.[42]

In the immediate post-war period, Chile was firmly within the sphere of United States influence. It became a prominent participant in several inter-American conferences, which eventually resulted in the establishment of the 1947 Inter-American Treaty of Reciprocal Assistance, the main cold war treaty in Latin America, and was instrumental in the creation of the Organisation of American States in 1948, which became a major tool for United States foreign policy in the region.

The close political relationship between the Chilean and American governments was further strengthened by the ratification of the Mutual Assistance Pact in 1951, which provided a direct channel of communication for the armed forces of the two countries. Yet, despite the close political links between the two countries by the end of the forties, their relationship was not always friendly. The main source of conflict revolved around copper policy. On the one hand, there was Chile's ever-growing need to increase her export revenue to maintain an adequate flow of state resources into investments and other expenditure. On the other hand, there was the United States government's determination to exercise full control over the location of the markets and the prices at which copper could be sold. A serious diplomatic row erupted between the two countries at the outbreak of the Korean War, when the price set by the United States government for Chilean copper sold in the United States was regarded by the Chilean government as unreasonably low. This row was temporarily settled by the Washington Pact in 1951, by which the United States agreed to a small price increase and allowed Chile to sell 20 per cent of the copper in the international market.[43] But this solution provided unsatisfactory for Chile. While on the one hand the government did not make an intelligent use of the 20 per cent quota, on the other, the price of copper in the international market rose to a much higher level than that allowed by the Washington Pact. Indeed, while the 27.5 cents per pound agreed in 1951 was then equal to the price prevailing in the London market and three cents higher than the United States domestic price, by 1952 the price in London had risen to 32.4 cents per pound.[44] These circumstances prompted the Chilean government to scrap the 1951 agreement and to enact, in February 1952, a law which gave direct control over the export of copper to the Central Bank. Thus, between 1952 and 1953 Chile marketed its copper directly at the price prevailing in the London market, which was 45 per cent higher than the price in the American market.[45] It is interesting to note that the decision to assume full control over the marketing of copper – a decision which with hindsight does not appear too radical – should have been made at the end rather than at the beginning of the period dominated by the economic policy of the Popular Front. In the event, as I shall explain in chapter 7, Chile's independent copper policy did not last long, and by 1955 the United States had once again regained control over the marketing of Chilean copper.

Agriculture: the Policy

While the income derived from copper exports was becoming increasingly inadequate to meet the levels of public expenditure, the decline in agricultural production caused a further drain on the already overstretched state revenues. In fact, agricultural output from 1932 to 1952 declined by as much as 16 per cent.[46] To compensate for this fall in production the government had to increase food imports, which created a further drain on the balance of payments, and had to resort to a system of price control which, in the absence of a comprehensive policy to increase agricultural production, further depressed the level of economic activity in the sector.

As I have explained above, in order to get the CORFO bill approved by the Congress, the Popular Front had to agree not to alter the *status quo* in the agricultural sector. In practice, CORFO adhered faithfully to the Popular Front's promise. It concentrated nearly 75 per cent of its resources in the manufacturing sector and in the promotion of basic industries to generate fuel and energy.[47] CORFO's assistance to the agricultural sector mainly took the form of subsidised credit for the acquisition of agricultural machinery. CORFO's almost exclusive concern with the manufacturing sector has led some commentators to conclude that, during this period, the state was presiding over two parallel but contradictory processes: a state-supported process of import substitution in the manufacturing industry and import de-substitution in the agricultural sector.[48]

The main consequence of the government's failure to incorporate the agricultural sector within CORFO's development objectives was that, by the end of this period, property and social relations in the countryside remained virtually unchanged. Land concentration ranked among one of the highest in the world, with nearly three-quarters of all land suitable for cultivation in the hands of a tiny number of large estates, *latifundia*; while a large number of small holdings, *minifundia*, had a share of only 2 per cent of the total arable land.[49] The *latifundia* accounted for 60 per cent of agricultural output and employed nearly 40 per cent of the agricultural labour force. Since nearly half of the *minifundia* were not economically viable, the *minifundistas* had to secure their livelihood by working for the *latifundia* on a seasonal basis.

The prominent role played by the *latifundia* resulted in an employment structure in which the wage relationship was not predominant. Even as recently as the late sixties, wages were the main part of the remuneration of only 50 per cent of the agricultural work force, while 20 per cent of rural workers received no remuneration at all as they were unpaid labour subjected to the *latifundia* regime. A further 25 per cent of agricultural workers were independent owners of small holdings, or sharecroppers.[50] Within the *latifundia*, wage relations were combined with some pre-capitalist forms of exploitation. Each *latifundia* generally had between twelve and twenty permanent workers, the *inquilinos*, who would agree to provide labour for a re-muneration made up of cash and kind. To fulfil their obligations the *inquilinos* had to supply the landowners with additional labour. The workers thus hired by the *inquilino* were euphemistically called volunteers and would often be members of the *inquilino* family. The landowners would generally not have any obligations with regard to the volunteers beyond providing them with a ration of food per day of work. The remaining labour requirements of the *latifundia* were satisfied by temporary wage workers who were either migrant workers or holders of *minifundia*.[51]

This mixed form of labour exploitation depended largely on the existence of the *latifundia*, which, in turn, was an essential component of the prevailing political system. From the twenties onwards, the *latifundistas* had managed to insulate the agricultural sector from even the mildest of social reforms. They successfully opposed the efforts by the Alessandri administration in the twenties and thirties to unionise agricultural workers. During the Ibáñez period, 1927–31, they lost none of their privileges despite the government's attacks on the landed oligarchy. Under the Popular Front government the *latifundistas* made use of their considerable influence in the Congress to obtain a guarantee from the government that development projects and political mobilisation would not be extended to the agricultural sectors. Finally, when the government of Gabriel González (1946–52), in its early years, decided to allow the establishment of peasants' unions, the reaction of the right-wing political establishment was so sharp that it not only brought about an immediate reversal of the unionisation process, but paved the way for the repression of the trade-union movement as a whole.

The success of the *latifundistas* in preserving intact property and social relations in the countryside cannot be attributed merely to the existing electoral system, that is, to the fact that they could always control enough seats in the Congress to exercise a permanent veto against government policy. In fact, the measures adopted by the Popular Front and by the two succeeding administrations in order to accommodate their economic policy to the conditions imposed by the *latifundistas* had the effect not only of further reinforcing their privileged status, but also of forging new ties between them and other strata within the dominant class, mainly in industry and finance. This came about as a result of the government's linking of price controls on foodstuffs and subsidies for food imports on the one hand to generous taxation and to credit policies on the other. To ensure that adequate supplies of food would reach the growing urban population the government imposed price controls on selected foodstuffs and subsidised food imports.[52] Since these measures acted, arguably, as a disincentive to increasing domestic production, the government compensated large landowners by taxing them at exceptionally low rates. Indeed, by the early fifties, the rate at which agricultural enterprises were taxed was one-fourth of the rate applicable to industrial enterprises.[53] This unequal treatment was achieved by not keeping the valuation of agricultural land – the basis on which agricultural taxes were estimated – in line with the rate of inflation.[54] In conjunction with this inequitable tax policy, state-subsidised agricultural credit was concentrated in the hands of the *latifundistas*. Moreover, there is some evidence to suggest that these monies were not invested in agriculture but were channelled back into the more profitable ventures in the manufacturing sectors.[55] Hence, state resources were not only used to subsidise private investment, but were contributing towards forging new ties between the landed oligarchy and the groups of industrialists within the dominant class. Thus, as a recent study shows, the landed oligarchy was so closely linked to industralists and bankers that they can only be regarded as inseparable elements of a single class.[56]

Some commentators have described the economic policy of the Popular Front as discriminating against the agricultural sector.[57] This description is accurate in so far as it focuses on the consequences of goverment policy on agricultural production and employment. Yet the shortcomings of this description become evident if one considers that during this same period the *latifundistas*, who presided over the collapse of agricultural production, received preferential treatment from the government. Indeed, it is because of the protection given by the government that the *latifundia* survived almost intact well into the sixties and were not swept away by the modernising influence of CORFO. By the early fifties, however, there was plenty of evidence and awareness that the decline of agricultural output was becoming a major obstacle to sustaining the rate of growth in manufacturing industry.

III   OVERVIEW

The economic policy of the post-depression period brought about chronic inflation. While in the twenties the average annual rate of inflation was 3 per cent, in the thirties the rate increased to 7 per cent per annum.[58] During the fourteen-year period in which the Popular Front economic policy was applied, the rate of inflation continued to increase, reaching an annual average of 18 per cent. During this period, the inflation rate never dropped below 8 per cent or went above 30 per cent per annum.[59] But these annual averages conceal the marked upward trend in the rate of inflation throughout the whole Popular Front period and beyond. Thus, while the annual average rate of inflation between 1940 and 1946 was 15 per cent, the annual average between 1947 and 1951 was 21 per cent. After 1952 inflation continued to increase, reaching an all-time high of 84 per cent in 1955. Apart from creating serious political problems for the government, this chronic inflationary process naturally had a negative impact on income distribution, which was in turn reflected in the impressive changes in the pattern of employment during this period.

Between 1930 and 1953, while the share of agriculture in total employment dropped from 37 per cent to 31 per cent, employment in manufacturing industry only increased from 16 per cent to 19 per cent.[60] The service sector, which by 1950 accounted for over 50 per cent of employment, had absorbed the largest share of new entrants to the labour market.[61] Most of the growth in the service sector had already taken place by the end of the thirties when, as a consequence of the rapid growth of factory production, jobs in handicraft were destroyed and the increase in factory employment had not compensated for this loss. Thus, between 1925 and 1940, the number of people employed in the manufacturing sector remained unchanged at 280,000, while the number of people working in handicrafts – that is, establishments employing less than five workers – fell from 200,000 to 140,000.[62] Those displaced from handicraft joined the growing number of workers in the service sector. It is important to note that employment in manufacturing only began to grow during the forties, when it increased from 238,000 in 1940 to 383,000 in 1950. Yet not all of this increase was due to the growth of factory employment. In fact, during this period and reversing the previous trend, employment in handicraft began to grow. It rose from 140,000 in 1940 to nearly 200,000 in 1950, when it still accounted for 50 per cent of total employment in manufacturing. These figures show that during the forties the growth of manufacturing employment was, to a large extent, due to a revival of handicraft rather than to the jobs created by the factories established or supported by the State.

The disappointing results in employment of the post-depression economic policy were matched by the income-distribution effect of this policy. Between 1940 and 1950, labour's share in domestic income rose from 42.4 per cent to 44.5 per cent.[63] Thus, the impact of the Popular Front's economic policy on the remuneration of labour was negligible. However these figures conceal a great disparity between two important groups within the labour force. During this period, salaries of white-collar workers increased by 46 per cent, while wages of manual workers increased by only 7 per cent.[64] Therefore, by 1950 white-collar workers, who comprised 10 per cent of the labour force, received nearly 20 per cent of income, while manual workers, who made up 60 per cent of the labour force, received 24 per cent of total income.[65] But not all manual workers did badly throughout the Popular Front period. Up until 1945, manual workers largely maintained the income gains they had achieved in the early years of the Popular Front government. But between 1946 and 1952, as the rate of inflation increased, their share of disposable personal income dropped from 25 per cent to 20 per cent.[66] Yet they were not all equally affected by this drop in real earnings. The earnings of workers in mining, public utilities and manufacturing industry continued to show a real rise even after 1948, while the net losers in terms of income were those in construction, transport, commerce and services.[67]

The drop in real wages which began in the mid-forties was accompanied not only by a general slow-down of economic activity, but also by a substantial drop in the critically-important copper revenues and by a sharp rise in the rate of inflation. However, by the early fifties, there was a sharp upturn in the economy caused by higher copper revenues because of the Korean War, and by an increase in manufacturing output brought about by the coming into operation of two important CORFO projects in steel and oil. But this economic boom was short-lived. Copper revenue dropped at the end of the Korean War, thus causing the rate of inflation to rise sharply from 12 per cent in 1952 to 56 per cent, 71 per cent and 84 per cent in the following three years.[68] Likewise, while manufacturing output had shown an impressive recovery in the first half of the fifties, reaching an annual average of 5.4 per cent, it fell dramatically to its lowest level ever during the second half of the decade.[69]

The economic recovery of the early fifties came too late to compensate for the lost of prestige of the Radical Party. Indeed by 1952, although the Radical Party's electoral support had not declined, no major party on the left or right of the political spectrum was willing to enter into an electoral alliance with them. These circumstances paved the way for the victory of General Ibáñez in the presidential election of 1952. In this new role as geriatric democrat, the dictator of the twenties won an overwhelming mandate to cleanse the political system of corruption, patronage and inefficiency.

During the fourteen-year period dominated by the Popular Front economic policy, the domestic base of production expanded and diversified. Most of the expansion was concentrated in manufacturing and was achieved mainly through the agency of the state. However, towards the end of the period, and despite a short-lived economic recovery, the pattern of growth had begun to lose its dynamism and was generating a dangerously high inflationary process. To a large extent, failure to achieve a sustained level of economic growth can be attributed to the fact that government policy did not fulfil the central objective of the Popular Front, namely to bring about the harmonious development of all sectors of the economy, based on a redistribution of income in favour of the poorest section of the population. Instead, the policy generated a lop-sided growth, in which state-supported industralisation, financed largely from copper-revenues, was combined with an agricultural policy which insulated this sector from the rest of the economy and stunted its growth. However, the state's capacity to support investment in manufacturing declined as income from copper exports decreased, and the fall in agricultural output made new demands on the already over-stretched fiscal budget. Thus, by the early 1950s the economic policy of the Popular Front had lost its original impetus and the need for a new economic policy was becoming increasingly more apparent.

Coalition Politics: 1938–1952

I   THE POPULAR FRONT IN OFFICE

UPON taking office, the Popular Front government announced that it would adopt a series of measures which included redistributing land, building houses for urban workers, providing clothing and free school meals for children, and dealing with the most urgent health problems of the poorer sections of the population.[1] However, the government could not have hoped to implement these measures through legislation since the majority of the seats in the Congress were controlled by the right-wing parties, which seemed determined to block government action. To put pressure on the Congress, the Popular Front adminis-tration stimulated and supported political mobilisation at the grass-roots level, while making full use of the considerable regulatory powers vested in the executive branch in order to circumvent the Congress.

The government's decision to rely on mass mobilisation as a means of exerting pressure on the Congress greatly enhanced its popularity and brought about a sharp increase in the levels of unionisation and strike activity. Thus, by the end of the government's first year in office, union membership had increased by nearly 40 per cent to 170,000, while the number of unions nearly doubled to 1,687.[2] The number of workers involved in strike action also rose sharply from 3,000 in 1937 to 10,000 in each of the following two years, reaching 18,000 in 1940.[3]

This sharp rise in political mobilisation, which benefited mainly the marxist parties and the marxist-controlled confederation of unions, the CTCH, caused considerable concern in right-wing circles. For it seemed to confirm their own propaganda describing the Popular Front as 'a consortium formed by Moscow-bought communists, by mental

59

and physical degenerates, by enriched oligarchs who despise the people, and by corrupt and displaced politicians'.[4] Yet, though right-wing parties agreed that the Popular Front government had to be opposed, they did not have a clear strategy to deal with it. The Catholic Conservatives advocated total opposition to the government since they regarded it as a coalition of freemasons and marxists determined to undermine Christian values as well as property rights in the agricultural sector. The Liberal Party, while also advocating opposition to the government, had a less rigid attitude. For they knew full well that their former allies, the Radical Party, had a strong and influential right-wing faction of which President Aguirre himself was a prominent member. Accordingly, they were more optimistic than the Conservatives that either the Radical Party would moderate the political aims of the Popular Front coalition or that the coalition itself would not last very long. The views held by the Liberals led in practice to the conclusion that, at least in the first instance, opposition to the government should concentrate mainly on making full use of the parliamentary mechanisms so as to force it to change its political objectives and, if possible, to separate the Radical Party from its newly-found marxist allies. This practical conclusion was reinforced by the fact that, in the aftermath of the Ibáñez dictatorship, the armed forces were still discredited and could not be regarded as a viable political option. Also, the army did not have any prominent leader, since the Alessandri administration had carried out a fairly effective process of restructuring in order to deal with potential breaches of army discipline.

The fact that the Right concentrated its opposition strategy mainly on parliamentary manoeuvres did not render their actions less effective. On the contrary, it merely strengthened their resolve to make use of their parliamentary majority so as to deflect the government from fully implementing its programme. Thus, the Right used its majority in the Congress to block government legislation, to approve bills which were designed to disrupt the government's economic policy, or to harass the government by initiating impeachment proceedings against government ministers. But the Right could not impose unwanted legislation on the government since it did not have enough votes to override a presidential veto. Likewise, only one of the three impeachment proceedings was successful, since the opposition could not muster enough votes in the Senate to approve the indictment. However, the Right was capable of blocking government legislation in the Congress, and in this area showed that it was not prepared to yield easily to government demands.[5]

The violent earthquake of January 1939 had the effect of giving the recently-installed government a breathing space, making it possible to get two major bills approved by the Congress: one bill made provision for the reconstruction of the areas devastated by the earthquake, and the other established CORFO, which played such a critical role in the formulation of the government's economic policy. But, as I have already explained in Chapter 4, during the political bargaining which led to the approval of the CORFO bill, the right-wing parties forced the government to agree to finance CORFO by imposing a surtax on copper exports rather than by increasing personal and company taxation. Moreover, they also made their support for the CORFO bill conditional on an undertaking by the government to suspend indefinitely the process of unionisation in the agricultural sector.

The government's willingness to bargain away such an important part of its programme encouraged the right-wing parties to keep up the pressure. This was reflected in their vicious propaganda against both the government and President Aguirre. The objective of this campaign was to describe the government as incompetent, irresponsible and bent on destroying democratic institutions. Thus, when in May 1939 the Popular Front organised a National Congress of Peasants which, predictably enough, recommended the redistribution of land, the right-wing press began to publicise false and alarmist reports about widespread riots and destruction in the countryside. In the same vein, the right-wing press claimed in May 1939 that Grove was about to stage a military coup to establish a marxist dictatorship.[6]

Attempts by the government to restrain the excesses of the opposition-controlled press were described by the right-wing parties as an abusive exercise of power and provided them with the necessary excuse to institute impeachment proceedings against the Minister of the Interior. But while the Right was severe in castigating the government for alleged abuse of power, it turned a blind eye and even encouraged military conspiracies organised by fascists and other ultra-right-wing groups. Indeed, when on 9 November 1939 the government arrested two retired officers and a pro-Franco youth leader, accusing them of conspiring to overthrow the government, they were ridiculed by the right-wing press which claimed that the real conspirators were to be found in the Popular Front itself.[7] Barely a month after this incident, there was an attempted military coup led by an army general, Ariosto Herrera, who had previously served as military attaché in Mussolini's Italy and who had close links with Ibáñez. Herrera's putsch, known as the 'Ariostazo', failed to generate enough support from within the armed forces and instead helped the government to consolidate its own base of popular support. Although the right-wing parties did not openly support the putsch and, indeed, were prepared to allow Congress to give the President emergency powers to restore law and order, they served notice to the government that unless there were changes in policy their attitude would not be the same. Thus, *El Diario Ilustrado*, the newspaper of the Conservative Party, while ostensibly condemning the attempted coup, suggested that it had been a justifiable response to government policy.[8]

Following the attempted military coup, the Right continued to refuse the government the necessary votes in the Congress to approve legislation. The political paralysis which ensued not only exacerbated the differences among the Popular Front parties, but created some distance between the government and its own base of political support. This was precisely the objective which the Right seemed determined to achieve as reflected in their propaganda, which often portrayed President Aguirre as a sincere democrat manipulated by power-hungry marxists. Their strategy yielded fruit in July 1940, when the President entered into a secret pact with the Conservative and Liberal parties in a desperate attempt to break the congressional deadlock. According to this pact the right-wing parties in the Congress would approve a series of government bills in exchange for political concessions from the government. The bills which the Right agreed to approve dealt with minimum wages for farm workers, salary increases, and the funding of national defence. In exchange, the government agreed to remove from office the cabinet minister who had applied administrative sanctions to the newspaper owned by the Conservative Party, to guarantee that it would not intervene in the forthcoming congressional elections, and generally to ensure that the democratic process would not be disturbed.[9]

This secret pact was never implemented: when the Communist and Socialist parties learned about it they rejected it outright, describing it as an act of indiscipline and disloyalty which endangered the very existence of the Popular Front coalition. Opposition from the CTCH and from within the Radical Party itself, mainly its youth section, persuaded President Aguirre to withdraw from the pact. However, political circumstances changed in the second semester of 1940. In a by-election held in November, the Popular Front candidate won a resounding victory in a hitherto Conservative stronghold of Valparaíso. This electoral victory was all the more important since it was achieved despite growing divisions within the Popular Front and the isolation of the President from his own coalition.

The results of this by-election created great concern in the right-wing camp, for it seemed to indicate that its decision to block government bills in the Congress was counter-productive as it was strengthening rather than weakening the electoral base of the Popular Front parties. Therefore, taking advantage of the fact that in the November by-election there had been disturbances resulting in the death of one person, they announced that they would not participate in the general elections due to take place in March 1941 because the government was not capable of effectively guaranteeing freedom at the polls.[10] Together with this electoral boycott, right-wing parties in the Congress approved a bill banning the Communist Party – which was promptly vetoed by the government – and voted to impeach the Minister of the Interior for failing to maintain law and order in the by-election campaign.

The announced electoral boycott posed a fundamental challenge to the legitimacy of the government and was an explicit invitation to the army to overthrow the government. President Aguirre was undoubtedly aware of the gravity of the situation; yet, he could not confront the challenge with a coherent policy backed by all the Popular Front parties. Indeed, while the Right was launching a frontal attack on the very legitimacy of the government, the Popular Front coalition was torn by a major row between the Communist and Socialist parties, which, in the months of December and January 1941, led to the final breakdown of the coalition. Against this background, it is not surprising that in December 1940, President Aguirre made major concessions to the Right in order to persuade it to give up its electoral boycott. These concessions included a promise to repress strikes in the countryside, to order the disbandment of trade unions in the state sector and to close down any newspapers, mainly left-wing, which threatened public order. The government also had to agree to an amendment of the electoral laws, giving the army full responsibility for maintaining law and order on election day.[11] Despite the government's willingness to make these major concessions the Right did not cancel its proposed electoral boycott until February 1941; that is, less than one month before the general elections and one month after the Popular Front coalition had for all practical purposes ceased to function.

The results of the 1941 general elections proved that the Right had good reasons to want to boycott them. For in those elections, the Popular Front obtained a truly spectacular victory. The Socialist Party obtained 20 per cent of the vote, thus nearly doubling the share obtained in 1937; and the Communist Party trebled its 1937 share, obtaining 12 per cent of the popular vote. The Radical Party, for its

part, slightly increased its share to 22 per cent. This meant that together with the Radical Party, Communists and Socialists controlled
more than 50 per cent of the vote, and with the other Popular Front
parties they controlled a majority of seats in both Chambers of the
Congress.[12] However, at this stage the Popular Front had collapsed
and the President had bargained away some crucial points of the government's programme. Hence, the threat of an electoral boycott by
the Right had achieved its objective.

That President Aguirre made concessions to the opposition parties
can be attributed to two main factors. On the one hand, he was basically in agreement with the spirit of the demands put forward by the
right-wing parties. As a wealthy landowner, he had always stood on
the right of his own party and had strongly opposed the establishment
of a political alliance with the Communist and Socialist parties.
Hence, it is not surprising that he should have been sympathetic to the
two main demands put forward by the right-wing parties: reducing
the intensity of political mobilisation and curbing the growth of the
marxist parties. On the other hand, that he was actually able to engage
in independent political manoeuvering was a consequence of the
political paralysis affecting the Popular Front coalition which was
caused by endless conflicts among its members. Although these conflicts were often triggered by petty rivalries, their underlying cause
was fundamental disagreement about who would lead the coalition
and who would control organised labour.

Conflicts within the Popular Front: Radicals vs Socialists

The conflicts over the leadership of the coalition involved the Socialist
and Radical parties. While the Socialists believed that they had a
better claim to leadership than the Radicals, the Radical Party, having
finally achieved control of the executive branch, was not prepared to
give in to the Socialists. The Socialists had reluctantly agreed to
support the Radical candidate in 1938, and were hoping that in the
following elections the presidential candidate would be a member of
their party. The Socialists' claim to lead the Popular Front was based
on the fact that since 1938, the Socialist party had been growing faster
than the Radical Party, and indeed by 1941, its share of the vote was
only marginally smaller than that of the Radical Party. The rivalry
between the Socialists and Radicals was expressed in their competition
for government jobs, in which the Radicals took the greater share; and
in their constant quarrels over the correct implementation of the
Popular Front's programme. During the first two years of government, the Socialists were constantly applying pressure to prevent the

Radical Party from deviating from the programmatic objectives of the coalition. Indeed, while the Socialists seemed prepared to go along with President Aguirre's decision to freeze the Popular Front's agrarian policies, they claimed full credit for the decision to establish CORFO. Also, mainly through the efforts of Salvador Allende, the Socialists were the main force behind the Popular Front's efforts to improve health and sanitary conditions.[13] The conflicts between Socialists and Radicals often led to cabinet crises – such as the one involving a major row between Allende, the government's Health Minister, and the Minister of Finance, a Radical, over the allocation of public funds for the free distribution of milk in schools.

Communists vs Socialists

The struggle between Communists and Socialists regarding which party should exercise hegemony over the labour movement sharpened considerably after the Popular Front came into office, and it was in fact the immediate cause for the break-up of the government coalition. The Socialists, who had assumed full cabinet responsibilities, viewed with suspicion the Communists Party's decision not to participate in President Aguirre's cabinet. The Communists justified their decision on the grounds that, by not participating, they were simply trying to dispel the notion put forward by the opposition that the Popular Front was a creature of the Third International. The Socialists, for their part, believed that the Communist Party's decision to stay out of the government was purely opportunistic as it would enable it to derive political benefits if the government suceeded, without assuming any risks if things went wrong. The Socialists were particularly concerned that the Communist Party would take advantage of the situation, as in fact it did, to undermine their position within the labour movement.

Relations between the Communist Party and the Socialist Party improved slightly when, in July 1940, they discovered the secret deal between President Aguirre and the right-wing parties. But this period of rapprochement was short-lived. Following the Nazi-Soviet Non-Aggression Pact in August 1939 – which was duly repudiated by the Socialist Party – the Communist Party lost its initial enthusiasm for the Popular Front and became increasingly critical of the explicitly anti-fascist views expressed by the members of the government, especially by representatives of the Socialist Party. The main target of Communist criticism was Oscar Schnake, the Socialist Minister for Development, who, after endorsing the position of the United States in the Inter-American Conference held in Havana in 1940, went on to

65

Washington to seek some form of financial compensation for the fall in the price of Chile's copper and nitrate exports. The Communists strongly criticised Schnake's trip to Washington, claiming – rightly as it turned out – that he had granted excessive concessions to the Americans without obtaining adequate financial compensation.

The Communist Party's attack on the Socialists created great concern within the Socialist Party for not only were the Communists purporting to portray the Socialists as having sold out to American imperialism, but the Socialists also suspected that the Radical Party, taking advantage of the situation, was siding with the Communist Party. Thus, in December 1940 the Socialist Party announced that it would withdraw from the Popular Front and would only return if the Communists were expelled. On 6 January 1941 the Executive Committee of the Popular Front declared that the Socialist Party's demand to expel the Communist Party was unacceptable. On that same night, the Central committee of the Socialists decided not to return to the Popular Front because, as they put it, 'it is inspired by the Communist Party, whose national and international policy is contrary to the interests of the country'. Shortly thereafter, the CTCH decided to withdraw from the Popular Front in order to preserve the unity of the labour movement. In its statement of resignation the CTCH vowed never again to participate 'in any political combination with this or any other name which the parties may form'.[14]

The collapse of the Popular Front coalition was greeted by the right-wing press as a long-overdue nullification of the class struggle.[15] However, the immediate political consequences of the break-up of the government coalition were less dramatic than expected. The Socialists, though formally out of the coalition, retained their three cabinet posts, while the Communists continued supporting the government without participating in the cabinet. Yet the breakdown of the coalition transformed the Aguirre government into little more than a caretaker administration. Indeed, by January 1941, the government had completely lost its original impetus and was unable to take any new political initiatives. These circumstances rendered futile the victory obtained by the left-wing parties in the congressional elections of March 1941.

After withdrawing from Popular Front the Socialists tried to persuade the Radical Party to form a broad alliance of left-wing parties without the Communist Party. The Radicals rejected the Socialists' proposal because they feared that the establishment of such an alliance would boost the popularity of the Socialist Party, thus strengthening its claim of becoming the leading party of the Left. Moreover, because the congressional elections were only a few weeks away, the Radicals could not afford to break off their ties with the Communist Party since this party provided them with a stable base of electoral support which they desperately needed to counteract the growth of the Socialist Party. Besides, the Communists were safe allies since, unlike the Socialists, they had no explicit ambition to run their own candidate in the presidential elections.

Radicals vs the Government

While electoral calculations gave the Radical Party a semblance of unity, relations between party and government rapidly deteriorated, reaching their lowest level during the first semester of 1941. The main issue was the direction of government policy, and it was expressed as a challenge to the presidential prerogative to appoint the members of the cabinet. Upon taking office, Aguirre had appointed most of his own supporters in the party's leadership to senior government posts. This had created a vacuum in the party's governing bodies, which was promptly filled in by members of the party's left-wing groups. The new leadership of the Radical Party became seriously concerned that the President's willingness to make concessions to the Right would not only weaken the government, but would also undermine the Party's electoral base. Thus, in an attempt to exercise more control over government policy, the Party began to demand a greater say in the composition of the cabinet. The President consistently rejected this demand on the ground that the presidential prerogative to appoint the cabinet was an essential feature of the regime established by the 1925 constitution, which could not be modified without jeopardising the whole political system. During the first two years of the Aguirre administration, the party reluctantly accepted the President's interpretation of his own constitutional prerogatives. However, in April 1941, when the government ordered the closure of the communist newspaper *El Siglo* in order to prevent a strike in the nitrate mines from spreading, the Radical Party ordered the five Radical ministers in the cabinet to resign in protest at the government's attack on civil liberties. The President made desperate attempts to persuade the Radical Party to change its decision. However, in the event, it broke away from the government, and the President was forced to accept the resignation of his own ministers.[16]

Collapse of the Popular Front

After Hitler's invasion of the Soviet Union in June 1941, relations between the Communist and Socialist parties improved, and both parties began to show a renewed interest in collaborating with the

67

government. However, by then, President Aguirre's health had seriously deteriorated, and he no longer had the political will or the strength to reconstitute the old alliance of left-wing parties. In November of that year, the death of the President re-opened old feuds as a new electoral campaign got under way.

During the three years of the Aguirre administration, the Right successfully managed to bend the hand of the government, restricting the scope of its political programme. The Right was greatly helped in this by the profound divisions existing within the coalition and by President Aguirre's willingness to make concessions. However, it should be noted that their strategy showed that they were determined to provoke an institutional crisis that would overthrow the government. That this did not happen was not because the Right showed any flexibility but because government concessions to the Right – mainly concessions over CORFO and the decision not to intervene in the agricultural sector – satisfied the interests of the bourgeoisie. To be sure, some extreme groups within the Right never accepted that the Radical Party could run the country or that the marxists should be allowed to participate in the political system. However, acceptance by the right-wing parties of the modified economic policy launched by President Aguirre, and continued by the following two administrations until 1952, is shown by the fact that, between 1942 and 1952, they were willing to participate in coalition governments with the Radical Party.

II   TWO MORE RADICAL ADMINISTRATIONS

Juan Antonio Ríos, 1942–1946

President Aguirre's successor, Ríos, was a member of the conservative wing of the Radical Party and held strong anti-communist views. Ríos' presidential nomination owed much to the fact that after Aguirre's death the right-wing groups within the Radical Party quickly regained control of the party apparatus. However, his nomination can also be explained as a reaction by the Radical Party to the policies pursued by its two former allies, the marxist parties. Indeed, while the Socialists announced that they would nominate one of their own leaders to run for President, the Communist Party was openly intervening in the internal affairs of the Radical Party in support of Gabriel González, the leader of the party's left-wing faction. Indeed, after González' bid for the party's nomination had failed, the Communist Party tried unsuccessfully to persuade him to break away from the party and run as an independent candidate of the Left.[17] Given these circumstances, it is not surprising that the nominee of the Radical Party was a man who represented the party's conservative groups and who seemed more inclined to form an electoral alliance with parties in the centre and on the right than with the marxist Left.

Ríos' candidacy was immediately supported by a group of dissident Liberals and by an assortment of small centrist parties, including the Falange. His opponent in the presidential race was General Ibáñez, who was supported by the Conservative and Liberal Parties. During his campaign, Ríos made it clear that he was not interested in reviving the old Popular Front alliance.

However, in order to keep Ibáñez out of office, the marxist parties were forced to give Ríos their unconditional support. Ibáñez' strength can be appreciated by the fact that although he only had the support of the Conservative and Liberal parties, he managed to obtain 44 per cent of the vote.

Ríos' first cabinet was a heterogeneous combination of parties which included the Socialist Party, the right-wing Liberals, the Radicals and Democratic Party. Not surprisingly, this unlikely coalition – which was typical of the period 1942–52 – soon broke up, leading to permanent cabinet instability. After a year in government and considerable internal debate, which provoked a split in the party, the Socialists decided to leave the cabinet and to pursue a more fundamental marxist line. Nevertheless, the Socialists continued supporting the government in the Congress through their participation in the Democratic Alliance, a loose parliamentary alliance which included Socialists, Radicals and Communists. The Democratic Alliance had the limited objective of supporting Ríos' legislative initiatives, and, as Ríos soon found out, it rarely functioned effectively in support of the government.

The Radical Party, for its part, again came into conflict with the President over the question of cabinet appointments. In fact, during two long periods, the Radical Party was in formal opposition to the government. Throughout this time, the Communist Party, which was following its new policy of national unity, gave its unconditional support to President Ríos, making every possible effort to avoid a permanent rupture between the President and his own party. In spite of the loyal support offered by the Communist Party, Ríos consistently refused to accept it as a member of the governing coalition. This state of affairs led to a complicated and unsettling pattern of political manoeuvring, which was to become the main feature of the eleven years following President Aguirre's death and which eventually led to a fragmentation and weakening of the party system.

The Ríos administration had to confront the economic and political consequences of World War II. The outbreak of the war in Europe had closed Chile's European markets, thus forcing the government to come to terms with the enhanced role which the United States was beginning to play in the Latin-American region. Although the Ríos administration placed Chile firmly within the sphere of influence of the United States, it did not do so without some hesitation and considerable misgivings. In 1940, President Roosevelt had approved the general policy of using the supply of arms and credit as a lever to obtaining political and economic cooperation from the Latin-American nations.[18] The United States wanted full access to strategic raw materials at low prices, offering loans from the Exim-bank in exchange. Chile had in fact obtained such a loan in 1940, after agreeing to a low price for its copper and nitrate exports. However, after the attack on Pearl Harbour, the United States began to demand greater political cooperation from the Latin-American states without offering economic incentives in return. The new policy of the United States was formally endorsed by the Latin-American states in 1942, when the meeting of Ministers of Foreign Affairs of the region adopted a decision recommending breaking off diplomatic relations with the Axis powers. The Ríos government complied with this resolution a year after it was approved and only after considerable pressure from the United States. Ríos' reluctance to break with the Axis powers was not due to fascist sympathies, as was probably the case in Argentina, but to the fact that the Chilean economy had been particularly badly hit by the low prices of its copper and nitrate exports. Besides, many politicians in Chile advocated a policy of neutrality as they were not convinced that Germany would lose the war.[19]

The end of the war aggravated Chile's economic problems since demand fell below its pre-war levels even though the price of copper went up.[20] This situation brought about an unprecedented upsurge of industrial unrest. Although in the first two full years of the Ríos administration (1943–4), the level of strike activity had been high, in the following two years it reached an alarming rate. Thus, while in the first two years, there was an annual average of 109 strikes, involving 43,000 workers each year, in the following two years (1945–6) the annual average of strikes was 187, involving about 96,000 workers each year.[21] The growing militancy of workers intensified the rivalry between the Communist and Socialist parties, putting considerable pressure on the Radicals as each tried to win them over to its side.

The conflict between Communists and Socialists came to a head in January and February of 1946, after Alfredo Duhalde, a Cabinet Minister, had taken over as Vice-President, replacing Ríos who was terminally ill. In order to deal with a strike in the nitrate fields, Duhalde decided to take strong administrative measures against the striking unions, a decision which was interpreted as a major attack on trade-union freedom. The CTCH responded by organising several protest rallies in different parts of the country. In Santiago, these demonstrations were violently repressed by the government, resulting in the death of several people. These events prompted the CTCH to call a one-day national stoppage, which was successful, despite efforts by the government to make it fail. This forced Duhalde to agree to lift the sanctions against the unions and to meet some of the strikers' demands. To speed up the implementation of this agreement, the CTCH decided to call another one-day national stoppage on 4 February. However, this time, the Socialists, who had supported the decision to strike, changed their minds when Duhalde invited them to join the cabinet.[22] They justified their behaviour by claiming that their presence in the cabinet would safeguard the government's promise to the nitrate workers.[23] The Socialist Party's decision not to support the strike led to the division of the CTCH and provoked violent clashes between Communist and Socialist workers. Henceforth, the Socialist-controlled CTCH supported the government, while the Communist-controlled CTCH, by far the larger of the two, opposed it.

The conflict leading to the division of the CTCH also created problems for the Radicals. Since the party had begun to swing to the left in anticipation of a presidential election imposed by Ríos' imminent death, they sided with the Communists and quit the government in protest against the handling of the nitrate dispute. When Ríos died, Duhalde found himself out of the Radical Party, with the Socialists keen to support him if he accepted to run for President. Duhalde accepted the presidential nomination, but changed his mind unexpectedly after the electoral campaign had started. Duhalde's sudden change of heart left the Socialists with an embarrassing political dilemma. They could not support the Radical candidate Gabriel González because of his association with the Communist Party and were not prepared to vote for either of the two right-wing candidates – though some prominent party members advocated supporting the Liberal candidate. Thus, to avoid further embarrassment and to maintain a semblance of unity, they decided to run their own candidate.

Gabriel González, 1946–1952

The winner in the 1946 presidential election was Gabriel González, the Radical candidate who had the support of the Communist Party.

González, who only obtained a plurality of the vote, owed his victory to the division of the right-wing parties, which could not agree on a common candidate. Thus, while González only obtained 40 per cent of the vote, the combined vote of the two right-wing parties was 47 per cent. On the other hand, the division within the Left does not seem to have affected González at all, since the Socialist candidate polled less than 3 per cent of the vote.

González took office in 1946 as a left-wing president supported by the Communist Party and by the largest wing of organised labour. However, he soon moved towards the right and began to apply severely repressive measures against the union movement and the Communist Party. By the end of his administration González had totally alienated both left- and right-wing parties. Thus, though by 1952 the electoral strength of the Radical Party was the same as in the late 1930s, the party was no longer able to play the game of coalition politics at which it had been so successful during the preceding fourteen years.

President González inherited the unresolved economic problems of the previous administration, and he was in a delicate political position, both domestically and internationally, because of the Communist Party's participation in the cabinet. González did not have a majority in the Congress, and his own Radical Party had not fully supported his decision to seek the support of the Communist Party. Indeed, shortly before the election, a small, but influential group of Radicals broke away from the party to establish the Radical Democratic Movement. At the same time some disaffected Radicals had joined forces with groups from the extreme right to form the Chilean Anti-Communist Association (Asociación Chilena Anti-Communista/ACHA), a paramilitary organisation determined to use any means to eliminate the Communist Party from the country's political scene.[24] On the international front, González' position was weak since the United States, which was beginning to articulate its new Cold War policy, was deeply concerned about the participation of the Communist Party in a democratically elected government. Since at the time, Chile was in desperate need of foreign finance, the United States had a powerful weapon to persuade González to give up his alliance with the Communist Party.

González made his first concessions to the Right, even before taking office. Because he had only obtained a plurality of votes his election had to be ratified by the Congress, which was formally entitled to choose between him and the runner-up, the Conservative candidate Eduardo Cruz-Coke, who had obtained 30 per cent of the vote. Since the Liberal Party had the necessary votes to decide the outcome of the election in the Congress, they made full use of their position. In exchange for supporting González in the Congress, the Liberals demanded three cabinet posts, as well as the right to approve beforehand any bill which the government might send to the Congress dealing with the question of rural unionisation.[25] The Radical Party accepted these demands, and thus González' first cabinet was an unlikely mix of Radical, Communist and Liberal ministers.

During the first months of the González administration, the Communists pursued a two-pronged strategy: on the one hand, they advocated wage restraint in support of government policy, but on the other, they made full use of their position in government to carry out a vigorous campaign of political agitation and organisation, which greatly enhanced their popularity. Their most spectacular success was in the countryside, where Communist support for the unionisation of peasants led in only two months to the establishment of 358 unions with a membership of 11,000.[26] Thus, while the Communist Party had already overtaken the divided Socialist Party in the 1945 congressional elections, by the end of 1946 their popular support was almost twice that of the combined Socialist vote.

The growth of the Communist Party greatly concerned the other political parties, particularly the Liberals, who felt betrayed by González. Indeed, the Liberals had good reason to believe that the President supported some of the Communist Party activities. For example, Communist Party policy in the rural areas had been triggered off by the government's decision to revoke an administrative order dating back to 1933, which had suspended the registration of rural unions. Thus, when the Liberals confronted the government with an ultimatum threatening to withdraw their support unless the Communists were expelled from the cabinet, the government, in order to placate them, decided to suspend the registration of new rural unions.[27] González also promptly gave in to the demands of the Liberals, but did it in a form which is typical of the political style prevailing at the time. Instead of completely breaking off with the Communists, he dropped them from the cabinet, but secured their continuing support by promising them that in due course they would be asked to return to occupy government posts.[28] Likewise, the government ban on rural unionisation took the form of a government bill, which was rushed through the Congress and approved in April 1947. This bill, purporting to regulate the union rights of agricultural workers, effectively banned rural unions for nearly twenty years, until 1967, when the law was changed.[29] Indeed, while this legislation

73

was in effect only twenty-eight rural unions were established with a membership of only 1,647.[30]

The departure of the Communists from the cabinet in April 1947 did not alleviate the government's difficulties. The United States maintained its pressure to secure a complete break with the Communist Party. Although the Truman Doctrine was announced only in March 1947, the United States had already for quite some time been pursuing a policy of closer military and political cooperation in the Latin-American region. A joint memorandum of the State, War and Navy Departments of the American government prepared in July 1945 stated that military aid to the region would involve 'The indoctrination, training and equipment of the armed forces of the other American republics' with a view to facilitating the defence of the hemisphere.[31] Later on, President Truman made it clear that international security in the hemisphere entailed solidarity measures to repel armed attacks from outside the continent, as well as attacks from within launched by the growing menace of internal Communism. Thus, in Chile the alliance between the Radical Party and the Communist Party was conspicuously out of step with the emerging foreign policy of the United States. Therefore, to secure a complete break between the government and the Communist Party, the United States maintained the informal embargo on credits to Chile, which had been in effect since González took office in November 1946.[32]

The international credit squeeze aggravated the already difficult economic situation, giving fresh impetus to industrial unrest. The continuous involvement of the Communist Party in support of strike action against government policy, together with its strident criticism of the government's endorsement of the United States' policy in the hemisphere, gave President González the necessary justification to break completely with the Communist Party. Thus, in August 1947, accusing the Communist Party of subversive activities, he sacked all the Communists who held posts in the state bureaucracy. Later on, in October of that same year, the government applied draconian measures to repress a legal strike declared by the Communist-controlled unions in the coal mines. At the same time, the government closed down the Communist newspaper *El Siglo* and broke off diplomatic relations with the Soviet Union.[33]

Once the González administration had given ample proof of its determination to repress the Communist Party and to align itself with the West in the emerging Cold War, the United States supported Chile's application for World Bank loans and supplied an Exim-Bank credit for twenty-three million dollars.[34] But González' tough anti-

Communist stance did not automatically bring an end to industrial unrest. For another whole year the government continued applying emergency measures to repress strikes and to destroy working-class organisations. This strong anti-labour policy crystallised in 1948 with the approval of the Defence of Democracy Act, a legislative enactment which banned the Communist Party, but which was also a fundamental attack on union rights and freedoms. This Act gave the government power to cancel the electoral registration of nearly 26,000 members of the Communist Party, to send the party's leaders into exile and to exercise direct political control over the composition and activities of the unions.[35] Following the promulgation of this shameful statute, President González appointed a new cabinet, which he called Cabinet of National Unity (*Concentración Nacional*), which included representatives from parties on both sides of the political spectrum, including a break-away faction of the Socialist Party. This cabinet remained in office until 1950, when it was swept away by a new upsurge of industrial unrest caused mainly by the government's attempt to apply a stabilisation programme at the cost of wage-earners.

By 1951, as it became clear that, in the absence of a major change of economic policy, the government's anti-labour stance had not succeeded in reducing inflation or the level of industrial unrest, González and the Radical Party began to distance themselves from the Right in a last-minute attempt to avoid defeat in the presidential elections that were due to take place in the following year. Thus, while in 1949 the Convention of the Radical Party had authorised the government to enter into alliances with any party willing to support democracy and to support the ban on the Communists; in 1951, the Party became more discriminating, requesting the government to form a broad left wing alliance, excluding the Communists, as well as their recent allies, the Conservative Party.[36] Despite these attempts at changing its right-wing image, the Radical Party was no longer capable of persuading any of the right-wing parties to form an electoral alliance to fight the 1952 presidential election. González' strong anti-labour stance, which had initially seduced some Socialists because of its anti-Communist slant, had nearly destroyed the electoral strength of the marxist Left, but had also alienated the working class from the government. Therefore, by the early fifties, when the Radicals tried to return to the centre of the political stage, they found that there was no major party willing to join forces with them. Some of the Socialists opted for supporting Ibáñez, while others formed an alliance with the Communist Party in an attempt to get Allende elected President. The right-wing parties, for their part, realising that the Radicals could no longer exercise any influence within the labour movement, lost interest in them and supported a man from their own ranks, thus reviving the old right-wing bloc which had been so successful during the second administration of Arturo Alessandri.

Fourteen years of political rule by the Radical Party had not only isolated the Radicals, but had also fragmented the political system. By the early 1950s, all major political parties were divided, and there was a great proliferation of political groups. This fragmentation weakened the party system, making possible in 1952 the electoral victory of General Ibáñez, who promised to cleanse the system of political corruption and to open a new era in the country's political history.

CHAPTER 6

Marxists in Coalition Politics: 1938–1952

FROM 1932 to the end of the 1940s the Communist and Socialist parties were prominent participants in the political process. In many respects, their behaviour was not unlike that of any other non-marxist party. For their actions seemed to be largely determined by the over-riding objective of participating, albeit as junior partners, in coalition governments led by the Radical Party. To secure this objective they campaigned vigorously to increase their electoral appeal, formed parliamentary alliances with non-marxist parties, subordinated the interests of the labour movement to their political ambitions, and occasionally even made use of their influence in government to attack and undermine each other. This commonplace parliamentary behaviour acquires special significance through the fact that despite their involvement in parliamentary politics, both Communists and Socialists sought, in different ways, to link their activities to their own programmatic objective of bringing about a revolutionary transformation of society and to their claim of representing the interests of the working class and the popular masses generally.

A preliminary assessment of the Communists and Socialists as actors in the political system would probably be negative. For while both parties played a crucial role in and out of government and made impressive electoral gains, they were in disarray by the end of the 1940s. The Socialist Party was deeply divided and had all but lost its strong electoral backing, the labour movement was split into two, the Communists were banned from politics and the government of the day was waging a vigorous campaign to weaken the labour movement and to eradicate marxist influence from the political system generally.

Political developments during this period do not bear out Communists' and Socialists' claim that they actually represented the interests of the working class. For despite the growing influence of the marxist parties the boundaries of the political system were not substantially altered. From 1932 to the late 1940s the size of the electorate in relation to the total population remained unchanged at around 10 per cent, agricultural workers continued to be denied the right to form unions, and the majority of workers in manufacturing industry did not, despite their links with the marxist parties, substantially improve their living standards. Thus, by the end of this period, not only was the working class facing serious economic difficulties, but the prospects of revolutionary change seemed to have faded forever. Indeed, the very survival of political democracy was in danger as the party system seemed unable to generate a viable coalition to confront effectively the populist threat of Carlos Ibáñez.

Given the circumstances of the late forties it would have been plausible at the time to predict that the heyday of marxism was over and that the labour movement was likely to remain divided for a long time to come. Yet, by the early fifties the labour movement came together again under a single organisation, the United Workers' Federation (Central Unica de Trabajadores/CUT), which was jointly controlled by Communists and Socialists. Shortly thereafter, Communists and Socialists formed an electoral alliance which was to last for more than a decade. This seems to suggest that the experience of the marxist parties in coalition governments was not entirely negative since by the early 1950s they were once again the dominant force of a unified labour movement and, together, they were still the leading force on the left of the political spectrum.

The itinerary of the marxist parties during this period raises some interesting questions. Why, for example, did the Socialists persist in defining themselves as marxist when both the populist and the social democratic routes were possible alternatives? Why were the Socialists unable to implement their several resolutions to follow a consistent marxist line and to refuse cabinet posts? Why were the Communists such loyal adherers to the international communist movement? How involved was the Comintern in the creation of the Popular Front? Why were the Communists so successful in maintaining party unity despite their changing political line? This chapter examines these and other issues.

I   MAIN EVENTS

In 1932 the labour movement was weak and fragmented. FOCH membership had plummeted to only a few thousand as a consequence of the severe repression under the Ibáñez government. The Communist Party had only recently re-emerged into legality, and it was not only isolated from other political groups, (because of its strict application of the Comintern's 'Third Period' line), but was still confronting a serious challenge from the Communist Party-Left, a Trotskyite party which had broken off from the Communist Party in 1931. However, by 1936 the left-wing parties had undergone a dramatic change. In 1933 a very popular Socialist Party resulting from the merger of several small socialist groups had emerged, and by then the Communist Party was no longer threatened by Trotskyism. The Popular Front was established in April 1936, and later that year the main segments of the labour movement came together to form the CTCH.

The united labour movement, together with the partnership between Communists and Socialists, was politically very effective as a means of coordinating opposition to the austerity programmes of the Alessandri government and as a vote-catching device. Thus, in the congressional elections of 1937 the recently created Socialist Party obtained an impressive 11 per cent of the vote, while the Communist Party obtained just over 4 per cent.

The victory of the Popular Front in the 1938 Presidential elections greatly strengthened the labour movement. In the first two years of the Aguirre administration the number of workers belonging to unions increased by 30 per cent, reaching nearly 162,000 in 1940. Moreover, as nearly two-thirds of all unions were affiliated to the CTCH, which in turn was jointly run by the Communist Party and Socialist Party, the increase in union membership greatly enhanced the influence of these parties among the working-class.[1]

Relations between Communists and Socialists as coalition partners in the Popular Front were less than cordial. The Socialists accepted cabinet posts in the Aguirre administration while the Communists decided not to take on cabinet responsibilities. After the Nazi-Soviet pact of August 1939 relations between the two parties turned sour. Eventually, in January 1941, the Socialists, after failing to persuade the Radical Party to expel the Communist Party from the coalition, decided to resign from membership in the Popular Front, though, interestingly enough, not from their cabinet posts. As the quarrel between Communists and Socialists intensified, the Socialists had to confront their first serious split when the ultra-left, 'non-conformist' faction, quit to form the Socialist Workers' Party. This new party, despite its radical rhetoric, soon entered into electoral alliances with the Communist Party, and by 1944 it dissolved itself, most of its members joining the Communist Party.

79

The conflicts among the leadership of the marxist parties had no effect on their electoral appeal. In the 1941 Congressional elections both Communists and Socialists increased their share of the vote: the Communist vote rose from 4 per cent to 12 per cent while the Socialist vote increased from 11 per cent to 17 per cent. Hitler's attack on the Soviet Union in June 1941 brought about a slight improvement in relations between Communists and Socialists as the Communist Party's interest in forming broad alliances against fascism revived. However, the election of a new President in 1942, following the death of President Aguirre, bought to an end the brief rapprochement between them. The Socialists tried, unsuccessfully, to persuade the Radicals to support a Socialist candidate, while the Communist Party made vigorous efforts, also unsuccessful, to secure the nomination of Gabriel González as the Radical Party's presidential candidate.

The Radical Juan Antonio Ríos, a man from the right-wing of the party and hostile to the Communists, won the 1942 presidential elections. The Socialists accepted cabinet posts in the Ríos administration, but soon resigned to reassess their political role and to adopt a stricter marxist line. The Communists, for their part, gave their unconditional support to Ríos, but were not offered cabinet posts.

The withdrawal of the Socialist Party from the Ríos administration was strongly resisted by some of its leaders, notably by Marmaduque Grove. This caused the second major split, when Grove and his followers eventually left the party to form the Partido Socialista Auténtico (PSA). Initially, Grove's party did considerable damage to the Socialist Party's electoral performance. Thus, in the 1945 Congressional elections the Socialists' share of the vote fell dramatically from 17 per cent in 1941 to a mere 7 per cent while Grove's party polled 6 per cent of the vote. However, by the late 1940s Grove's party had disappeared, and Grove himself had quit politics. It must be noted, though, that by 1945, the Communist Party, whose share of the vote had dropped only slightly from 12 per cent in 1941 to 10 per cent had become the largest marxist party. By then it also controlled 60 per cent of all unions and was the dominant group in the CTCH.

Late in 1945 President Ríos became terminally ill and was replaced on an interim basis by Vice-President Alfredo Duhalde, a member of the Radical Party. In January 1946 the Socialists accepted cabinet posts in the Duhalde administration and were soon involved in a major conflict with the Communists and the CTCH. This row eventually led to the split of the CTCH, with the Communists retaining control of the larger section.

After the death of President Ríos, the Community Party supported the Radical candidate González, and the Socialists, unable to find an acceptable ally, had their own candidate. González won the election with only a plurality of the vote, while the Socialist candidate obtained a bare 2.5 per cent of the vote. González appointed three Communists to cabinet posts, but this friendship was short-lived. Less than six months after taking office they were asked to resign their cabinet posts, and a year later, in 1948, the Communist Party was banned from politics altogether. These events brought about yet another division within the Socialist Party, when a small group led by Bernardo Ibáñez accepted cabinet posts in the González administration. This split created confusion. Although the dissidents were a tiny minority, a procedural manoeuvre enabled them to retain the full name of the party, Socialist Party of Chile. The main party was thus forced to change its name to Popular Socialist Party (PSP). This division did not greatly damage the electoral base of the PSP as the dissidents only accounted for 3 per cent of the vote; however, it created considerable confusion among the rank and file of socialist trade unionists since those who led it were leaders of the Socialist-controlled CTCH.

Another internal conflict developed in 1950 when the PSP decided to back General Ibáñez in the forthcoming presidential elections. On this occasion, a small group of prominent leaders, led by Salvador Allende, left the party to join the Socialist Party of Chile. Allende and his followers soon took over the party's leadership and entered into an alliance with the banned Communist Party. This new alliance supported Allende in his first bid for Presidency in 1952. Thus, by the early 1950s, Grove's party had disappeared from the political map, and the Socialists were divided into two main parties: the PSP and the SP of Chile. The former, accounting for the bulk of the Socialist vote, had taken the populist option offered by the candidacy of Ibáñez, the dictator of the 1920s; while the latter, a party without a significant following, had taken the first step towards the establishment of what was soon to become a durable alliance between the two marxist parties.

II THE SOCIALIST PARTY

In many respects, the Socialists' behaviour from 1932 to 1952 appears to have been most erratic. In the early days they participated in a left-wing parliamentary alliance which excluded the Communists, and later they formed the Popular Front in alliance not only with Communists, but with the hitherto right-wing Radical Party. In the years following the electoral victory of the Popular Front the Socialists seemed unable to follow a consistent line as their appetite for high office overshadowed their long-term programmatic objectives. Their opportunistic behaviour brought about a series of divisions which seriously weakened the party's popular base without diminishing their seemingly inexhaustible interest in participating in coalition governments.

Some observers have described their behaviour during this period as typically populist.[2] This description is, on the face of it, plausible as in the early days the Socialists greatly benefited from the enormous popular appeal of their leader, Marmaduque Grove, which went well beyond working-class constituencies to include a large number of middle- and lower-middle-class voters.[3] It was because of this broad appeal that they were able to establish their electoral presence throughout the country at a much faster rate and with greater ease than did the Communist Party. Yet, in practice, they did not abandon their marxist ideology nor did they give up their attempts to become the vanguard of the proletariat in a revolutionary process which was to culminate in socialist revolution. Some observers who emphasize the populist trends during the early years of the Socialist Party note with regret that they eventually opted for marxism as, in their view, the populist road would have yielded greater political dividends.[4] Although this is an interesting suggestion, an analysis of the political context shows that the populist alternative was not, at the time, viable.

Populist Impulse Frustrated

It is arguable that when the Socialist Party came into existence in 1933 conditions were ripe for the emergence of a powerful left-wing populist movement. The economy was in ruins as a consequence of the world depression, and the party system was in disarray after four years of dictatorial rule by Ibáñez. It is therefore not surprising that, in June 1932, Air Commander Marmaduque Grove managed to stage a successful military coup against the government of President Juan Esteban Montero, which had been elected only eight months earlier on 4 October 1931. Grove promptly established a military junta and proclaimed a Socialist Republic. His experiment was, however, short-lived. After twelve days in office another member of the Junta, Carlos Dávila, took over and sent Grove into internal exile. Less than four months later, Davila himself had to give way to the democratically-elected government of Arturo Alessandri.

Grove's coup had many features which, at least in Latin America, have been associated with populism.[5] That is, it was led and supported by middle-class groups impatient to achieve social and economic change, which did not, however, fully accept either communism or liberalism. Grove also enjoyed overwhelming support from the mass of urban poor and organised workers. His populist inspiration was confirmed by the dramatic measures he took during his brief spell in office, such as returning to the poor, free of charge, their pawned clothes and working tools, including sewing machines.[6]

Three factors may account for Grove's failure to consolidate his position as leader of a left-wing populist government. Firstly, despite his left-wing inclinations, Grove had in the past worked closely with Ibáñez, and both Ibáñez and the armed forces, in general, were regarded with considerable suspicion by the leadership of practically all political parties. Secondly, Grove and his movement did not enjoy the support of the Communist Party, which, though weak at the time, still had considerable influence within the labour movement. At the time the Communist Party was applying the Comintern's 'Third Period' line and regarded itself as the natural leader of any movement towards socialism. Moreover, Grove himself was profoundly anti-communist, a feature which, in the absence of a coherent alternative ideology, merely emphasized similarities with Ibáñez. Thirdly, and perhaps most important, some of Grove's close middle-class supporters, mainly young university graduates, perhaps shared his anti-communism, but were not anti-marxist. Their anti-communism stemmed from the sectarian ultra-left policies of the Communist Party in the late twenties. At an ideological level, Grove's supporters, such as Oscar Schnake and Eugenio González, had either already embraced marxism or were soon to do so. Moreover, many of these radical youths had had first hand experience of repression or, at the very least, were aware that Ibáñez' repression of working-class and popular organisations had been carried out under the anti-party banner. Thus naturally, they were not against the re-establishment of a party parliamentary system.

The economic policies advocated by the Socialists during the Aguirre administration reveal more concern with the technical aspect of development, than with mobilizing the masses in a populist direction. The Socialists were in fact the driving force in the government's attempt to modernise industry through the agency of CORFO. That this was an overriding concern of the Socialists is reflected in the passion with which Oscar Schnake, the Socialist Minister for Development, embraced the pro-Allied line taken by the United States at the Inter-American Conference held in Havana in 1940. Schnake's views on this not only alienated him from the Communists, who, because of the Nazi-Soviet Pact had already turned against the Popular Front, but also from an important segment of public opinion which was reluctant to abandon the policy of neutrality, both on political and economic grounds. Schnake's argument in favour of siding with the Allies was simply that unless Chile and other countries in the Latin-American region continued to count on trade and financial support from the United States they would confront an economic and political crisis as serious as the one they had experienced during the world depression. According to Schnake, neutrality amounted to collective economic suicide. Thus, to safeguard stability in the region and to ensure economic development, it was necessary to accept United States leadership in matters of foreign policy.[7]

Underlying Schnake's views was the conception that industrial development should take priority over other areas of government policy. Whether or not this was the correct approach, it was nonetheless, at the time, perfectly consistent with the political constraints of the Popular Front's administration. As explained in Chapter 3, above, the Popular Front's objective of achieving the harmonious development of all economic sectors was frustrated by the opposition parties in the Congress as they all but excluded agriculture from the reach of the government's economic policy and severely limited the financial resources of CORFO. Given these circumstances it is not surprising that Schnake concentrated all his efforts on securing finance for CORFO while neglecting to use the agrarian issue as a populist platform. Instead he concentrated on industrial development projects, most of which only came into operation in the early 1950s. This approach to economic policy may perhaps be described as technocratic, but it would be inaccurate to describe it as populist.

The Socialist Party's acceptance of the Popular Front's economic policy further undermined the party's populist impulse. For, together with circumscribing the scope of the government's economic policy, the opposition parties also ensured that the boundaries of the political system remained unchanged. Indeed, between 1938 and 1949 there was practically no increase in the size of the electorate, which remained at about 10 per cent of the total population. Thus, the Socialist Party's scope for increasing its electoral and popular support was greatly reduced. The non-Catholic middle-class vote was firmly controlled by the Radical party. Indeed, one of the remarkable features of the period is the stability of the Radical Party's electoral strength. Moreover, the Catholic middle-class constituencies which, in principle, should have been attracted by the Socialist Party's brand of

84

populism were still loyal to the traditional right-wing parties, and even the recently-created Falange was unable to establish itself there. The Socialists certainly had some scope for increasing their support among working-class voters and in fact did quite well amongst them. However, here they had strong competition from the Communist Party. Thus, while the Socialists managed to obtain 20 per cent of the vote in 1941, it was not enough for them to do anything but continue their involvement in electoral and coalition politics.

Socialist support for Ibáñez in the 1952 Presidential elections could well be regarded as a sign of the Socialist Party's persistent populism. Yet, as explained in Chapter 8 below, when the Socialists joined the Ibañista movement they had only recently completed a lengthy process of ideological clarification resulting in a reaffirmation of their commitment to marxist principles. Accordingly, their objective in joining the Ibañista movement was to transform it into a marxist revolutionary vehicle. Since they soon realized that this was not easy, they quit the government and concentrated on the task of unifying their party.

A Marxist Party

It could well be argued that if the Socialist Party was unable to take the populist route, it should have taken the seemingly easy option of becoming a Social Democratic party to the left of the Radical Party and at arms-length from the Communist Party. For, after all, by the mid-1940s the feud between Socialists and Communists had reached such acrimony that a reconciliation between them seemed unthinkable. Moreover, by 1947 the Radical Party had already moved so far to the right that the transformation of the Socialist Party into a left-wing Social Democratic Party committed to improving the living standards of working people would have probably been regarded as the natural step for a party desperately in need of a clearly-defined political role. Yet, instead, the Socialist Party continued to declare itself a marxist party with, as its ultimate goal, the revolutionary transformation of society.

To understand the Socialist Party's continuing allegiance to marxism it is necessary to take into account its relationship with the Communist Party and organised labour. As already explained, when the Socialist Party came into existence the Communist Party was politically isolated, its influence in the labour movement had declined and it had been weakened by the split of the Trotskyites from the party. By contrast, the Socialist Party was full of vitality, enjoying considerable

85

popularity and rapidly expanding its influence in the labour movement. Thus, the possibility of establishing itself as the dominant – if not the only – political force on the left was not unrealistic.

During the decade preceding the establishment of the Socialist Party, the dominant influence in the labour movement had been marxism. By 1919 the POS had taken over and had radicalized the FOCH, and from 1922 the organisational structure for the labour movement was almost one and the same with that of the Communist Party.[8] This identity between party and union probably accounts for the decline of the Communist Party and of the labour movement. However, the enormous influence of marxist ideology in the labour movement during its formative years is probably important in explaining not only why the Socialists embraced marxism, but also why competition between Socialists and Communists for influence in the labour movement probably had the effect of reinforcing their commitment to marxism. It must also be noted that by the mid-1930s the Trotskyites had wound up their party and joined the Socialist Party, and this must have certainly strengthened the party's ideological commitment to marxism.

The economic policy pursued by the Socialists as members of the Aguirre government was, as already noted, probably somewhat technocratic and not based on a thorough marxist analysis of local conditions. Yet, as members of the cabinet, the Socialists acted with loyalty to the government and were committed to seeing the Popular Front's programme implemented. Their behaviour was consistent with their conviction that the modernisation of the economy – at least of the industrial sector – was a necessary prerequisite for bringing about a socialist transformation at a later stage. In this respect, the Socialist Party was not only politically more consistent than the Communist Party, but also more to the left.

The Socialist Party had grounds for regarding the Communist Party as opportunistic and unreliable. The Communist Party's decision not to accept cabinet posts in the Aguirre government was seen as an indication that the Communists were not fully committed to the government's programme, but were merely using their membership in the Popular Front as a means of increasing their popularity without assuming responsibility for the consequences of government policy as a whole. To the Socialists the definitive proof that the Communists were unreliable political partners and that their leftism was insincere came after the signature of the Nazi-Soviet Non-Aggression Pact. For, after the Soviet Union concluded this agreement with Hitler the Chilean Communists suddenly lost interest in the Popular Front and began to criticize government policy, accusing Oscar Schnake of selling out to American imperialism because of the strong pro-Allied stance which he adopted at the Inter-American Conference of 1940. The Communist Party's allegation that the Socialists had sold out to imperialism was all the more invidious since only a few months earlier, following the line of the Comintern, they themselves had praised, as progressive, President Roosevelt's Good Neighbour policy.[9] Therefore, it is not surprising that in December 1939 the Socialists demanded the expulsion of the Communists from the Popular Front.

The Communist Party's behaviour during the Aguirre administration seemed to confirm the view widely held among Socialists that the Communist Party was not capable of pursuing a coherent marxist policy because of its subordination to the dictates of the Third International. The Socialist Party was therefore largely justified in dismissing the Communist Party's claim to be a genuine marxist party and in trying to establish itself as the only marxist party truly representing the immediate and historical interests of the working class. However, they did not launch a massive campaign of popular mobilisation and agitation to achieve this. Instead, they made use of the party system and of the existing political process to undermine the Communist Party's electoral base and lessen their influence within the labour movement. In the event, the Socialists not only failed to achieve this objective, but by 1946 found themselves politically isolated and with a significantly-reduced electoral base.

The Socialists were not unaware of the dangers involved in participating in governments led by the Radical Party or in making use of the electoral process to compete with the Communist Party. In fact, when Aguirre offered cabinet posts to the Socialists there was a serious debate about whether the offer should be accepted. The youth section and at least one provincial branch strongly opposed it on the ground that it would divert the party away from its main objective of bringing about a socialist revolution. They forcefully reminded the party that it should not confuse participation in a bourgeois government with the actual exercise of power.[10] The majority of the party, however, accepted claiming that the presence of Socialists in the cabinet would ensure that the Radical Party remained loyal to the Popular Front's programme.[11]

The Socialists' decision to accept cabinet posts did not settle the debate concerning participation in bourgeois governments. During Aguirre's first year in office those opposed to participation began to operate as a faction calling themselves Non-conformists. Eventually, in 1940, they left the party to form a rival Socialist Party, the Socialist

Workers' Party (SWP), which, describing itself as a revolutionary marxist party, accused both Socialists and Communists of betraying the interests of the working class in pursuit of narrow electoral objectives.[12]

The Socialists also accepted cabinet posts during the first months of the Ríos administration. By 1943, however, they had decided to withdraw from the government and to take more seriously their role as a marxist party committed to revolutionary socialism.[13] This decision was the product of a protracted internal debate which had started in 1941 and which, in many respects was the continuation of the one begun in 1938 by the Non-conformists. It stemmed from a profound dissatisfaction with the party's role, both in the Aguirre and the Ríos administrations, and an awareness that rivalry with the Communists was leading nowhere as neither party was capable of displacing the other from the political arena. This process of ideological clarification culminated in 1945, when the party adopted a new line, the People's Front Line. According to this, the party would no longer concentrate exclusively on parliamentary politics, but, instead would pursue policies based on the interests of the working class.[14]

This new approach to politics did not, however, bring to an end rivalry with the Communists. For, at the time, the Communists were advocating a temporary freeze on the class struggle to confront the fascist threat. Such was the Communists' enthusiasm for the policy of national unity, which had been officially proclaimed by the international communist movement after the winding up of the Comintern in 1943, that they advocated a truce with the landed oligarchy and to this end dropped from their programme the demand for land redistribution.[15] The Socialists strongly opposed the Communists' new conciliatory policy and accordingly, continued to regard themselves as the only truly marxist political group. Hence, not surprisingly, in 1943, when the Communists approached them with a proposal to merge they politely refused, arguing that conditions were not yet ripe.

Given the lengthy debate preceding the adoption by the Socialist Party of the People's Front Line, it seems surprising that in January 1946 – less than eight months after its formal approval – they accepted cabinet posts in the interim administration of Vice-President Duhalde, thus not only renouncing their recently-formulated policy, but also provoking a major division within the labour movement. Although this decision blatantly contradicted their political line, there are at least two factors explaining their behaviour: their rapid decline in the polls and the growing electoral strength of the Communist Party. Indeed, as the Socialists were busy moving their party further to the left under a more explicit marxist policy, their electoral strength plummeted from 20 per cent in 1941 to 7 per cent in 1945. The party's poor performance in the 1945 Congressional elections was largely caused by the exceedingly good results obtained by Grove's party in Santiago.[16] However, at the time, this could not have given the Socialists much comfort since by 1945 the Communists, with 10 per cent of the vote, had become the largest marxist party. Hence, by now, the Socialists had been overtaken by the Communists, and were also facing competition from another Socialist Party, the one created by Grove.

The Socialists had some reason to believe that their participation in the Duhalde administration would help them regain their electoral strength. For Duhalde, whose labour policies had brought about the division of the labour movement, had been expelled from the Radical Party. This prompted the Socialists to back Duhalde's candidacy to the Presidency on the assumption, not altogether unreasonable, that he would attract most of the Radical voters and would also have the support of other smaller parties such as the Falange Nacional and Democratic parties. Unfortunately for the Socialists, this 'Third Front' electoral alliance did not materialise since Duhalde, quite unexpectedly, decided to drop out of the race, thus leaving them without a candidate and politically isolated.

After their failure to defeat the Communists through alliances with non-marxist parties, the Socialists once again vowed to pursue their objectives without forming alliances with bourgeois parties. This time, however, they also decided to draft a new political programme. The new programme, approved in 1947, is an interesting document. For while it confirms the party's adherence to marxism and repudiation of the Communist Party's pro-Soviet line it does not succeed in putting forward an original approach to socialist politics in accordance with the needs of the country.[17] Indeed, although the programme strongly rejects any form of totalitarianism as contrary to the principles of socialism, it does not abandon the concept of dictatorship of the proletariat, although interestingly enough, the phrase itself does not appear in the text. This is because the programme discusses the type of social organisation which will obtain once the existing state has withered away, without describing the political forms to be used during the period of transition to a socialist society. It is true that there is a reference in passing to the compatibility between the libertarian ideals of socialism and the process of socialization of production. Yet, this reference cannot be interpreted as the rejection of the notion of the dictatorship of the proletariat since the programme qualifies it with the rider that the libertarian objective of socialism will be safe-guarded not by the existing democratic forms, but by the strength of working-class organisations.

The new programme, despite its shortcomings, probably helped the party to cope with the consequences of the brief, but eventful Communist participation in the González administration. For although during this period the Communists acted as if their main objective was to wipe out the Socialist Party, the party, on the whole responded to this threat and to the ensuing anti-communist campaign launched by the government with dignity and maturity. The majority of Socialists in fact refused to be drawn into the anti-Communist camp, realizing that government policy, prompted as it was by the outbreak of the Cold War, was as much anti-union and anti-Left as it was anti-communist.

III   THE COMMUNIST PARTY

The behaviour of the Communist Party between 1932 and 1952 was in many respects no less erratic than that of the Socialist Party. While at the outset the Communist Party rejected any form of alliance, it later changed its line to become an enthusiastic proponent of the Popular Front. But its enthusiasm with alliance politics did not last long. By 1939 it had distanced itself from the ideals of the Popular Front only to emerge a few years later as the main advocate of a policy of national unity, which envisaged a political truce with the parties of the bour-geoisie so as to further the struggle against fascism. By 1945, however, it had abandoned this policy in favour of an intensification of mass mobilisation so as to secure, in alliance with other progressive parties, a bourgeois national revolution as the first stage in the path to social-ism. This policy of mass mobilisation was, however, abandoned in 1947, when, following the line of the international communist move-ment, it called for an orderly retreat so as to secure the stability of democratic institutions.

The Communist Party's drastic changes of policy were primarily, though not exclusively, the consequence of its strict observance of the ever-changing political line of the international communist move-ment. The party's unquestioned loyalty to the principles of proletarian internationalism as interpreted by the Comintern and the Communist Party of the Soviet Union (CPSU), greatly exacerbated the latent con-flict with the Socialists. It was arguably a factor contributing to the division of the labour movement in 1946, and eventually threatened the unity of the party. This section examines why the Communist Party came to be such a loyal member of the Comintern and how it attempted to reconcile domestic policies with international obligations.

Proletarian Internationalism

After the fall of Ibáñez, the Communist Party was once again allowed to function legally. It was then following the 'Third Period' line of the Comintern, according to which socialist revolution was on the immediate agenda as the process of disintegration of capitalism had already begun.[18] In pursuit of this line, it had refused to join other parties in their struggle against the Ibáñez government. This policy not only alienated working-class support, but also isolated it from other progressive political groups fighting for the restoration of democracy.

The return to legality did not change the Communist Party's position. At its national conference held in July 1933 it defined the nature of the revolution as a bourgeois democratic revolution against the landed oligarchy and imperialism. This bourgeois democratic revolution was, according to the Communist Party, the first stage in a continuous and uninterrupted process towards a socialist revolution. Hence its call for the creation of a united front 'from below' which, under the leadership of the party, would be the vehicle for conquering power.[19] This conception of the revolution left no room for alliances with the parties of the bourgeoisie.

To some extent the re-opening of the channels of political participation in the early 1930s appears to have reinforced the party's political isolation and its fear that it was rapidly becoming encircled by political groups which, using left-wing rhetoric, were determined to undermine its revolutionary platform. Thus, at its 1933 national conference, the Socialist Party was identified as the main obstacle blocking communist efforts to build a strong and truly revolutionary party. The Socialist Party – or 'Grovismo', as the communists described the Socialists – was essentially a bourgeois party with close links with the landed oligarchy and imperialism, and, as such, its main objective was to strengthen capitalism.[20]

At their 1933 conference they also called for a re-assessment of the role of Luis Emilio Recabarren, the former leader and founding father of the party. Although they did not completely repudiate him, they came close to it by describing him as a liberal who had in fact delayed the process of building a truly Marxist-Leninist party.[21] Recabarren's alleged liberalism stemmed from his involvement in parliamentary politics and his interest in forming political alliances with non-marxist parties. Moreover, Recabarren had always insisted that as a socialist he was also a patriot. Recabarren's nationalism was also strongly rejected by the conference, which approved a resolution declaring that the Soviet Union was the only fatherland party members should recognise.[22]

The Communist Party's intense loyalty in 1933 to the principles of proletarian internationalism, as expounded by the Comintern, may be explained by the party's recent history. As explained in Chapter 3, above, Trotskyism became a major divisive issue within the Communist Party as early as 1924, and it was not finally resolved until the early 1930s, when the Trotskyites formed another party. This new party did not make a great impact, and by 1935 its members had joined the Socialist Party. However, in its early party years the Communist Party must have regarded the Trotskyites as a serious threat. In fact, in the 1931 presidential elections both parties ran candidates, and they each obtained practically the same share of the vote, around 1 per cent.

Another factor, not related to the issue of Trotskyism, which may explain the Communist Party's strong internationalist line in the 1930s concerns the relationship between the Chilean Communists and the Comintern. As already explained, the political transformation of the POS into the Communist Party of Chile met with little internal resistance. Hence, not surprisingly, both the internal organisation and the party's behaviour within the political system were not significantly different from those of the old POS. After all, the POS had been active for a decade before it sought affiliation with the Third International, and during that time it had established firm roots within the labour movement.

The fact that, in Chile, by contrast with other Latin-American countries, the Communist Party already had a well-established working-class following when it applied for membership in the Third International must have been regarded with some suspicion by the Comintern. Besides, in the eyes of the Comintern there was probably a close link between the party's organisational weakness and the powerful Trotskyite faction within it. Thus, by the late 1920s, under the supervision of the South American Bureau of the Comintern, it underwent major internal changes, transforming it into a truly Leninist party. In 1928, this process was near completion, the Comintern finally granted it full membership. Thus, not surprisingly, when it returned to legality, its loyalty to the Comintern and the Soviet Union was beyond any doubt.

The isolationist position adopted by the Communist Party in 1933 was, however, not only the consequence of its adherence to the dictates of the Comintern. For, accustomed as it was to being the only left-wing party with solid backing among the working class, it must have seen the emergence of the Socialist Party as a major threat which had to be eliminated. But the Communists soon realized that the popularity and influence of the Socialist Party among the popular masses continued to increase, despite their propaganda and their efforts to present the Socialist Party as yet another bourgeois party. Besides, the Socialist Party, as an emergent and dynamic political force, soon assumed the leadership of the left-wing opposition to the Alessandri administration by a political alliance – the Left-wing bloc – which included the old Democratic party, dissident Radicals and the Trotskyites.

The Socialists' success in bringing about a semblance of unity among left-wing parties underlined the futility of the Communist Party's anti-socialist position. Moreover, the forceful anti-labour policies of the Alessandri administration, which, as explained in Chapter 3, treated Socialist workers and their leaders no more gently than their Communist counterparts, was bound to generate solidarity at the grassroots level, which made the official Communist line all the more difficult to sustain.

The Comintern and the Popular Front

Given the evolution of left-wing politics during the first half of the Alessandri administration, it is not surprising that the Communist Party found it so easy to change its policy when, in 1935, the Comintern called for the formation of broad anti-fascist fronts. For it is arguable that, had the Comintern not given the green light to forming alliances with bourgeois parties, the Communist Party would never have managed to recover the political influence it had enjoyed in the 1920s. That the Comintern's change of policy led to a revival of the Communist Party's political fortunes does not mean that the Popular Front was engineered by Moscow. The unity of the Left was the culmination of a process linked to the evolution of domestic politics since the downfall of Ibáñez.

The view that the Popular Front was a creature of the Third International has been forcefully argued by Eudocio Ravines, a one-time Communist, who, as agent of the Comintern in South America, spent time in Chile working for the Communist Party.[23] Ravines' views have been very influential not only because of the important position he

93

occupied in the Comintern, but also because his interpretation fits the widely-accepted conception of Popular Fronts as mere Trojan horses designed to enhance the influence of communist parties. Recent historical research, however, has shown that his interpretation of the Comintern's role in the creation of the Popular Front in Chile is, if not wrong, at least greatly exaggerated. For at the time, the Comintern appears to have been more concerned with events in other Latin-American countries, such as Cuba and Brazil, than in Chile, where it was supposedly putting its Popular Front strategy to a test.[24]

Whether or not the creation of the Popular Front was engineered by Comintern agents, the fact is that once it was established the Communists consistently subordinated their domestic political priorities to the ever-changing political line of the Comintern. Thus, after the Nazi-Soviet pact of 1939 the Communists became critical of the Popular Front government, only to change their position in 1941, after Hitler's invasion of the Soviet Union, when they began advocating a freeze on the class struggle to defeat the Axis powers.[25] Their shifting political position not only revived the latent conflict with the Socialists, but intensified it. For in their efforts to influence domestic political events along the lines set by the Comintern the Communists always found themselves at odds with the Socialists. Hence their attacks on the Socialist Party were prompted by the need to justify their adherence to Comintern policy. For example, in 1939 the Communists began to criticize the pro-Allied policy of the Popular Front's government, blaming it exclusively on the Socialists and describing them as lackeys of United States' and British imperialism.[26] Later on, in 1942, after they had embraced the Allied cause, they sought, albeit in vain, an alliance with the Radical Party, while refusing to support the candidacy of Oscar Schnake, the Socialist Party leader. Instead, – under the banner of the National Party – they became loyal supporters of President Ríos, who was not only prominently anti-communist, but also critical of his party's alliance with the marxists.

Mass Mobilisation

Following the Teheran conference of 1943, in which Stalin, Roosevelt and Churchill invited other countries to join the family of democratic nations as they divided the world into spheres of influence, the Communist Party began to flirt with the ideas put forward by Earl Browder, the leader of the Communist Party of the United States.[27] Browder advocated maintaining the anti-fascist front of the war years on the assumption that class collaboration was now possible because capitalism and socialism had begun to march together in the interest of peace.[28] Browderism, however, did not become the Communist Party's official line. Instead, again taking its cue from Moscow, the Communist Party resolved at its 1945 congress that it was now possible to work towards a bourgeois democratic revolution in alliance with other progressive forces sharing the objective of fighting imperialism and the landed oligarchy. At this congress the party also decided to undertake a vigorous campaign of mass mobilisation to strengthen and unite all members of the oppressed classes.[29] These resolutions paved the way for Communist participation in the González administration.

That in 1946 the Communists decided to accept cabinet posts in the González administration can be attributed to the fact that this was probably the first time since 1936 that they could easily reconcile their loyalty to the international communist movement with their domestic political role as the leading party of the working class. For while on the one hand the González administration appeared committed to fulfilling the national democratic tasks corresponding to the first stage of the socialist revolution, on the other hand the Socialists, whose electoral support had plummeted to a mere 7 per cent no longer appeared as a serious threat to the Communists. But the success of the Communists was brief. They soon found themselves ousted from the government and from the political system altogether. Also, they were confronted with the problem of reconciling their loyalty to the international communist movement with the internal dynamic of the process of mass mobilisation which they had so successfully promoted. This unexpected turn of events brought about the first serious breakdown of party discipline since the late 1920s.

An Orderly Retreat

As already explained, the Communist Party did extremely well during the first months of the González administration and increased its electoral support from 10 per cent to 17 per cent. From this position of strength, it proposed that the government should broaden membership in the cabinet to include all progressive forces, such as the Falange, willing to help in the implementation of the programme.[30] The Radicals not only refused this proposal, but instead asked the Communists to quit the cabinet. This snub made a travesty of the Communist Party's assumption that there existed progressive forces seriously committed to fulfilling the moderate task of building a truly national bourgeois democracy. The fact that the Communists had been forced to leave the government when they were at the height of their popularity was deeply resented by many party members, among them Luis Reinoso, who also happened to be a prominent leader. According to Reinoso, this was a serious setback, and to overcome it he proposed that the party should take the offensive and step up the process of mass mobilisation which had been so successful.[31]

The exclusion of the Communists from the González government, and later on from the political system altogether, posed a difficult dilemma for the party. Its political line called for the support of bourgeois democracy combined with a policy of mass mobilisation. Yet the new domestic context made it impossible for it to continue its policy of mass mobilisation unless it changed the forms of struggle, opting for illegal methods if necessary. Reinoso's view was that mass mobilisation should be maintained so as to expose the limitations of the political system and perhaps eventually to topple the government and make a direct bid for power. But the party rejected his proposal on the grounds that it was unrealistic and ultra-leftist. The official view was largely shaped by international developments relating to the emergence of the Cold War. Indeed, in September 1947 the Soviet Union had created the Cominform, which, apart from re-affirming the division of the world into irreconcilable camps, called upon the international communist movement to support the foreign policy objectives of the Soviet Union in the interest of a lasting democratic peace. In the new context of the Cold War this call entailed a retreat of the working-class movement to give the Soviet Union time to consolidate its hegemony over the new popular democracies in Eastern Europe and to catch up with the United States in the atomic race.[32] In Chile, the Cominform line required giving up the policy of mass mobilisation and supporting the prevailing political system.

In 1951, while the Communist Party concentrated its efforts on trying to secure a return to legality, Reinoso and his followers were expelled. By this time restrictions on party activities had been *de facto* relaxed, although the political ban was not officially lifted until 1958. The Communist Party's decision to give up its policy of mass mobilisation and to opt instead for the more limited objective of securing the re-establishment of full political rights was consistent with the Cominform's line. However, it is doubtful whether in the circumstances, a more radical line, such as the one advocated by Reinoso, would have been successful. For the labour movement was divided, the Socialist Party was fragmented and the United States government was closely following political developments in Chile and would not have hesitated to intervene – as it did a few years later in Guatemala – to prevent a communist take-over. In any event, in 1951, the Communist Party unequivocally reaffirmed that its immediate aim was the achievement of full bourgeois democracy as the first stage on the road to socialism.

IV OVERVIEW

The consequences of the participation of Communists and Socialists in coalition govenments between 1938 and the late 1940s were, at least from the standpoint of the ideals of the Popular Front, largely negative. For throughout this period there was no substantial re-distribution of income in favour of the wage-earning population; growth by manufacturing industry was uneven and largely off-set by a dramatic decline in agricultural output; and dependence on the external sector increased, thus making the economy all the more vulnerable to changes in the international situation.

From the point of view of the unity of the labour movement, one of the bases on which the Popular Front was launched in 1936 the record is no more favourable. For while initially Communists and Socialists managed to unite the labour movement under the CTCH, by the mid-1940s rivalry between them brought about its division, thus setting the stage for the enactment of anti-labour legislation, which remained in force well into the 1950s.

Perhaps one of the most disastrous consequences of Communist and Socialist participation in coalition governments was in fact that each, in turn, made use of its influence in the state apparatus to eliminate and destroy the other. Thus, during the Duhalde administration the Socialists were, if not directly at least indirectly, responsible for gaoling more than one hundred Communists, including the editor of the party's newspaper.[33] The record of the Communists in the González administration only a few months later was no less shameful as they made use of their newly-acquired political influence to attack Socialist-controlled unions and to harass members of the Socialist Party who held posts in the state bureaucracy.[34]

With the benefit of hindsight it may be argued that the consequences of marxist participation in coalition governments could have been different if, instead of allowing petty party rivalries to dominate their behaviour, they had demanded full implementation of the Popular Front's programme and if they had vigorously campaigned for an extension of the franchise and for the unionisation of agricultural workers. It must be noted, however, that the failure of Communists and Socialists to pursue their programmatic objectives was largely a consequence of the formidable influence the right-wing parties had in the political system at the time which, in turn, was a fair reflection of the dominant social and economic interests in the country at large. For as explained in Chapter 3, the right-wing parties had the necessary number of votes in the Congress to block any government initiative and were unwilling to compromise on issues which they regarded as essential. These issues included two of the most important objectives of the Popular Front, namely, the unionisation of agricultural workers and the restructuring of the tax system. Such was the determination of the right-wing parties to defend what they regarded as their fundamental interests, that they announced an electoral boycott when the Aguirre government attempted to use popular mobilisation as a means of putting pressure on the Congress to approve its programme. Thus they clearly showed the Radicals that the defence of their interests took precedence over the preservation of democracy.

The Radical Party's willingness to comply with the conditions of the Right stemmed not only from that fact that to some extent their economic interests coincided, but also from the fact that in political terms the combined forces of the right-wing parties were larger than its own. Indeed, between 1932 and 1949 the combined electoral strength of the right-wing parties was between 30 and 40 per cent of the vote, while that of the Radical Party oscillated between 18 and 27 per cent. The fact that the Radical Party was able to win the Presidency three consecutive times between 1938 and 1952 was largely a result of its ability to form coalitions with both right – and left-wing parties. It is significant, however, that when its electoral strength was at its peak in the late 1940s, it was no longer able to form a viable electoral alliance with either right- or left-wing parties.

A fundamental feature of the relationship between the Radical Party and the marxist parties from 1932 to 1952 was that the Radical Party never attempted to build an independent base of support among workers in manufacturing and mining. Thus, the marxist parties' almost exclusive control over organised labour, rather than electoral strength, provided them with access to political power and influence. Labour's split between the Radical Party and the marxist parties was acknowledged by Gabriel González when he explained that his party had agreed to an alliance with the marxist parties mainly because of their influence among organised workers.[35]

The Radicals, however, were not mere passive beneficiaries. For while they had an interest in securing support from the CTCH, they also had an interest in promoting the conflict between and within the two marxist parties so as to ensure a leading position in the coalition government of the period. They therefore made full use of their position to play one party off against the other, as well as to deepen the internal differences within the Socialist Party.

By the late 1940s, the seemingly inexhaustible ability of the Radicals to benefit from the conflict between Communists and Socialists came to an end. In 1946, after the division of the CTCH, the Radicals made what appeared to be a durable alliance with the Communists, which enabled them to ensure the electoral victory of Gabriel González. Not surprisingly, shortly after his victory, González made a solemn pledge that no human or divine power would ever force him to break his links with the Communist Party.[36] Yet, less than a year later, González expelled the Communists from his government, arguing that they were trying to establish a monopoly over the working class.[37] After breaking with them he sought to legitimise his government among the working class by taking measures to boost the Socialist-controlled CTCH. However, by this stage the credibility of the Radicals among workers was very low, and the Socialist leaders who had joined the government were unable effectively to mobilise support at the grassroots level. Thus, without the support of organised labour, the Radical Party was unable to continue presiding over the game of coalition politics at which it had been so successful since 1938. Indeed, by 1952 the Radicals found themselves politically isolated, despite the fact that in electoral terms they were as strong as before.

The negative consequences of participating in coalition governments was to shape the type of alliances the marxists were to form in the 1950s, when they created the Popular Action Front (Frente de Acción Popular/FRAP). For the FRAP represented, largely, a rejection of the type of coalition politics as practised from 1932 to 1952.

PART II   A NEW BEGINNING

CHAPTER 7

The Ibáñez and Alessandri Administrations

THE election of General Ibáñez in 1952 marked the beginning of a twelve-year period during which government policy seemed explicitly designed to overturn the policies of the preceding decade. Indeed, both the Ibáñez (1952–8) and Alessandri (1958–64) administrations made a determined effort to reverse the pattern of state intervention initiated by the Popular Front and to reduce the excessive politicisation of social life, so prevalent during the previous period. Ironically their policies did not bring about the expected results. Although they went a long way towards liberalising certain areas of economic activity, the economic role of the state had in fact increased by 1964. Public expenditure and the state's share in investment had risen while government regulation of prices, production and labour had intensified. Likewise, on the political front, these two administrations, whose popular appeal was based on an anti-party stance, in fact strengthened the party system. Thus, while the Ibáñez and Alessandri administrations failed to liberalise the economy, they unwittingly brought about a revival of politics and the party system. This chapter explains the apparent contradiction between the stated aims and unintended consequences of the policies of these two administrations.

I   THE IBÁÑEZ ADMINISTRATION, 1952–1958

In 1952 General Ibáñez achieved an impressive victory in the presidential election. His Ibañista movement obtained 46 per cent of the votes, thus winning a clear majority over the three other candidates on the right, left and centre of the political spectrum. Ibáñez' victory should be attributed to the crisis affecting the party system rather than to what is often described as his enigmatic appeal.[1] Indeed, the

Ibañista movement, made up of fragments from all the major political parties, had a short life. It emerged unexpectedly in the months preceding the 1952 election only to collapse less than three years later. Its heterogeneous composition was reflected in its vague political programme. It promised to eradicate political corruption, to pursue a more independent foreign policy, and to increase the power of the executive branch. Although the vagueness of this programme could have been an asset, Ibáñez, already old, showed little interest in giving it a coherent content.

Ibáñez' failure to transform his massive electoral support into a powerful political movement should not be exclusively attributed to his weakness as a political leader. In fact, to a large extent, his government did not have a chance to implement its programme because from the very beginning it had to concentrate all its attention on the continuously-rising rates of inflation. While in the last year of the previous administration the annual rate of inflation had been 12 per cent, in the first three years of the Ibáñez government inflation rose to unprecedentedly high levels, reaching 56 per cent in 1953, 71 per cent in 1954 and 84 per cent in 1955. This inflationary process, brought about by the collapse of copper prices after the Korean War, had a serious impact on the income of the wage-earning population, thus increasing the militancy of the trade-union movement and undermining the government's popularity. The government's inability to control inflation during its first three years provided a focus around which the established parties in the Congress reconstituted their political strength.

The problems caused by the rising rate of inflation were further complicated by the links which the government began to forge with General Perón in Argentina. Ibáñez, a great admirer of Perón, had drawn much of his own political views from Perón's *justicialista* movement. Once in office, he seems to have wanted to create closer links with Argentina to strengthen his bargaining position with the United States. But Perón's objectives regarding Chile were more ambitious. Early in 1953 during a visit to Chile, he proposed the immediate signature of a treaty to consolidate the political and economic unity between the two countries.[2] Although his offer was rejected, it created a major political uproar, providing the anti-Ibáñez forces with a powerful weapon to use against the government. Apart from reviving strong anti-Argentinian feelings, Perón's candid admission of his foreign policy objectives introduced doubts about whether the Ibáñez government could safeguard the country's sovereignty and territorial integrity. The question of Peronism led to the appointment of a special congressional committee, which found that the activities of several local journalists, politicians and labour leaders were financed directly by the Argentinian government. These findings added fuel to the political scandal which had been brewing since Perón's visit in 1953.[3] Thus, while Ibáñez saw his attempt to forge stronger links with Argentina as a useful complement to his other political objectives, in practice it back-fired mainly because the uncontrollable inflationary process had already seriously eroded his popularity. Peronism in Chile was therefore a factor which greatly contributed towards the decline of the Ibañista movement and the strengthening of the party system.

The Ibañista movement was made up of an assortment of political groups including left-wing corporativists, marxist socialists and right-wing nationalists.[4] The axis of the Ibañista movement was the Agrarian Labour Party, the PAL, a party created in the 1930s as a right-wing alternative to the old Conservative and Liberal parties. During the 1940s the PAL had little political success. However, in the early 1950s, after a major split which allowed them to shed their right-wing image, they supported Ibáñez and for a few years became the largest and most important political party in the country. But PAL's sudden growth did not endow the Ibañista movement with greater ideological coherence. In fact, its heterogeneous composition, combined with the absence of adequate leadership provoked bitter battles within the government camp, leading to a succession of cabinet changes and culminating in 1955 with the disintegration of the Ibañista movement. Most of the political groups which had supported Ibáñez returned to their parties on the right and the left, some joined the Falange Nacional while others remained loyal to the government.[5] From then on, as Ibáñez began to rely on the right-wing parties for political support, the government's economic policy became more coherent, but bore no resemblance to its original nationalist populist image. The two main components of this economic policy were a new framework to regulate copper mining and a programme of economic stabilisation to reduce the rate of inflation.

A New Copper Deal

Since the early fifties relations between Chile and the United States had been strained by the continuous conflict over copper revenues. In Chapter 4 I explained how, despite the government's willingness to follow the lead of the United States in the Cold War, the attempt by the United States government to impose controls on the price of

Chilean copper exports at the outset of the Korean War had led to a major row between the two countries. The election of General Ibáñez in 1952 had added yet another element of uncertainty in the relations between the two countries since Ibáñez had not only promised to follow a more independent line in foreign policy, but as a Senator in 1951 he had voted against the ratification of the military pact with the United States.

The end of the Korean War brought about a reduction of Chilean copper exports from 350,000 metric tons to 290,000 metric tons, and was the immediate cause of the rise in inflation.[6] These circumstances weakened the government's resolve to exercise control over the marketing of copper and paved the way for the approval in 1955 of a new regulatory framework for it. The objective of this new copper legislation was to increase output and investment by reducing and stabilising the taxation of the United States copper companies operating in Chile. For some time United States copper companies had argued that the high level of taxation which affected their operations was the main reason for the drop in production and for Chile's declining share in world copper markets. In fact, by the early fifties the rate of taxation of these companies was 80 per cent while Chile's share in the world's copper market had dropped from 20 per cent in 1944 to 13 per cent in 1953. The new copper legislation reduced the basic rate to 50 per cent and introduced a 25 per cent surtax which declined as production exceeded a given base level. It also liberalised depreciation allowances, permitting the rapid depreciation of new investment up to a rate of 20 per cent per year.[7] Finally, it returned to the United States companies full control over the marketing of copper.

In the five years which followed the approval of the new copper legislation, production increased by 50 per cent. However, critics opposed to this new regime pointed out that the increase resulted from favourable conditions in the international markets, since the expected new investment in copper had failed to materialise. Moreover, they also pointed out that tax revenues from copper had effectively decreased because the base triggering the reduction in taxation had been set at a very low level.[8] The new copper legislation had in fact given the United States copper companies all the concessions that they had been expecting without demanding in return a firm commitment from them to increase their investments.[9] Thus, as this new regime created a safe climate for foreign investment, diplomatic relations between Chile and the United States improved. The government could now expect advice and general support from the United States to tackle its problem of inflation.

The Stabilisation Programme

By mid-term, in 1955, the full impact of the collapse of the copper markets in 1953, became evident. As the rate of inflation continued to rise and Ibáñez' popularity fell dramatically, government revenue was insufficient to finance even current expenditure. The problem was further complicated by the fact that automatic re-adjustment of salaries for public sector employees equal to the rate of inflation was required by law. Moreover, the inflationary crisis had contributed towards strengthening the solidarity and militancy of the trade-union movement, which, under the leadership of the recently-established CUT, began to demand that workers in the private sector should receive pay increases similar to those in the public sector. Between 1953 and 1955 the government tried several times to bring inflation under control, but failed mainly because the groups supporting Ibáñez could not agree on a long-term policy acceptable to them all. However, by 1955 after the Ibañista movement had effectively disintegrated and the government had begun to follow right-wing policies, a package of measures was introduced to stabilise the economy along the lines suggested by the International Monetary Fund and the United States government.[10]

The government's policy to fight inflation was designed in the United States by Klein-Saks, a firm of consultants which also advised the government on its implementation. The programme recommended by the Klein-Saks mission was based on a diagnosis that inflation was caused by excessive demand and accordingly recommended that public expenditure and pay increases should be reduced and stiff credit restrictions should be imposed. It recommended the removal of government controls in foreign exchange, trade and prices. It proposed phasing out production subsidies, increasing income tax and reforming the system of public administration. This programme not only had the blessing of the United States, as it followed closely the recommendations previously made by the IMF, but was also warmly welcomed by local industrialists for they believed that a reduction of government intervention in the economy would stimulate investment and growth. To ensure the success of this stabilisation programme, in 1955 the government issued a decree severely restricting trade-union rights and banishing some trade-union leaders to remote islands.[11]

The implementation of the stabilisation programme fell short of the recommendations made by the Klein-Saks mission. The government concentrated mainly on keeping pay increases below the rate of inflation. In the first year that it was applied, pay increases were restricted to 60 per cent of the rate of inflation in the previous year. The labour movement responded with a call for a general strike, which the government crushed with strong repressive measures.[12] The government was unable to achieve a significant reduction with regard to other items of public expenditure although it kept their growth within manageable limits.[13] The severe contraction of economic activity brought about by these measures, a consequence foreseen by the Klein-Saks mission, weakened the government's resolve to pursue the implementation of the other aspects of the programme which included new taxes and the elimination of subsidies. Indeed, as soon as economic activity started to slow down, the industrialists, who had so keenly supported wage reductions, began to put pressure on the government to maintain state subsidies and other special measures of support. Likewise, the right-wing parties in the Congress refused to increase the levels of taxation. Thus, by the end of 1957, as the date of the next presidential election came closer, the government quietly abandoned its stabilisation programme.

Results

The programme of economic stabilisation brought inflation down from 84 per cent to 25 per cent. However, at this new level the annual rate of inflation was still several points higher than the average rate for the three years before Ibáñez came into office.[14] The decrease in inflation was accompanied by a slump in the economy, which affec-ted mainly the manufacturing and construction industries, and by a sharp drop in the rate of investment despite the fact that the govern-ment's new deal for copper had created a more attractive climate for foreign investment.[15] Although some price controls and government subsidies were phased out, the programme did not achieve economic liberalisation.

The strong measures taken against the trade-union movement in 1955 and 1956 account for the success in the enforcement of the new incomes policy. But weakening of the trade-union movement did not bring about social peace. Indeed, in 1957, as it was becoming clear that the costs of the stabilisation programme were borne mainly by wage earners, violent riots erupted in the streets of Santiago, which were all the more worrying to the government as they had been sparked by a student demonstration and were not ostensibly control-led by any political group. Although the context was different, the 1957 riots must have reminded General Ibáñez of the student-led demonstrations, which, twenty-six years earlier had forced him out of office and into exile in Argentina. It is therefore not surprising that in his last year in office, after it became clear that the right-wing parties in the Congress would not support the full implementation of the stabilisation programme, Ibáñez should have made yet another political turn. He now supported legislation lifting the ban on the Communist Party and reforming the electoral system. The electoral reform introduced the official ballot paper, thus safeguarding the secrecy of the vote and going a long way towards eliminating the practice of vote-buying. The immediate impact of this reform was to increase the level of electoral participation, which had declined sharply in the two general elections held during the Ibáñez administration. Indeed, while between 1952 and 1957 the rate of electoral abstention had increased from 13 per cent to 32 per cent, by 1958 it was reduced to 17 per cent. Also between 1957 and 1958 the proportion of the population registered to vote rose slightly by three points to an all time high of 21 per cent.

By 1958, as the Ibáñez phenomenon faded away, the party system began to recover. In the presidential election held during that year the four main candidates were supported by established political parties. However, the circumstances surrounding that election reveal that the recovery of the party system was still far from complete. Indeed, Alessandri, the candidate supported by the right-wing parties, obtained 31 per cent of the votes, thus narrowly defeating Allende, the candidate of the newly established FRAP, a coalition of the Communist and Socialist parties, who obtained 29 per cent of the vote. The right-wing victory, as well as the spectacular achievement by the marxist candidate, owed much to the fact that more than one-third of the vote had been split between the Christian Democratic Party, obtaining 21 per cent of the vote, and the Radical Party, 15 per cent. But there were three other factors contributing to the narrow victory of the right-wing candidate. Firstly, the left-wing candidate was unable to attract the female vote; indeed, the left-wing candidate obtained the largest share of the vote among men, 32 per cent, but only 22 per cent of the vote among women, thus finishing in third place.[16] Secondly, since the electoral reforms had made vote-buying more difficult, the right-wing parties sponsored the campaign of a fifth candidate, a defrocked priest, who enjoyed considerable popularity among left-wing supporters in one of the provinces. Also, the right-wing parties made some financial contribution towards supporting the candidate of the Radical Party in order to prevent a major swing from the Radical Party to the left-wing candidate.[17] Thirdly, the victory of the right-wing party owed much to the electoral appeal of their candidate, which was based on the same anti-political banner so successfully exploited by Ibáñez. This time however, although the candidate did not hold a party card, he was a member of the political and business establishment and a life-time supporter of the right-wing parties. Yet because his anti-political stand was basically technocratic, he did not pose a threat to the party system in the same way as the Ibañista movement had done in 1952. Alessandri's rejection of party politics stemmed from his managerial perspective, which was reinforced by a long career as a leading spokesman for the private sector. Thus by the end of the Ibáñez administration, although the party system had regained strength, it had not yet fully recovered.

II   THE ALESSANDRI ADMINISTRATION, 1958–1964

A Managerial Economic Policy

During his six years in office Alessandri was loyally supported by the right-wing parties, the Conservative and Liberal parties. By mid-term he was also supported by the Radical Party. Alessandri maintained his image as a non-political President by refusing to accept direct intervention by the political parties in the appointment of his cabinet and other top government jobs. These posts were filled by individuals who, described as technical experts, were mainly drawn from among the top managerial layers of industry and finance. The technical outlook of this new team was supposed to bring efficiency and austerity into the administration of the state. But Alessandri's attempt to keep his administration at a safe distance from the political parties did not last long. By mid-term, as opposition inside and outside Congress became unbearable mainly because of the collapse of the government's economic policy, he was forced to accept direct involvement of the parties at cabinet level. Thus, by the end of his six years in office, he found himself presiding over an ill-fated attempt to form a long-term alliance between the right-wing Conservative and Liberal parties and the ubiquitous Radical Party.

When Alessandri took office in 1958 the annual rate of inflation had nearly doubled from 17 per cent in 1957 to 33 per cent. But while the government team regarded inflation as serious, they were more interested in dealing with the root of the problem than its symptoms. In this view, it had its roots in the Popular Front's economic policy, which had been more concerned with raising the standards of living of the wage-earning population than with increasing production. The heavy tax burden and intense government regulation brought about by the Popular Front had suffocated the private sector, creating major disincentives to new investment. Accordingly, the Alessandri team believed that to increase production it was necessary to free the market from the restrictions imposed by state intervention. But consistent with their managerial approach, they did not transform the objective of economic liberalisation into an article of faith. Their programme actually called for two successive steps; the first was to re-activate the economy by increasing public expenditure; and the second to introduce measures of economic liberalisation, together with an incomes policy to keep pay increases below the rate of inflation.[18]

The programme of economic liberalisation concentrated mainly on the elimination of foreign exchange and trade controls. Following a 30 per cent devaluation, the rate of exchange of the peso was frozen, and restrictions on the movement of capital were lifted. Also, most non-tariff import restrictions were removed and tariff rates were reduced. To compensate for the negative effect which the over-valued currency would have on non-mineral exports, the government introduced several measures designed to operate as export incentives. Finally, to stimulate new investment the government introduced a liberal foreign investment regime and transformed CORFO from a pioneer of new investment projects into a provider of credits for the private sector.

Return to Politics

In practice, the economy did not respond as envisaged by the government. Imports grew faster than expected and exports remained practically stationary. Moreover, a spectacular increase in foreign debt generated a huge deficit in the balance of payments, which, in less than three years, depleted the Central Bank's supply of foreign exchange and prompted a major reversal of policy, including a reinstatement of exchange and foreign trade controls as well as currency devaluation. The collapse of Alessandri's economic policy may be attributed to several miscalculations and misjudgements. It was based on the assumption that foreign borrowing would make a major contribution towards raising investment levels. But since the government feared that a sudden inflow of foreign exchange would have a negative effect on the rate of inflation, it decided to encourage imports. But relaxing import controls brought about a flood of imports which had no relation to the growth of exports. Thus, between 1959 and 1961, the value of exports remained virtually unchanged, while the value of imports increased by more than 50 per cent and the balance of trade, which at the beginning of the period had a surplus of forty-two million dollars, showed a huge deficit of 153 million dollars by 1961.[19] The increase in the value of imports was accompanied by a sharp rise in the share of imports in the Gross National Product, from 9.6 per cent in 1959 to 14 per cent in 1961.[20]

An important factor accounting for the spectacular growth of imports during this period was the government's decision to maintain a fixed rate of exchange, which resulted in a gross over-valuation of the peso. It has been estimated that in 1961 the peso was over-valued as much as by 45 per cent.[21] This unrealistic rate of exchange also caused a severe drop in the value of non-mineral exports. The government had expected that, initially, most of the imports would be financed by foreign loans and that, eventually, export revenues would begin to pay for an important proportion of the import bill. However, since export revenue did not increase as expected, the growing demand for imports continued to be satisfied by foreign loans. Hence, between 1959 and 1961 the current account deficit multiplied ten-fold from 25 to 246 million dollars which, because of the unsatisfactory developments of the capital account balance, generated a deficit of 135 million dollars in the balance of payments.[22]

By the end of 1961, the depletion of foreign exchange from the Central Bank caused a financial panic which led to a three-week ban of foreign exchange transactions and culminated in the introduction of a dual exchange rate and the re-imposition of some controls on foreign trade. The introduction of a dual exchange rate provided a much-needed breathing space, but as it involved only a partial devaluation which did not affect the exchange rate for the importation of goods, the pressure on the balance of payments persisted. It was only in October of the following year that the government finally decided on a 38 per cent devaluation.[23] The October devaluation was accompanied by the introduction of yet more foreign trade controls and by a more explicit policy of price controls. By the end of 1962, as inflation rose from 10 per cent in 1961 to 28 per cent and strike activity increased, the government formally abandoned its liberalisation policy.

The fear that a major currency devaluation would push the rate of inflation upwards was a major factor underlying the government's decision to delay the fateful moment of devaluation. In fact, while the liberalisation policy was in fact preparing the ground for a major balance of payments crisis, the government was enjoying remarkable success in its stabilisation policy. Between 1959 and 1960 the rate of inflation was reduced from 33 per cent to 5 per cent, and even though in 1961 the rate of inflation actually doubled, it was still well below the average annual rate of inflation of the 1950s. The government's reluctance to devalue was naturally related to the political implications of such a decision. On the one hand, the groups supporting the government were deeply divided on this issue as the number of firms and individuals who had debts payable in dollars had grown as a consequence of a series of measures taken by the government to stimulate domestic savings. On the other hand, the government was aware that a sharp upsurge in the rate of inflation would further strengthen the militancy of the labour movement which had in fact been growing since 1959.

The fact that Alessandri allowed the balance of payments to reach a crisis point before reversing his economic policy was not because his managerial outlook prevented him from seeing its political consequences. On the contrary, in December 1961, long before the crisis came to a head, he had made some significant moves towards political compromise in order to ensure the long-term viability of his economic policy. During the middle of 1960, after some disquiet among the right-wing parties about a proposed tax increase to finance the reconstruction of areas devastated by an earthquake earlier that year, there was an important cabinet change resulting in the removal from office of Roberto Vergara, the chief architect and the main co-ordinator of the government's economic policy. Although Vergara was replaced by another non-political minister, the new appointee did not play the same prominent role of his predecessor. Moreover, Vergara's departure gave the government a more moderate political image, thus making it easier for the parties supporting the government to confront the general elections of March 1961. By August 1961, when there was already plenty of evidence that a major financial crisis was imminent, Alessandri made yet another attempt to salvage his economic policy by strengthening his political support. This time he gave cabinet responsibility to the political parties and, significantly enough, appointed a member of the Radical Party as his Chief Economic Minister. Despite these efforts, his economic policy had completely collapsed by the end of his fourth year in office.

The government's decision to devalue in October 1962 was followed by the much-feared increase in the rate of inflation and the expected wave of strikes in support of higher pay settlements. The strikes which took place at the end of 1962 were part of a growing trend of labour militancy which had begun to take shape in the late 1950s and early 1960s. When Alessandri took office, the trade-union movement had still not fully recovered from the severe repressions it had suffered during the Ibáñez administration. In fact, during his first year in office he did not face any serious labour unrest. However by 1960, as the government attempted to introduce a stricter incomes policy, the labour movement under the leadership of the CUT began to stiffen its resistance. In 1960, the CUT rejected the attempt to impose a 10 per cent limit on pay settlements, demanding instead 38 per cent and backing this demand with a wave of strikes which culminated with a call for a general strike. Eventually, the conflict was resolved when the government agreed to a 15 per cent limit on pay settlements. Trade-union opposition to the government's incomes policy was kept up during the remaining four years of the Alessandri administration.

The statistics on strikes for the period 1959 to 1964 show how trade-union militancy evolved during the Alessandri administration. In 1960 and 1961, when the labour movement began to mobilise against the incomes policy, the annual number of strikes was 260. This figure represented a 50 per cent increase from the 1959 level. In 1962 and 1963, the turning-point for the Alessandri administration, the annual number of strikes increased to 400, and by 1964 it had increased yet again to 564. Thus, between 1959 and 1964 the annual number of strikes increased by more than three times.[24] To a large extent the increase in trade-union militancy was fuelled by the government's futile attempts to resolve the crisis by cabinet re-shuffles rather than by broadening its social base. Yet, the militancy of the trade-union movement did not pose an immediate threat to the established order since at that stage the marxist parties had re-asserted control over the movement and were unequivocally steering it in the direction of electoral politics.

After the 1962 devaluation the government lost its sense of direction, becoming very much a caretaker administration until the end of its term in office in 1964. Matched against its own objectives, its record was poor. For it failed to control inflation, it did not make a lasting impact on the productive system and ended up by increasing the role of the state in the economy. The changes in the rate of inflation followed closely the evolution of the government's economic policy. After a spectacular success in 1960, when the rate of inflation was brought down from 33 per cent to 5 per cent, inflation soon re-appeared reaching an annual rate of 10 per cent in 1961, 28 per cent in 1962 and 45 per cent in each of the last two years of the government's term in office.[25] Likewise the liberalisation in the movement of capital and imports did not generate the expected upsurge in the rate of investment. Instead of attracting foreign direct investment, the liberalisation policy generated a massive flow of short-term loans which, by the end of the period, had contributed towards trebling the foreign debt. Between 1959 and 1963, as the foreign debt rose from 569 million dollars to 1,677 million dollars the cost of servicing this debt rose from 10 per cent to nearly 30 per cent of the annual export revenue.[26] Moreover, despite the massive amount of foreign goods which flooded the market, the share of capital goods in total imports dropped from 37 per cent to 35 per cent, while consumer goods increased their share in total imports from 29 per cent to 32 per cent.[27] The reluctance of the private sector to respond favourably to government incentives was, as always, compensated by greater state support of investment. Thus, during the Alessandri period, the contribution of public investments to total investment continued its upward trend, jumping from 52 per cent to 58 per cent.[28] At the same time, as the role of the state in supporting investment continued to increase, a growing proportion of public investment, over 30 per cent in 1964, was financed by external borrowing.[29] Thus by the end of the administration in 1964, while the local bourgeoisie continued to rely on the state to support the process of capital accumulation, the state had become increasingly dependent on foreign loans to perform this crucial function.

CHAPTER 8

Legacy of the 1950s

THE Alessandri and Ibáñez administrations set out to liberalise the economy and to cleanse the political system of corruption and inefficiency. However, as explained in the preceding chapter, they both failed in their objectives. Instead of liberalising the economy, state intervention increased; instead of radically transforming the political system, the ailing party system revived. Because this revival took place in a stagnant economic environment, the parties critical of the system obtained the greatest political dividends. This process culminated in the presidential elections of 1964, when the two candidates calling for a fundamental reform of the socio-economic system – the Christian Democrat Eduardo Frei and the Socialist Salvador Allende obtained more than 90 per cent of the popular vote. In the event Frei obtained a clear majority for his proposed 'Revolution in Liberty'. To understand the dynamics of the political radicalisation which took place this chapter examines some aspects of the country's political and economic developments from 1952 to 1964.

I   POLITICS

During this period the marxist parties, as well as the political system generally, underwent major changes. At the outset, the marxist parties were deeply divided and largely excluded from the political system. By the mid-1950s, however, they had overcome their differences and were once again playing a prominent role. Likewise, there were new developments within the political system. Changes in the electoral laws brought about an increase in political mobilisation which, in turn, dramatically altered the balance of forces. As electoral calculations became more complex and political discourse more radical, a re-alignment of political forces took place which threw the Christian Democratic Party (CDP) into political prominence and nearly eliminated the old right-wing parties from the political map. This section examines developments leading to these events.

Marxists and the Labour Movement

When Ibáñez took office in 1952, the divisions and conflicts between and within the two marxist parties seemed to follow the same pattern as during the late forties. Conflict between Communists and Socialists, which, in 1946, had led to the division of the trade-union movement, was still alive and in some respects had intensified. The 1948 ban on the Communist Party and the subsequent wave of repression aimed at trade-union activities had not had a cohesive effect on the marxist parties. Moreover, the decision of the Socialist Party to support the candidacy of Ibáñez had caused yet another split within its ranks. This time a small but influential group left the party to form an electoral alliance with the Communist Party, which supported Allende in the presidential election of 1952. Thus, at the beginning of this period, while the PSP was participating in the Ibáñez government and a small group of Socialists had begun to gravitate around the Communist Party in search of an electoral alliance along the lines of the old Popular Front, the labour movement was still deeply divided. However, these divisions did not last long. Before the end of the decade the labour movement had reunited, all the factions of the Socialist Party had come together and the Communist and Socialist parties had established a durable electoral alliance.

The participation of the Socialists in the Ibáñez government was brief, lasting only 6 months. It represented their last attempt to pursue a political strategy without, and largely against, the Communist Party. Their participation was also to some extent consistent with the newly-found political identity which the party had begun to develop in the late 1940s. For the Ibañista movement represented a rejection of the type of coalition politics which had prevailed since the collapse of the Popular Front in 1941, and its massive electoral appeal stemmed from an intelligent, albeit demagogic, use of anti-imperialist and anti-oligarchical slogans. The Socialists were obviously aware that the Ibañista movement lacked coherence, but hoped that they would be capable of steering it towards the left in a revolutionary direction.[1] They also regarded their participation as a golden opportunity to establish themselves as the leading force within the labour movement.

During their brief spell in office the Socialists tried unsuccessfully to persuade the government to adopt a left-wing course. In the Ministry of Labour the Socialist Minister implemented pro-labour policies, causing considerable disquiet among industralists, who promptly called for the removal of the marxists from the cabinet. In the Ministry of Mining the Socialists tried to continue the independent policy on the marketing of copper exports which had begun in the early 1950s. They received little co-operation in these two areas of policy from other groups in the heterogeneous Ibañista Movement and practically no support from the President himself. Moreover, as the economic situation deteriorated and inflation began to rise, they realised that they would soon be called upon to enforce unpopular stabilisation measures which would undermine their own base of popular support. Their early departure from the Ibáñez government thus allowed them to preserve their left-wing credentials, and facilitated their reconciliation with the other wing of the Socialist Party and with the Communist Party.

Emergence of the CUT

By the time the Socialists left the Ibáñez administration, the trade-union movement had once again reunited under the Central Unica de Trabajadores (CUT). The creation of CUT in 1953 was preceded by a large increase in labour militancy. While in 1950 the number of people involved in strike action was 44,000, the annual average for the following three years was 109,000.[2] The increase in militancy revived the union movement, and was also the catalyst for its re-unification. White-collar workers in the private and public sectors played a leading role in this process for they were now beginning to feel the full impact of inflation on their salaries. Since they enjoyed greater political freedom than manual workers, who had been the main target for González' repressive politics, their activity became the focus around which the labour movement was re-united. They first created a nationwide federation of state and private employees. They then established institutional links with trade unions in the manufacturing and mining sectors and played a leading role in the negotiations which led to the establishment of the CUT.[3]

The political programme of the CUT was unequivocally marxist, bearing more resemblance to FOCH's programme of the early 1920s than to its conflict-ridden predecessor, the CTCH. But unlike FOCH, the CUT programme sought to keep the trade-union movement free from political intervention by parties and government alike. Thus, the programme called upon the movement not only to defend the immediate interests of their members but to further the class struggle so as to bring about a socialist transformation of society. But it also made it clear that for the sake of preserving the unity of the labour movement, trade unions should maintain their independence from the government of the day and from all political parties.[4] Thus, while the CUT's programme acknowledged that the ultimate objective of the labour movement was political, it also sought to keep the unions away from the divisive influence of party politics, which in the 1940s had led to the break-up of the CTCH.

The fear of government intervention in the trade-union movement was confirmed when, less than a month after the creation of the CUT, Ibáñez appointed one of the members of its management committee to the cabinet. The CUT reacted swiftly by expelling the individual concerned and reaffirming the principle that CUT officers could not hold government appointments.[5] After the Socialists left the government, the CUT's relations with Ibáñez turned sour. The growing rate of inflation brought about a new wave of strikes, culminating in 1954 in a general strike after the government had taken severely repressive measures against the unions, including the imprisonment of Clotario Blest, the CUT's Secretary-General. An important factor contributing towards preserving union independence was the government's unsuccessful attempt at dividing the labour movement following the advice of prominent Argentinian politicians belonging to the Peronista movement.[6] But while the CUT found it relatively easy to resist the influence of the Ibáñez government, keeping the labour movement free from political interference by the marxist parties was to prove more difficult.

The Left Unites

After the Socialist Party left Ibáñez' government, the three main marxist parties – the two Socialist parties and the Communist Party found themselves, for the first time since the early 1930s, opposing a government which could no longer tempt them into sharing the spoils of office and which seemed determined to divide and repress the trade-union movement. These new circumstances, together with the fact that the trade-union movement was already united around the CUT, acted as a catalyst for the reconciliation of the marxist parties. The major step towards the unity of the left was the creation of the Popular Action Front (Frente de Acción Popular/FRAP) in 1956. The FRAP was a loose political alliance between the Communist and Socialist parties, along with two other small parties, the Democratic National Party and the People's National Vanguard. As an electoral alliance the

FRAP proved to be surprisingly effective. In 1958, only two years after its establishment, Allende, the FRAP's candidate, nearly won the presidential election. This surprisingly good performance radically transformed the electoral prospects of the marxist parties. Now they no longer had to play second fiddle to the Radical Party, or to any of the other parties at the centre of the political spectrum, since they could realistically envisage winning a presidential election with a candidate of their own. These bright electoral prospects made it unthinkable for any of them to break away from the FRAP. Indeed, the electoral alliance between Communists and Socialists lasted, albeit with some changes, until the end of the Allende government in 1973.

Electoral Politics and the Party System

Neither Ibáñez nor Alessandri had managed an effective challenge to the party system. As a consequence, they had been eventually forced to play the game of parliamentary politics with the existing political parties. Because they both carried out distinctly right-wing economic policies, political forces re-aligned along well-defined ideological lines. Contrary to what had happened in the late 1940s when it had been possible to form broad coalitions which included governments made up of right-wing and marxist parties, by 1964 the right and left of the political spectrum had become irreconcilable extremes with the centre parties gravitating around them. The process of ideological clarification, prompted by the more clearly-defined nature of government policy, brought greater cohesion to the party system. By the early 1960s, the extraordinary fragmentation of the party system, begun in the early 1940s and reaching its peak in 1953, when there were nearly thirty-two political groups represented in the Congress, had changed dramatically. In the general election of 1961 the number of parties electing representatives was only seven.[7]

The cohesion and growing strength of the party system did not however make electoral calculations less complicated. In the 1961 congressional elections, the FRAP, with only 30 per cent of the vote, became the largest electoral bloc in the country. However, the informal alliance between the two right-wing parties, Conservative and Liberal, also accounted for 30 per cent of the vote.

The rest of the votes were controlled by the centrist parties, the Radical and the Christian Democratic Parties, with 21 per cent and 15 per cent respectively. However the politics of these centre parties were not centrist. Indeed, while the Radicals had supported the Alessandri government in alliance with Liberals and Conservatives, the Christian Democratic Party had become increasingly left-wing. Because the combined electoral strength of the Radicals and the right-wing parties would give them a clear majority over the FRAP, in October 1962 they created an electoral alliance, the Democratic Front, which nominated a member of the Radical party to represent them in the presidential election. But despite its bright electoral prospects the Democratic Front was not successful. In a by-election which took place six months before the presidential election in a predominantly right-wing rural area, the Democratic Front was categorically defeated by the FRAP, which obtained 39 per cent of the vote as against 33 per cent by the Democratic Front.[8] As a consequence of this electoral defeat, Conservatives and Liberals scrapped the Democratic Front and supported Eduardo Frei, the CDP candidate, who obtained 56 per cent of the vote against 39 per cent by Salvador Allende, the FRAP candidate.

Transformation of the Falange

The creation of the Christian Democratic Party (CDP) in 1957 was one of the most important political events of this period. The CDP originated in the early 1930s when a group belonging to the Conservative Youth broke away from the party to form the Falange Nacional. During its first twenty years, from the early 1930s to the mid-1950s, its electoral impact was insignificant, as it never obtained more than 4 per cent of the popular vote. Nevertheless, because of the nature of the coalition-style politics prevailing in the 1940s, it exercised considerable influence, holding key cabinet posts in several coalition governments.

After the collapse of the Ibañista Movement, the Falange suddenly emerged as one of the major political parties in the country. In the general election of 1957 it obtained 9.4 per cent of the vote, which was more than treble the figure it had achieved in the 1953 general election. After this spectacular performance it merged with other Social Christians and Ibañista groups to form the Christian Democratic Party. The following year, the CDP candidate in the presidential election finished third, obtaining 21 per cent of the vote thereby defeating the Radical Party candidate who obtained 15 per cent. In the municipal elections of 1960, the CDP obtained 14 per cent of the vote, thus becoming the fourth largest political party; in the 1961 general elections, with nearly 16 per cent of the popular vote they became the third largest, and by 1963, with 22 per cent of the vote, they had become the largest party in the country.

The Falange's evolution during the 1950s follows closely the general trends of the period. After participating for a short time in the González administration, it supported the Radical candidate in the

1952 presidential elections. Following Ibáñez' overwhelming and un-expected victory and the poor performance of the Radical candidate – who was third, with less than half of Ibáñez' vote, finishing several points behind the right-wing candidate – it decided to change its strategy. The new strategy involved abandoning its previous practice of participating in coalition governments and in alliances with other parties and concentrating instead on broadening its popular base of support. To this effect, the party convention of 1959 called upon its members to adopt an aggressive approach at the grassroots level and to increase the number of new recruits among working-class constituen-cies. This new independent political line was further ratified when at the same convention the party rejected a motion calling for greater cooperation with the marxist parties.[9] This change of strategy was its first attempt at finding an independent political role and establish-ing itself as a competitor in a field hitherto controlled by the marxist parties. Thus, as a centrist party, it was markedly different from the Radical Party. For while the Radical Party had never attempted to establish a working-class base and had relied on the marxist parties for support, the Falange was determined to take over the base of support from the marxists so as to push them out of the competition and become an independent political alternative.

Expansion of the Electorate

The beginning of the electoral growth of the CDP in 1957 coincided with the collapse of the Ibañista movement. At this stage, the vast majority of CDP supporters were urban, middle and lower-middle class. In terms of electoral statistics, the CDP appears to have grown mainly at the expense of the right-wing parties. The results of the 1953 congressional elections, in which the groups supporting Ibáñez obtained more than one-third of the vote, had seriously affected all major parties, except the Socialist Party. The share of the vote of the right-wing parties dropped from 41 per cent in 1949 to 22 per cent in 1953, and that of the Radical Party from 22 per cent to 13 per cent. In the general elections of 1957, while the Radical Party recovered lost ground, achieving once again 22 per cent, the right-wing parties with 29 per cent recovered only half their 1949 strength. But the electoral strength of the CDP cannot be solely attributed to its ability to win votes away from the right-wing parties. In fact by the late 1950s it had succeeded in attracting a large following among the urban poor, mainly among non-unionised workers in the service sector, and had managed to gain some influence among agricultural workers in the central zone, largely owing to the hard work of a few dedicated activists. The CDP's opposition to the unpopular economic policies of President Alessandri had undoubtedly contributed towards making the party appealing to working-class voters. Indeed, in many respects the opposition of the CDP and of the FRAP were almost identical.

The most important factors underlying the growth of the CDP between 1952 and 1964 were the changes in the composition and size of the electorate. From the return to democracy in 1932 until 1949 the size of the electorate doubled so that in the 1952 presidential elections the number of registered voters was 1.1 million, representing nearly 18 per cent of the population. Between 1952 and 1964 the process of electoral mobilisation continued unabated. After the introduction of the single official ballot paper in 1958, which reinforced the secrecy of the vote, the percentage of the population registered to vote increased from 18 per cent to 23 per cent in 1961. But the largest increase in the size of the electorate took place between 1961 and 1964, when it increased from 1.8 million to 2.9 million people. This was largely a consequence of a change in the electoral laws, which made registration compulsory. Thus, while in 1952 only 46 per cent of those eligible to vote had actually registered, by 1964 this figure had risen to 90 per cent. By 1964 the proportion of the population registered to vote was 35 per cent, while in the late 1940s it had only been 9 per cent.[10]

The substantial increase in electoral registrations which took place during this period, particularly during the second half, was accompanied by a marked and sustained increase in the rate of electoral participation. While in the general elections of 1953 and 1957, 70 per cent of those registered to vote actually participated, in the general elections of 1961 the rate of participation increased to 75 per cent and in the municipal elections of 1963 it increased again, reaching 80 per cent of the registered voters. A further point that should be noted to understand the electoral mobilisation during this period is that most of the newly-registered were women and members of the lower strata among the urban working class and agricultural workers. Indeed, the effect which compulsory registration had on female registrations was remarkable. The first time that women participated in a presidential elections was in 1952. On that occasion only 40 per cent of the women eligible to vote actually registered. This low level of female registration remained fairly stable until 1962, when the law made electoral registration compulsory. This had the effect of increasing the number of female registrations to nearly 75 per cent of those eligible to vote.[11]

Electoral Calculations in a New Context

The rapid growth of the electorate introduced confusion and uncertainty in electoral calculations. During the 1940s the distribution of votes among the main political parties was roughly as follows: the right-wing parties controlled around 40 per cent of the vote, the marxist parties between 15 per cent and 25 per cent and the Radical Party around 20 per cent. The rest of the vote was scattered among smaller parties. In terms of the constituencies of the various party groupings, the picture was roughly as follows. The right-wing parties drew their urban support from a mix of entrepreneurs, liberal professionals and lower middle class. The Conservative Party's ability to attract lower-middle-class voters was based on their self-professed Catholicism. The right-wing parties also controlled the bulk of the vote in rural areas because of their control over the land. Since the rural areas were grossly over-represented in the Congress, the right-wing parties enjoyed privileged access to political influence.[12] The fairly stable 20 per cent vote controlled by the Radical Party during the 1940s was mainly urban-based and strongly linked to the middle – and lower-middle classes in the state bureaucracy. The Radicals were also influential in some areas in the far south and north of the country. In the south, their support stemmed mainly from the wheat-growing land-owners, whose interests often clashed with those of the land-owners of the central region, who, controlling the best of the country's agricultural land, were at the centre of the *latifundia* system. Support for the Radicals in some provinces in the north of the country, mainly Coquimbo, had been traditionally connected to small- and medium-sized mining. Electoral support for the marxist parties consisted largely of the organised working class in mining, manufacturing industry and construction. The Socialists also drew support away from the Radical Party among the lower-middle class in some professions, mainly education, and in the service sector generally.

To a large extent, the straightforward distribution of votes among the various political groupings during the 1940s was a consequence of the fact that the electorate was small and its size remained fairly stable, at about 9 per cent of the population. However with the rapid growth of the electorate between 1952 and 1964 came two new constituencies, which greatly complicated the hitherto simple process of electoral calculation. On the one hand, there was the female vote, comprising half of the electorate, and on the other, there were the new male voters, a large proportion of whom belonged to the lowest-paid groups among urban workers. These two new constituencies were eventually captured by the CDP and were to form the backbone of its popular support.

In 1952, the first time that women voted in a presidential election, the female vote was concentrated mainly on the winning candidate Ibáñez (43 per cent) and on the runner-up supported by the right-wing parties (32 per cent).[13] In the 1958 elections, after the collapse of the Ibáñez movement, there was a notable swing in the female vote in favour of the Christian Democrats. Although on that occasion the candidate of the Christian Democratic Party finished in third place, among women he obtained the second largest share of the vote (24 per cent). Since female support for the right-wing parties between 1958 and 1964 remained fairly stable, at about 30 per cent, it is safe to assume that the CDP attracted half of the female constituency away from the Ibañista movement. The popularity of the CDP among women voters reached its peak in the 1964 presidential elections, when Frei obtained 63 per cent of female votes against 32 per cent obtained by Allende, the FRAP candidate.

The spectacular popularity of the CDP among female voters merely illustrated its enormous success in attracting a large number of the new electors who registered after the electoral reforms of 1962. This group, comprising nearly one-third of the electorate, consisted mainly of the lowest-paid non-unionised workers in urban and rural areas. That the CDP could compete so effectively with the marxist parties for the vote of this new constituency gave it the necessary impetus towards becoming, by 1963, the largest party in the country and the alternative to the traditional right- and left-wing parties.

The sudden growth of the CDP to being the largest party with a political appeal stretching across class boundaries, posed a new and difficult challenge to the Communist and Socialist parties. For until then, they had been accustomed to occupying a hegemonic position among working-class voters and, since the 1958 electoral reform, they had established themselves as a major political force in the country-side. During the fourteen years of political rule by the Radical Party (1938–52), Communists and Socialists had never had serious competition for the vote of the urban working class. The Radical Party had never attempted to exercise direct electoral influence over this group, for they had always assumed that they could count on its support by forming alliances with either one of the marxist parties. This implicit understanding came to an end when the Communist Party was outlawed in 1948 and it could not be revived because of the political changes which took place in the following ten years. By the 1960s the working-class electorate had changed not only in size, but also in composition. In the 1940s, because the electorate was small (10 per cent of the population) the proportion of registered voters who also belonged to unions was very high. In fact, while the total electorate consisted of roughly 500,000 people, the number of workers belonging to unions was 250,000. Given the control which political parties exercised over the trade-union movement, it is safe to assume that the vast majority of unionised workers were also registered voters. Therefore, the control which Communists and Socialists exercised over the trade-union movement also ensured for them the bulk of the vote of organised workers. However, by the early sixties the rapid growth of the electorate altered the correlation between registered voters and unionised workers. Indeed, while in the 1940s the size of the trade-union movement was equal to 50 per cent of the electorate, in the early 1960s only 10 per cent of the electorate belonged to unions. Moreover, between 1952 and 1964 the size of the electorate trebled, but the number of unionised workers remained practically unchanged so that the actual proportion of the workforce belonging to unions dropped from 12 per cent to 10 per cent. Thus, by the early 1960s, the control which the marxist parties exercised over the labour movement could no longer guarantee access to political influence in the parliamentary system.

The CDP Challenge

Communists and Socialists were slow to grasp the political implications of the changes in the relative size of the electorate and the trade-union movement. In the 1964 elections they maintained their control over the vote of organised workers, mainly in manufacturing, mining and construction.[14] However, among the vast number of newly registered working-class voters, the marxists had to confront tough and largely successful competition by the CDP. Christian Democrats made substantial gains here thanks to their skilful use of left-wing slogans and to their superior financial resources. Their success among this new group is a major factor explaining their victory in the 1964 presidential elections. It seems therefore, that, in the short term at least, the expansion of the electoral system had the effect of destroying the hegemonic position of Communists and Socialists among working-class voters.

The CDP's electoral challenge elicited different responses from the various political parties. On the left, it became a major source of controversy between Communists and Socialists. While the Communist party regarded the electoral success of the CDP as a conclusive argument in favour of broadening the FRAP, the Socialists did not agree as they were aware that an electoral alliance with the CDP would relegate them to a subordinate position. On the right, the sudden growth of the CDP, in conjunction with the erosion of the popularity of the Alessandri government, prompted the establishment of the Democratic Front, a theoretically-promising electoral alliance which proved impractical long before the 1964 elections. After its collapse the right-wing parties were forced to offer their unconditional support to the CDP candidate so as to prevent the victory of the marxist candidate. Hence it is not surprising that the CDP candidate in 1964 should have vowed not to change one iota of his programme to please the right-wing voters.

The seemingly uncompromising position of the CDP belies the complicated politics of the period preceding the 1964 presidential election. The spectre of a democratically-elected marxist government in Chile had haunted the United States government since 1958, when Allende was narrowly defeated in the presidential elections. Moreover, in the late 1950s and early 1960s, Fidel Castro's victory in Cuba and the election of President Kennedy in the United States brought about important changes in United States policy in the region. To prevent Castro's revolution from spreading, Kennedy put forward a new policy, the 'Alliance for Progress', which was based on the assumption that the most effective way of fighting communism in the region was by promoting economic development and democracy. Hence, United States military aid and advice on counter-insurgency tactics were supplemented by generous development aid.[15]

From the perspective of inter-American relations, the 'Alliance for Progress' constituted a belated and unsatisfactory response to the Latin-American governments' old aspiration of having a regional version of the Marshall Plan. But the emphasis of the 'Alliance for Progress' on the virtues of democracy had a special significance for Chile. Indeed, since Chile had one of the few democratic governments, as well as the strongest marxist political movement in the region, it became an ideal testing ground for the principles of the 'Alliance for Progress'. United States policy towards Chile had therefore two main objectives: an immediate objective, aimed at defeating the marxists through the ballot box; and a long-term objective, which envisaged destroying the social base of support of the marxist parties through the modernisation of the country's social and economic structures.

The main obstacle to achieving the first objective stemmed from the division between the main non-marxist parties. As already noted, by

1961 the FRAP with 30 per cent of the vote had become the largest electoral bloc in the country and was therefore in a position to make a serious bid for the Presidency. Since the right-wing parties controlled 30 per cent of the votes and the Radical and Christian Democratic parties around 20 per cent each, on paper at least, there were several electoral combinations which could have defeated the marxists. But in practice, the establishment of these alliances proved to be difficult and, consequently, a source of great concern to the United States.

The right-wing parties decided to confront the 1964 presidential election in alliance with the Radical Party. Together, they controlled just over 50 per cent of the vote. The CDP, which had been building its electoral strength on the basis of its claim to represent an alternative to the traditional right- and left-wing parties, could not at the time afford to enter into any form of electoral alliance. Although the Kennedy administration had strong sympathies for the CDP, as it was the party most in tune with the objectives of the 'Alliance for Progress', the policy of the United States government in Chile was to provide financial and logistical assistance both to the Democratic Front and to the CDP. After the collapse of the Democratic Front in 1963, the United States government gave its full support to the CDP candidate, by financing nearly half of the party's electoral campaign.[16]

There were two main reasons prompting such massive American intervention in the 1964 election. Firstly, the introduction of the single official ballot paper in 1958 had made vote-buying very difficult, thereby increasing the importance of political propaganda and mobilisation. The United States had the resources and experience to make an enormous impact in this domain, especially since the main issue was defined as a choice between marxism and democracy. Secondly, United States support for the CDP candidate was, paradoxically enough, meant to ensure the smooth continuity of democratic institutions. Indeed, after the collapse of the Democratic Front, when it was clear that the right-wing parties had no chance of winning the election, there was a serious threat of a right-wing inspired military coup preventing the election from taking place. The Central Intelligence Agency office in Chile managed to dissuade the conspirators from carrying out their planned coup, pointing out that the victory of the CDP candidate was assured.[17] But the United States government and the right-wing parties realized that an electoral victory by the CDP was not enough to keep the marxists out of office. Indeed, because the constitution provided that the election of the President would be determined by the Congress in the case that no candidate won an absolute majority of the vote, they feared that the CDP, following its populist instincts, would enter into a parliamentary alliance with the marxist parties to secure a favourable decision by the Congress. To prevent this from happening, the United States government poured massive resources in support of the CDP candidate so as to ensure not only that he would win the election, but also that by obtaining an absolute majority his access to office would not require political negotiations in the Congress.

United States intervention in the 1964 election concentrated mainly on financing a campaign depicting the horrors of communism and linking the Chilean Marxists to human rights' violations in states in the Soviet bloc. According to a United States Senate report, the sums spent by the Kennedy administration in this campaign amounted to over half of the total budget of the CDP candidate.[18] This anticommunist campaign was successful on two counts: on the one hand, the CDP candidate did obtain more than 50 per cent of the vote, thus making unnecessary the Congress' involvement in the election of the President; and on the other hand, it contributed towards deepening the antagonisms between the CDP and the marxist left, thus making it unlikely that any form of alliance could develop between them during the Frei administration and beyond. Hence, American intervention did secure the continuity of democracy, but it was also a forceful reminder that its support was not unconditional. Despite all these problems, the new CDP administration opened an important chapter in Chile's political history.

II THE ECONOMY

When the CDP took office in 1964 inflation was once again on the rise. The preceding administration had applied a stabilisation programme which brought inflation down from 33 per cent in 1958 to a post-war record low of 5 per cent in 1960. But, as a serious balance of payments crisis began to develop the government was forced to abandon its stabilisation programme so that by 1963 inflation had risen to 45 per cent; that is, twelve points above the 1958 level. Attempts to liberalise the economy had brought about some measure of rationalisation to the pattern of state intervention, particularly in the areas of price control and foreign trade, but it did not greatly reduce the level of state intervention in the economy. Indeed, while in the early fifties the share of public investment in total investment was 40 per cent, by the early sixties the public sector accounted for 50 per cent of investment.[19] Likewise, public expenditure continued to rise, reaching 20 per cent of GNP by 1960; that is six points higher than in 1940. But despite the greater involvement of the state in the economy, growth rates remained at disappointingly low levels. While during the forties GDP grew at an average annual rate of 3.9 per cent, in the decade of the fifties the annual average dropped slightly, to 3.5 per cent. However, because in the fifties there was a marked increase in the rate of population growth, from 1.8 to 2.5 per cent a year, per capita GDP increased by only 1 per cent a year by comparison with 2 per cent during the forties.[20]

The problems created by the low rates of growth during the fifties were further aggravated by the fact that, during this decade, the process of concentration of the population in urban areas continued unabated. Indeed, at the beginning of the decade 60 per cent of the population lived in urban areas, and by the end of the decade this figure had increased to 67 per cent, of which more than half lived in Santiago.[21] These demographic changes, combined with a stagnant economy, brought about a major increase in the rate of unemployment. Thus, in 1952 unemployment in the Greater Santiago area was 4 per cent; from 1955–9 the average annual rate was 8 per cent.[22] A special source of concern was the bleak employment prospects in manufacturing industry. While in the 1940s employment in manufacturing industry increased at an annual rate of 33 per cent, in the 1950s the annual average rate of increase was less than 1 per cent. Thus, while manufacturing industry in the 1940s generated an annual average of 9,000 new jobs, in the 1950s it only generated an annual average of 500 jobs.[23]

The loss of dynamism of manufacturing industry which, as explained in Chapter 4, had begun in the late 1940s continued throughout the 1950s. Although in the first five years of the decade industrial production grew at an annual average rate of 5.4 per cent, mainly because of the CORFO-sponsored steel and oil projects, in the second half of the decade it registered a negative growth rate of 0.4 per cent.[24] Thus, between 1945 and 1960, the contribution of manufacturing industry to GDP remained practically stationary at 23.1 per cent and 24.8 per cent respectively.[25] Besides, some of the structural features of the manufacturing sector did not make its growth prospects very encouraging. By the early sixties, of the 447,000 persons employed in the manufacturing sector only 54 per cent were employed in factories (defined as enterprises employing five or more workers). The remaining 46 per cent of the workforce were employed in handicrafts.[26] Factories accounted for the bulk of industrial production and capital. However, there were great disparities within this category. While nearly 70 per cent of the 6,000 units classified as factories were tiny units employing less than twenty persons, only 3 per cent of them were large factories employing 200 or more workers. However, this small percentage of large enterprises, comprising 190 units, accounted for 44 per cent of factory employment.[27] Within the small group of large enterprises there were also discrepancies in size as twelve units accounted for 40 per cent of production of large enterprises, and for 20 per cent of all factory production. Besides, only nine units concentrated 45 per cent of the capital of all large enterprises, accounting for 25 per cent of the capital of all factories.[28] According to the 1957 industrial census, the top twenty manufacturing firms accounted for nearly 39 per cent of the gross value of manufacturing production, 20 per cent of employment and 52 per cent of the sector's fixed capital.[29] These high levels of concentration in industry were combined with a typically under-developed structure of production. Indeed, by the early sixties 60 per cent of the country's industrial output consisted of traditional consumer goods while capital goods and consumer durables accounted for only 10 per cent.[30]

Manufacturing industry's failure to play a dynamic role in promoting economic growth ran parallel with the continuous decline of the agricultural sector. While there was a marked increase in mechanisation, mainly because of the liberalisation of imports, agricultural employment and production continued the steady decline which had begun in the late thirties. Between 1950 and 1960 the share of agriculture in employment dropped from 32 per cent to 31 per cent, while its share of GDP dropped from 11.6 per cent to 9.8 per cent.[31] During this period property relations remained unchanged, despite an agrarian reform law which the Alessandri government had enacted in return for badly-needed foreign exchange, at the suggestion of officials in charge of the administration of the United States foreign aid programme, the 'Alliance for Progress'. The stagnation of agricultural production created serious political and financial problems for the government as demand for foodstuffs increased as a consequence of the acceleration in the rates of population growth and urban concentration. The growing food deficit was compensated by imports, mostly subsidised by the United States' programme under Public Law 480. Thus, while by 1956 the value of food imports was equivalent to 9 per cent of the value of non-agricultural exports, by 1962 it had increased to 22 per cent.[32]

In the export sector copper continued to be important, generating over three-fourths of the export sector's revenue. Although the volume of copper exports increased from 322,000 metric tons to

460,000 metric tons per year from 1950 to 1960, these figures were still below the export levels achieved during the boom period of World War II.[33] This insufficient increase in copper production was combined with a decline in the share of copper value retained by the Chilean state. Thus, while in the first half of the decade, Chile retained on average around 72 per cent of the CIF value of the unit of copper exported, in the second half of the decade its share had dropped to 60 per cent and remained at this level throughout the first three years of the sixties.[34] The poor performance of the copper sector was all the more disappointing as the copper legislation of 1955 had been hailed as a promising new deal which would yield substantial and immediate benefits.

The failure of Ibáñez' and Alessandri's economic policies between 1952 and 1964 is magnified when the poor performance of all sectors of the economy is set against the spectacular rise of the foreign debt. Between 1958 and 1963, foreign currency debt trebled from 569 million dollars to 1,677 million.[35] Thus, by 1963 the cost of servicing the debt was equivalent to nearly 30 per cent of the annual value of exports, that is, three times higher than the average prevailing at the time for less developed countries.[36]

The pattern of income distribution in the early 1960s was still highly concentrated, with 50 per cent of earners sharing 15 per cent of income and 5 per cent of earners taking nearly one-third of total income.[37] But despite this regressive pattern of income distribution the share of labour in renumeration made remarkable progress, increasing from 38 per cent in 1952 to nearly 48 per cent in 1964.[38] This gain was partly due to the introduction of minimum wage legislation for agricultural and industrial workers in 1953 and 1956 respectively, and to the greater political strength of the working-class under the CUT. It is interesting that, whereas white-collar workers had increased their share of disposable income during the 1940s, and the income share of manual workers had declined, during the Ibáñez and Alessandri administrations white-collar workers lost ground to manual workers; and among manual workers, agricultural workers were beginning to make important income gains because of the widening of the electoral system.[39]

CHAPTER 9

Revolution in Liberty

THE CDP called its programme a 'Revolution in Liberty' as it combined substantial economic and social reforms with major changes to the political system. The programme was conceived as a long-term political enterprise lasting at least three decades. Given that Frei, the CDP's presidential candidate, had had such a decisive victory at the polls – 56 percent – the possibility of thirty years of political rule by the CDP was, at this time, not altogether unrealistic. However, the CDP lasted only one term in office, and in 1970, after a humiliating defeat in the presidential elections, it handed over power to its archrivals, the marxist parties. In spite of this failure, the six years of the CDP administration offer interesting insights into the functioning of Chile's political system; and they were a foretaste of problems which the Allende administration had to confront. This chapter is divided into two main sections. Section I discusses the intellectual background to the CDP's political programme. Section II examines the main developments during these six years.

I CDP – BACKGROUND

Ever since its emergence in the mid-1930s as a breakaway faction of the Conservative Party, the Falange (as the CDP was then called) had sought to occupy a position equidistant from the traditional Right and the two marxist parties. The economic consequences of the world depression had greatly impressed the party's middle-class leadership, all of whom were then university students belonging to the youth section of the Conservative Party. Since the Conservative Party claimed to represent the only channel for Catholics in politics, it is not surprising that the Falange's break with it took the form of a dispute over the correct interpretation of the social doctrine of the Catholic Church. According to the Falange's interpretation of the Papal Encyclicals, mainly *Rerum Novarum* and *Quadragesimo Anno*, Catholic social doctrine rejected the extreme manifestation of liberal individualism espoused by the local Conservative and Liberal parties, as well as the denial of human individuality implicit in the ideology of the marxist parties. In their place, the Falange put forward a conception of society in which individual and community are regarded as inseparable elements of the same organic whole, linked by Christian solidarity. In practical terms the Falange's conception of society involved a recognition of the conflict between capital and labour, together with a plea to overcome it through a redefinition of the rights and duties inside and outside the capitalist enterprise. Hence their conception of the social function of private property and their advocacy of communitarianism as an alternative form of social organisation.[1]

The political philosophy of the Falange was strongly influenced by the writings of the French Catholic philosopher Jacques Maritain.[2] But, apart from its solid grounding in Catholic social philosophy, its ideology in the early years was based on a thorough and original attempt to interpret Chile's changing social and economic realities after the great depression. It was in this early period that the Falange began to express serious political and intellectual interests in reconciling the need for greater economic growth with real social justice. It was also during this period that Eduardo Frei made his greatest contribution towards shaping the ideology of the Falange by writing several books and articles in which he argued that it was necessary to exercise more effective control over the country's natural resources and made a strong plea for the modernisation of production in agriculture.[3] However, during the forties, the intellectual pursuits of the Falange leaders were pushed to the background as they became prominent actors in the complex game of coalition politics, participating in several cabinets during the Ríos and González administrations. However, by the early fifties, after realising that participation in coalition governments did not yield significant electoral dividends, the party decided to follow an independent centre-left political line, keeping a safe distance from the Radical Party and directly competing with the marxist parties.

After the collapse of the Ibañista movement in the mid-fifties a few scattered Ibañista groups merged with the Falange and with other progressive Catholic groups to form in 1957 the Christian Democratic Party. The creation of the CDP gave the party a more pluralistic outlook, particularly among non-Catholic and lower-middle-class voters, even though its core was Falange. But together with these institutional changes there took place a significant renewal of political ideology. For in the mid-1950s there appeared a group of economists who linked the emerging theory on economic development, elaborated by the recently established United Nations Economic Commission for Latin America (ECLA), to the political philosophy of the CDP. These economists, under the leadership of Jorge Ahumada, revived the Falange's critical tradition, which had remained dormant since the early forties, when Frei and the rest of its leadership had become involved in coalition politics. Ahumada's main work, *En vez de la miseria* (*In place of poverty*), was first published in 1958 and immediately became the most influential source of CDP ideology. His diagnosis of Chile's economic plight is based on ECLA's analysis of under-development in peripheral economies. Thus, it starts by identifying the structural imbalances among the various sectors of the economy, paying particular attention to the inefficiency of the agriculture sector and to the country's excessive dependence on mineral exports, which is described as one of the main factors responsible for the chronic inflation affecting Chile since the early thirties. Since these imbalances act as a brake on the process of industrialisation, there follows a plea to introduce major structural reforms which, propelled by a substantial redistribution of income, would be coordinated by the state under a well-designed plan.[4] So far Ahumada's analysis follows closely ECLA's analysis of under-development.[5] However, its originality lies in the fact that he took it one step further into the realm of politics, thus infusing ECLA's technocratic analysis with real political substance.

According to Ahumada, the problem of economic growth cannot be resolved independently of the social and political factors affecting the process of development. In his view the efficacy of technical measures applied to correct economic imbalances depends largely on the existence of a healthy and vigorous socio-economic context. The two main political problems which Ahumada identifies as obstacles to change in the case of Chile are participation and representation. According to him, the problem of participation stems from the fact that the political system did not provide adequate mechanisms to channel the interests and aspirations of the majority of the people, while the problem of representation is related to the fact that the prevailing institutional structure over-represented sectional interests, mainly at the trade-union and business levels, thus distorting the content of the political process. To remedy these problems Ahumada calls for a gigantic effort of popular mobilisation to provide new forms of political participation, which would enable people to maintain a permanent and active presence in the political arena. This in turn, would contribute towards the successful implementation of the technical measures necessary for reviving economic growth.[6]

Ahumada's conception of a link between economic and political development – an original insight three decades ago – became the cornerstone of the CDP's 'Revolution in Liberty'. Indeed, its programme of government combined the well-known developmentalist goals of increasing state control over natural resources, modernising property relations in agriculture, and redistribution of income, with the political aim of introducing fundamental changes to the political system so as to adapt the institutional structure to the economic changes that would be introduced. It was the mix of these economic and political objectives that made the CDP's programme of governments so threatening to the rest of the political parties.

The political reforms advocated in the CDP's programme of government included three main points: firstly, it called for the creation of a vast network of grassroots organisations at the neighbourhood level to serve as channels of political participation between the community on the one hand and the state or council authorities on the other. This programme was known as Popular Promotion, and it was aimed mainly at the unorganised urban poor, which the CDP called marginals. Secondly, it envisaged a reform of trade-union legislation which would act as an incentive to increasing the levels of unionisation, but which, at the same time, would free the trade-union movement from its dependency on political parties. Thirdly, it envisaged a series of constitutional amendments which would give the executive branch exclusive legislative initiative over key matters of economic policy.

Bearing in mind the enormous electoral mobilisation which had taken place before Frei came into office, combined with the failure of the two preceding administrations to revive economic growth, the political programme of the CDP was a coherent attempt at redefining the economic and social boundaries of the political system. For apart from the theoretical conviction about the need to link economic and social development, the CDP was aware that the spectacular support it had achieved in the 1964 presidential elections would quickly evaporate unless it was able to translate it into effective political power. The CDP's awareness of this political dilemma is clearly expressed in one of Frei's first speeches as President: 'electoral power is not enough to satisfy the needs of the people. Electoral power is only a part of political power in general, which also includes economic and cultural power. If a nation is to be really democratic, the people should have access to all the forms of power and participate in their exercise.'[7]

Given that, at the time of this speech, Frei was also the leader of the largest and most energetic political movement in the country's history, it is little wonder that both right- and left-wing parties, regardless of whether they believed in the forthcoming 'Revolution in Liberty', regarded the CDP as a very serious threat.

The one important point which CDP ideologues failed to define clearly at the outset of the Frei administration was the notion of communitarianism, which was the form of social organisation meant to replace capitalist property relations and the alternative to collectivist socialism. Not surprisingly, arguments about the precise definition of communitarianism featured prominently during the party's six years in office.

II   CDP – ADMINISTRATION

Initial Strategy

When the CDP took office in November 1964, it only had a very small proportion of seats in both houses of the Congress. Since elections to renew the whole of the Chamber of Deputies and half of the Senate were due to take place four months later, it concentrated all its efforts in trying to transform its enormous popularity with the electorate into a parliamentary majority to implement its 'Revolution in Liberty'. This short-term political objective had the practical effect of ruling out any early attempt at forming an alliance with other parties in the Congress. This same consideration also made it impractical for other parties to envisage a coalition with the CDP. Besides, in the aftermath of its massive electoral victory, the other political parties were carefully reassessing their position. The two right-wing parties which had been forced to vote for the CDP to keep the marxist candidate out of office desperately needed to regroup their traditional electorate so as to reassert their political identity. Indeed, as I explained in Chapter 8, the CDP had made significant inroads into the right-wing vote in the period preceding the 1964-elections. The Communists and Socialists for their part were still recovering from the shock of having been defeated by such a large margin and had not yet decided how to respond to the new government. Besides, since the CDP's electoral campaign, heavily financed and inspired by American Cold War strategists, had relied on anti-marxist and anti-communist themes, relations between them were at their lowest.

The general election of 1965 gave a resounding victory to the CDP;

with 42 per cent of the vote it was confirmed as the largest political party. However, the allocation of seats in the Congress that ensued were not so favourable. In the Chamber of Deputies, it managed to obtain a majority of seats (55 per cent); while in the Senate, mainly because only half of the seats were renewed, it obtained less than one-third of the seats. Although these results did not give it a working parliamentary majority, it maintained its policy of refusing alliances with any of the major political parties, claiming that such an alliance would compromise its political programme. Its principled position regarding political alliances – which had been consistently followed by the party since the 1950s – was also quite reasonable given the strategy which it intended using to implement its programme. Indeed, because its short-term objectives could be largely achieved without relying on the Congress, the government did not really need to enter into any form of alliance with either right- or left-wing parties.

The government's strategy had two main components: a short-term expansionary policy designed to revive the economy, bringing about a gradual process of income re-distribution and greater price stability; and a long-term policy which included basic political reforms. To implement the short-term policy the government did not need to rush into political alliances since this policy called for the adoption of measures regarding which the Congress had limited jurisdiction – such as increases in public expenditure – or which the Congress would not have dared reject – such as the approval of a generous incomes policy. The long-term policy, on the other hand, required congressional participation as some of the proposed reforms required new legislation. However, given the nature of the government's approach to its long-term policy, a permanent alliance with any of the major parties was also impractical. Indeed, because it had decided to concentrate its efforts on two main areas of policy – copper and agriculture – over which it was sure to receive support from either the right- or the left-wing parties, it was reasonable for the government to expect that in time its bills would be approved by the Congress, without the need of a permanent alliance. The government was naturally expecting that within its first two years in office it would be able to consolidate its overwhelming electoral power, thus forcing would-be opponents in the Congress to follow a conciliatory and flexible path. This was not unrealistic since it was in a position to implement several of its populist policies, particularly those concerning the establishment of grassroots organisations, without needing Congress' approval.

The government's calculations about the behaviour of the Congress were right. For, after a lengthy parliamentary procedure, the Congress approved – almost unchanged – all its proposals to reform the copper and agricultural sectors. However, its strategy started to crumble mainly because its short-term economic policy did not work as expected. Indeed, not long after taking office, it realised that its short-term policy was not proving effective as a tool for controlling inflation. Because it feared that inflation would reappear in force, it decided to reduce public expenditure in the key areas of housing and public works. This decision had the effect of depressing the economy and undermining its popularity. Moreover, it continued promoting the process of political mobilisation among agricultural workers and the urban poor, who, in the new context of expenditure cuts, became increasingly more radical. These circumstances exacerbated the divisions within the CDP, pushing the left- and right-wing factions into more intransigent positions. Thus, by the end of its term in office the government had all but forgotten its slogan of the 'Revolution in Liberty', and, as it became exclusively concerned with maintaining law and order, the left-wing groups broke away from the party.

The objective of the short-term economic policy was to reactivate the economy through an expansion of demand, induced by increasing public expenditure and remunerations. The government also introduced a gradual programme of stabilisation, which was meant to eliminate inflation within a five-year period.[8] Its views on growth and stability provided a logical link between its short-term policy and its programme of structural reforms. According to the government, one of the main factors accounting for the failure to achieve sustained growth was the vulnerability of the economy to changes in the conditions of foreign trade. While fiscal revenues were still largely dependent on export revenues, domestic production relied heavily on imports. Thus, sharp changes in the conditions of foreign trade produced shock waves throughout the economy, creating strong inflationary pressures and eventually causing a drop in economic activity. The solution proposed by the government to this vicious circle of stagnation and inflation called for an increase and a diversification of domestic production. To achieve this, it proposed to increase export revenue by doubling the producton of copper and by modernising the domestic economy, particularly the agricultural sector. Hence the need to introduce major reforms in the copper and agricultural sectors and the close link existing between the short- and long-term policies.

Results of the short-term economic policy were encouraging. There was an increase in the overall level of economic activity and inflation was brought down. Thus, while in the first two years in office production grew at a cumulative rate of 12 per cent, the rate of inflation was reduced from 46 per cent in 1964 to 23 per cent in 1966. These results were achieved without creating a fiscal deficit, mainly because of the favourable conditions prevailing in the copper markets and the successful re-negotiation of the huge foreign debt inherited from the previous administration. In spite of these good results, the re-activation programme began to run into difficulties because, contrary to expectations, the private sector did not increase its investment.[9]

Since the private sector was unable to match production to the expanding levels of demand, the government found it increasingly difficult to keep prices down. Indeed, while the government had expected that, by 1966, the annual rate of inflation would be reduced to 15 per cent, the actual rate stood at 23 per cent. Since these early warning signals were accompanied by a rapid exhaustion of idle capacity in manufacturing industry, the government began to fear that inflation would soon run out of control. Confronted with this dilemma, the government followed the advice of its economic team and cut public expenditure, restricted credit and reduced the flow of imports.[10] These measures brought about a temporary relief from the inflationary pressures, but at the cost of greatly depressing the levels of economic activity and slowing down the process of income redistribution. Thus, before the end of its second year in office, the government's popularity began rapidly to decline. This situation was particularly serious since the two most important government bills had not yet been approved by the Congress.

Chileanisation of Copper

One of the main objectives of the CDP government was to integrate the copper sector into the rest of the economy. According to government estimates, copper production needed to be doubled so as to provide a more stable financial base to support new investment projects in other sectors of the economy.[11] During the electoral campaign, Frei had been studiously equivocal about the kind of copper regime which his government would introduce. Although in contrast to the marxist candidate, he had not promised to nationalise the property of the two American companies – Kennecott and Anaconda – which accounted for more than 80 per cent of the country's copper exports; he had, however, called for greater state involvement in the mining sector. The uncertainty over Frei's copper policy was a major concern to the companies. For they feared that under pressure from his own party, he might introduce a new mining legislation which might in fact amount to what American investors describe as 'creeping expropriation'. To prevent this from happening Kennecott decided to act swiftly offering to sell the government a 51 per cent share in its operations in combination with a scheme to finance the expansion of copper production. Kennecott's offer came immediately after Frei's election, while his party was still celebrating its victory and long before the government had decided on how to implement its programme. Since Kennecott's proposal contained a ready-made package, including greater state control and a planned increase in production, the government accepted it without hesitation.

Acceptance led to an agreement between the government and Kennecott, establishing a jointly-owned company in which the government held 51 per cent of the shares and Kennecott 49 per cent. The sum paid to Kennecott for 51 per cent of its operations in Chile was more than twice its book value. Besides, the agreement also revalued by more than four times the remaining 49 per cent of the operations still owned by Kennecott. The tax rate for the new company was reduced from 80 per cent to 44 per cent, and the price of copper for tax purposes was fixed at around 30 cents a pound. Under a separate management contract, administration of the new company remained in the hands of Kennecott.[12]

Under this new agreement Kennecott was considerably better off than under the previous regime. Firstly, because it increased the value of Kennecott's shares by four times. Secondly, because it entitled the company to received revenues from an operation which was due to increase its exports by 50 per cent. And thirdly, because the external financing which Kennecott had promised to arrange was not an additional burden to the company. Indeed, this sum was made up of a loan of 110 million dollars from the Exim-Bank, guaranteed by the Chilean State, and an eighty million dollar loan from Kennecott, guaranteed by the United States government under its foreign investment insurance programme. It should be noted that the eighty million dollars which Kennecott lent to the new company was equal to the amount paid by Chile for the purchase of 51 per cent of its operations.

The government tried to persuade Anaconda, the other major copper company operating in Chile, to enter into a similar joint venture agreement, but was not successful. Anaconda agreed to form a joint venture with only one of its newest and smallest mining projects, but refused to sell any part of its larger operations. However, Anaconda did agree to expand production and in exchange obtained tax advantages similar to those enjoyed by the Kennecott joint venture.

Initially, the government's copper policy was only opposed by the marxist parties, which described it as a sell-out to imperalism and insisted on the need for full nationalisation of Chilean copper. However, opposition grew rapidly, particularly within the CDP, as it became obvious that the foreign companies were making enormous profits as a consequence of the new policy. These profits were brought about by the fact that the price fixed by the government to calculate the taxation of the new companies was rapidly becoming obsolete as a consequence of the price boom caused by the escalation of the Vietnam War. Indeed, the price used by the government for the purposes of taxation was about 50 per cent below the price of copper in the London market. A similar price disparity existed between the price of copper in the United States and the London market. The price of copper in the American market, where Chile sold 15 per cent of its exports, was kept artificially low by a series of measures taken by the American government to protect supplies during the Vietnam War. Hence, while copper sold in the European markets generated larger-than-expected profits for the American companies, copper sold in the United States was in fact subsidising the American war effort in Vietnam.

The financial consequences of the new copper policy caused great embarrasment to the government. Because the policy had been adopted at the suggestion of the American companies with the full backing of the United States government it seemed as if the Chilean government had been duped into accepting a joint venture scheme which was contrary to the national interest. To remedy this, in February 1966, the government entered into an agreement with the United States government, whereby the price of Chilean copper sold in the United States was increased only slightly in exchange for a low interest loan. But this agreement lasted for six months, and in August of 1966 the government decided to adopt the quotation of the London market only as the basis for determining the price of copper exports. Shortly thereafter, Chile together with other copper producing countries, established the Council of Copper Exporting Countries.[13]

The measures taken by the government to offset the unfavourable consequences of its copper policy did not satisfy its critics. As the end of Frei's term of office came into sight, the CDP began to exert great pressures on the government so that it would review its copper policy.

The government initially resisted these pressures, but this merely added fuel to the growing feeling within the CDP that the correct policy was outright nationalisation. However, instead of following the path of nationalisation, the government introduced a tax surcharge on the price of copper and persuaded Anaconda to agree to sell its operations in Chile over a period of several years. Although President Frei described this new policy as 'agreed nationalisation' (*nacionalización pactada*), not even his own party took this label seriously, and the proof of this is that the programme of government of the CDP candidate in the 1970 election called for the full nationalisation of copper.

Agrarian Reform

The agrarian reform of the CDP was the first serious attempt to alter the relations of production in agriculture. Together with a new regime for copper, it was the programme to which the government assigned top priority. The government's objectives in the agricultural sector were twofold: to achieve a substantial increase in agricultural production and thus contribute towards easing pressure on the balance of payments; and to initiate a process of land redistribution, which would create 100,000 new proprietors among the landless peasants during President Frei's term of office. To achieve these objectives the government believed that agricultural workers had to become actively involved in the political process. A first step towards this was to promote the establishment of agricultural unions, which, for all practical purposes, had been outlawed in 1947 during the González administration.

The consensus within government circles about the need to carry out a comprehensive reform of the agricultural sector proved difficult to translate into detailed legislation. The drafting of the bill was delayed by nearly a year as there was disagreement within the government regarding its scope. The agricultural experts occupying key posts in the Ministry of Agriculture wanted the legislation to give the government broad powers to expropriate land so a speedy and inexpensive process of agrarian reform could be carried out. These views were not shared by President Frei and right-wing groups within the CDP. They believed that a radical agrarian reform law was not only technically unnecessary, but might prove to be politically unwise as it would undermine the confidence private investors had in the government's commitment to respect private property.[14] Eventually the agrarian reform bill was submitted to the Congress, which in turn took more than a year to approve it. Thus, when the government began implementing its provisions the Frei administration was well into the second half of its term in office and was starting to face serious economic difficulties.

The Agrarian Reform Act provided that holdings of more than eighty basic irrigated hectares (BIH) or its equivalent, would be expropriated. Compensation was calculated on the basis of the tax assessed value of the property and only 10 per cent of this amount was due in cash. The balance was paid over twenty-five years. The amount payable in cash was reduced to 5 per cent or 1 per cent in cases of poorly-worked or abandoned land. The expropriated land would be exploited under a transitional arrangement called '*asentamiento*' which had some features of a cooperative, but was strictly controlled and assisted by state agencies. By the end of a three-to-five-year period, the members of the *asentamiento* could choose either to divide the land into individual holdings or to establish a communal form of exploitation along the lines of a cooperative.[15]

Apart from the specific Agrarian Reform Act, the government sponsored legislation to facilitate the process of unionisation among agricultural workers. As a result, the number of agricultural workers belonging to unions increased from less than 2,000 in 1964 to 114,000 in 1970.[16] Thus, by 1970, more than 30 per cent of agricultural workers belonged to unions. This unionisation law was the single most important political achievement of the CDP government. For it gave a basic political right to a group of workers hitherto denied access to the political system. The full impact of this important political change was not to be felt until the Popular Unity period.

The government began the implementation of its agrarian reform at a time when Frei had completed nearly half of his term in office and his government had started to reduce public expenditure. These circumstances created a major conflict between President Frei and the CDP officials in charge of carrying out the reform. The main issue was the pace of the reform process. While the economic policy of the government acted as a brake on land expropriation, officials pressed to accelerate the process in order to satisfy the growing militancy among agricultural workers. Since this conflict was never resolved, it had the effect of seriously weakening the government and widening the gap between President Frei and his party. It was in fact one of the main factors underlying the breakaway of its left-wing faction, the *Rebeldes*, from within the CDP to form the Movimiento de Acción Popular Unitaria (MAPU), which was to become a member of the Popular Unity. Nonetheless, despite these problems, the Frei government expropriated 15 per cent of all agricultural land, benefiting nearly 30,000 persons.

Conflicts within the CDP

The government's decision in late 1966 to apply the brakes to its re-activation policy, giving priority instead to curbing inflation, added fuel to the increasingly bitter conflict between the left-wing groups in the CDP, the *Rebeldes*, and President Frei. The conflict was about the definition and scope of the government's programme of structural reforms. The *Rebeldes*, as I have already explained, were critical of the new copper policy, and did not share the government's timid approach to the implementation of agrarian reform. They called upon the government to assume an unequivocal left-wing position and advocated closer links with the marxist parties. They were suspicious of the well-known right-wing orientation of many of Frei's closest advisers in the key ministries of the Treasury, Economics, and Labour, and were frustrated by the fact that they had been appointed to relatively junior government posts, from where they had little hope of determining the overall direction of government policy.

The influence of the *Rebeldes* in the CDP grew rapidly during the first years of the Frei administration. In August 1965, only a year after the government took office, they already had the support of 46 per cent of the members of the party's National Assembly. But they were not the only group within the CDP critical of the government. In 1966, a new group within the party appeared, the so-called '*terceristas*', who represented a milder form of opposition to some of the government's key policies. By mid-1966 *Rebeldes* and *terceristas* already represented the majority of the party, although at that stage the party was still in the hands of groups loyal to President Frei. It was therefore not surprising that in 1967, as the party's electoral support dropped from 42 per cent to 36 per cent and the economy began to slow down, the *Rebeldes* managed to win the presidency of the party. This set the stage for a serious confrontation between the government, which was steadily moving to the right, and the CDP, which was veering towards the left.

Confrontation with the leadership of the CDP took place in the last months of 1967, and it was about the government's proposals for wage re-adjustments for the following year. These proposals reflected the government's overriding concern with inflation and the declining rate of investment in the private sector. To deal with these problems the government proposed to pay 50 per cent of the pay increase in government bonds to form a national development fund. To ensure compliance with this policy, it also proposed a temporary suspension of the right to strike in support of economic demands.[17] The new leadership of the CDP strongly opposed this policy and after lengthy negotiations managed to persuade the government to pay only 25 per cent of the pay increases in bonds. Despite the willingness of the party leadership to compromise with the government the rank and file of the party continued their opposition to the policy. At this stage the CUT launched a nationwide campaign of partial stoppages and strikes in protest against the proposed policy. This campaign culminated with a one-day general strike, which was strongly repressed, with five demonstrators dead and scores injured.[18]

The government was deeply embarrassed by the strong opposition its policy had met with in its own party. This prompted the pro-Frei groups within the CDP, acting with the active encouragement of the President, to take measures to oust the *Rebeldes* from the leadership of the party. Thus in the early months of 1968 Frei managed to regain control over the CDP. Yet this failed to resolve the political problems the policy had created. Indeed, because all the parties in the Congress had declared their opposition to the government's proposal, the government had no choice but to withdraw the bill from the Congress. This decision led to the resignation of the Minister of Economics and chief architect of the government's policy, Sergio Molina. Eventually, after a brief period of cabinet instability and confusion, the government finally gave up trying to introduce this controversial incomes policy. Frei cleverly used the conflict to dislodge the left from the leadership of the CDP, yet on balance his government suffered a major defeat as it not only had been forced to give up its fight against inflation, but could no longer count on the loyal support of the CDP to carry out its programme of structural reforms.

The conflict between the government and the *Rebeldes* brought into the open the different views about communitarianism within the CDP. The *Rebeldes* defined it as a form of socialism based 'on the principle that land and productive goods should belong to the workers'.[19] According to them communitarian socialism was different from state socialism 'in its assertion that the role of the state is subsidiary to the self-management of the workers'.[20] Thus, the *Rebeldes* advocated not only a more radical programme of structural reforms, but also called upon the government to introduce self-management immediately in state-controlled enterprises so as to begin building the foundations for a communitarian society.

The chief pro-government ideologue within the CDP, Jaime Castillo, strongly objected to the use of the phrase 'communitarian socialism'. In his view, this phrase was redundant, because communitarianism implied socialism, and it was misleading, because of the historical link existing between the notion of socialism and the real experience of totalitarian collectivism.[21] Castillo also introduced a more precise definition of the transition to the communitarian society. This new definition was, interestingly enough, quite similar to the Communist Party's conception of the stages in the march towards socialism.[22] According to him, the communitarian society would be built in two distinct stages. In the first stage the state would play a central role by increasing control over the economy and promoting the political mobilisation of the masses. In the second stage, grassroots organisations would become real organs of political power, and thus a truly cooperative society would be ushered in.[23] Since, according to this argument, the Frei administration was carrying out the first stage, it was premature to consider the introduction of self-management. Moreover, government ideologists began also to redefine the concept of self-management, a notion which occupies such a central place in the CDP's views about how the class struggle in a capitalist society will be overcome. By the middle of Frei's term in office, the government's leading industrial relations spokesman began to argue that changes in the management of capitalist enterprises would not necessarily be a requisite in a future communitarian society.[24] Moreover, he also categorically rejected the *Rebeldes'* demand for the immediate introduction of self-management in state-owned enterprises. In his view the best administrators of these enterprises were state officials as they were capable of representing the interests of the community better than the workers of the enterprises concerned.[25]

Government and the CUT

A central objective of the CDP government was to alter substantially the balance of forces within the political system so as to create the conditions necessary for launching the party's long-term project of building a communitarian society. An important step towards achieving this objective was to break the dominance of the marxist parties over the trade-union movement and to cut the traditional links between the right-wing parties and the local bourgeoisie. During its first months in office, the government seemed determined to pursue this critical political objective. However, as President Frei began to distance himself from his own party and the threat of inflation led to a shift in priorities, the government quietly abandoned its plan. Failure to pursue this important political objective inflicted permanent damage on the CDP's image as an alternative to the established political parties and as an agent of revolutionary change.

The trade-union policy of the CDP was contained in a bill which the government introduced to the Congress shortly after taking office. This bill removed the legal obstacles barring public employees from forming unions, legalised federated wage bargaining and made it possible for workers to establish more than one union per industrial establishment. According to the government the objective of the bill was to facilitate the growth of the trade-union movement within a pluralist framework. Therefore, while it recognised that practically all workers, including public sector employees, had a right to form a union, it also eliminated any form of compulsory union membership. Communists and Socialists supported most of the provision of this bill, but strongly opposed the sections allowing for the existence of more that one union per industrial enterprise on the grounds that it would weaken and divide the hard-won unity of the labour movement.[26]

The Communists' and Socialists' fears that the government was determined to divide the trade-union movement were confirmed when there appeared a new trade-union confederation, the Comando Nacional de Trabajadores, which, enjoying full government support, began to act in direct competition with the CUT. Communists and Socialists had different views about how to deal with this threat. The Communists wanted to encourage CDP participation in the CUT so as to frustrate the government's divisive moves. They proposed to allocate five of the twenty-one seats of the CUT's ruling council to the CDP. Since this proposal entailed calling off the forthcoming council elections its approval required the Socialists' agreement. But the Socialists, who were in no mood to make concessions to the CDP, particularly concerning the trade unions, rejected the proposal on the grounds that it overestimated the real strength of the CDP among the unions affiliated to the CUT. In the event, the Socialists' view prevailed, but this incident provided the CDP with an excuse to withdraw from the CUT. Thus, in August 1965 they walked out of the CUT, and the government began to intensify its efforts to establish a separate labour confederation.[27]

At the congressional level, the government could afford a confrontation with the marxist parties over the trade-union bill as it could count on the right-wing votes to secure its approval. However, strong opposition to the bill began to build up from where the government least expected it; that is, from within the CDP. The *Rebeldes* who, as I explained above, controlled nearly half of the seats in the party's national assembly, began to question the wisdom of the proposed union policy and soon joined in with the marxist parties, arguing that the bill would weaken organised labour. The strength of the opposition within the CDP persuaded the government to withdraw it from the Congress, thus one of its most important programmatic objectives was abandoned. Interestingly enough, the marxist parties and the left-wing groups within the CDP were at the same time supporting the government's bill on agricultural unions, which contained provisions almost identical to those of the trade-union bill.[28]

By mid-term, after the government had shelved its trade-union bill and given up its attempt at creating an alternative organisation, the CDP rejoined the CUT. From then on, relations between the CUT and the government became surprisingly good. This was largely because of the Communist Party, which was trying to build bridges between the CDP and the left-wing parties so as to prepare the ground for an electoral alliance in anticipation of the next presidential elections. The new attitude of the CUT towards the government was evident at the time of the *'Tacnazo'*, a strange form of military *pronunciamento* which occurred towards the end of 1969. This episode, which involved only a handful of senior officers, was ostensibly prompted by dissatisfaction among the military over their salaries and poor equipment. Since the majority of the armed forces remained loyal to the government the incident did not, in the short run, have major repercussions.[29] The CUT offered unconditional support to the government and called upon the working class to defend it. This show of loyalty was acknowledged by the government, and shortly thereafter it entered into an agreement with the CUT on incomes policy. This agreement marked the first official recognition of the CUT. It is ironic that recognition, albeit belated, should have taken place under the Frei administration which had originally intended to undermine it.

Government and the Right

Relations between the CDP government on the one hand and the right-wing parties and associations representing the interests of the local bourgeoisie (hitherto called business associations) on the other were largely determined by the spectacular impact the CDP had on the electoral strength of the traditional right-wing parties. Indeed, between 1961 and 1965, while the CDP more than doubled its electoral strength from 16 per cent to 44 per cent, the share of the vote of Conservatives and Liberals dropped from 31 per cent in 1961 to an all time low of 13 per cent in 1965. But despite their disastrous electoral performance, the right-wing parties still had considerable political leverage since they controlled a disproportionately large number of seats in the Senate, which the government needed for legislation to be approved by the Congress. But the CDP's success forced Conservatives and Liberals to reassess their political future. This led in 1966 to the creation of the National Party, which resulted from the amalgamation of the two traditional parties, Conservatives and Liberals, with other right-wing nationalist groups, most of which had, at one time or another, been part of the Ibañista movement. Following the inspiration and leadership of those nationalist groups, the new party gave up the upper-class image of the traditional right to assume the role of an aggressive and efficient middle-class party. Their immediate objective was to regain the electoral terrain which they had lost to the CDP.[30]

The prospect of building up a modern right-wing party was welcomed by the various associations representing the local bourgeoisie. However, it did not help them resolve the immediate problem posed by a new government committed to carrying out a vast programme of structural reform. Moreover, representatives of industry had already become disillusioned by the right-wing parties' inability to protect their interests effectively against what was perceived to be the ever-growing economic powers of the state. By the early fifties, when the era of coalition politics led by the Radical Party had reached its apogee, a strong dissident movement emerged from within SOFOFA, the leading association of industrialists, which openly criticised its leaders for depending on the traditional right-wing parties to represent its interests. Instead, it called upon SOFOFA to deal directly with government authorities.[31] Discontent among representatives of business associations continued to grow during the Ibáñez administration. However, this trend was temporarily interrupted in 1958, when Alessandri opened up a brief period of close cooperation between the government and the private sector. Therefore when Frei became President the representatives of business associations were not completely unprepared to assume a more direct political role in defence of their interests.

The most important immediate challenge which business associations confronted during the Frei administration stemmed from the government's agrarian reform programme. Although most industrialists were sympathetic to the idea of agrarian reform, they did not believe that the principle of redistributing property should be applied to other sectors of the economy. Therefore, as the more radical groups within the CDP started to gain influence within the party, leading industrialists began to fear that, in the near future, the government might want to take over other sectors of the economy. These circumstances prompted the business associations to close ranks behind the SNA, the leading landowners' association, in its campaign to limit the scope of the agrarian reform law. Although the SNA did not persuade the government to change the terms of the agrarian reform bill, the government was nonetheless forced to give ample assurances to business associations that it would not attempt the same type of reform in other sectors of the economy.[32]

Apart from agrarian reform, representatives of the business associations also regarded the long-term plans with some suspicion. For they believed that the government was determined to undermine their influence within the state by furthering the divisions within the private sector. This belief was reinforced by some of the policies the government adopted.[33] Firstly, it set up a coordinating committee to handle relations with the private sector, thus effectively by-passing the existing business associations. Secondly, it sponsored the establishment of independent associations for small- and medium-sized industrialists in manufacturing and in commerce, thus institutionalising the divisions within the private sector. Thirdly, it used every means possible to neutralise the influence of business associations in public and quasi-public bodies. And fourthly, it made generous concessions to attract foreign investors, particularly in the mining sector, which were deeply resented by the business associations since the majority had no direct links with foreign capital and all of them had seen their profits shrink as a consequence of the government's incomes policy.[34]

Business associations responded to the government by organising a gigantic conference designed as a celebration of private enterprise and meant to bring together, under a single organisation, every capitalist enterprise in the country, regardless of its size. The conference took place in December 1967 and turned out to be little more than a media event as not many owners of small- or medium-sized enterprises actually participated in it. That the conference failed to link all capitalists in a single organisation was unimportant. Indeed, by the end of 1967, the right-wing forces had already recovered their political confidence and through the recently-formed National Party had recovered a large proportion of the votes lost to the CDP. Moreover, at the time the conference took place, the government was already on the defensive and could no longer be taken seriously as a threat to private property.

Political Consequences

The government's mid-term decision to apply the brakes to its economic policy was not accompanied by a similar decision in the area of political mobilisation. Here, it continued supporting the rapidly-growing process of unionisation and promoting the establishment of thousands of grassroots organisations to benefit mainly the urban poor. Thus, during the CDP period, the number of workers belonging to unions doubled, reaching 550,000 in 1970 and representing just under 20 per cent of the workforce.[35] Alongside this spectacular increase, its achievement in the popular promotion programme was no less impressive. Under this programme, the government sponsored the establishment of 20,000 grassroots organisations, which included more than 3,000 neighbourhood committees, 6,000 mothers' associations and 6,000 sporting clubs. The programme also offered training courses on matters of community interest to nearly 7,000 people.[36]

The rapid political mobilisation during this period was one of the major achievements of the CDP administration. However, as the economic situation began to deteriorate and the dreaded inflationary process reappeared, the newly-organised groups became the government's worst enemies. Indeed, during the last three years of the Frei government, the number of strikes increased from 1,100 in 1968 to 1,800 in 1970, while the number of workers involved in strike activity increased from 300,000 to 656,000.[37] The groups of workers most heavily represented among the strikers during this period were those in the agricultural and building sectors; that is, workers who had been recently organised and who had weak links with the traditional membership of the CUT, which consisted mainly of workers in the manufacturing and mining industries.[38]

The growing militancy at the fringes of the labour movement was accompanied by the emergency of new forms of struggle such as land seizures, squatters' settlements and even some factory occupations. The seizure of agricultural land as a means to back up economic demands or to speed up the expropriation process increased sharply from only six reported cases in 1967, to twenty-seven in 1968 and 148 in 1969. Likewise, by 1969 the urban poor began to rely on direct action as a means of resolving their housing problems. Thus, in 1969, there were thirty-five reported cases of land invasions to establish squatters' settlements. Also, by the end of the Frei administration, workers and students had begun to resort to the occupation of buildings with alarming frequency. Thus, for example, in 1966 there were 166 occupations by students, and in 1969 there were 121 cases of factory occupations.[39]

This massive popular discontent erupted during the second half of the government's term of office. At that late stage, the other political parties were already making plans for the forthcoming presidential elections, so the government could not hope to find allies in the Congress. On the other hand, the right-wing forces had already regrouped around the National Party and were confident that the patrician figure of Jorge Alessandri would secure them a victory in the 1970 elections. Besides, the Right did not believe that Frei had the political strength, or the will, to restrain the more radical elements within his own party. The Right in fact no longer believed that the CDP could make a useful contribution in the fight against marxism since it was itself veering in that direction. On the other hand, an alliance between the government and the Left was also unthinkable. Although the Communist Party was keen to contain the level of mobilisation, any attempt at an alliance with the government would have been vetoed by the Socialists and consequently would have broken the hard-won unity between Communists and Socialists. Besides, the marxist parties were deeply involved in promoting popular discontent against the government as it allowed them to establish a foothold in the unions and grassroots organisation created under the auspices of the CDP.

The isolation of the government was underlined by the fact that, because of the ideological differences existing within the CDP and the tactics employed to resolve them, it could no longer count on the unconditional support of the whole party. Therefore, by the end of its term in office, the government was alone in trying to reconcile two conflicting sets of policies. On the political front, it was applying a law and order policy, which the Right found too mild and the Left too repressive. On the economic front, the government's attempt to slow down the pace of structural reforms was regarded as too drastic by the Left and not drastic enough by the Right. These policies eventually eroded the popularity and electoral base of the CDP.

The political revival of the Right was largely based on the government's failure to maintain law and order effectively. The National Party's call for a stronger government generated impressive political dividends. Indeed, by 1969 the National Party had already become the second largest political party in the country and could boast an electoral support for the Right which had increased at a spectacular pace from 13 per cent of the electorate in 1965, to 21 per cent. The displacement of the CDP vote to the Left was no less spectacular, although it was somewhat more complex as, together with a strengthening of the electoral support of the marxist parties, there appeared a new and crucially important group of non-marxist voters supporting socialist policies.

Between 1965 and 1969 the Communists and Socialists, riding on the wave of popular discontent, managed to make important gains among groups largely controlled by the CDP, such as agricultural workers, working-class women and the recently-organised urban poor. Thus, the combined electoral strength of the Communists and Socialists increased from 23 per cent of the electorate in 1965 to nearly 32 per cent in 1967. But during this same period, there was a steady radicalisation of the left-wing groups within the CDP, which culminated in 1969, when they broke away to form the MAPU. The leadership of the MAPU was made up of middle-class Catholic intellectuals and technocrats who were frustrated by the reformism of the CDP and deeply committed to the notion of a communitarian society. Although the parliamentary strength of this group was insignificant, it took away from the CDP more than 20 per cent of agricultural workers' support for the CDP. However, MAPU's impact on the political system was far greater than its actual numerical strength would suggest. For its very existence effectively nullified the CDP's characterisation of all political forces to its left as communist-dominated with totalitarian objectives. There were also important changes within the Radical Party. These changes were preceded by a fierce ideological debate, which involved a re-affirmation of the party's Social Democratic ideology of the thirties in a clear attempt to oppose the CDP from the left and to revive the Popular Front alliance with the marxist parties.

The cumulative effect of all these developments was to legitimise a more radical alternative to the CDP's 'Revolution in Liberty'. While in 1964 CDP propaganda had succeeded in isolating the marxists from the rest of the political system, six years of CDP government had given a new political respectability to the marxist parties by making their views acceptable to large groups of white-collar workers, intellectuals and members of the liberal professions. Likewise, the genuine disappointment of these groups with the CDP's experiment in communitarianism made their newly-acquired socialist convictions more credible to the marxist parties, thus the way was paved for the creation of the Popular Unity, an electoral coalition which included marxist and non-marxist parties. This re-alignment of political forces culminated in the 1970 presidential elections, when the CDP candidate obtained 28 per cent of the vote, finishing in third place at a considerable distance from the winning candidate, Allende, who obtained 36.8 per cent of the vote and the runner-up Alessandri, who obtained 35 per cent of the vote.

Economic Consequences

The roots of the electoral defeat of the CDP in 1970 can be traced to the failure of the government's economic strategy. For the government never quite managed to harmonise the various levels of its economic policy and did not anticipate the contradictions which some of its long-term policies would generate. As I have already explained, by the end of its second year in office, the government realised that because its short-term policy was not stimulating new investment by the private sector the rate of inflation would not be easy to keep under control. This situation prompted the government to cut expenditure in some programmes so as to ease inflationary pressures. The consequences of this were mixed. On the one hand, inflation was momentarily contained. In fact, during the government's first three years in office the annual average rate of inflation dropped consistently from 47 per cent in 1964, to 30 per cent during the government's first full year in office 1965, to 24 per cent in 1966 and to 19 per cent in 1967.[40] But since expenditure cuts had only been partial, and investment by the private sector showed little signs of recovery by the end of 1967 the government decided to introduce a strict incomes policy to keep inflation at bay.

After the government was forced to withdraw its proposed incomes policy from the Congress, the average annual rate of inflation once again began to rise, reaching 28 per cent in 1968, 32 per cent in 1969 and 34 per cent in 1970. Thus, by the end of its term in office the rate of inflation was rapidly approaching the same level, 40 per cent, as during the last two years of the Alessandri administration.

The decision to cut expenditure did not affect all items of public expenditure in the same way. Public expenditure in building and public works was the worst hit, while long-term productive investment and expenditure in social development, such as education, was left practically untouched. The government was aware that this pattern of expenditure cuts would in the short-term reduce the level of growth – as in fact it did – but expected that this would provide the basis for healthy economic growth and development. As the most senior economic aide of the period explained: 'when confronted with a choice between development and growth, we chose development'.[41]

The government's concern with the long-term development prospects is illustrated by the changes which took place in the composition of public investment. Between 1964 and 1968, the proportion of public expenditure devoted to productive investment rose from 33 per cent to 40 per cent, while the proportion spent in infrastructure dropped from 13 per cent to 12 per cent.[42] Besides, the government financed a major expansion of the educational system, with special emphasis on primary education.[43] But its determination to favour development-oriented programmes belies the fact that it was unable to persuade the private sector to increase its investment. Indeed, virtually all the increase in the rate of investment which took place during this period came from the public sector. Therefore, during the government's term of office, the share of public investment in total investment rose from 54 per cent in 1964 to 75 per cent in 1970.[44]

The changing balance between public and private sector investment is shown by changes in the pattern of investment in fixed capital in industry during this period. While the state accounted for 22 per cent of total investment in fixed capital in industry in 1963, the year before Frei took office, by 1970 its share had risen to 57 per cent.[45] The growing importance of public investment in this area was accompanied by an interesting change in the composition of private investment. During the period 1963–70 the share of the private sector in fixed capital investment in industry dropped from 78 per cent to 43 per cent, while the share contributed by foreign investment actually increased from 3 per cent in 1963 to 16 per cent in 1970.[46] The implications of the rapid penetration of foreign capital in industry had not been fully worked out by government officials as it was a new and largely unexpected phenomenon. However, it was welcomed by the government because, apart from contributing towards compensating for the falling rate of investment by local capitalists, it was helping to revive the ailing process of growth, particularly in manufacturing industry. There thus developed an informal alliance between the state and multi-national companies, which led to a rapid growth of the branches of industry producing capital goods and consumer durables. This was reflected in the changing structure of industrial production. While in 1963 the share of consumer durables and capital goods in industrial production was only 10 per cent, by 1970 their share had increased to 22 per cent.[47] However, the new dynamic branches of industry proved incapable of increasing the overall levels of industrial growth. Indeed, in the second half of the 1960s, industry grew at an annual average rate of only 3.6 per cent while in the first half of the decade, the annual average rate of growth had been 7.3 per cent.[48] Moreover, throughout the 1960s industry created a disappointingly low number of jobs. In fact, it provided only 22 per cent of the new jobs created during the decade, lagging well behind the service and commerce sectors, which absorbed 28 per cent and 30 per cent of new employment respectively.[49] The new pattern of industrialisation, based mainly on expanding the production of consumer durables with the help of foreign capital, not only failed to revive industrial growth, but soon had to confront the characteristic obstacles derived from a small national market. In fact, because of the inequitable distribution of income, the market for the new consumer durables comprised little more than 10 per cent of the population.[50] To help in the marketing of these products the government launched a campaign to promote industrial exports and was a major proponent of the Andean Pact, a sub-regional scheme of economic integration. Industrial exports did in fact increase as their share in the value of total exports rose from 8 per cent in 1960 to just over 12 per cent in 1970.[51] However, participation of the firms producing consumer durables in this export drive was disappointingly low, partly because their products were not competitive in international markets, but mainly because they had to comply with export restrictions imposed by the parent company abroad or by their foreign licensers.[52] Thus, the penetration of foreign capital in the manufacturing industry created two sets of problems for the government: on the one hand, it sharpened the contradictions between the structure of industrial production and the existing pattern of income distribution; and on the other hand, it restricted the government's capacity to direct the process of industrial growth.

Although the Frei government failed to secure a second term for the CDP, some of its achievements are impressive. Apart from the agrarian reform and the massive programme of political mobilisation, it introduced important reforms rationalising the administration of the tax system and foreign trade. Also, through a responsible control of the budgetary process, it achieved a substantial reduction of fiscal deficit, from nearly 5 per cent of GDP in 1964 to just over 1 per cent GDP in 1969. Important progress was made in health, education, social security and housing. By the end of the Frei administration most children had the opportunity of completing primary education, the social security system had been greatly extended to benefit nearly 70 per cent of the active population and state agencies were contributing greatly towards resolving the housing problem. Finally, the government's concern with the redistribution of income had some success, as the share of labour in total income increased from 48 per cent in 1964 to 53 per cent in 1969.[53]

To some extent, the CDP's failure to secure a second term in office may be related to the fateful decisions which the government took at mid-term. As already explained, at that stage the government chose to sacrifice part of its re-activation programme to prevent inflation, decided to slow down its programme of structural reform without giving up its efforts at political mobilisation, and did nothing to prevent its general political isolation. These measures did not contain inflation, as expenditure cuts had only been partial, and did not deflect popular pressure for more structural reform, as the programme of political mobilisation was allowed to continue unchecked. Therefore, when popular discontent began to grow, the government found no sympathetic allies in the Congress and was encircled by dangerously high levels of political mobilisation. To resolve these problems the government relied on authoritarian measures too mild to repress the popular movement effectively and too strong to arrest the CDP's electoral decline. With hindsight perhaps it could have avoided political defeat had it confronted head-on the political implications of its mid-term decisions. That is, had it opted either to reduce the pace of change with the explicit support of the right-wing parties or to accelerate the implementation of its programme with the support of the marxist parties. However, at the time, these options were politically unthinkable.

CHAPTER 10

Marxists in a New Political Context

BETWEEN 1952 and 1970 Communists and Socialists were faced with problems which were notably different from those of the preceding decade. While in the 1940s their position as sole representatives of organised labour had not been challenged, they now had to confront vigorous and successful competition from the CDP for support among organised workers, and newly-registered voters in urban and rural areas. Also, and largely as a consequence of the re-alignment of political forces which began during the late 1950s, Communists and Socialists now emerged, for the first time, as serious contenders for the Presidency, thus abandoning their hitherto subordinate role in coalitions led by the Radical Party. The changing international context also brought about problems for the marxist parties. In the forties the main issue dividing them on the question of proletarian internationalism was the special relationship existing between the Communist Party and the Communist Party of the Soviet Union. The Sino-Soviet conflict and the emergence of a marxist revolutionary government in Cuba introduced a new dimension to the conflict between the two parties.

Given the political conditions prevailing from 1952 to 1970 it is not surprising that there was a considerable amount of argument and conflict between the two parties. Yet, unlike what had happened in the 1940s, they now not only maintained their electoral alliance for nearly fifteen years, but broadened it, forming the Popular Unity, which was to lead to the electoral victory of Salvador Allende.

This chapter explains how and why the alliance between the two Marxist parties turned out to be so durable. The first section examines some aspects of FRAP policies from 1952–70. The second and third sections respectively explain how the Socialists and Communists reconciled their conflicting ideological perspectives and how each responded to the pressing domestic and international issues of the day.

I FRAP

Taming the Labour Movement

When the FRAP was created in 1956 the political strategies of Communists and Socialists were notably different. That of the Communists, known as the national liberation front, was based on the conception of a socialist revolution with two clearly defined stages. The first would prepare the ground for socialism by freeing the economy from the fetters of imperialism and the landed oligarchy. During this stage, the process of democratisation within the existing capitalist state would be furthered by a political alliance between working-class parties and those groups within the bourgeoisie whose interests were in conflict with imperialism and the local oligarchy. This stage, also described as the national democratic stage of the revolution, would last for an unspecified time, but would be followed by a second stage, in which the working-class parties would conquer power and begin a period of socialist transition.[1] The line developed by the Socialists in the early fifties, known as the Workers' Front Strategy, rejected the two-stage approach to the revolution as well as any alliance with parties representing bourgeois interests. The Workers' Front Strategy started from the assumption that the local bourgeoisie was incapable of carrying out the democratic tasks as set out by the Communist Party in the first stage of the revolution. Accordingly, it described the socialist revolution as an uninterrupted process led, from the start, by the working class.[2]

In its objectives, the FRAP was closer to the Communist Party's national liberation strategy than to the Socialists' Workers' Front Strategy. For, as explained in Chapter 8, the FRAP was committed to a broad alliance with all anti-oligarchical forces. Despite this bias towards the Communist position, the Socialists accepted the FRAP because, insofar as it did not include the Radical Party or the CDP, it was in their view consistent with their Workers' Front Strategy.

The FRAP, however, was not intended as a vehicle for resolving ideological differences between Communists and Socialists. It was merely an alliance representing their decision to pursue their own electoral strategy. Nonetheless, the FRAP's unexpectedly good performance at the polls in the 1958 presidential elections had a great impact on their political behaviour. For now that winning the Presidency through elections had became realistic they began to concentrate all their energies on their electoral ambitions. This new electoral orientation was expressed mainly in their policies towards the trade-union movement, where they had to face two main problems. The first was an increasingly militant and independent trade-union movement, which did not automatically follow the directions of the central committees of either party, and the second, which was largely a consequence of this militancy, was the fact that neither the Radical Party nor the Christian Democratic Party were willing to participate in the CUT. To deal with these issues, Communists and Socialists adopted a trade-union policy consisting of two related elements. On the one hand, they sought direct control over CUT's leadership; and on the other hand, they toned down the CUT's radicalism to make it more acceptable to non-marxist parties. Thus, while the Marxist parties pursued an independent electoral strategy, which, insofar as it rejected alliances with the centre parties, can be described as isolationist, at the trade-union level they reasserted their direct political influence, albeit within a pluralistic framework.

When the CUT was created in 1953, the trade-union movement vowed to pursue a socialist strategy, independent of all political parties. During its first five years, it managed to maintain a certain degree of autonomy from the marxist parties. Strike decisions were taken by the CUT's management committee and were not subject to veto by the central committees of the parties. During this early period, it had major confrontations with the government, including three general strikes against Ibáñez' economic policies.

However, after the unexpectedly good results for Communists and Socialists in the 1958 presidential elections, their grip on trade-unions became tighter. Moreover, during the early part of the Alessandri government they had both realised that the uncontrolled militancy of the trade-union movement could create embarrassment and damage their electoral chances. The worst offender in this respect was Clotario Blest, the Secretary-General of the CUT, who had consistently rejected the economic stabilisation programmes of the Ibáñez and Alessandri administrations. A devoted Catholic, he was not a member of a political party and was a staunch advocate of trade-union independence. In the early sixties, after a visit to Cuba, he became an outspoken admirer of the Cuban revolution, which, in the Chilean context meant that he did not believe in the electoral road to power. On all these counts, Blest did not satisfy the immediate needs of the Communist and Socialists parties. To force him out of office, they instigated a series of manoeuvres which culminated in 1961, when they overturned a call for a general strike by the CUT's executive committee. Since this move amounted to a vote of no-confidence, Blest felt that he had no choice but to resign. In his letter of resignation he attacked – in no uncertain terms – the electoral strategy pursued by the Communist and Socialists parties.[3] After his resignation CUT leadership remained tightly under the control of the Communist and Socialists parties. Although the chances of Blest ever becoming a local revolutionary leader were slim, his refusal to subordinate the interests of the labour movement to the demands of the electoral process were singularly out of step with the views of the two marxist parties.

The objective of broadening the CUT's membership to include the Radical Party and the Christian Democratic Party raised a delicate political issue. Initially, these parties had participated in the movement leading to the establishment of the CUT. However, towards the end of the 1950s, they withdrew, claiming that it was a marxist-controlled organisation which did not pursue trade-union objectives. To entice them back to the CUT, Communists and Socialists sponsored several amendments to the CUT's programme which resulted in toning down its political profile. The more explicit marxist principles were dropped and a new section was added proclaiming that the short-term objectives of the labour movement were to achieve social equality and greater efficiency.[4] After the approval of these amendments in 1962, the Radicals and Christians Democrats once again participated in the CUT's management committee. The distribution of seats was as follows: the Communist Party controlled six seats, the Socialist Party five, the Christian Democratic Party three and the Radical Party one.[5] Thus, the CUT could no longer be described as a purely marxist organisation, although it was still firmly controlled by the Communist and Socialist parties.

Response to the Frei Government

The CDP's victory in the 1964 presidential elections was a major blow to the electoral strategy which Communists and Socialists had pursued since the creation of the FRAP coalition in the mid-fifties. As already explained, FRAP was the largest electoral bloc in the country during the early sixties and was therefore regarded as the most likely winner of the 1964 elections. The confidence which Communists and Socialists had about their electoral possibilities is reflected in their concern about what they would do if the bourgeoisie refused to acknowledge their electoral victory. However, things did not work out as expected because the right-wing parties, scared by the growing strength of FRAP, abandoned their own candidate in support of the CDP candidate. This last minute move made it possible for the CDP to obtain more than 50 per cent of the votes, thus shattering the hopes of the marxist parties and exposing the shortcomings of their electoral strategy.

The lessons which Communists and Socialists drew from the electoral defeat were remarkably different one from the other. The Communists argued that FRAP had been unable to attract large sectors of the working class. They therefore proposed that it should broaden its popular base through alliances with progressive sectors of the bourgeoisie.[6] The Socialists, for their part, drew radical conclusions. In their view, the defeat of the FRAP coalition had shown that it was an illusion to expect that the working class could achieve power through the ballot box. According to them, only revolutionary violence would be capable of securing this objective. In the meantime, before the advent of the final armed confrontation with the bourgeoisie, all means available, legal and illegal, should be used to further revolutionary objectives.[7]

Despite the different views held by Socialists and Communists regarding the CDP administration, their response to it was not notably different. In the Congress they had much the same policy towards government proposals. They both supported, albeit with reservation, the agrarian reform; they voted against the new copper legislation; they were united in their opposition to the proposed reform of trade-union law; and they fought fiercely against the government's proposed income policy in 1967.

In the early days of the government there was an important disagreement between Communists and Socialists concerning CUT policy towards the CDP. At the time, CDP trade unionists did not have a strong representation in the CUT. The Communist Party, believing that CDP participation should be encouraged, proposed a method of appointing members to CUT's ruling council which would have given the CDP more seats than its actual strength warranted. The Socialists rejected this proposal on the ground that it was an unacceptable compromise. The Communist Party gave in to the Socialist Party's demand, and as a consequence the CDP walked out of the CUT and attempted, unsuccessfully, to form a separate trade-union confederation. This disagreement between Communists and Socialists was soon forgotten in the face of the government's attempt to introduce new trade-union legislation, which they regarded as undermining their predominant influence among organised workers in manufacturing industry and in mining.

The response of the marxist parties to the military uprising of October 1969 was, significantly, quite different. On that occasion, the Socialist Party, adopting an ultra-left position, called upon workers 'not to defend the bourgeois institutional structure, but to mobilise in support of their own social and political demands'.[8] The Communist Party, on the other hand, along with the CUT, rallied behind the government to defend the constitutional order.[9] In the event, the overwhelming majority of left-wing supporters followed the lead of the Communist Party and the CUT, thus furthering Communist prestige in left-wing circles and exposing the Socialist Party's position as empty ultra-left rhetoric.

II   THE SOCIALIST PARTY: A FRUSTRATED STRATEGY

In Search of an Independent Marxist Position

There was a marked radicalisation of the Socialist Party from 1952 to 1970. After adopting the Workers' Front Strategy in the mid-1950s, it followed a line which was consistently to the left of the Communist Party. It not only refused to enter into alliances with the centre parties, but also, by the mid-1960s, repudiated the electoral process, declaring that revolutionary violence was inevitable. Yet despite this rhetoric, its practice was, as ever, consistent with its parliamentary traditions. For it happily joined in with the Communists in taming the labour movement, it campaigned for a moderate political programme in the 1964 presidential elections, and finally, in 1969, agreed to enter into an alliance with the Radical Party and other non-marxist parties to form the Popular Unity, an electoral alliance ostensibly committed to the electoral road to socialism.

The discrepancy between theory and practice could, to some extent, be attributed to the party's chronic opportunism. It does, however, reflect a more serious and perhaps even tragic political dilemma. For during this period the Socialist Party sincerely tried to formulate and implement an independent marxist strategy different both from that of the Communist Party and social democracy generally. Its failure to achieve its objective is, however, related more to the nature of the revolutionary process which it was attempting to further than to opportunistic proclivities. In any event, once it became clear at the practical level that there was no easy alternative to the Communists' strategy, it followed their lead while, at the ideological level, embracing the view that violence was the only way to a socialist revolution. In the process, the party gave up its claim to a genuine national marxist approach to socialism, opting instead for a line which, ideologically, was a mix of Castroism and Trotskyism, while, at the practical level, it was primarily parliamentary. To understand the nature of the political dilemma which the Socialists confronted it is necessary to examine the basis of the Workers' Front Strategy and to ask why the Socialists were unable to implement it.

The Socialists formulated the Workers' Front Strategy in the mid-1950s. Ideologically influenced by Trotksy's views about the nature of a socialist revolution in backward countries, it was based upon a rejection of the notion that the national bourgeoisie had an independent role to play in the process leading to the socialist revolution. This was so because the local bourgeoisie was weak and had close links with imperialism and the landed oligarchy. Accordingly, the Socialists called for the creation of a broad alliance including intellectual and manual workers which, under the leadership of the parties of the working class would carry out a national democratic revolution. Thus, the way would be open to a socialist revolution that would erupt in a single uninterrupted process. The Socialists, therefore, did not reject the traditional communist view that it was necessary to carry out a national democratic revolution against imperialism and the landed oligarchy before a socialist revolution could begin. They did, however, reject the communist two-stage approach and regarded the revolution as an uninterrupted process which, though having a national democratic phase, would from the outset be carried out directly by the parties of the working class.[10]

Insofar as the Worker's Front strategy identifies capitalism, rather than imperialism, as the main target of the revolutionary process, and calls for the creation of a united front 'from below', its lineage can be traced to a variety of radical currents within marxism. However, its originality stemmed from the fact that it was to be implemented largely through parliamentary means. The Socialist Party therefore was faced with the problem of how to give concrete political content to its strategy in a milieu dominated by short-term electoral considerations.

In some respects the Socialists rightly regarded the FRAP as consistent with the Workers' Front Strategy since it excluded the centre parties and was controlled by the marxist parties. But the FRAP was only an electoral alliance, and the Socialists were aware that the Communists were keen to include the Radical Party and the CDP.

Thus, initially, the Socialists strongly criticised the purely defensive approach adopted by the FRAP and demanded more aggressive policies.[11] Yet, exactly what the Socialists wanted the FRAP to do, apart from campaigning to increase its electoral support, was never clearly stated. For while the Socialists were critical of the Communist Party's attempt to keep the FRAP strictly within the bounds of legality, they were equally critical of the ultra-left groups which called for an armed insurrection.[12] Unfortunately, because the Socialists did not propose a coherent alternative policy for the FRAP, they found themselves, ultimately, fully accepting the game of electoral politics as the only means of struggle for the FRAP.

In their search for a coherent set of policies for their Workers' Front Strategy, the Socialists, at one time or another, borrowed from and were influenced by a whole range of marxist approaches to revolutionary politics, except for that of the Communist Party of the Soviet Union. The influence of Trotskyism on the development of the Workers' Front Strategy has already been noted. Also, in the early 1950s, the Yugoslav experience was studied with great interest by the Socialist leadership. This model provided them with a notion of the party which rejected the Bolshevik concept of the party as the exclusive representative of the popular masses. In its place, the Socialist Party put forward the notion of the party as a democratic unit, a nucleus of a broader organisation of revolutionary forces.[13] The Yugoslav model also provided the Socialists with a blueprint for the organisation and participation of workers in production and social affairs generally. This model did not, however, have any real impact on the politics of the Socialist Party as it had no immediate relevance to the Chilean context. Undoubtedly, its appeal was largely based on the fact that it was a rejection of Stalinism.[14]

Maoism also appealed to some members of the Socialist Party leadership, notably to Clodomiro Almeyda, who was to be Foreign Minister under Allende.[15] Yet once again, this particular interpretation of marxism was not entirely relevant to the Chilean experience. For while maoism emphasises the importance of peasants in the socialist revolution – an aspect greatly neglected by Chilean marxists – it is ultimately based on a social formation in which the industrial base is negligible and, accordingly, peasants constitute a majority of the working population. Maoism had some impact among party intellectuals, but was never a major force with the political organs of the party. It is therefore not surprising that at the height of the Sino/ Soviet conflict the party should have adopted a resolution proclaiming its neutrality and declaring that the conflict showed that the international communist movement was rapidly becoming obsolete.[16]

The Cuban revolution was undoubtedly influential. For it was the first time in Latin America that a socialist movement succeeded in taking power in defiance of both the local oligarchy and the United States. In 1961, the nineteenth congress of the Socialist Party sent a message of greetings to the Cuban people, stating that their experience proved the inevitability of the socialist revolution in the rest of Latin America and confirmed that the Workers' Front Strategy was essentially correct.[17] But they were cautious not to endorse Fidel Castro's view that armed struggle was the only means to power.[18] This caution was based on the fact that the party had great expectations that the FRAP candidate would win the forthcoming presidential elections of 1964. Nonetheless, among the intellectuals and the youth sections of the Socialist Party, the Cuban revolution was a model which offered more hope than did the FRAP's elusive electoral path. Thus, not surprisingly, after FRAP's decisive defeat in the elections, the party fell under the control of its more radical wing, which declared that the electoral road was permanently blocked and that armed struggle was inevitable.

Before the 1964 elections, however, the Socialists were still hopeful about the electoral road. But they were worried, naturally, that in the event of a FRAP victory the parties of the bourgeoisie would refuse to recognise it and opt instead for a military coup. On this point, the Socialists had reason to believe that the Communists, having decided after the twentieth congress of the Communist Party of the Soviet Union that socialism could be achieved through peaceful means, would not be prepared to wage battle if the bourgeoisie refused to accept defeat. This suspicion contributed towards re-igniting the conflict between the parties, the Socialists believing that the Communists would not be prepared to use force because of their adherence to Moscow's policy of containment of revolutionary movements in Latin America.[19]

A Marxist Debate

The revival of conflict between the marxist parties was prompted by the Socialists' continuous critical appraisal of the communist notion of proletarian internationalism and, more specifically, by the Communist Party's electoral success after its return to legality in 1958. Indeed, in the first election following their return to legality – the council elections of 1960 – the Communists obtained almost as many votes as the Socialists. In the 1961 congressional elections, they did marginally better than the Socialists, obtaining 11.4 per cent of the vote, against 10.7 per cent for the Socialists. Their electoral success was reinforced by their growing influence in the trade-union movement. Indeed, by 1962, they had gained control of the majority of seats in the CUT's management committee, putting the Socialists into second place.

The Communist Party's electoral growth was particularly worrying to the Socialists because they knew that the political orientation of the FRAP would eventually be determined by the larger party. In this respect they had reason for concern since the Communists were beginning to argue that membership of the FRAP should be broadened to include all political parties which, though not socialist, agreed with its objectives.[20] Eventually, in the early part of 1962, as the tension increased, a major polemic erupted between them.

The two main issues in this polemic were the Communists' unquestioned loyalty to the directives of the Communist Party of the Soviet Union and their conception about the peaceful road to socialism.[21] On the first point, the Socialists restated their well-known objections to the Soviet style of internationalism. In their view, Soviet domination of the international communist movement contradicted basic marxist principles as it involved subordinating the historical interests of the working class to the national security of states in the Socialist bloc. According to the Socialists, this type of internationalism was based on a dogmatic attitude which regards as infallible any government belonging to the socialist bloc while characterising as heretical any soicalist movement which does not. In place of this internationalism, the Socialists called for the democratic integration of all socialists in a movement which would not attempt to exercise control over its members. The Communists strongly rejected the suggestion that they were manipulated by the Communist Party of Soviet Union. According to them, the communist movement has always been internationally based, and the role of the Soviet Union was that of a directive centre, which did not involve interference in the internal affairs of the national parties. But instead of dwelling on this point, the Communists concentrated their arguments on safer terrain: the peaceful road to socialism. On this point, the Socialists had accused them of using the concept as a means of glorifying bourgeois democracy 'instilling in the masses misplaced trust ... in the normality of democratic institutions and in the correct functioning of the mechanism of political representation'.[22] In reply the Communists stated that their conception about the peaceful road involved a belief in the possibility of introducing revolutionary changes with the support of a mass movement and without resorting to armed insurrection or civil war. It did not involve a rejection of other forms of violence such as general strikes, struggles in the street and seizures of land or occupations of factories. The concept of the peaceful road to socialism did not therefore imply strict respect of bourgeois legality. The Communists concluded their defence with a reminder to the Socialists that to the extent that they were committed to securing a victory for the FRAP candidate in the forthcoming elections they were also committed to the peaceful road to socialism.

After several public exchanges, Communists and Socialists decided to conclude their debate in private so as to avoid irreparable damage to their political alliance. Indeed, the right-wing press had thoroughly enjoyed the controversy about the role of the Soviet Union and had naturally been sympathetic towards the Socialists on this point. But if this argument was won by the Socialists, the Communists won the other. Indeed, in June 1964 the Socialists formally accepted the Communist Party's interpretation of the peaceful road to socialism.[23] They did not, however, attempt to reconcile this decision with their own Workers' Front Strategy: that issue was postponed because of the forthcoming presidential elections.

Practice versus Theory

The electoral defeat of 1964 brought about a major shake-up within the leadership of the Socialist Party. Raúl Ampuero, the Secretary General and architect of the Workers' Front Strategy, resigned and the key posts in the party hierarchy fell into the hands of more radical groups, mainly Trokskyites, which looked upon the Cuban revolution as the source of political inspiration. This brought to an end the Socialist Party's attempt to forge an independent marxist political line different from that of the Communists and – though still within the parameters of parliamentarism – different also from that of traditional Social Democratic parties. Under the influence of these radical groups, it repudiated the electoralist approach pursued by the FRAP on the eve of the presidential elections and declared that the working class would only conquer power by preparing itself for the inevitable armed confrontation.[24] Thus, by the mid-1960s, the Socialists formally abandoned efforts to find an alternative path to power, adopting instead the traditional view of radical marxists that armed struggle is inevitable. Under this new ideological influence, it also declared itself a Leninist organisation committed to the principles of democratic centralism.

The new-found radicalism of the Socialist Party was, however, largely rhetoric. The party did not in fact become Leninist and did not really abandon its parliamentary strategy. However, the new wave of radicalism brought about the expulsion of Raúl Ampuero, who was perhaps the only Socialist leader to take seriously the party's commitment to developing an original and independent Marxist approach consistent with local conditions. Interestingly enough, Salvador Allende, who was closely identified with the electoralist line attributed to the Communists, and who therefore should have been the main target for the new radical groups, managed to survive virtually unscathed.

Allende survived the radical onslaught by making oral concessions to the radical groups, while maintaining his traditional unreserved adherence to the electoral road and his close personal links with the Communist Party. Allende was in fact aware that the ultra-left groups were themselves divided and would not find it easy to translate their views of armed struggle into a coherent alternative to the parliamentary road. In any event, drawing from his own experience as a prominent member of the party since its inception, Allende rightly concluded that the radicals would only last until the eve of the forthcoming presidential election.

To establish his revolutionary credentials, Allende became an outspoken admirer of the Cuban revolution, played a prominent role in the establishment of OLAS, the Latin American Solidarity Organisation created in Cuba in 1966 after the tricontinental conference and designed to promote socialism in the region.[25] That he manged successfully to reconcile his support for the armed struggle in Latin America with his advocacy of the electoral road in Chile owed a great deal to the fact that, by 1963, Castro himself had toned down and qualified his views about the nature of the revolutionary struggle in Latin America. Indeed, in 1963, under pressure from Moscow, Castro openly conceded that the armed struggle, though the norm, was not inevitable as conditions vary from one country to another.[26] Even 'Ché' Guevara in his famous book *Guerrilla Warfare* conceded that in countries where constitutionalism prevailed the working-class would not necessarily have to resort to violence.[27] Thus, with the explicit approval by the leaders of the Cuban revolution, Allende could effectively reconcile his continuing support of the electoral road in Chile with his acceptance of the armed struggle elsewhere in the region.

By the end of the Frei administration the Socialist Party was forced to accept that, despite the rhetoric, it had not in fact abandoned the parliamentary road. In 1969, when the Socialists became aware that an alliance between Communists and Radicals was imminent, they were forced to accept their arch-enemies, the Radicals, as partners in the coalition known as the Popular Unity. To justify this decision they stated that they were prepared to form a revolutionary front with any party or group committed to substituting capitalism with a socialist order.[28] But this was little more than a hollow concession: underlying this change of heart was the growing awareness that ultra-left rhetoric had not yielded electoral dividends. Although the party increased its electoral support from 10.6 per cent in 1965 to 12.8 per cent in 1969, in the same period the Communist Party did far better, increasing its support from 12.7 per cent to 16.6 per cent. Besides, during this period, it lost many members from its youth section to the ultra-left group, the Left Revolutionary Movement (Movimiento de Izquierda Revolucionaria/MIR) which, though small, had a special appeal in that it actually practised the extra-parliamentary tactics advocated by the Socialists. Thus, although by joining the Popular Unity the Socialist Party objectively accepted the viability of the electoral road, ideologically it continued to accept the inevitability of the armed struggle.

III   THE COMMUNIST PARTY: A SUCCESSFUL STRATEGY

By contrast with the Socialists, the Communists regarded FRAP as the ideal vehicle for pursuing their national liberation strategy. FRAP was not after all committed to bringing about socialism, but only to undertaking a limited programme of reforms that fitted within the Communist Party's concept of the bourgeois national democratic stage of the revolution. Besides, the Communists regarded FRAP as a broad political alliance, which would not necessarily exclude the Radicals or Christian Democrats. They were therefore strong supporters of FRAP. During this period the Communists were quite successful: the ban on them was lifted; their electoral strength rose rapidly from 9 per cent in 1960 to 16.6 per cent in 1969; they became the leading force within the union movement; and finally, in 1969, their objective of broadening FRAP was fulfilled when the Popular Unity was established as a broad alliance which included the Radical Party and other non-marxist parties.

The success of the Communists' strategy during this period is all the more remarkable since, internationally, they had to contend with the split in the international communist movement and, domestically, they had to face simultaneously an increasingly successful CDP and a dangerously radical Socialist Party. This section explains the Communist Party's response to the conflicting political pressures it experienced during this period.

Proletarian Internationalism

In its international policy the Communist Party aligned itself firmly with the CPSU in the Sino/Soviet dispute, agreed with the Brezhnev doctrine as applied by the Soviet Union in Czechoslovakia in 1968, adopted a cautious policy towards the Cuban revolution and firmly rejected the increasingly prevalent view among Latin-American marxists about the inevitability of armed struggle in the region. Yet, despite the fact that the actual policies suggest unquestioned loyalty towards the Soviet Union, the party was not completely immune from the conflict dividing the two leading marxist powers.

Throughout the 1950s the Communist Party had maintained good relations with the Communist Party of the People's Republic of China. There had been several cultural exchanges between them, and Luis Corvalán, the Secretary General, had often praised the achievements of the Chinese revolution. By the early 1960s, however, as the Sino/Soviet conflict unfolded, the Chinese Communists began a vigorous campaign to enhance their influence in Latin America. In Chile, the China News Agency opened an office to distribute information, free of charge, praising China's political, economic and cultural developments. These materials were naturally welcomed by party members in Chile, since hitherto, news from and about China had been unobtainable locally. Eventually, a pro-Chinese group appeared within the party, which began to criticise the party's excessive concentration on the electoral road and its failure to establish a significant presence among agricultural workers.[29]

It is difficult to assess the impact which maoism had on the Communist Party as information on dissent within the party has always been difficult to obtain. Although many members most likely regarded the Chinese revolution with a great deal of sympathy, only a handful – mainly intellectuals – would have been prepared to rely on Mao's teaching to criticise their own party's political line. Yet, the reaction of the party hierarchy to maoism was strong and unequivocal. In March 1963, the party's central committee notified the rank and file that the line of the Communist Party of China was incompatible with that of the international communist movement as expressed in the Moscow declarations of 1957 and 1960.[30] By October of that same year seven members were expelled because of pro-Chinese activities, and Luis Corvalán launched an attack on the Chinese Communist Party, accusing it of intervening in the internal affairs of his party.[31]

The Communist Party's reaction to maoism within the party could be regarded as exaggerated given the fairly small influence it had on party members. However, it was rightly concerned that maoism combined with the influential views of Castro and Guevara concerning revolution in Latin America, could easily disrupt party discipline or threaten the political line pursued by FRAP. Indeed, since Castro's revolution had not been communist-inspired, the Communist Party's initial reaction to it had been cautious. Moreover, even in December 1961, when Castro declared himself Marxist-Leninist, the Communist Party maintained its caution because at the time Castro held the view that the only viable path to power was the armed struggle. Castro's views on the armed struggle had been welcomed by the Chinese partly because they coincided with their own and partly because they were inconsistent with Soviet policy in Latin America.

The prospect of a serious threat to party discipline did not, however, materialise. For while the Communist Party was ridding itself of maoist influence, the Soviet Union and Cuba reached an understanding about the nature of the revolution in Latin America which placed Cuba firmly within the Soviet camp. In a joint communique issued in April 1963 after an official visit by Castro to the Soviet Union, the governments of Cuba and the USSR declared that the strategy towards socialism in one country or another has to be decided by the people of the country concerned without external interference.[32] Castro's implicit acknowledgment that there was a peaceful road strengthened the official line and contributed towards defusing the incipient radicalism within the party. Thus, by June 1965, the Communist Party was in a position unequivocally to pledge permanent solidarity with the Cuban revolution.[33]

By the late 1960s it was clear that maoism was not a threat either to the Communist Party or to FRAP. The decline of maoism in Chile can be attributed largely to the fact that Cuba, despite its formal acceptance of the Soviet line, offered a closer and more relevant source of inspiration to local left-wing groups critical of the electoral road. Besides, since maoists had ideological differences with pro-Castro groups concerning aspects of revolutionary theory, the possibility of an alliance between them and other radical groups had all but disappeared by the late 1960s.

The maoist challenge and the emergence of the Cuban revolution had the effect of further reinforcing the Communist Party's loyalty to the Soviet Union. Thus, the Communist Party gave its unqualified support to the Soviet Union in Czechoslovakia, disregarding the fact that in domestic electoral terms support on this delicate issue was very risky. In the event, the electoral strength of the Communist Party was unaffected by its policy on Czechoslovakia, and though it created a certain amount of tension with the Socialists, this was soon forgotten.

Domestic Politics

The Communist Party's greatest achievement during this period was its ability to maintain good relations with the Socialists despite their new-found radicalism, while simultaneously building bridges with non-marxists, leading eventually to the transformation of FRAP into the Popular Unity. Its success, however, was at some cost: for while, on the one hand, to maintain its alliance with the Socialist Party, it had to make concessions to their radical position; on the other hand, it had strongly to reaffirm its commitment to the prevailing political system in order to inspire confidence in non-marxist parties. This created a certain ambiguity in the rhetoric and behaviour of the Communist Party which, as I explain in Part III, was carried over to the time of the Popular Unity government.

In its policy towards the Socialists the Communist Party concentrated on two main objectives: maintaining the unity of the Left as embodied in FRAP, and ensuring that the Socialists adopted a policy of constructive opposition towards the CDP administration. The rationale of this policy was based on the Communist Party's views about the nature of the CDP administration and the prospects for a future left-wing government. According to the Communists, there were contradictory forces operating within the CDP administration. For while objectively the government represented the interests of the bourgeoisie and imperialism there were influential groups within it sincerely committed to introducing structural reforms. Moreover, the government enjoyed widespread popularity and support among workers in urban centres and in the countryside. Thus, they advocated an opposition policy which would support the progressive initiatives of the government – such as the agrarian reform – but would firmly oppose those measures which favoured imperialism – such as the government's copper policy – or tended to break the unity of the labour government – such as the government's trade union policy.[34]

The Communists regarded their alliance with the Socialists as essential for safeguarding the interests of the working class both at the political and the trade-union levels.[35] But the Communists did not commit themselves unconditionally to this alliance. Indeed, they strongly hinted that they would not be inhibited from furthering their links with other progressive forces, including those within the CDP, if the Socialists refused to adopt a flexible and tolerant policy towards CDP supporters.[36]

The Communists' strategy was successful. For while on the one hand the Socialists' behaviour towards the CDP remained largely within the parliamentary framework and was in fact constructive, on the other hand, the Communists' flexible and tolerant approach invigorated the radical groups within the CDP and the Radical Party. Indeed, there is little doubt that the cooperative position adopted by the Communist Party during the Frei administration made it possible for the radical groups within the CDP to advocate closer links between the government and FRAP, and later on – after they had left the CDP – to join the marxists in a political alliance. A similar case was that of the Radical Party, which, by the end of the Frei administration, had already moved to the left in the political arena and eventually agreed to join the Popular Unity.

An interesting aspect of the Communists' policy during this period was their attitude towards the Catholic Church. In contrast to the Socialists, who continued their anti-clericalism, claiming that the church, together with the CDP, was working for the survival of capitalism, the Communists were seriously trying to understand the new phenomenon of Catholic reformism.[37] The marxists had of course good reason to be suspicious of the church. For in the past, it had consistently taken sides with the conservative forces and in particular with the landed oligarchy. Moreover, in the early sixties, when FRAP emerged as the largest political bloc in the country it took the side of the CDP and declared illegitimate any form of cooperation between Christians and marxists.[38] In contrast to the Socialists, however, the Communists did not react by completely rejecting the new political role assumed by Catholics under the CDP.

The Communists were careful not to attack the church. Instead, they respectfully requested it not to become directly involved in party politics. Moreover, the party also made a serious effort to understand the new reformist trends among Catholics. To do this it relied on the work of Orlando Millas, one of its leading ideologues. In essence Millas' conclusion was that despite the fact that the reformist trends in the Catholic Church were meant to preserve the capitalist system, the new progressive political outlook advocated by the CDP and the church was a welcome development. Accordingly he recommended that the Left should establish links with the new mass of Catholic reformists so as to win them over to more radical positions.[39]

Once again the tolerant and reasonable policy advocated by the Communists proved successful. For by the end of the 1960s the

175

church had quietly dropped its anti-marxism and was now simply advocating greater support for the poor through carefully planned social reform. This was partly a consequence of changes which had taken place in Latin America following the conference of bishops at Medellín in 1968.[40] But it was also prompted by the fact that, contrary to what had happened in 1964, by the late 1960s the Catholic vote was divided between the traditional right-wing parties and the CDP.

Unarmed, but not Peaceful

On the general question of power the Communists – probably under pressure from the radical wing of the Socialist Party – introduced a distinction between the peaceful and the unarmed road to socialism, claiming that they advocated the unarmed path. According to them this path rejected violence as the dominant form of struggle, but did not completely exclude its use in other forms such as land seizures, illegal strikes and street demonstrations.[41] In 1969 the Communist Party also introduced a slight amendment to its programme and statutes concerning the nature of the first stage of the revolution – the national liberation stage. In the past the Communist Party had defined the objectives of this stage as anti-imperialist, anti-monopolistic and anti-feudal. In 1969, after a lengthy procedure which had lasted four years, the Communist Party replaced the term anti-feudal with agrarian, thus acknowledging, albeit belatedly, that capitalism had already penetrated the countryside. In 1969 the Communists also incorporated into their programme a phrase by which they acknowledged that the revolutionary transformation envisaged during the first stage was, though not yet socialist, 'in the perspective of socialism'.[42] They also acknowledged that this first stage of the revolution could well be brief. Thus the Communists contributed towards setting the stage for the Popular Unity.[43]

PART III   POPULAR UNITY

CHAPTER 11

Programme and Initial Reactions

THE Popular Unity won the presidential elections by a narrow margin. Salvador Allende obtained 36 per cent of the vote; while the runner up, Jorge Alessandri, the candidate of the Right, obtained 35 per cent, Rodomiro Tomic, the CDP candidate, was third with 28 per cent of the vote. This surprising electoral result is often explained by the fact that the non-marxist vote was divided. In fact, in contrast to what happened in 1964 when the right-wing parties supported the CDP candidate in order to defeat the marxist candidate, in 1970 the Right decided to run its own candidate. The self-confidence of the Right was not unfounded; its electoral strength had been growing at a spectacular rate, from 12 per cent in 1965 to 20 per cent in 1969; and its presidential candidate was probably the most popular politician in the country at the time. Besides, after the Frei administration, the Right had become convinced that the CDP was no longer effective in containing the marxist threat. The CDP, for its part, had in fact ruled out an electoral alliance with the Right by nominating Tomic as its candidate, a man on the left of the party, who ran on a platform which was not unlike that of the Popular Unity.

From a broader political perspective, the narrow victory of the Left is less surprising than the electoral results would seem to indicate. Indeed, as already noted, by 1970 the political arena was highly polarised as a consequence of the sharp increase in political mobilisation and of the slow-down in the rate of economic growth. Thus, the candidates for the Presidency offered a clear choice to the electorate: the right-wing candidate openly advocated reversing the reformist policies of the Frei administration and re-affirming the principles of discipline and authority; the Popular Unity and the CDP candidates proposed, albeit with some important differences, to accelerate the pace of economic reforms so as to continue implementing policies of income redistribution to benefit the poorer sections of the population. In the event, the Popular Unity's more radical alternative prevailed at the polls by a narrow margin. However, this narrow electoral victory should not obscure the fact that in 1970 more than two-thirds of the electorate voted in favour of radical reform, while only one third supported the conservative option offered by the Right.

I   THE OPPOSITION: OPTIONS AND RESPONSE

The electoral victory of the Popular Unity presented the opposition parties with an unexpected dilemma. According to the constitution, if no candidate obtained an absolute majority then the Congress had to choose between the two candidates with the largest number of votes. Since Allende only obtained 36 per cent of the vote, the Congress was supposed to choose between him and the runner-up Alessandri. In the event, the Congress – with the vote of the CDP and the Popular Unity parties – elected Allende, thus following the well-established practice of opting for the candidate who had in fact won on election day.

On the surface, this decision can be easily explained, for the CDP and the National Party, the new right-wing party created in 1966 by the merger of the Conservative and Liberal Parties, had not agreed on a common strategy to keep Allende from office. While the National Party wanted to elect Alessandri as a tactical move in order to call for another presidential election; the CDP decided to vote for Allende in exchange for an agreement with the Popular Unity on a constitutional amendment meant to strengthen democratic freedom. However, such an explanation is inadequate. After all, the CDP and the National Party could have exercised their constitutional right by electing Alessandri in October 1970, thus preventing Allende from taking office. Why did they not make use of what – with hindsight – seems to have been a golden opportunity? Undoubtedly, the answer to this is that had they attempted to keep Allende out of office by a parliamentary manoeuvre they risked provoking a bloody confrontation out of which the Left was likely to emerge as the winner. Although this explanation correctly identifies one of the problems which the CDP and National Party confronted, it does not account for the novel situation in which the anti-Allende forces found themselves after the election.

To answer the question, the factors contributing towards shaping what was to become a solid and united opposition to the government have to be discussed, and especially the role of the National Party and the CDP within this process. For throughout the three years, these parties were the main forces mobilising public opinion and legitimising action against the government. Other actors and political groups – notably, the United States and the guild movement (*gremialismo*) – also played an important role in opposing the government, but they had to subordinate their specific objectives to the tempo and pace set by the two main opposition parties.

In the following paragraphs, I explain why the extra-constitutional option of keeping Allende out of office by force – favoured by the United States government and by some ultra-right groups in the country – could not be successfully implemented. Then, I show how this had the effect of reasserting the importance of the party system and of forcing the United States to re-examine its policy towards the Popular Unity. I then explain why the two parties adopted different policies to deal with the new government, and I argue that these policies both competed against and complemented each other. Their different policies were to make it possible for them to form a powerful bloc supported by the *gremios* at the grassroots level and benefiting from the anti-Allende activities carried out by the United States inside and outside Chile.

The Extra-Constitutional Option

In the immediate post-electoral period, as fears of financial crisis were voiced by members of the outgoing administration and all sides were putting pressure on the military to define their position, an ultra-right group, Patria y Libertad (PL), emerged which openly demanded that Allende be prevented from taking office by any means. Patria y Libertad was led by Pablo Rodríguez, an obscure but ambitious law professor. He won considerable sympathy among the right-wing public as he was the organiser of the first anti-marxist demonstration shortly after the election. In his speeches, he made ample use of well-known nationalist and fascist ideas, but he was careful not to identify his movement with reactionary anti-communist Catholic groups such as those sponsored by the Brazilian movement *Tradición, Patria y Familia*.

The emergence of PL was accompanied by a mild outbreak of right-wing terrorism, mainly designed to provoke the military into action and to warn the middle classes of the chaos that would ensure if Allende was allowed to take office. The views held by PL were not at all different from those held by some leaders of the National Party, who, in their youth, had been members of the MNS and whose anti-

Communist views were well-known, Indeed, not long before the 1970 presidential election, the leader of the National Party, Onofre Jarpa, had called for the banning of the Communist Party and of other marxist groups.[1] Thus, it is likely that Jarpa not only welcomed the emergence of PL, but it is probable that he and other members of the National Party were closely involved in its activities. But whether or not these links were strong, the fact is that PL failed to persuade the National Party to opt for an extra-constitutional solution to prevent the marxist threat. Instead, the National Party chose to continue playing the game of parliamentary politics and to accept, albeit grudgingly, Allende's election by the Congress. PL was thus forced to withdraw temporarily from the streets and to discontinue its terrorists activities.

The failure of PL to change the course of constitutional politics is not surprising since at the time the United States government had also failed to secure the same objective. The reaction of the Nixon/Kissinger team to Allende's electoral victory has been well documented and is aptly summarised by the following statement attributed to Henry Kissinger: 'I don't see why we need to stand by and watch a country go Communist due to the irresponsibility of its own people'.[2] The United States government therefore quickly designed a plan to keep the Popular Unity out of office. It consisted of two main elements: firstly, a determined effort to instigate a military coup and secondly, an attempt to block Allende's election by the Congress through pressure and bribery of individual members of the Congress. The United States government also had a long term plan, inspired by ITT, to bring about a major economic crisis.[3]

The Nixon/Kissinger Plan

The idea of a military coup undoubtedly had many supporters within the National Party, as well as within the CDP. However, the armed forces were not at that stage prepared to take such an important step. The serious breaches of military discipline which had taken place during the last two years of the previous administration, culminating with the 'strike' at the Tacna barracks in Santiago, had brought about important changes at the top of the military hierarchy. In 1968 Frei appointed a new commander-in-chief, General René Schneider, who concentrated most of his efforts on re-establishing discipline in the rank and file. His objective was to re-affirm the principle that the military should not intervene in politics and should respect constitutional procedures. Schneider's success in fulfilling this task can perhaps be attributed to the fact that the recent events at the Tacna regiment had brought into the open the divisions existing within the military, thus underlying the fact that a political intervention by the armed forces would, at that stage, divide them even further and lead to a bloody civil war. In any event, so confident was Schneider about the success of his task that, some six months before the presidential elections, he explicitly committed the military to non-intervention, stating that if no candidate obtained an absolute majority of the popular vote, it was up to the Congress to select the next President and that the military would respect its decision, whatever it might be.[4] This restatement of a basic principle of constitutional government, upheld by the Chilean armed forces since 1932, became known as the 'Schneider doctrine'.

That the armed forces accepted the 'Schneider doctrine' in the critically important post-electoral period can, to some extent, be attributed to the much-praised professionalism of the Chilean armed forces. However, there are other reasons which may be more relevant to explaining why, at that crucial moment, they did not intervene. In the first place, a military coup would have split the armed forces. Support for Allende would have been forthcoming not only from the few officers with known left-wing sympathies, but from many others who sincerely believed that electoral results had to be respected. In the second place, any form of military intervention which ignored the outcome of the electoral process would have sparked massive popular support for the Left, thus transforming an inevitable conflict into a bloody civil war. In the third place United States support for a military coup, well-known at the time, did not necessarily make this a popular option among the military. For the Chilean military, reared as they were on a strict Prussian tradition, firmly believed in operational autonomy and had little respect for armies in other Latin-American countries which seemed to be always willing to act as puppets of the United States government. Besides, in the mid-sixties the United States had decided to transform Latin-American armies into counter-insurgency forces. This decision was deeply resented because it involved reducing United States supplies of conventional equipment which the Chilean military regarded as essential for fulfilling adequately the task of safe-guarding national sovereignty[5]. Finally, a military coup was effectively ruled out after an attempt by right-wing groups to kidnap General Schneider ended with his assassination. This event, which took place after the CDP had officially decided to vote for Allende in the election by the Congress, caused great consternation within the armed forces, transforming the so-called 'Schneider doctrine' into a temporary symbol of unity.

United States Policy: a Change of Course

The alternative plan considered by the United States government was to buy enough votes in the Congress to secure the election of Alessandri. Its aim was to undermine the agreement which the Popular Unity and the CDP were negotiating at the time. However, it was abandoned because it was not only impractical, involving as it did a large number of individuals, but it was also dangerous, for it was unlikely that the origins of the funds for such intervention could have been kept secret. In the highly politicised climate, such massive bribery by a foreign power, intended to subvert the normal course of democratic politics, would not only have increased popular support for the Popular Unity, but most likely would also have caused a split within the CDP.

Since the two possible ways of blocking Allende's access to office were ruled out, the United States government was forced to come to terms with the vagaries of Chile's constitutional procedures and party politics. President Nixon was thus forced to be patient with a country which, according to Henry Kissinger, had been foolish enough to elect a marxist President. In the meantime, United States policy concentrated on two long-term objectives: undermining the government's economic policy, and ensuring that opposition parties were kept well supplied with money and other resources to wage an effective ideological war against the government.

In regard to the economy United States' policy was largely based on the proposal made by ITT in September 1970. Its objective was 'to make the economy scream'.[6] However, initially, the means at the disposal of the United States government were limited. The fact that the Allende government had been democratically elected and was trying hard not to annoy the American administration, effectively ruled out the imposition of a trade boycott and other forms of economic sanctions. This is why, in the first instance, the United States government concentrated, quietly, on blocking loans to Chile from public and private sources. Later on, when Allende's copper nationalisation transformed the question of compensation into a major issue between the two countries, United States pressure could be exercised more openly, particularly in regard to the negotiations over Chile's foreign debt. Also, the legal conflict over the nationalisation of copper brought about some disruption to Chile's copper trade as the American companies which had been expropriated challenged the legality of the nationalisation process in United States and European courts.[7] It must be noted that the economic blockade the United States imposed on Chile did not extend to military sales. On this front, the flow of resources originating in the United States continued uninterrupted.[8] At the ideological level, the CIA carried out what it regarded as the defence of Chilean democracy through covert action. It included generous financial subsidies to selected opposition newspapers and political parties. Direct financial support to opposition groups was supplemented by an abundant supply of anti-communist material to organs of the media controlled by the opposition.[9] These activities have been recently justified by Nathaniel Davis, the United States ambassador at the time, as indispensable means to protect democracy from the marxist threat.[10]

The National Party: A Constitutional Option

Aware that Allende could not be kept out of office by force or bribery, the National Party proposed an alternative to the CDP. It consisted in joining their parliamentary votes to elect Alessandri as President. He would then immediately resign so that a new election would have to be held. In this new election, the National Party and the CDP, re-enacting their 1964 alliance, would vote for Frei. This proposal was, on paper, quite sensible because it would have made it possible to get rid of Allende through a constitutional procedure, and because it would have given the electorate a second chance to decide who should be the country's President. However, the CDP, for reasons which I examine below, was not tempted by the proposal and decided instead to vote for Allende. The National Party's reaction was interesting. Instead of attacking the CDP, it expressed great concern and disappointment, pointing out that the CDP was deluding itself into believing the marxist party once in office would respect democracy. But it also declared it was willing to wait for the CDP to change its policy and join in the struggle for freedom in the fatherland.[11]

In a curious way, the CDP's decision to vote for Allende in the Congress was probably welcomed by the National Party. For it needed time to consolidate its spectacular electoral achievements since its establishment in 1966. As I have explained in Chapter 9, the National Party's objective was to recapture the vote which had been lost to the CDP in the early sixties. To this effect, the National Party declared itself a middle-class party and began to distance itself from the old-fashioned oligarchical image of the Conservative and Liberal parties. Thus, the fact that the CDP had decided to support the Popular Unity candidate in the Congress provided the National Party with a golden opportunity of becoming leader of the opposition. Accordingly, even before the Allende government had had a chance to settle in, the National Party had mobilised its powerful propaganda machinery to proclaim that the Communist Party had already begun implementing its plan of leading the country towards the dictatorship of the proletariat.[12] But the National Party did not rely exclusively on propaganda. Its leader, Onofre Jarpa, was aware that a sudden political swing to the Right would not be brought about through the ballot box. He therefore concentrated on the intermediate organs of functional representation, the so-called guilds (*gremios*), in which government policies could be confronted at the point of implementation.

Gremialismo

The National Party's interests in the guild movement, *gremialismo*, was not new. A powerful right-wing *gremialista* movement had in fact emerged in 1965 at the Catholic University, the traditional bastion of right-wing support. The *gremialista* movement was ostensibly established to counter the growing politicisation of university life under the influence of the CDP-led student union (FEUC), and to everyone's surprise it became extremely popular. By 1969 it had managed to win the presidency of the FEUC away from the CDP.[13]

The enormous success of the *gremialista* movement at the Catholic University owed more to the fact that it provided a focus of protest against what was perceived as the arrogant and sectarian attitudes of the CDP than to its ideology, which was a fairly crude variety of corporatism. This fact could not have been missed by the National Party, as Jaime Guzmán, the leader of the movement, as well as his close associates, had been either members of the old Conservative and Liberal parties or were the sons, or nephews, of prominent right-wing personalities. Under the able leadership of Guzmán, the *gremialista* movement spread from the Catholic University to other universities.

The *gremialista* movement was not a fascist organisation and had no immediate plans to displace the National Party from national politics. Indeed, at a national level, the *gremialistas* largely accepted the National Party's leadership, and did not regard membership in the party as incompatible with participation in their movement. They concentrated their efforts at intermediate bodies, where they could effectively undermine the electoral strength of the CDP. In this respect, the work of the *gremialistas* became a useful complement to the tasks which the National Party set for itself. This was reflected in the close cooperation which developed between the National Party and the *gremialista* movement during the 1970 presidential campaign.

In June 1971 Jarpa called for a massive mobilisation in defence of freedom and democracy, but not through traditional political rallies or marches. Instead, he called upon his supporters to use every organisation to which they belonged to mobilise opposition against the government. Thus, echoing the *gremialista* movement, he called for mobilisation through parents' associations, universities, professional societies, trade unions and guilds.[14] Jarpa's call was promptly picked up by the leading employers' organisations in industry, agriculture and commerce.[15]

The grassroots approach the National Party adopted did not lead them to neglect the more traditional terrain of struggle: the Congress. There they strongly and consistently denounced alleged abuses of power by the government and attempted to initiate impeachment proceedings against several cabinet ministers. Initially these proceedings were unsuccessful because the CDP refused to support them. However, by the end of Allende's first year in office, the CDP was to change its mind.

The Christian Democratic Party

The response of the CDP to the electoral victory of the Popular Unity was also complex. Two important factors contributed to shaping this response: firstly, that the CDP was the single largest party in the country; and secondly, the existence within the party of two important factions, which had radically different views about the prospects for democracy under a marxist-led coalition government.

As the largest party in the country, the CDP had a special interest in the long-term survival of the party system and would therefore not have benefited from a violent interruption of constitutional procedures. Moreover the fact that important groups within the party had strong views for and against closer cooperation with the Popular Unity made it impossible for the party to consider an early alliance with either the National Party or the Popular Unity. The Conservative faction led by Frei, the most popular figure in the party, was profoundly anti-marxist and was initially unwilling to make any concessions to the Popular Unity. On the other hand, the progressive wing of the party, led by the former presidential candidate, Radomiro Tomic, and including most of the party's youth and peasant sections, acknowledged defeat in the elections and called upon the party to co-operate with the Popular Unity administration. Shortly after the elections, Tomic in fact took the bold step of visiting Allende to congratulate him on his victory. Hence, the existence of these two important factions made it difficult for the CDP to side with the National Party or the Popular Unity without risking party unity.

It is not surprising therefore that the CDP rejected the National Party's proposal to join forces in the Congress and elect the runner-up

Alessandri. However, it must be noted that when the party formally considered this proposal, as many as 40 per cent of the members of its ruling council voted to accept it.[16] Therefore, the CDP's decision to vote for Allende in exchange for a constitutional amendment, described as a Statute of Democratic Guarantees (SDG), must be seen as an attempt to reconcile the conflicting views within the party.

The Statute of Democratic Guarantees

The constitutional amendment proposed by the CDP was designed to make more explicit the provisions of the constitution in matters concerning the protection of certain civil rights. The CDP claimed that the amendment was a necessary precaution to ensure that the Popular Unity's intended social and economic reforms would be carried out through democratic procedures. The CDP expressed special concern over the proposal to establish new organs of popular representation, and over proposals on education and the media.[17]

Negotiations between the Popular Unity and the CDP over the constitutional amendment were brief but intense. The text which was finally approved was practically the same as that originally proposed by the CDP. Its most important provision dealt with the status of political parties, freedom of the press and education, the right to participate in activities of the community and the structure of the armed forces. The amendment gave constitutional status to political parties and set limits on the power of the legislators to regulate them. Political parties were also to have free access to state-controlled media and access on equal terms to privately-owned media. The right of every person to establish means of communications was recognised and the expropriation of any privately-owned organ of the media was made conditional to the enactment of special legislation, which would require for its approval the vote of at least two-thirds of the members in each house of the Congress. In education, the amendment provided that the state-controlled system of education should have no official party-political orientation. The SDG also included a section recognising the right to participate in all spheres of social life, providing that this right was exercised through organisations established by law. Finally, it introduced a clause clarifying that in the armed forces decisions on admission requirements and staffing levels could only be made by the authorities of the existing institutions.

On the face of it, the SDG did not introduce any major change to the constitution. It merely clarified the scope of civil rights already recognised by the constitution and provided that only by law could the exercise of these rights be restricted. Indeed, the National Party justified its refusal to vote in favour of the SDG on the ground that it did nothing to change the basic structure of the constitution.[18] The Popular Unity also regarded the SDG as a fairly innocuous measure, which would not seriously interfere with the implementation of a socialist programme. In any case since the amendment was primarily concerned with the immediate problem of securing CDP support for the election of Allende by the Congress, acceptance of the amendment by the Popular Unity must have seemed a minor, even ridiculous, concession to make. The Popular Unity was also aware that approval of the SDG by the Congress would further legitimise the Allende government in the international arena, thus making it more difficult for the United States to subvert the country's democratic process. Hence Allende's suggestion that the decision to accept the SDG was purely tactical.[19]

A Neutral Standpoint

The fact that the SDG did not explicitly introduce major changes in the composition and power of the organs of the state does not mean that it was a totally innocuous document.[20] The amendment actually had the effect of severely undermining the powers of the President, and of the executive branch generally. However, this fact went largely unnoticed at the time, at least as far as the Popular Unity was concerned. Apart from a detailed description of the civil liberties already protected by the constitution, the SDG reaffirmed the principle that only by law could civil liberties be restricted. This obvious restatement of a generally-accepted principle in fact had the effect of casting a shadow of doubt over the constitutionality of many powers traditionally vested in the executive branch. This was so because in practice, since the enactment of the 1925 constitution, the President had in fact been recognised as having broad powers to regulate the exercise of some basic civil rights. Thus, for example, until 1970, the exercise of the right of assembly was regulated by a mere executive decree. Likewise, an executive decree regulated broadcasting activities, and, according to this decree, the President had wide-ranging powers to restrict the operation of privately-owned radio stations. After the approval of the SDG, it was arguable that all these previously enacted executive decrees had been implicitly repealed and the President no longer had the power to regulate the exercise of basic civil liberties. These and other similar issues posed by the constitutional amendment were naturally not mentioned by the CDP when it negotiated with the Popular Unity. However, they were soon to become main issues on which the CDP was to base its opposition to the government. For its part, the Popular Unity was not greatly concerned with the broader legal implications of the amendment, not only because of the political reasons already mentioned, but because it did not explicitly restrict the considerable powers of the President in the area of economic regulation.

From the CDP's point of view, the SDG was useful not only because it made reconciliation possible between the two sides within the party, but also because it was a useful weapon to oppose government policy from a seemingly neutral position. The right-wing faction in the CDP regarded the SDG as indispendsable for protecting democracy from the well-known totalitarian tendencies of certain marxist parties. Their leading spokesman explained that, despite the Popular Unity's commitment to democracy, some aspects of its programme implicitly threatened the continuity of democracy and civil liberties.[21] For its part, the progressive groups within the CDP regarded the approval of the SDG as the first step in the process of cooperation between the party and the new government. In fact, even before the CDP officially decided to vote for Allende in the Congress, Tomic had pledged his support to the Popular Unity's programme of radical reforms.[22] The SDG greatly contributed to preserving the unity and cohesion of the CDP because ostensibly it was only concerned with maintaining political democracy – an issue which united the whole party – and not with the preservation of capitalism – an issue which divided the party. The party made it abundantly clear that voting for Allende in exchange for the approval of the Statute of Democratic Guarantees in no way involved approval – or disapproval – of his political programme. That was an issue on which the party reserved its position. Its apparent neutrality contributed to uniting the party in a particularly difficult moment. This neutrality was also useful as it allowed the party to assume the role of umpire in the game of political democracy. In its new role, it could challenge the democratic behaviour of the government without running the risk of identifying itself with the economic interests affected by government policies. The SDG was thus a powerful ideological tool, which could be effectively used to criticise government policies and which the government could be reasonably expected to respect, as it had been approved with the vote of the Popular Unity parties.

While the National Party and the CDP may have been shocked by the electoral results, their different responses to the new situation does not reveal confusion or hesitation.[23] Indeed, both parties reacted in a manner consistent with their objective position within the party system and with the interests that they each purported to represent.

Moreover, their different policies were interesting in that they were competitive and complementary. They were competitive because each party had to take into account its specific electoral interests in the event of the system of political democracy surviving beyond the six years of the Popular Unity administration. In this respect, as I have shown, each of the parties had good reason to believe that it had the best chance to win the next presidential election. But their policies were also complementary because they were based upon the same ideological assumption; that a government coalition led by marxists was bound to behave undemocratically. The seemingly tenuous link between the initial policies of the National Party and the CDP was to become, later on, the basis on which the two parties would unite to form a solid and inflexible anti-government bloc.

It is important to point out, at this stage, that the fact that the United States was forced to act in Chile mainly through the existing party system and to accommodate its objective to the peculiarities of local political development, explains why it is so difficult to assess the exact impact of its policies on the breakdown of democracy. Indeed each separate action carried out or attributable to the United States government, whether it involved blocking financial assistance to the government, delaying debt negotiations or financing anti-government strikers, cannot be easily described as having a decisive impact on the final outcome. However, as I show below, action by the United States government, as well as by United States-owned multi-national companies, had a cumulative effect, which, together with the rapidly converging policies of the opposition, undoubtedly contributed towards bringing about the government's collapse.

II THE PROGRAMME

The Popular Unity came into existence in 1969 as an electoral alliance made up of three main parties – the Communist, Radical and Socialist parties – and three small political movements – the Social Democratic Party (SDP), the Independent Popular Action Party (API), and the Movimiento de Acción Popular Unitaria (MAPU). Its creation was made possible by a compromise between Communists and Socialists over two issues which had divided them since the early fifties. Socialists gave up their opposition to forming an alliance with parties which, according to them, represented the reformist aspirations of the bourgeoisie, and the Communists accepted that the Programme of Government of the Popular Unity should state that the new government's objective was to prepare the ground to initiate a socialist transition.

But this compromise was more apparent than real, inspired as it was mainly by electoral calculations. On the one hand, the Socialists, who only recently had solemnly rejected the electoral road, had a last-minute change of mind when they realised that an electoral alliance between Communists and Radicals could easily attract the CDP, thus leaving them out of the political game altogether. Indeed, Tomic had emphatically stated that he would decline his party's nomination – as in fact he did, but later on changed his mind – unless he was the candidate of a united left-wing coalition representing a broad popular alliance. The Communists welcomed his proposal, and were prepared to support a CDP candidate, but did not believe that he was suitable. In this context, it is not surprising that the Socialists should have seen an alliance with the Radical Party as the lesser of two evils. On the other hand, while the Communists were not keen to include the word socialism in the Programme of the Popular Unity, the reference that was made was sufficiently vague to be consistent with its views regarding the two stages of the Socialist revolution. Thus, while the Programme stated the central objective of the Popular Unity was to destroy the power base of monopoly capitalism and of the landed oligarchy 'in order to begin the construction of socialism', it did not specify exactly when the process of transition would begin.[24] Besides, any misgivings that the Communists may have had about the radical nature of the programme must have vanished when Salvador Allende, a well-known Socialist moderate, was nominated as the Popular Unity's presidential candidate.

The Popular Unity's Programme was based on a radical critique of the Christian Democratic Party's 'Revolution in Liberty'. According to the Programme, six years of piecemeal reforms by the CDP had failed to resolve basic social and economic issues, had not increased the overall rate of economic growth, and had deepened the country's dependency on multi-national firms and other foreign economic interests. Hence, the Popular Unity's call for a more radical programme of action to replace the prevailing economic structure. In the new economy it envisaged, the commanding heights would be controlled directly by the state in what was described as the area of social property. This area would include large-scale mining, strategic industrial monopolies, foreign trade, banking, insurance and large firms in key sectors such as distribution, energy and transport. Alongside the area of social property, it contemplated the existence of two others: the area of private property, made up of small and medium-sized firms; and the area of mixed property in some selected technologically-advanced sectors of production, in which state and private capital, mainly foreign, would form joint ventures. To complete the restructuring of the economy, it proposed to accelerate the land reform initiated by the previous administration and to broaden its scope so as to integrate fully the agricultural sector within the rest of the economy.

To ensure that the transformation of the economic structure would bring about an effective transfer of power to the people the Popular Unity proposed the creation of a new 'popular state'. This new form of state was to provide the framework for the effective participation of the people in political affairs. The central organ of this new political order would be the Popular Assembly, a single chamber of elected representatives, which was to replace the existing Congress. The Assembly was conceived as the central organ of power, meant to eradicate the evils of parliamentarianism and to keep close control over the use of power by the executive. The Assembly would also appoint supreme court judges and would have supervisory powers over the whole of the judiciary.

The Popular Unity's proposals in specific matters of policy such as education, health and housing were all consistent with the overriding objective of bringing about a more equitable distribution of resources and of introducing democratic procedures at all levels of social life. In matters of national defence and foreign policy its programme was cautious. With respect to the armed forces, the programme made a vague reference to the need to make them participate directly in the tasks of economic development, but did not call for any major changes in their composition or structure. In general foreign policy matters, the Programme called for a review of the country's treaty commitments, 'in particular those treaties of reciprocal and mutual aid and other similar pacts which Chile has signed with the United States'.[25] However, it also made clear that the new government would not attempt to play one super-power against another and would follow a strict policy of non-alignment.

The Popular Unity relied on the strength and flexibility of the existing political institutions to achieve its objective. Thus, the structural changes proposed by the Programme would be implemented through constitutional amendments, legislation and ultimately through a plebiscite. The Popular Unity was therefore committed to accomplishing everything through the rules and principles of the prevailing constitutional order. But the duty to act within the limits of the constitution was understood to be shared by the Congress. Hence Allende's warning: 'it depends to a great extent on the realistic attitude of the Congress whether or not the legal system of capitalism can be succeeded by a socialist legal system without there being a violent rupture in the judicial system, which could give rise to those arbitrary acts and excesses which we wish to avoid.'[26] Congress' approval would be secured by the strength of the political organisations of the proletariat, which, in alliance with peasants, the urban poor and the middle class, would act as a democratic pressure group. According to the Programme, this broad alliance for socialism could be easily established because the Popular Unity's policy would only threaten the interests of a tiny minority, consisting of a few landowners and a handful of individuals controlling the commanding heights of the economy. Since the policies would benefit the vast majority of the population, Congress and other organs of the state could not afford to ignore the demands of this truly democratic movement for socialism.[27]

The optimistic views of the Popular Unity concerning a democratic response by the organs of the state was combined with a favourable assessment of the existing body of legislation. Thus, according to Allende, although on the whole the prevailing political system was unjust as it legitimised an oppressive social and economic order, some laws enacted by this system had a truly progressive content. According to the Popular Unity, these laws had been enacted by the Congress as a result of organised pressure from the working class, and would therefore provide the basis for the implementation of the new government's programme.[28] Hence, a flexible and responsive democratic process and an institutional structure with some progressive laws would facilitate the implementation of the Popular Unity's second model for the transition to socialism.

Conflicting views about the Programme

As noted in Chapter 10 above, one of the main ideological differences which existed between the Communists and Socialists concerned the nature of Chile's socialists revolution. The Communists, upholding the view of the national liberation front, conceived the revolution as a process involving several stages. During the first stage, the so-called national-democratic stage, the popular forces, in alliance with political parties representing progressive forces of the bourgeoisie, would carry out national-democratic tasks, involving measures against the landed oligarchy, imperialism and monopoly capitalism. After these tasks were fulfilled, the second stage of socialist transition would follow. The Socialists, for their part, rejecting the notion that an alliance with a fraction of the bourgeoisie was either possible or desirable, conceived of the revolution as a single process in which the national-democratic and socialist tasks would be carried out simultaneously. To this effect, they called for the creation of a Workers' Front, consisting of an alliance of only those political parties which represented the interests of the proletariat and the popular masses.

Since the early fifties, these conflicting conceptions about the nature of the socialist revolution figured prominently in the ideological debates between Communists and Socialists. The establishment of the FRAP in 1956 had a moderating effect in the dispute between the two parties, but did not change their respective positions. That an alliance between them lasted owes more to the demands of the electoral process than to an ideological rapprochement between them. Indeed the policies they pursued under the aegis of the FRAP can be interpreted as short-term trade-offs between the two conflicting ideological perspectives.

Insofar as the FRAP was an electoral alliance and the socialist revolution was not on the agenda, differences between the two marxist parties on the nature of the revolution had no impact on their daily practice. However, after the Popular Unity won the presidential elections, the Communist and Socialist parties could no longer afford to rely on the traditional ideological trade-offs which had accounted for the FRAP's longevity. As leading members of a government coalition committed to bringing about a socialist transformation of society it was imperative for them to have a common view regarding the enterprise upon which they were embarking and the steps that they would be expected to take. Unfortunately, this ideological unity was not achieved; instead, during their three years in office, they continued to have conflicting views about the Popular Unity programme and the forms of implementation. Given the peculiar conditions under which Allende's government was operating, this disagreement was, if not irresponsible, at least dangerous.

As already noted, the Programme stated that the Popular Unity government would 'initiate the construction of socialism'. This phrase was acceptable to both Communists and Socialists, but because it was ambiguous each party interpreted it in accordance with its own preconceived ideas about the nature of the revolution.

According to the Communist Party's interpretation of the Programme, the govenment's task was to isolate the principal enemies of the revolution: imperialism, local monopolists and landed obligarchy. The electoral victory had, according to the Communists, made it possible for the Popular Unity to gain control over the most dynamic and powerful part of the state apparatus, but had not fully resolved the question of state power. To displace the reactionary forces from the key positions in the state apparatus, the Communists advocated a policy of class alliances, to be carried out with due respect for the existing institutional framework and through the party system.[29] This policy involved two main aspects: on the one hand, a firm condemnation of any attempt by the ultra-left to use extra-parliamentary means of struggle and, on the other, a determination to arrive at an understanding with the CDP so as to enable the government to fulfil its principal task.[30] Thus, although the Communist Party had accepted the reference to socialism in the Programme, its views on the tasks of the Popular Unity and the means to achieve them showed that, on the whole, it had not abandoned its national liberation strategy.

The Socialists interpreted the Popular Unity's programme as a restatement of their own Workers' Front Strategy. Shortly after Allende took office, Carlos Altamirano, the recently-elected leader of the party, reaffirmed his conviction that the socialist revolution was a single process and that in his view, the Popular Unity was called upon to fulfil not only the national-democratic tasks against the local oligarchy and imperialism, but also socialist tasks.[31] Accordingly, there was no room in the coalition for bourgeois parties, even for those which presented themselves as progressive. Indeed, according to Altamirano, bourgeois reformism, as represented and practised by the CDP, was the principal enemy of the revolution. For the CDP, with its populist ideology of income redistribution, was destined to become the axis around which the Right would re-group its forces. The Socialists acknowledged the CDP's considerable influence among sections of the working class, but did not believe that their support could be gained by making concessions to the CDP leadership. The correct policy they argued was immediately to transfer power to working-class and other popular organisations as this would not only increase and broaden support for the government, but would also facilitate the task of socialist construction.[32]

It is important to note that although the Socialist Party was ideologically to the left of the Communist Party, its position was different from the MIR, the ultra-left group. The MIR had not supported the Popular Unity candidate in the presidential elections but neither had it called upon its supporters to abstain. As a critic of the electoral orientation of the Left, not only did it refute the road to socialism as proposed by the Popular Unity, but was profoundly sceptical of Allende ever winning the elections. After the victory, the MIR announced that it would support all the anti-capitalist measures that the new government might take, provided that the Popular Unity did not enter into an alliance with the CDP. However, according to the MIR, political and military confrontation with the bourgeoisie was inevitable and imminent. Therefore, the main task of the Left was to prepare the masses for this confrontation and to begin immediately by transferring power to working-class and other grassroots organisations.[33]

In some respects, the MIR's position was similar to that of the Socialist Party. Both parties advocated transferring power to the popular masses, and they both flatly rejected the idea of an alliance between the Popular Unity and the CDP. However, they differed on several fundamental issues. While the MIR believed that the electoral victory had placed the Left in a strong position to launch an assault on the state and to conquer power, the Socialists argued that the revolutionary process leading to the conquest of power had already begun. On the basis of this assumption, the Socialists believed that a speedy implementation of the Popular Unity's programme, with no concessions to the CDP, would fundamentally change the balance of forces, thus making it possible for the proletariat to conquer state power. The MIR, for its part, did not believe that the conquest of power could take place within the framework of the existing state structure, regardless of the speed at which the Popular Unity implemented its programme. Hence its call for military and political preparations in anticipation of the inevitable confrontation to resolve the question of power.

CHAPTER 12

Popular Unity: The Party of Government I

I POLITICAL CONSTRAINTS

Nature of the Coalition

Upon taking office, Allende had to confront the task of transforming the Popular Unity into an effective decision-making body. This was difficult, not only because, as an electoral alliance, the Popular Unity had been hastily put together, but also because its membership was not homogeneous, either in size or in ideology. Indeed, the bulk of the coalition's electoral strength was derived from three of its six members: the Communist, Socialist and Radical parties. In the general election of 1969, the combined vote of these three parties had in fact reached 41 per cent, that is, 5 per cent more than Allende had obtained in the 1970 presidential elections.

In these same 1969 electoral results, the largest of the three parties was the Communist Party, with 15.9 per cent of the vote, followed by the Radical and Socialist parties with 13 and 12.2 per cent of the vote respectively. These figures indicate that the marxist parties accounted for more than two thirds of the electoral strength of the coalition. The electoral contribution of the other three parties, the API, the SDP and the MAPU, was negligible, although they played an important political role as they gave the coalition a democratic and pluralistic image which the Communists and Socialists were keen to cultivate. The API and SDP were tiny political parties with no expectations of developing into larger political movements. However, their political importance stemmed largely from the fact that the handful of seats which they controlled in the Congress, added to those of the other government parties, made it possible for the Popular Unity to uphold the President's veto power and thus block unwanted legislation. The MAPU was the only one of the three with a potential for growth. It was formed by CDP dissidents who had broken off from the party in 1969. It derived its support mainly from the youth section and from the agricultural workers' unions affiliated to the party. It was also seen by the other members of the coalition as a vehicle for channeling the support of Catholics who, whilst supporting the Popular Unity's objectives, may have been inhibited from voting for a marxist.

The complex nature of the coalition explains why all its members, despite differences in size and ideology, had a claim to be treated as equal partners. This claim to equal treatment was reflected in cabinet appointments and in the decision-making procedure adopted by the Popular Unity. In the appointment of cabinet ministers the principle of proportionality was applied. Thus, members of the three big parties in the coalition were appointed to ten out of fifteen cabinet posts. The Socialist Party, the smallest of the big three according to the 1969 electoral results, was by far the most successful in the allocation of cabinet posts. Socialists were allocated four cabinet posts: Interior, Foreign Affairs, Housing and the Government's Secretariat. Besides, Pedro Vuskovic, a fellow traveller, who later joined the Socialist Party, was appointed Minister of Economics. The Communist and Radical parties each obtained three cabinet posts. Communists were appointed to head the Treasury, Labour and Public Works departments; while the Defence, Education and Mining departments were assigned to the Radical party. A member of the MAPU, Jacques Chonchol, a leading expert in agarian reform, was appointed to the Department of Agriculture. A member of the API was appointed to the Justice Department, while the SDP obtained two cabinet posts in the departments of Health and Land. To prevent government departments from being taken over by the ministers' party, the Popular Unity decided that the second most senior post in each department, the post of Under-Secretary, was to be held by a member of a different party from that of the minister.

The procedure the Popular Unity adopted to take decisions was based on the principle of unanimity. Not surprisingly, this method proved to be inefficient for it transformed the Popular Unity into a forum where its members would voice their disagreements over government policy, but which rarely took decisions. Moreover, even when decisions were made – such as those concerning the size of the state-controlled sector of the economy, measures to deal with inflation, or plans for the reform of education – they were often poorly-structured compromises, which had the effect of merely transferring policy disagreements from the level of formulation to the level of policy implementation. Hence, contradictory interpretations of policy flourished, causing great embarrassment to the government and increasing the distrust and sectarian behavior among members of the different sections within the coalition. Given the complex structure of the Popular Unity as a decision-making body, it is not surprising that Allende should have chosen to surround himself by advisers who did not belong to any of the Popular Unity parties. His political adviser, Joan Garcés, was a visiting academic from Spain; his chief economic adviser, Pedro Vuskovic, also an academic, was an economist who had worked for the United Nations Economic Commission for Latin America; and his legal adviser was Eduardo Novoa, a well-known criminal lawyer. It should also be pointed out that Allende's personal security was not organised by the Popular Unity parties but by individuals close to the MIR, the ultra-left organisation.

Composition of the Congress

Allende's unenviable position was further complicated by the fact that the Popular Unity parties did not control the majority of seats in the Congress. Indeed, none of the three electoral blocs which had competed for the presidency in 1970, the Right, the CDP and the Popular Unity, had overall control in either the Chamber of Deputies or in the Senate. This posed a problem for Allende, not only because of his government's commitment to carry out a major programme of reforms through legislation, but also because the forthcoming general elections, which would renew all the seats in the Chamber of Deputies and half the seats in the Senate, were not due to take place until March 1973; that is, more than two years after he had taken office. The two obvious possibilities for resolving his dilemma were to enter into an alliance with another party in the Congress or to call for a plebiscite.

The only party with which the Popular Unity could have made an alliance was the CDP. However, at the time, both sides to this hypothetical alliance would have regarded it as unrealistic. For there were groups in the CDP, mainly those close to Eduardo Frei, and in the Popular Unity, mainly the Socialists, for whom such an alliance would have been unacceptable as a matter of principle. The idea of a plebiscite was considered by the Popular Unity, shortly after it took office, but was discarded as impractical.[1] The mechanism of the plebiscite had in fact been introduced into the constitution by an amendment approved during the last year of the Frei administration. Thus, not even the law that was supposed to regulate it had been enacted. The plebiscite was conceived as a means of resolving conflicts which might arrive between the President and the Congress in the course of the approval of a constitutional amendment.[2] Had Allende decided to call for a plebiscite, he would have had to initiate a procedure, which, even assuming good faith on the part of the opposition parties, would have taken at least eight months to complete. Moreover, had the President sought through a plebiscite to dissolve Congress and call for a general election, the Popular Unity parties probably would have done very well; but given the vagaries of the Chilean electoral system and the overall balance of forces, it is unlikely that they would have obtained a majority of seats in the Congress. The idea of the plebiscite was therefore neither attractive nor practical.

Having rejected the option of a plebiscite and the possibility of forming a parliamentary alliance with the CDP, the government decided to begin implementing its programme, relying mainly on the broad regulatory powers vested in the executive branch. This was not an unreasonable decision since the balance of forces in the Congress created a paralysis of the legislative procedure which the government expected to exploit to its advantage. Although, together, the CDP and the National Party controlled more than 50 per cent of the seats in both houses they were short of the two-thirds majority required to override the President's veto. Thus, even in the event of an alliance between the CDP and the National Party, they would have been unable to approve legislation without the implicit consent of the President.[3]

The government's decision to implement its programme without first defining its position towards the CDP was also prompted by the fact that the two main parties in the coalition had different views about how to deal with the CDP. While the Communist Party was favourable to the idea of reaching some form of agreement with the CDP so that the government could have a working majority in the Congress, the Socialist Party completely ruled out such an alliance since, in its view, the CDP was a bourgeois party which would never agree to the socialist measures the Popular Unity government intended to take. Seen from this perspective, the government decision to initiate its programme without first defining its position towards the CDP was, interestingly enough, acceptable to both the Communist and Socialist parties, albeit for different reasons. The Communists regarded it as necessary for preparing the ground for negotiations with the CDP. They expected the Popular Unity's popularity would increase as soon as its policies began to take effect, thus it would have the upper hand in negotiations with the CDP over legislative measures. The Socialists, on the other hand, believed that the government's decision was consistent with their own political line and expected that, in due course, the progressive elements within the CDP would break away from the party to join the political forces backing the government. Thus, while the Communist Party believed that the government was preparing the ground for an alliance with the CDP, the Socialist Party believed that the government was preparing the ground for breaking up the CDP.

II STRATEGY: BACKGROUND

Shortly after the Popular Unity's electoral victory, Allende appointed Pedro Vuskovic to liaise with the authorities of the outgoing administration. Allende also asked Vuskovic to prepare a programme of action for the new government. Vuskovic was Director of the prestigious Institute of Economics of the University of Chile and had previously served at ECLA, the influential United Nations agency in the field of development economics. His credentials were those of a highly-qualified technical adviser who did not, at the time, belong to any political party.

Vuskovic, together with a small team of economists, submitted to Allende a document containing a programme of action.[4] This document was approved by the Popular Unity parties, and when Allende took office, Vuskovic was appointed to the cabinet to preside over the implementation of the government's economic policy.

Vuskovic's document contained a detailed policy for economic re-activation, which the government later implemented. But his team did not regard these neo-Keynesian measures as an end in themselves: they were meant to facilitate the implementation of the structural reforms. The assumption underlying his proposals was that the reactivation programme would make it possible to carry out a revolutionary transformation of society without disrupting the normal functioning of the economy, hence making it possible to maintain and improve the living standards of the working class, on whose electoral support the government depended. In this respect, his team did not regard their proposals as mere technical advice, but rather as a coherent strategy for the transition to socialism.[5]

Vuskovic's team did not produce a detailed statement on the crucial question concerning how to implement the programme of action. This was probably because the government could rely largely on the regulatory powers vested in the executive branch to put it into effect. As regards the proposals on structural changes, Vuskovic's work was complemented by the work of another group of technical experts led by Eduardo Novoa, an independent lawyer who later became Allende's legal adviser. According to Novoa, the Popular Unity did not need to obtain congressional approval to begin implementing its programme of structural reforms since existing laws gave the President broad powers to regulate economic activity.[6] Novoa's advice was a perfect complement to the programme of action prepared by the economists and contributed towards reinforcing Vuskovic's view that his team had in fact designed a viable strategy to bring about a socialist transition.

The Initial Policy

The government's initial policy was a short-term programme of economic reactivation based on a generous incomes policy and a substantial increase in public expenditure, mainly in public works and housing.[7] To implement it the government sought and obtained congressional approval for its incomes policy – a matter which the CDP could hardly afford to oppose – and for its budget – an area in which the powers of the Congress were seriously restricted.[8] Salary increases to public-sector employees were set at 35 per cent, a figure equal to the rate of inflation for 1970. Although this figure was only binding on the public sector it provided a lead which was generally followed in wage negotiations in the private sector.

Such an expansionist economic policy was based on several expectations about the behaviour of certain economic variables. According to government officials, the existence of above-average rates of idle capacity in the industrial sector, resulting from a mild recession during the final two years of the previous administration, made it reasonable to expect that the private sector would be capable of responding fairly quickly to the expansion of demand, thus absorbing the inflationary pressure which the incomes policy was bound to generate. It was also expected that the increase in public expenditure in housing and public works generally would act as a catalyst to mobilise economic activity in the private sector.[9] The government hoped to keep inflation within reasonable limits by means of a strict enforcement of price controls. This would be complemented by maintaining a fixed rate of exchange for the escudo in order to stabilise the cost of raw materials and other imports needed by industry. Since the fixed rate of exchange greatly over-valued the escudo, the government introduced a series of administrative controls over foreign trade.

Increase in public expenditure was to be financed by an increase in tax revenues. The government expected that an increase in copper production would yield greater tax revenues and that the overall improvement in economic activity would increase the yield of indirect taxes collected by the Treasury. The government naturally expected that its income policy would create a sharp imbalance between demand and supply of basic consumer goods, mainly foodstuffs. To deal with this, it had at its disposal an unusually high level of monetary reserves so that any shortages in the market would be covered by imports, without necessarily increasing the country's foreign debt.

According to the government's chief economic adviser, the objective of the short-term economic policy was to prepare the ground for transferring the commanding heights of the economy to the area of state property.[10] This transfer of property was to be achieved through legal procedures, as promised by the Popular Unity's programme. In its early days, the government seemed prepared to honour its promise: it proposed a constitutional amendment to nationalise copper, announced that it would introduce a bill to nationalise banks and other sectors of the economy and continued implementing the land-reform legislation approved during the previous administration. The cautious approach it adopted was also evident in other areas of policy making. Thus, to contain the growing political mobilisation which led to land seizures in the countryside and to the occupation of urban plots and factories, the government announced that it would use persuasion rather than repression. To prove its good intentions, it proceeded to wind up the riot-police unit. Such a non-conflictive approach was also followed in its foreign policy. Thus, contrary to its programme, it did not denounce treaties such as that of the Organisation of American States; it maintained, and in some respects intensified, the existing military links with the United States; and continued participating in the much-criticised American foreign aid programme, the 'Alliance for Progress'.[11] In this context its decision to establish diplomatic relations with Cuba and the People's Republic of China had largely a symbolic value.

Short-Term Economic Policy: Results

By the end of the government's first year in office, some indicators showed impressive achievements. The rate of inflation fell by thirteen points to 22 per cent, industrial production increased by 13 per cent, unemployment in Santiago stood at an all time low of 4.2 per cent and the share of labour in GNP rose by five points to 59 per cent. However, these achievements were overshadowed by other economic indicators showing that control over some economic variables was more limited than expected. The government's reactivation policy had generated an unprecedented expansion of demand which could not be met by domestic production. As a consequence, the government began to rely heavily on imports to meet demand for foodstuffs at a time when other external factors were beginning to impose serious constraints on the balance of payments. Meanwhile, a huge fiscal deficit had developed as a consequence of overspending and an unexpected drop in revenue. This deficit was financed by domestic borrowing, leading to a dangerously high increase of the money supply. Since the production bottlenecks which had caused sporadic shortages by the end of 1971 were likely to continue and the huge fiscal deficit was creating strong inflationary pressures, the government was confronted with the option of either continuing to support the existing levels of production, thereby risking an inflationary explosion, or taking measures to reduce the fiscal deficit at the cost of slowing down production and bringing about shortages of basic consumer goods. The government was aware of the political risks involved in taking either option, as well as the difficulties involved in striking a balance between the two.[12]

Many of the difficulties the government had to face during its first year in office can be attributed to miscalculations about the behaviour of key economic variables such as tax and export revenues or current expenditures. Such a managerial assessment of the Popular Unity's economic policy must be treated with caution since the highly politicised context in which the policy was implemented makes it difficult to examine economic decisions from a purely technical point of view. Nonetheless, its economic policy was based on assumptions and expectations which, for reasons beyond the control of the government and the opposition, did not obtain in practice.

The government's reactivation package was based on the assumption, familiar enough, that its incomes and public expenditure policies would increase demand, thus stimulating growth in production. However, in fact, the government's incomes policy brought about an expansion of demand that was far greater than expected. Indeed, after taking into account inflation, disposable income in 1971 increased by 30 per cent.[13] This was largely because the limits set by the government for wage re-adjustments were not respected.

The objective of the incomes policy was to compensate workers fully for inflation in the previous year. Accordingly, the government set a mandatory 35 per cent target for pay increases in the public sector. Since it did not have the power to make this target obligatory for the private sector, it enlisted the support of the CUT. In December

1970, the CUT formally agreed to the target set and undertook to ensure that the union movement would respect it in the forthcoming wage negotiations. However, neither the public nor the private sector complied with it. In the public sector remunerations increased by 40 per cent, while in the private sector the average increase was 50 per cent. This wage explosion, combined with a large increase in social benefits, mainly family allowances, led to an increase of the share of labour in GNP from 54 per cent in 1970 to 59 per cent in 1971. Hence, in one year the Popular Unity achieved the goal which it had planned to reach in six years.[14]

The spectacular increase in labour's share in income benefited all income groups, not just the poorest groups as the government had intended.[15] Nonetheless, this brought about an important shift in the pattern of demand for basic products, mainly foodstuffs. While in 1969 and 1970 the demand for foodstuffs had increased by 1.1 per cent and 1.3 per cent respectively, in 1971 it had increased by 13.7 per cent. According to calculations carried out at the time by an international research institute, about 70 per cent of this new demand was directly attributable to the government's incomes policy.[16] Meanwhile, as demand for food was increasing by 13.7 per cent, domestic production of food only increased by 6.7 per cent. The deficit was met by imports, and, as a consequence, the total volume of foodstuffs and beverages imported in 1971 increased by 43.5 per cent, while their costs increased by 55 per cent.[17]

The strain which the higher-than-expected import bill was putting on the balance of trade further aggravated the government's fiscal problems. Initially, the government had estimated that, in order to launch its programme of economic reactivation, a fiscal deficit of 20 per cent was acceptable. It expected to reduce this deficit in the future, as the state assumed control over the commanding heights of the economy and production was re-structured and made more efficient. In practice, however, government estimates proved to be badly off-the-mark. The fiscal deficit in 1971 was more than twice the amount originally budgeted, reaching nearly 50 per cent of effective income.[18] However, contrary to the claim often made by Allende's critics, the miscalculation leading to the deficit was the result not so much of overspending, as of a huge and largely unexpected drop in fiscal revenue.[19] It has been estimated that while the drop in expected revenue accounted for 90 per cent of the fiscal deficit, overspending – mainly on salaries – accounted for only 10 per cent.[20]

The fall in income was mainly due to the fact that taxes yielded less than expected. Although the revenue collected through indirect taxes increased by just over 15 per cent, the yield of direct taxes dropped by the same amount.[21] Thus between 1970 and 1971 tax revenue was virtually unchanged, despite the fact that in the same period public expenditure increased by almost 40 per cent.[22] The lower-than-expected yield of direct taxes was mainly because of the government's miscalculation in its estimates concerning the price and production of copper. The estimate for the price of copper in the 1971 budget was based on the rather favourable market conditions prevailing in 1970; however, in 1971 copper prices dropped by nearly 24 per cent. Likewise, production of copper in 1971 turned out to be 15 per cent lower than what the government had expected.[23]

The failure to reach production targets in copper can be attributed to two main factors. Firstly, it was caused by the production policies introduced by the United States-owned companies in the period immediately preceding nationalisation. The government's allegations that this caused a major setback in production was confirmed by the two independent technical reports it commissioned.[24] Secondly, it was caused by the innumerable difficulties arising from the transfer of administration after the nationalisation of copper.[25]

The fiscal deficit was financed almost entirely by domestic borrowing. This form of financing practically doubled the growth rate of money issued by the Central Bank, leading to a 119 per cent increase in the money held by the private sector.[26] During 1971 the inflationary pressures resulting from the rapid growth of the money supply were contained by the expansion of domestic production and by imports. However, by mid-1971, some constraints appeared in the productive structure, which showed that the government's assumptions about the levels of idle capacity, though accurate on average, did not apply equally to all sectors of industry. Hence, there were production bottlenecks which led to sporadic shortages of basic consumer goods. Likewise, the reliance on imports to maintain adequate levels of supplies on the market was rapidly draining the foreign exchange reserves.

The reliance on imports to meet the growing demand for food did not greatly increase the value of the import bill. Indeed, in 1971 the import bill increased by only 5.6 per cent.[27] Nevertheless, despite this small increase, there was a balance of trade deficit of eighty-eight million dollars because the value of export revenue had fallen by 10 per cent.[28] More dramatic than the increase were the changes in the composition and value of imports. While in 1970 foodstuffs and food industry imports accounted for 14 per cent of the value of imports, representing 9 per cent of export earnings, in 1971 they accounted for

19 per cent of the value of imports, representing 16 per cent of export earnings.[29] The change in the composition of imports was achieved at the cost of reducing the import of capital goods, which, in 1971, represented only 24 per cent of the value of all imports, while in the previous year it had accounted for 29 per cent.[30]

The capacity to import in 1971 had been based on the existence of an abundant supply of foreign currency reserves. However, during 1971 foreign sources of credit dried up as a consequence of the informal boycott applied by the United States government and by United States-owned banks. Thus, while in 1970 the net disbursement of foreign loans to Chile was 234 million dollars, in 1971 it only reached 28 million. Moreover, because throughout 1971 the government continued servicing the 2.5 billion foreign debt inherited from the previous administration, the net resource-flow between Chile and foreign lenders was negative, amounting to 52 million dollars.[31] This factor, combined with the rise in the import bill and the fact that foreign investment had also dried up, led to a balance of payments deficit of 299 million dollars, which was all the more shocking since in the previous year the balance of payments had shown a surplus of 100 million dollars.[32]

Towards the end of 1971, as pressure on the balance of payments was building up and it became apparent that the private sector was not re-investing the substantial profits obtained from the reactivation policy, the government began to consider the possibility of a devaluation. This topic was taboo to the Popular Unity since for years the marxist parties had been strongly opposed to the International Monetary Fund-induced devaluations applied by previous administrations. This is why, upon taking office, as proof of its determination to carry out an independent economic policy, the government announced that it would apply a fixed exchange-rate policy. The government expected that any imbalances arising from this policy could be controlled by the broad regulatory powers which the Central Bank had over foreign trade. But the government's attempt to regulate imports through the Central Bank proved more difficult than expected as it could hardly afford to reduce imports of foodstuffs and raw materials for industry, the two items which had accounted for nearly 70 per cent of all imports. Indeed, a restriction upon the importation of food would have hit hardest the lower-income groups that the government wanted to favour; while industrial imports could only be restricted at the cost of slowing down economic re-activation, on which the whole of the government's programme rested. Despite these difficulties, by the end of 1971, as domestic production began to slow down and applications for import licenses continued to increase, it became clear that it was no longer possible to rely exclusively on the regulatory powers of the Central Bank. The government was therefore forced to take the painful decision to devalue the escudo.

The December devaluation was a timid step, characteristic of the Popular Unity's decision-making style. It introduced a multiple rate of exchange, which, on average, devalued the escudo by 30 per cent. However, because the multiple rate of exchange had been carefully designed to minimize the impact of the devaluation on the cost of items of popular consumption – the main items on the import list – the devaluation did not achieve its goal of restraining imports and instead created strong inflationary expectations.

III POLITICAL STRUGGLE: YEAR ONE

Responses to Popular Mobilisation

The government confronted a spectacular increase in the level of popular mobilisation during its first year in office. By 1971 the number of strikes had increased by 50 per cent, while instances of direct action, mainly the occupation of agricultural land, factories, urban plots and educational establishments more than trebled during the same period.[33] The sharp rise in political mobilisation was undoubtedly brought about by the fact that the popular masses were aware of the government's sympathy towards their demands for economic and social improvements, as well as to the fact that the government had announced that it would not use force to deal with strikes or occupations. To some extent, the government's generous incomes policy also contributed towards increasing the level of political mobilisation. Indeed, this policy, which was obligatory only for public sector workers, prompted unions in the private sector to make huge wage claims leading in turn to lengthy negotiations often culminating in strikes and/or occupations. It should also be noted that workers used strikes and occupations to put pressure on the government to speed up the process of expropriation. This was particularly the case in the agricultural sector where, according to a survey carried out at the time, the objective of more than one-third of the 1300 cases of occupation reported in 1971 had been to secure the expropriation of the respective holding.[34] Such politically-motivated occupations also occurred in the industrial sector, although not with the same intensity.[35]

Having rejected force as a way of repressing strikes and dealing with occupations, the government was left with little but the power of persuasion. Thus in November 1970 Allende put his own political reputation on the line when he unexpectedly showed up at a construction site where a low-income housing estate was being built and attempted to establish a dialogue with the group which had occupied it.[36] Also, in order to deal with the alarmingly high rate of land seizures in the countryside, the government transferred the headquarters of the Department of Agriculture to Cautín, one of the provinces most seriously affected by land occupations and other acts of violence. However, these well-intentioned gestures did not resolve the underlying problem. Thus, less than three months after taking office, the government, recognising that its policy of persuasion had not worked, sent a bill to the Congress, which provided for the imposition of mild criminal sanctions on ringleaders of occupations, only when, as a result of the occupation, property had been damaged.[37] The intention of the government was to rely on the law as a deterrent, to avoid using direct repression. Not surprisingly, the opposition parties did not support the bill in the Congress, thus forcing the government to decide whether it should rely on the police to contain the growing popular mobilisation.

Taking over the Commanding Heights

As the government could not afford to repress its own supporters and was unable to persuade them to give up using strikes and occupations as political weapons, it began to give in to their demands. This would often take the form of an intervention decree by virtue of which the government would take over the administration of a farm, or industrial enterprise, in order to resolve the conflict and restore public order. Because of the government's peculiar role in these situations, the issuing of an intervention decree came to be regarded by workers as an expropriation or nationalisation. This led to a situation in which industrial conflicts were often artificially created so that the government was forced – or provided with the excuse – to issue intervention decrees.

There is little doubt that some of the parties within the Popular Unity, notably the Socialist Party, made use of strikes and other forms of political agitation in order to prepare the ground for government intervention.[38] Once the government had decided to issue the decree, workers would then demand that the enterprise in question should remain within the area of social property. The moderates within the Popular Unity, mainly the Communist and Radical parties, together with President Allende, openly criticised indiscriminate occupations and reaffirmed the Popular Unity's pledge that nationalisation would take place through legislation. However, not a single member of the coalition opposed the extensive use of intervention decrees, so that eventually the whole of the Popular Unity began to regard the enterprises affected by intervention measures as part of the new area of social property.[39]

It should be noted that the widespread use of intervention and requisition decrees during the government's first three months in office taught it an invaluable lesson on the extent to which the powers vested in the executive branch could be used to carry out its 'nationalisation' programme. Thus, the government began to use other mechanisms as well, such as the direct purchase of shares, the requisition of industries and the expropriation of certain enterprises. It began to use the administrative measures with caution, yet, by March 1971 their use had become firmly established policy. As a result, by the end of its first year, the government claimed to have nationalised the bulk of the country's mineral resources (including four United States-owned copper companies), more than 80 per cent of the banks, a large number of enterprises in the manufacturing sector and nearly 2.5 million hectares of agricultural land.[40]

By the end of 1971, the number of manufacturing enterprises controlled by the state had increased from 43 to 138, and the state accounted for over 20 per cent of production and 20 per cent of employment in manufacturing.[41] In the agricultural sector, the government applied the existing land-reform legislation, but greatly accelerated the pace of expropriations. Indeed, after one year in office the Popular Unity expropriated as much land as the previous government had in six years; and after eighteen months in office, it had expropriated all the land which could be expropriated under the terms of the existing law. While the previous administration had carried out 1,400 expropriations which accounted for 3.5 million hectares of land, the Popular Unity, during its first year, carried out another 1,400 expropriations which transferred 2.5 million hectares of land to the state sector. Thus, by the middle of 1972, the state controlled around 35 per cent of agricultural land, which in turn accounted for 20 per cent of employment in the sector.[42]

The fundamental economic changes the government introduced during its first year were all the more impressive since they were largely achieved without involvement by the Congress. Except for the nationalisation of copper, the government formed a new area of social property, relying exclusively on powers which the constitution and existing legislation had vested in the executive. Copper was national-ised by a constitutional amendment unanimously approved by the Congress and representing the culmination of the process began by President Frei in 1965.[43] Banks were transferred to the state sector through the purchase of shares by CORFO, the State Development Corporation. The expropriation of agricultural land was based on the existing Agrarian Reform Act, but its pace was greatly accelerated by a liberal interpretation of some of its provisions, including the wide-spread use of the intervention decrees mentioned above.[44] In the manu-facturing sector, administrative measures of intervention or requisition were applied to some 200 firms. Although, in some cases these mea-sures did not last more than a few months, by the end of 1971 about 138 firms were still under government control.[45] The practical effect of these two measures were the same: a state-appointed manager would take over the administration of the enterprise and the measure would remain in force until such time as the government deemed it to be necessary.

IV   REACTION OF THE OPPOSITION

The National Party

The nationalisation policy the government applied openly contradicted its pledge to carry out a programme of structural reforms through legislation. Yet Allende, as well as other leaders of the Popular Unity parties, mainly Radicals and Communists, continued to reaffirm this pledge promising that, in due course, the government would send several nationalisation bills to the Congress. The National Party con-sidered the nationalisation policy as evidence of the government's totalitarian inspiration and of its determination to abolish democratic freedom. It pointed out that the proliferation of occupations and other acts of violence, particularly those in the agricultural provinces of the south, were instigated by government officials to justify the issuing of intervention decrees designed to deprive people of their property. It also criticised the government's reluctance to use force against occupiers of private property, describing this as a challenge to police authority.[46] The government's decision to grant an amnesty in favour of several members of the MIR convicted of terrorist offences during the pre-vious administration was, according to the National Party, further evi-dence of the Popular Unity's determination to undermine democracy by making a travesty of the legal process. Thus, by March 1971 the National Party had instituted impeachment proceedings against two government ministers – Labour and Justice – on the grounds that they were in breach of their duty to respect the constitution and the law.

The Christian Democratic Party: a Dilemma

The Christian Democratic Party's response to the government's initial policies was more complex and ambiguous than that of the National Party. Throughout the government's first year in office, the CDP, still under the influence of progressive groups, constantly reaffirmed its commitment to socialism, albeit of a communitarian type, and claimed that its position was one of constructive opposition. This constructive approach was to some extent reflected in the parliamentary debate on the nationalisation of copper. Here the progressive groups of the CDP firmly supported the constitutional amendment sponsored by the government, thus preventing attempts by some of its right-wing members to use the debate as a means of scoring points against the government.[47] The support which the progressive groups within the CDP were willing to give the Popular Unity was acknowledged by Allende and the leaders of the Communist Party, who openly declared that closer cooperation with the CDP was a necessary pre-condition for the success of the Popular Unity government. Indeed, Tomic, writing after the military coup, has revealed that he and other CDP leaders maintained close personal contact with Allende. According to him, in December 1970, when the recently-elected chairman of the CDP visited Allende, he asked the President to help him and his party to become 'better Allendistas'.[48] But the progressive groups encountered many obstacles in their attempts at achieving this. Some of these obstacles came from within the party, while others came from the government itself.

Within the party, the progressive groups had great influence in the formulation of policy and in the election of party officers. However, the right-wing groups counted on the former President, Frei, the undisputed leader of the party and a man who was not prepared to make any concessions to the Popular Unity government. Through Frei, the right-wing groups had abundant financing, from domestic and international sources, which gave them access to the national press and radio.[49] Apart from their superior material resources, the right-wing groups also had the support of an impressive team of parliamentarians, many of whom owed their political careers to Frei. But perhaps the greatest obstacle the progressive groups encountered was the Popular Unity government itself. Indeed, in the internal conflict within the CDP the only way in which the progressives could make their views prevail was by showing that they were in fact capable of influencing the government, particularly regarding its nationalisation policy. Since on this and other points, the government seemed unwilling to compromise, it became increasingly difficult for the progressive wing to persuade the rest of the party to negotiate with the government.

The early conflict between the CDP and the government over the nationalisation of banks was to determine the nature of their relationship for the rest of the period. The Popular Unity had declared its intention to nationalise the banking sector in its programme. Although the CDP was not in principle against this, it had reservations, mainly over the need to safeguard bank employees and the general public from the dangers of a state-run monopoly. To calm the CDP's fears as well of those of the financial community, in December 1970 Allende announced that his government would shortly introduce a bill nationalising banks and establishing the rules which would govern this sector of the economy. This news was naturally welcomed by the CDP. However, not long after making this announcement, CORFO began to buy shares in the banks. The government explained this as an emergency measure intended to avert financial chaos and reaffirmed its pledge to send a nationalisation bill to the Congress. In the event, however, the government did not need to nationalise through legislation since in less than twelve months it had gained control of over two-thirds of the banks through the direct purchase of shares. This move caused great frustration among the progressive sectors within the CDP as it made a travesty of their efforts to cooperate with the government. As a consequence, the right-wing groups within the CDP were strengthened, and the whole party united in criticising what it described as the reckless manner in which the government was carrying out its programme of economic reforms.[50] This critical view about the political style of the Popular Unity was also borne out by the widespread use of intervention and requisition decrees in other sectors of the economy.

The discrepancy existing between the statements in which the government announced a particular course of action and its actual policy was worrying to all groups within the CDP. To the right-wing groups it was evidence that the Popular Unity was not serious about its own self-proclaimed legal road to socialism and that it would eventually lead the country towards a dictatorship of the proletariat. Such was the view held by Frei who, only ten months after the government had taken office, described the Popular Unity as a tool of the Communists, serving their totalitarian objectives.[51] Although the progressive groups would not at that stage have agreed with Frei's assessment, they were concerned that the failure to obtain anything but oral concessions from the government would not only affect their own credibility, but would cause a major crisis within the party. They naturally feared that the tactics of the Popular Unity would eventually either divide the party or push it towards the right.[52] This concern about the party's future led them to close ranks with the right-wing groups within the party, and this explains why the party appeared so united in its opposition to policy proposals made by the Popular Unity, even when some of these proposals should have appealed to the progressive groups.

For example, in the agricultural sector, the Popular Unity proposed the creation of Centre of Agrarian Reform (Centros de Reforma Agraria CERAS) as a transitional solution to organising production in holdings expropriated under the Agrarian Reform Act. Although the CERAS were perfectly legal and, from a technical point of view, probably justified, the CDP strongly rejected them and campaigned against them through the peasant unions under their control.[53] This action did not prevent the government from continuing to establish CERAS; however, it opened up new divisions among agricultural workers and greatly contributed towards creating a negative image of the CDP among the rank and file of the Popular Unity parties. CDP opposition to them was prompted by fear – partly justified – that the government would use them to undo the achievements of the agrarian reform under the Frei administration. Also the CDP regarded them as a weapon which Popular Unity parties could use to undermine its own influence within the recently-formed unions of agricultural workers.

The CDP's reaction to the government's proposals to create neighbourhood tribunals was similar to its reaction to the CERAS. The idea of creating neighbourhood tribunals was part of the government's attempt to introduce self-regulatory mechanisms in shanty-town areas, which would contribute towards maintaining public order without resorting to the police or to ordinary courts. Theoretically, this proposal was based on the simple idea that informal procedures for the administration of justice, based on participation by the local community, are more effective in repressing petty crimes and other forms of anti-social behaviour than the inefficient system of criminal justice prevailing in most less-developed countries.[54] However, the bill was strongly opposed by all major groups within the CDP on the grounds that it was a totalitarian idea, inspired by the experience of the Soviet Union and designed to undermine the authority and independence of the judiciary.[55] In view of this opposition, the government was forced to withdraw the bill from the Congress.

Opposition to the neighbourhood tribunals by the right-wing of the

CDP was predictable enough. However, that the progressive groups within the party were also opposed revealed the extent to which the CDP as a whole distrusted the political intentions of the government. Such was the distrust existing between the CDP and the government that, when the Supreme Court in an astonishing decision refused to lift the parliamentary immunity of a senator accused of being implicated in the assassination of General Schneider, the CDP, instead of criticising the court, launched a vociferous attack against a government minister who had expressed misgivings about that decision.[56]

The assassination of one of the most senior members of Frei's inner circle, carried out in June 1971 by members of an ultra-left organisation, contributed to weakening further the progressive group's position within the CDP. The final blow came in July 1971 when they were unable to persuade their party, or the Popular Unity, to form an electoral alliance to contest a by-election. Instead, the CDP ran its own candidate, who willingly accepted the support of the National Party. Its decision to accept electoral support from the National Party caused great anger and frustration among the progressives and led to the resignation of a small but influential group of leaders. These resignations were warmly welcomed by the Popular Unity, particularly by the Socialist Party, which saw them as confirmation that division within the CDP was inevitable.[57] However, the resignations caused only a minor dent in the strength of the party in the Congress. In fact, these resignations represented divisions within the ranks of the progressive members of the CDP rather than a division of the party. They did not affect the balance of forces at the national level, but they did mark the beginning of the party's steady move to the right.

Taking the Power Away from the President

The developments which, by mid-1971, led to a shift in position of the CDP, did not bring about an instant change in its tactics as an opposition party. For, while it became more openly critical of the government, it still refused to form a bloc with the National Party. The impeachment proceedings which the National Party brought against Vuskovic, the Minister of Economics, in September 1971, challenging the legality of nationalisation procedures employed by the government, provided the CDP with an opportunity to define its own independent opposition strategy. Until then, it had consistently refused to go along with the National Party's attempt to impeach cabinet ministers, but had been unable to offer an alternative strategy. As a result, the National Party was slowly beginning to assume the leadership of the opposition and was successfully re-establishing old links with the various employers' associations as it called for widespread grassroots resistance against government policies. These developments were naturally a cause of great concern to the CDP, but the allegations against Vuskovic provided it with the opportunity of taking an independent stand by making demands on the government to change its policy.

The main allegation in the impeachment proceedings against Vuskovic was that the procedures the government used to carry out its nationalisation policies were illegal – a point on which the CDP and the National Party agreed. However, instead of supporting the impeachment in the Congress, the CDP entered into direct negotiations with the government. As a result, the government promised to send a nationalisation bill to the Congress promptly in exchange for the CDP's abstention in the vote on the impeachment against Vuskovic.[58] In the event the CDP kept its promise, but the government did not, mainly because the Popular Unity parties could not agree on the content of the nationalisation bill.[59] Interpreting this delay as yet another example of bad faith, the CDP introduced in the Senate on 14 October 1971, a constitutional amendment taking away from the President the regulatory powers on which the government's nationalisation policy was based and declaring null and void any new purchase of shares by the government in private enterprises. The amendment provided that there would be three areas of property in the economy: social property, owned by the state, mixed property, and private property. But it also established that firms could only be brought into the area of social property by nationalisation, duly authorised through special legislation.[60] Prompted into action by the CDP's move, the government finally produced its own bill providing for the nationalisation of just over 250 enterprises, mainly in the manufacturing and commercial sectors. However, coming after the constitutional amendment proposed by the CDP, it had no chance whatsoever of being approved by the Congress.

Opposition Strategies Converge: the 'Empty Pots' March

The constitutional amendment sponsored by the CDP was such a fundamental challenge to the government's nationalisation policy that it was difficult to conceive how there could be any compromise between the CDP and the government. This situation had the effect of strengthening the position of the Socialist Party and other radical groups within the Popular Unity. The National Party announced it would support the amendment, thus assuring its approval. But the National Party continued to put pressure on the CDP to take more effective and co-ordinated action against the government. In this respect, the government's announcement in October 1971 that it intended to buy shares in the Compañía de Papeles y Cartones, a company which had monopoly control over the production and supply of paper, provided the National Party with a welcome opportunity to strengthen its links with the CDP.

Since both parties regarded the transfer of the company – known locally as the *Papelera* – to state control as a major threat to freedom of the press, their supporters launched a well-funded campaign, ostensibly designed to persuade shareholders not to sell to the government, but which in fact made use of the issue to mobilise public opinion against the government. Thus, small but well-publicised demonstrations were staged and a 'freedom fund' was established to help individual shareholders, who for economic reasons might have been forced to sell. But apart from the *Papelera* issue, the occasional shortages of basic consumer goods, mainly foodstuffs, became the most effective way of mobilising public opinion against the government. Thus, in early December, a march of some 2,000 women, mostly upper-middle class, carrying empty pots, was responsible for the issue of shortages being put on the agenda of the opposition and causing a major political problem for the government.

The 'empty-pots' march was presented as a spontaneous demonstration by housewives against an insensitive government determined to sacrifice the needs of the family to obtain its totalitarian objective. However, the spontaneity of the march was, to say the least, doubtful. Its participants were from the rich suburbs of Santiago; the only working-class women there were their maids. The march was carefully staged to achieve maximum publicity. The presence of Fidel Castro in Chile at the time ensured wide international coverage for the march. Besides, in a calculated act of provocation, the women marched under the protection of young members of Patria y Libertad and of the National Party, equipped with helmets and sticks. They achieved the response they had hoped for. Pro-government sympathisers were provoked into action and sporadic confrontations, lasting several hours, developed between the two sides.[61] To deal with this, the government, against the advice of Castro, declared a state of emergency, entrusting the military with the task of restoring law and order.[62] Led by General Pinochet, as head of the emergency zone, the military promptly restored law and order.

Taking advantage of the events surrounding the 'empty-pots' march, the CDP initiated impeachment proceedings against the Minister of the Interior, accusing him, *inter alia*, of failing to guarantee the right of assembly.[63] This time, the CDP, reversing its previous policy, also decided to participate with the National Party in an anti-government rally. However, even at this stage, the CDP still tried to distance itself from the National Party, pointing out that its participation was meant as a defence of basic civil rights, rather than a critique of the government's economic policy, however much they disagreed with some aspects of it.[64] But despite this disclaimer, the CDP and the National Party formed a *de facto* electoral alliance, which enabled them to defeat the Popular Unity candidates in two by-elections held in January 1972. The following month the Congress – with the vote of the CDP and the National Party – approved the CDP's constitutional amendment, thus paving the way for what was to become a major confrontation between Congress and the executive.

V   A REVOLUTIONARY STRATEGY?

The appointments of Vuskovic and Novoa as Minister of Economics and Legal Adviser to the President respectively would seem to indicate that the government had fully accepted their programme of action. This was true regarding the proposals on economic re-activation. However, as already noted, the government acted with considerable caution – even hesitation – on the proposals concerning the use of the President's regulatory powers to bring about changes in the ownership and control of the means of production. This could be regarded as a purely tactical consideration, since the government could not afford to proclaim openly that its nationalisation programme would be carried out without the intervention of the Congress. However, the government's attitude can be more clearly attributed to the differences existing between the Communist and Socialist parties. The Communists could not fully support a policy which in effect denied a meaningful role to the Congress since they believed that this would alienate the CDP, thus making impossible their goal of isolating and neutralising the local oligarchy and imperialism. The Socialists, for their part, supported this policy, but were unable to relate it to their own conception about the nature of the revolutionary process since they were aware that Vuskovic's measures did not amount to an alternative strategy for the conquest of power. In the absence of such a strategy the Socialists could not afford to repudiate the parliamentary system on which the Popular Unity's programme was based.

That Vuskovic's programme of action eventually became the basis of the Popular Unity's initial economic policy can be attributed simply to the fact that it was the only coherent proposal available to the government. Besides, although the two leading members of the coalition did not fully accept his programme, they did not reject it either. The Communists supported the requisition and intervention measures, but interpreted them as sanctions which the government had the right to impose against capitalists who had misbehaved.[65] This interpretation, or rather rationalisation, enabled the Communists to reconcile government policy with their own conception about the need to form an alliance with the CDP. The Socialists, for their part, supported the use of intervention and requisition decrees because, in their view, these measures would increase popular support for the government, thus weakening and finally eroding the base of support of the CDP.

The apparent economic and political success of the government's initial policy served to enhance Vuskovic's authority within the Popular Unity, giving credibility to his claim that this was indeed a revolutionary policy. By the end of Allende's first year in office, the Socialist Party had completely succumbed to the appeal of this policy and began to regard almost as counter-revolutionary any proposal for changing it. However, contrary to what the Socialist Party believed, the revolutionary potential of the government's initial policy was ambiguous, for though it generated massive popular support for the government, it did not succeed in changing the traditionally electoralist orientation of left-wing supporters.

The electoral success of the government during its first months in office was remarkable. During this short period, the government increased its electoral support by 10 points, thus accounting for nearly 50 per cent of the vote by April 1971. The Popular Unity parties naturally attributed this success to the virtues of the government's economic policy. However, this policy, based as it was on the manipulation of a few economic variables, was contributing towards reinforcing a style of political mobilisation which was ill-suited to the circumstances of the time. Indeed, the apparent ease with which the Popular Unity achieved its goal of increasing electoral support gave credence to the notion that support for the government could be achieved through clever manipulation of state power, rather than through direct political work at the grassroots level. Hence, the nearly fourteen thousand Popular Unity committees created during Allende's electoral campaign and supposed to form the basis of a people's power disappeared soon after he took office.[66] As the Popular Unity parties adopted a predominantly electoral style of popular mobilisation, they began to take for granted that working-class voters would automatically support them, thus neglecting to take into account the influence of the

CDP among them. Moreover, that the government proved to be such an effective vote-catcher led the Popular Unity parties to a senseless and often sectarian competition for votes, as the relative size of each party within the coalition determined the influence it would have on policy-making and the allocation of governments posts.

The initial economic policy had an interesting impact on the way the government defined its stance towards the opposition. Because this policy was based on the manipulation of regulatory legislation, the government began to act as if its economic achievements were immune from all political response by the opposition. It seemed to believe that as long as opposition parties acted within the law, they would not be capable of undermining Popular Unity policies. Hence, it is not surprising that when the opposition began to show its real strength, the government was not capable of responding with a coherent policy.

The great expectations placed by the Popular Unity on its economic policy also explain its ambiguous behaviour towards the CDP. On the one hand the government openly proclaimed its desire to reach an agreement with the CDP on its nationalisation programme, while on the other, the expectation that the populist appeal of its economic policy would soon provoke a significant split within the CDP led it towards complacency during its first year in office. It is well known that the Socialist Party expected that, sooner or later, the CDP would split right down the middle, thus making it unnecessary to enter into a parliamentary deal with the CDP. But there is also evidence that the Communist Party expected the CDP would split, although they openly advocated an early settlement with them.[67]

CHAPTER 13

Popular Unity: The Party of Government II

I   ELECTORAL COMPETITION AND POLITICAL FRAGMENTATION

By the end of 1971, as the opposition strategies of the CDP and National Party began to converge, the Popular Unity parties and the government started showing signs of political fatigue. Although in the municipal elections of April 1971 the Popular Unity parties increased their electoral backing by nearly 15 points, from 36 per cent to 50 per cent of the vote, they had not been able to transform these gains into effective support for the government. In fact, after only twelve months in office and despite its electoral success, the Popular Unity was weak and divided. Electoral competition among members of the coalition had deepened their ideological differences, and, as a consequence, the government had virtually lost its capacity for taking decisions. Membership in the Popular Unity had increased from six to eight parties as the result of divisions within the Radical Party and the MAPU. In both cases the splits had been prompted by the fact that a small group within each of the parties rejected what they perceived as a dangerous ideological evolution towards marxism. The disaffected Radicals formed the Partido de Izquierda Radical (PIR) and MAPU dissidents joined the group which, in August 1971, had left the CDP to form the Izquierda Cristiana (IC). Both the PIR and IC joined the Popular Unity and were each given a share of cabinet and other government posts. Although the Popular Unity did not overtly lose any support as a consequence of these divisions, the political fragmentation at the party level was symptomatic of more serious problems at the grass-roots level.

The electoral success of the government in 1971 had been brought about by the enormous political mobilisation triggered off by the mere

existence of a socialist President, rather than by any specific achievement of the government. The government was then confronted with
the difficult task of channelling this massive political energy towards
the realisation of its programmatic objectives. However, neither the
government nor the Popular Unity as a coalition was capable of putting forward a policy which would have allowed them to transform the
militancy of the masses into constructive political participation to
strengthen the position of the government. Instead, each party was
left on its own to compete against other members of the coalition for
the newly-found left-wing supporters. As a result, electoral competition among the parties intensified, leading to bitter disputes at local
and trade-union levels, and to the development of sectarian practices
to secure government jobs for their members. This type of electoral
mobilisation not only failed to control and channel the growing militancy of the masses, but increased it. Indeed, the proliferation of
occupations and other forms of direct action, initially prompted by
real economic grievances, was soon instigated by some of the Popular
Unity parties – mainly the Socialist Party – as a means of enhancing
their electoral influence among industrial workers and peasants and of
forcing the government to adopt more radical economic policies. Faced
with this situation, the government's attempt to dissuade its supporters
from taking direct action was a complete failure. Instead, it was the
government that was 'persuaded' into action by the militants and
forced to issue intervention decrees to restore law and order.

Underlying the electoral competition among the Popular Unity
parties were the well-known differences between the Socialist Party
and the Communist Party. The Socialist Party believed that the
government should act quickly and take over the commanding heights
of the economy by all the means at its disposal, without waiting for an
agreement with the CDP. The Communist Party, for its part, believing that agreement with the CDP was essential for securing the implementation of the Popular Unity's Programme, advocated restraint and
condemned the indiscriminate use of factory-and land-occupation.
But the Communist Party was either unable or unwilling to control
effectively the radical elements within the Socialist Party. Throughout
the first year in office, the Communist Party acted as if the Socialist
Party's radical position was due to the influence of the MIR among its
leadership. Hence it concentrated its attacks on the MIR, describing
them as agents of United States imperialism and attempting to dis-
credit its leaders.[1] This type of attack not only increased the popularity
of the MIR among the rank and file of Popular Unity supporters, but
also missed the point, since neither the MIR nor other ultra-left groups

were responsible for the growing militancy of the popular masses. Hence, attacking the MIR – whose national political influence was negligible – did not resolve the problem at hand. Indeed both the MIR and the Socialist Party, as well as the Communists, were simply riding on a wave of popular mobilisation triggered off by Allende's victory, which could not be controlled through traditional methods of electoral competition.

The events surrounding the 'empty-pots' march of December 1971, combined with the impending approval by the Congress of the constitutional amendment sponsored by the CDP, forced the Popular Unity to reassess its position. Symptomatic of the Popular Unity's weakness was its humiliating defeat in the two congressional by-elections held in January 1972. However, by far the most important factor prompting the Popular Unity into action was the realisation that its short-term economic policy had reached a dangerous deadlock and that unless it was modified the economy would not grow and inflation would reappear in force.

II UNFOLDING OF THE POLITICAL STRUGGLE

Re-assessing the Strategy

The political and economic problems the government confronted by the end of its first year prompted a formal meeting of all the Popular Unity parties to re-assess their strategy. The meeting was held at El Arrayán, a suburb of Santiago, and its agenda was largely based on a document prepared by the Communist Party, which was later leaked to the right-wing newspaper *El Mercurio*. In it, the Communist Party acknowledged that the political and electoral strength of the government had been weakened and suggested that this was because of the Popular Unity's failure to isolate its main enemies, the landed oligarchy, the local monopolies and imperialism. This fundamental strategic failure had made possible the establishment of an informal alliance between the National Party and right-wing groups of the CDP. To prevent this alliance from consolidating there should be negotiations with the CDP over the Popular Unity's nationalisation programme. These negotiations would thus neutralise the CDP and provide the Popular Unity with an institutional channel to reach the popular masses supporting the CDP.[2]

At the Arrayán meeting, the Popular Unity tackled the crucial problem of how to correct the imbalances which its economic policy had generated. Two possibilities were considered: the first was to ease goverment control over the economy, thus allowing market forces to operate more freely; and the second was to apply more specific measures of economic regulation, thus increasing control over the economy. The first possibility was discarded since the prevailing view was that in the forthcoming year, 1972, as the nationalisation of the commanding heights of the economy was completed, the government would have at its disposal the means to apply direct and effective controls over prices and production, thus correcting the imbalances of the previous year.

The Popular Unity's confidence in being able to continue using the regulatory powers of the executive branch while attempting to reach agreement with the CDP on its nationalisation policy was not altogether groundless. Indeed, shortly before the Arrayán meeting, the government had made a major concession in its efforts to reconcile its nationalisation policy with the CDP's position. It published a list in which the number of enterprises to be nationalised was reduced from 250 to 90. This list of named enterprises was meant to restore confidence among those members of the local bourgeoisie whose companies were not listed, and to provide a basis for negotiations with the CDP. Having made this concession it is not surprising that the Popular Unity decided that – in conjunction with opening up negotiations with the CDP – priority should be given to transferring to state control the ninety enterprises and to completing the expropriation process in the agricultural sector. Accordingly, although concerned about the size of the budget deficit, the Popular Unity parties regarded it as an evil to be tackled as soon as their nationalisation programme had been implemented. This explains why, at the Arrayán meeting, the Popular Unity did not take the most obvious financial measure; namely another devaluation of the escudo.[3]

The CDP's Constitutional Amendment

Shortly after the Arrayán meeting the Congress approved the CDP-sponsored constitutional amendment. As expected, the government vetoed it. The veto accepted the principle that nationalisations should be carried out by law, but provided that the enterprises on the government's list would be nationalised immediately. Thus, the government expected the veto to provide the basis for negotiations with the CDP.[4] Negotiations between them commenced not long after the Arrayán meeting. However, it soon became clear that not all the Popular Unity parties were keen to reach an agreement with the CDP along the lines of the decision taken at Arrayán. By mid-February, the central committee of the Socialist Party issued a statement effectively disassociating the party from the talks the government was about to begin with the CDP. In its statement, the central committee advocated more participation by the popular masses in the revolutionary process initiated by the Popular Unity, but strongly rejected the notion that this participation could be brought about through 'super-structural agreements' with the leadership of political parties, which, in daily political practice act in a reactionary manner.[5] This statement, apart from undermining the spirit of the agreement reached at Arrayán, openly contradicted the policy advocated by the Communist Party in the document it put forward there. Nonetheless, despite the serious policy disagreements, talks between the government and the CDP over the question of the veto were held in March 1972. Given the circumstances discussed above, it is not surprising that the talks failed to produce an agreement.

The collapse of the talks was surrounded by controversy, the CDP claiming that agreement had at one time been reached, but that the government had unexpectedly backed down. The government, for its part, giving credence to the CDP's allegations, stated that the Popular Unity representatives had acted outside their brief.[6] Since the negotiations had been conducted by members of the PIR, and the government's interpretation of the negotiations questioned the political and moral integrity of the individuals concerned, the PIR decided to break away from the Popular Unity and join the opposition.[7] Their departure from the Popular Unity did not affect the balance of political forces as this was a tiny party with an insignificant representation in the Congress. However, in broader political terms, the events surrounding the PIR episode were a reflection of the Popular Unity's chronic inability to implement collective decisions.

The policy disagreements prevailing within the Popular Unity were undoubtedly an important factor accounting for the collapse of the talks between the government and the CDP. However, it must be noted that the CDP's inflexible position made a successful outcome unlikely. Indeed, on 2 March, shortly after the government had sent the Congress the veto containing its list of ninety enterprises, the CDP, together with the National Party, issued a statement, which essentially defined the long-term institutional strategy the opposition was to follow until the military coup. Taking advantage of an ambiguous and highly controversial clause in the constitution, the opposition parties declared that the President's veto could be rejected by the Congress by a simple majority of votes. The government, on the other hand, argued that Congress required two-thirds of the votes to reject the veto. But the opposition argument went one step further, for it also claimed that if the Congress rejected the veto, the government should either accept its decision or call for a plebiscite. The opposition parties also declared in their statement that the recently-established Constitutional Tribunal did not have jurisdiction to resolve the conflict which might arise if the government held – as in fact it did – a different view.[8] Thus, in early March 1972, the opposition had already outlined in clear terms the itinerary which the conflict between Congress and the executive was to follow during the next eighteen months. The extent to which the CDP was committing itself to an inflexible policy is underlined by the fact that this document also accused the government of preparing the violent overthrow of the rule of law and democracy.[9]

Early in March the opposition parties and other groups began to coordinate policies more closely. At a meeting hosted by the President of the Confederation of Employers' Organisations (Confederación de la Producción y del Comercio), leading figures of the CDP joined members of the National Party and of Patria y Libertad to discuss the erosion of traditional values, such as the family, Christian religion and respect for the fatherland. The Popular Unity described the meeting as subversive and linked it to a conspiracy to topple the government, involving the notorious General Viaux.[10] In recent years, General Pinochet has claimed that it was around this time, April 1972, that he and other senior officers began to consider seriously the possibility of a military coup.[11] At the time, however, the opposition parties dismissed the government's accusations as an attempt to divert attention away from the catastrophic consequences of its economic policy.[12] Given the close involvement of the CDP with the National Party and Partria y Libertad what is surprising is not that the talks with the government failed, but that they took place at all. The explanation for this lies in the fact that, at that stage, the CDP could not afford to adopt an unequivocal opposition policy for fear of losing its working-class support.

In March the government resumed the requisitioning of industries, despite the fact that it was simultaneously conducting delicate negotiations with the CDP over the veto. During that month, seven firms were 'nationalised' by the government through the requisition process: that is, more firms than in any other month to date except for May 1971, when the government had taken over the administration of twelve textile firms.[13] Two explanations can be advanced to justify this obviously contradictory behaviour on the part of the government. The first would attribute the new wave of requisitions to a conscious attempt by the leadership of the Socialist Party to boycott negotiations with the CDP. This explanation is consistent with the policy statement issued by the Central Committee in mid-February, which I have already discussed. It also appears to be confirmed by the fact that requisition decrees were issued by the Department of Economics, which at the time was firmly controlled by Vuskovic, who had fully identified himself with the radical leadership of the Socialist Party. The second explanation would interpret the requisitions as an attempt by the government to show the strength of its commitment to the nationalisation of the ninety enterprises on its list, thus warning the CDP that it would not accept delaying tactics. Both explanations are plausible; I am inclined to favour the first although there is no conclusive evidence in support of either.

By deciding to concentrate on the nationalisation of the ninety enterprises the government had in fact placed its future in the hands of the CDP as agreement on the veto was the only legal way for it to achieve this objective. After the collapse of the negotiations, the CDP moved closer towards consolidating its incipient alliance with the National Party, and even some well-known progressives in the party openly expressed doubts about Allende's democratic convictions.[14] But, while failure of the talks had in fact foreclosed the possibility of a compromise within the constitutional framework, it did not lead to a major shift in the position of either government or the CDP. On the contrary, it increased the ambiguity in the behaviour of both sides.

Populism and Market Shortages

After the collapse of the negotiations, the government had no legal mechanism at its disposal to fulfil its nationalisation programme. It was therefore forced to continue paying lip-service to the idea of a negotiated settlement with the CDP, while still relying on its *de facto* nationalisation policy, consisting of intervention and requisition decrees. Thus, the official statements by the government became more contradictory than ever as, on the one hand, it continued to advocate strict observance of the rule of law, while attempting, on the other, to provide revolutionary leadership to the working class. Likewise the CDP, instead of immediately embracing right-wing positions, maintained one foot firmly within the opposition camp and the other within its own vaguely-defined universe of communitarian socialism. This enabled it to participate in anti-government demonstrations with the National Party in which they ridiculed government allegations about military conspiracies and accused the government of instigating violence and intimidation.[15] At the same time, it presented itself as the champion of the working class, advocating the right of workers to participate fully in the administration of nationalised enterprises and supporting huge wage claims, which they knew would further contribute to disrupting the government's economic policy.[16] Thus, as the government simultaneously made use of the ideologies of order and revolution, the CDP started to combine reactionary and populist ideologies.

It was relatively easy for the CDP to adopt a populist approach during the wage negotiations which took place in the first quarter of 1972. Wage settlements were far greater than the targets already agreed between the government and the CUT as a consequence of strong inflationary expectations and lack of discipline within the rank and file of the Popular Unity. Thus in 1972, the targets the government had set for its incomes policy were again overshot. While it recommended increases of 22 per cent, the rate of inflation in 1971, actual wage increases reached 34.6 per cent in the private sector and 47.7 per cent in the public sector.[17]

Another reason for the CDP to adopt a populist posture was the forthcoming elections to renew the leadership for the CUT. Held in late April, they were the first direct elections ever held by the CUT. Until then, senior posts had been allocated to political parties on the basis of a quota representing their assumed strength in the union movement. Since the early 1960s as the CDP increased its influence among organised workers, this method had consistently under-represented the CDP and over-represented the Socialist Party.

The results of the CUT elections were as follows: Communist Party 33 per cent, Socialist Party 29 per cent and CDP 25 per cent.[18] These results were significant since they confirmed that the marxist parties no longer exercised exclusive control over organised workers. Indeed, only a year earlier, the CDP had been allocated 20 per cent of the seats in the CUT executive. After these elections, the CDP could claim the same share of seats as the Socialist Party. Moreover, in the province of Santiago, the CDP won the elections by a comfortable margin, thus taking control over that influential branch of the CUT.[19] Thus, while the Popular Unity parties continued to have majority control in the national executive the leader of the CUT in the important province of Santiago was a Christian Democrat.

The Socialist Party and Communist Party responded differently to the electoral results of the CUT. The Socialist Party, which had in fact been the main loser, purported to ignore the significance of the results, presumably on the ground that workers who voted for the CDP would soon realise their mistake and join the ranks of the Popular

Unity. The Communist Party, on the other hand, saw these results as confirmation of their long-held view regarding the need to establish a dialogue with the CDP. An article in *Principios*, the Party's theoretical journal, in May 1972, notes that the Popular Unity should re-affirm the primary role which unions should play in the representation of working-class interests.[20] Coming only weeks after the results of the CUT elections, this statement was not only a friendly gesture towards the CDP, but also a reminder to the Socialist Party that the Communist Party was prepared to recognise the real influence of the CDP in the labour movement.

The poor results obtained in the CUT elections was one problem among the many worrying the Communist Party. In the article mentioned above, the Communist Party refers to the increasing isolation of the government, a theme also mentioned in its February document. According to the Communist Party, the government was rapidly losing support from among social groups and classes which should otherwise be supporting the Popular Unity's anti-imperialist struggle. The primary task was therefore to make substantial concessions in favour of these groups so as to strengthen the government's base of support.

The Communist Party, together with the Radical Party and President Allende himself, were concerned at the strength of anti-government feeling expressed by white-collar workers both in the state and in private sectors. Undoubtedly, the newly-found militancy among this group of workers, described by some as the middle strata, had not occurred spontaneously, but had been instigated by the increasingly well co-ordinated political campaign of the opposition.[21] However, the government was aware that they had genuine grievances, which provided a focus for the activities of the opposition. In the first place, given the high inflationary expectations prevailing at the time, white-collar workers felt at a particular disadvantage by comparison with the traditionally better-organised manual workers, who by flexing their industrial muscle knew that the government would eventually give in to their demands. Thus, in May, the government confronted six major strikes in the state sector, two of which included workers in the newly-nationalised copper mines and three involved white-collar workers.[22] In the second place, rising inflation was slowly making the price control system redundant, bringing about undesirable consequences for the government. On the one hand, shopkeepers were becoming increasingly alienated from the government as they could not comply with the artificially low official prices for basic consumer goods. On the other hand, the near breakdown of the price control mechanism led to shortages of goods in the market and to the emergence of a black market in which these same goods would be traded at about two or three times their official value.[23] Since the middle-income groups were the most seriously affected by shortages – as the black-market was cleverly manipulated by the opposition – it is not surprising that they turned against the government. In the third place, insecurity among middle-income workers was further reinforced by sporadic acts of violence, mainly in the agricultural sector, and by the continuing use of factory occupations and other forms of direct action as ways of pressurizing the government. All this was magnified by the opposition-controlled media, which naturally, linked the shortages of consumer goods and social unrest to a carefully prepared plan to introduce a totalitarian system of government.[24]

Early in June, the Popular Unity parties once again held a high-level meeting to consider changes to the government's economic policy. This meeting – held in Lo Curro, a Santiago suburb – was successful. For the first time, the Popular Unity parties were able to agree to change along the lines advocated by Allende and by the Communist Party. The most important decision they took was to restore the balance between supply and demand through a re-adjustment of prices, rather than through administrative measures as advocated by the Socialist Party. This market-orientated adjustment also required further devaluation of the escudo, as well as strict observance of the government's incomes policy. They also agreed to assign top priority to improving the management of 'nationalised' enterprises and to increasing levels of production, particularly in the copper and agricultural sectors. Finally, it was agreed that the government should again try to reach an agreement with the CDP on the question of the veto.[25]

A New Round of Negotiations

Negotiations between the government and the CDP were held immediately after the Lo Curro meeting and lasted for nearly one month. The government was aware that this was the last chance it had to secure parliamentary approval of its nationalisation programme. The youth section of the CDP, also aware of the importance of the negotiations, called for the creation of a broad alliance to support democratic socialism and prevent armed confrontation.[26] During the negotiations the government made important concessions: it agreed to reduce to eighty the list of enterprises to be nationalised, it agreed to introduce some of the CDP ideas on workers' management in the administration of nationalised industries; and it conceded that the powers of

231

the government to intervene and to requisition industries should be limited.[27] Despite the progress made during the course of the negotiations, the CDP executive council did not endorse them, and in early July it ordered its senators to vote against the government veto. This surprise decision, allegedly prompted by the direct intervention of Frei, brought about an angry exchange between the negotiators.[28] In constitutional terms, however, it effectively marked the end of the Popular Unity's legal road to socialism, for after the Senate had rejected the presidential veto, it was inconceivable that Congress would ever approve the government's nationalisation programme. Moreover, after the Senate vote, the President was, according to the interpretation put forward by the opposition, legally bound either to promulgate the constitutional amendment approved by the Congress, or to call for a plebiscite.

After the collapse of the second round of negotiations with the government, the CDP moved unequivocally towards the National Party. The ambiguity in the behaviour of the CDP throughout the CUT elections and during the June negotiations with the government had now disappeared. In July, the CDP joined with the National Party, voting in favour of the impeachment of the Minister of the Interior. It also introduced another constitutional amendment, which, purporting to protect the small landowners and to guarantee freedom of commerce, was in fact meant to curtail severely the government's capacity to re-structure agricultural production and regulate the distribution of basic consumer goods.[29] The CDP's move to the right was formalised with the establishment of the Democratic Confederation (Confederación Democrática CODE), an electoral alliance uniting all anti-government parties.

Meanwhile, as the opposition centralised and coordinated its political activities, other organs of the state began to express more explicitly their distaste for government policies. The Comptroller-General, an independent civil servant entrusted with the function of controlling the legality of government actions, had, since the middle of 1971, consistently ruled that requisition decrees were illegal. To reach this conclusion, he had changed his formalistic approach to legal interpretation to one inspired by American legal ideology which emphasised the purposes and objectives of the law.[30] The government overcame this obstacle by issuing 'insistence decrees', which effectively overruled his interpretation. However, the individuals and companies whose property had been affected by requisition decrees sought and obtained the judiciary's protection. By mid-1972, the judiciary, relying mainly on the new approach to legal interpretation developed by the Comptroller-

General had already begun to challenge the legality of government requisition orders and to impose serious restrictions on the powers of state-appointed managers.[31] Thus, apart from the continuing constitutional conflicts between government and the Congress over the majority necessary for rejecting the President's veto, there now appeared another conflict which was to contribute to undermining even further the legitimacy of the government's nationalisation policy.

Disintegration of the Popular Unity

While the failure of the negotiations had the effect of bringing the opposition closer together, for the government the effect was the opposite. The Socialist Party, which had never had expectations about the outcome of the negotiations, held a plenary meeting in July, at the end of which one of the members of the central committee declared that, in view of the failure of negotiations, the Popular Unity had begun to consider other means of securing the implementation of its programme.[32] Shortly thereafter, the local branch of the Socialist Party in the province of Concepción, together with the MIR and the other members of the Popular Unity, except the Communist Party, held what was to be the first meeting of a self-styled People's Assembly, which called for the immediate dissolution of the Congress and the creation of popular power.[33]

The People's Assembly of Concepción had serious political implications for the government, which went well beyond the revolutionary rhetoric of the participants. Concepción was the third largest industrial city in the country and as such had an important concentration of industrial workers who traditionally supported either the Communist or Socialist parties. Since the early 1960s, it had also been the home-base of the MIR, and the focus of radical political activity by agricultural workers, members of the traditional proletariat and students. Although the Communist Party and the Socialist Party had different views about the MIR they both accepted that the existence of the Popular Unity government implicitly ruled out of order the MIR's ultra-left tactics. This fragile understanding between them was shattered with the advent of the People's Assembly. For, at that meeting, the local branches of all but one of the Popular Unity parties accepted the basic assumption underlying the political position of the MIR; namely, that the natural allies of the proletariat were not the middle strata, as represented by the CDP in the Congress, but the peasants and urban poor. Hence the call for the dissolution of the Congress and the creation of popular power through a new revolutionary alliance.

The People's Assembly of Concepción was promptly disowned by the Popular Unity parties at the national level. However, aware that it was more than just a passing episode, Allende sent a letter to each of the Popular Unity parties demanding unequivocal support for the government and reminding them that popular power would not come about through divisionist tactics based on a romanticised and unrealistic view of reality.[34] The Communist Party replied to Allende's letter, reaffirming its loyalty to the government and to the principles on which the Popular Unity was based.[35] The Socialist party, though pledging its support to the government, refused to condemn the members of its Concepción branch, thus suggesting it was not entirely in disagreement with the ideas put forward at that meeting.[36] From then on, the Socialist Party began to play more openly the comfortable role of left-wing opposition to the government, while maintaining its members firmly in key government posts. The Socialist Party's ambiguous position not only contributed to giving credence to the opposition's claim that the government was committed to extremist policies, but also contributed to undermining even further the efficacy of government action.

Implementing the New Economic Policy

Implementation of the economic policy changes agreed at Lo Curro began in August, a most unfavourable political moment for the government. After replacing Vuskovic at the Department of Economics by another member of the Socialist Party more in tune with the new political objectives, and appointing Orlando Millas, the Communist theoretician who had inspired the Lo Curro agreements, to head the Department of Finance, the government ordered a major devaluation of the escudo. This devaluation maintained the system of multiple exchange-rates, bringing down the value of the escudo by 33 per cent for export trade and by 85 per cent for import trade.[37] Responding to the devaluation and anticipating major changes in prices, the private sector withdrew basic consumer goods from the market. To prevent panic the government immediately granted generous price re-adjustments to firms in the private sector, while it considered a level at which it would set the prices of goods produced by the state sector.

The impact of this price increase was immediate and devastating. Prices increased between 30 per cent and 150 per cent, and the accumulated rate of inflation peaked from 28 per cent in the first six months of the year to 100 per cent in the nine months up to September. The inflationary pressure released by these measures took the government by surprise, provoking sharp criticisms from within the Popular Unity parties, mainly the Socialist Party, and generating a wave of unrest among government supporters as inflation began to erode the income gains that had been achieved during the government's first year in office. The opposition quickly took advantage of the growing discontent brought about by the upsurge of inflation and began demanding that the government should compensate wage earners for their income losses. Confronted by this two-pronged opposition, the government lost its nerve and decided to stop implementing the new economic policy. It also introduced a bill in the Congress giving each worker a supplementary bonus to compensate for inflation. The opposition approved the government's bill, but refused to give it adequate financing. Thus, the government's attempt to change the course of its economic policy ended in shambles: it had generated inflation without resolving the fiscal deficit and had not given the government greater control over production and distribution in the nationalised sector of the economy.

The political weakness of the Popular Unity encouraged the *gremios* to intensify their action. By the end of August shopkeepers had held a one-day national strike in protest at the death from heart attack of one of their members, which they attributed to abusive behaviour by government officials. Lorry drivers, for their part, were threatening a national strike unless granted substantial increases in freight rates and special treatment by the Central Bank to import badly-needed tyres and spare parts for their lorries. Taking advantage of this wave of discontent, the opposition parties launched a major offensive.

In September, while Allende was denouncing the existence of a military conspiracy against his government, leading members of the CDP were accusing the President of being directly responsible for the climate of hatred prevailing in the country.[38] They were also claiming that the democratic forces in the CODE were ready to defend the country against the totalitarian threat posed by the government.[39] Later in the same month, the National Party began to argue that the Allende government could no longer guarantee fair elections in the forthcoming general elections of March 1973.[40] This claim was a more elaborate version of an allegation put forward earlier by Patricio Aylwin, a leading senator on the right wing of the CDP, according to which the government was slowly losing its claim to political legitimacy.[41]

The National Party quickly grasped the significance of this charge against the government. On 6 October one of its leading spokesmen in the Senate declared that his party had come to the conclusion that the government was no longer involved in isolated breaches of the law, but in a systematic and carefully-planned attempt to undermine the constitution. Hence, according to the National Party, the government had already become illegitimate.[42] Thus at a CODE rally held on the eve of what was to become a major offensive by the opposition against the government, the leading speakers called for an end to purely oral accusations, demanding instead immediate action.[43] Following this rally, the lorry drivers called for an indefinite national strike in protest against the establishment of a state-owned transport agency in one of the southern provinces. This action by the lorry drivers took the government by surprise as it had only recently agreed to meet their demands for higher freight tariffs and easier access to foreign exchange to buy spare parts. The lorry drivers were immediately supported by the National Party and CDP, and shortly afterwards they were joined in their strike by taxi drivers, shopkeepers, the Association of Owners of Small Industries, the Secondary Students' Federation, the Law Society, the Medical Association and an assortment of professional and technical associations.

Initially, the lorry drivers put forward specific demands relating to their work. However, at the end of the first week of the strike, they established a centralised command and began to put forward demands on behalf of the CDP and the National Party: mainly, that the government should enact immediately the constitutional amendment reversing the government's nationalisation programme, that grassroots organisations should not be involved in the distribution of consumer goods, and that administrative measures against opposition-controlled media should be lifted.[44] But the well-coordinated strike, which counted on financial and logistical support from the CIA, was met by an unprecedented mobilisation of left-wing supporters in defence of the government.[45] Industrial production was maintained as workers prevented the lockout of big and medium-size firms. Likewise, companies under government control continued work as usual. Moreover, through voluntary work, Popular Unity supporters kept the channels of distribution open as far as they could, ensuring that basic goods would reach the consumer in the poorer sections of the main cities. Government control over the banking system ensured normal operating in this critical sector. The October strike in fact gave a boost to the newly-formed *cordones industriales* and *comandos comunales*, two grassroots organisations which were to play a prominent role during the final months of the Allende administration.

To maintain public order during the strike the government placed most of the country under the control of the armed forces. The opposition strongly criticised it for doing this, claiming that it was using the armed forces to achieve political ends. However, they were disappointed to discover that the military remained obedient to the government throughout the conflict. Two factors may explain this. On the other hand, that the government received such overwhelming support from the Popular Unity parties and from grassroots organisations throughout the country must have impressed the military. Moreover, this support was expressed in such a militant and disciplined manner that even the government was surprised. On the other hand, that the National Party and the CDP did not agree on the ultimate objective of the strike must have disconcerted them. Indeed, while the National Party was openly seeking to provoke a military coup so as to establish an efficient nationalist government, the CDP, aware that it would play only a subordinate role in such a proposed government, toned down its support for the strike and called upon its supporters to wait until March 1973, the date of the forthcoming congressional elections, to settle their political accounts with the government.[46]

Meanwhile, as the CDP and the National Party adopted different tactics, the strike began to lose momentum. On 2 November, Allende appointed a cabinet which included three senior members of the armed forces. General Prats, the Commander-in-Chief of the army was appointed Minister of the Interior and entrusted with the task of resolving the strike. Four days after the new cabinet took office, the strike had come to an end. By resorting to the military, the government had found the solution to a conflict which had lasted for nearly one month, and it was also a solution acceptable to the CDP. However, it was now nearly the end of 1972, and the government had still not been able to introduce the badly-needed changes to its economic policy and now found itself in the peculiar situation of having to share power with the military.

III   POWER-SHARING: MILITARY ENTER THE CABINET

The military agreed to serve in Allende's cabinet in order to restore social peace and to ensure that the forthcoming general elections of March 1973 would be free and fair. The results of that election did not alter the balance of forces in the Congress. However, the prolongation of the deadlock radicalised both sides of the political divide. On the government side, the inconclusive results strengthened the radical wing of the Socialist party, which called upon the government to carry out a truly proletarian revolution without regard to the legal niceties of

parliamentary democracy. On the opposition side the results strengthened those who believed that a military coup was the only solution
to the crisis. In the event, the opposition managed to expose and exploit
the growing divisions within the Popular Unity and to lead successfully
a seventy-day strike by copper-mine workers against the government.
Meanwhile, as the politicians declared that the rule of law and democracy had collapsed, the last remaining loyalist officers were removed
from office. By early September, the military had made their final
move and had toppled the government.

The Prats Cabinet

Soon after taking office as Minister of the Interior, General Prats
ordered the strikers back to work, but declared that he would consider
their economic grievances and would not take reprisals against them
or their organisations. The opposition parties, mainly the CDP, viewed
with great alarm the speed with which General Prats resolved the strike
and feared that because of him the armed forces would begin to side
with the government. These fears were undoubtedly confirmed when,
in an interview with a left-wing weekly, General Prats declared that
the political action of the popular masses was legitimate and that
Popular Unity politicians understood that the army's mission was to
serve the fatherland and not the interests of a particular social class.[47]
The CDP confronted Prats in the Congress, reminding him that he
was supposed to play a neutral role in the cabinet and that he should
not take sides with the government. General Prats, demonstrating
remarkable skills as a parliamentarian, replied that, while the role of
the armed forces in the cabinet was politically neutral, he and the
government would not allow another strike of the magnitude of the
October one as this could seriously endanger national security.[48]

Aware that it would be too risky to use the impeachment proceedings against General Prats, the opposition initiated impeachment proceedings against the Minister of Finance, Orlando Millas, accusing
him of taking reprisals against strikers. Since the alleged reprisals had
been taken by the Minister of Finance, acting in close cooperation
with General Prats, the articles of impeachment were meant to serve
notice to the armed forces that Prats was compromising their political
neutrality. Prats reacted swiftly, claiming that the allegations against
his cabinet colleague had no legal basis and that he fully agreed with
the arguments set forth by Millas in the Congress in defence of his
behaviour.[49]

The fears of the opposition were not groundless. Participation of the
military in the cabinet at such a critical moment could easily have

been used by the government to further its aims. Indeed, although the military refused to sign requisition decrees, thus disassociating itself from the government's *de facto* nationalisation policy, the opposition rightly saw the dangers involved in their excessive concern with the need to re-establish order, both in the political and in the economic spheres. For while order in the political sphere effectively meant re-straining anti-government demonstrations, order in the economic sphere meant destroying the basis of the black market, hitherto the opposition's main weapon against the government. Thus, the presence of the military in the cabinet provided the government with the means to resolve its two most pressing problems; an opportunity which the government did not have before the October strike.

The Prats-Millas Plan

In January the government announced measures to regulate the distribution of basic consumer goods. They involved rationing the distribution of about thirty basic consumer goods and assigning an important role to the armed forces in the distribution of these goods through a newly-established National Distribution Secretariat.[50] Together with these measures, the government introduced a new nationalisation bill in the Congress, reducing the number of firms it intended nationalising from ninety to fifty-four and providing that all firms already subject to government intervention but not on the new list would be returned to their owners.[51] These measures were known as the Prats-Millas plan and were strongly criticised both by the opposition parties and by the left wing of the Popular Unity.

The opposition ignored the new nationalisation bill as it had no chance of being approved by the Congress. Instead it concentrated its attacks on the proposed distribution system, describing it as dictatorial. According to the opposition, the new system of distribution was typical of totalitarian regimes, in which political subjection of peoples was achieved through controlling their basic needs. They singled out for attack the Supply and Prices Committees (Juntas de Abastecimientos y Precios/JAPs), grassroots organisations created by the government to assist in the process of distribution. The opposition described these organisations as illegal, on the grounds that they were called upon to perform a public function for which they were not authorised, and politically dangerous, as they were vehicles through which the marxist parties would exercise direct control over consumers and shopkeepers.[52] The new distribution scheme was only partially implemented and did not succeed in resolving the problem of distribution. Two reasons account for the failure of the scheme: firstly, the strong campaign mounted by the opposition, which secured a boycott from the majority of shopkeepers; and secondly, the fact that a successful implementation of the scheme would have required an organisational effort beyond the government's capabilities.[53]

Opposition fears that the Prats-Millas plan was the first step towards the creation of an alliance between the government and the military were quickly dispelled when the Socialist Party and the MAPU strongly opposed the new nationalisation bill on the grounds that they had not been consulted before its publication and that the contents of the bill were, in any case, unacceptable to them. Allende replied in sharply-worded letters stating that their allegations were unfounded since all the members of the Popular Unity had in fact participated in the drafting of the new bill and reminding them of their collective responsibilities as members of a government coalition.[54]

The reason why the Socialists opposed the new nationalisation bill was similar to that of the opposition parties. For the Socialists, too, feared that the new bill was part of a political plan involving the military, the Communist Party and Allende, which was designed to stop or even reverse the revolutionary process and to prepare the ground for a political compromise with the CDP. The Socialists, apart from rejecting the nationalisation bill, argued that the fascism of the extreme Right could not be distinguished from the fascism prevailing in the CDP and that it was illusory to expect that, at that late date, a compromise would be successful.[55] The Popular Unity had only one choice: to press forward with the implementation of its programme so as to secure full transfer of power to the people. Hence the slogan 'avanzar sin transar', 'forward without compromising'.

In ideological terms the differences between Socialists and Communists were not new and had already surfaced in mid-1972 over the People's Assembly of Concepción. Yet the difference now was that the conflict had a direct bearing on the conduct of the campaign for the March elections, now in full swing. While the Communist Party emphasised the need to increase production and to run nationalised industries more efficiently, the Socialist Party called upon the government to continue implementing its programme without entering into agreements with the enemies of the revolution. This fundamental difference between the two leading members meant that the Popular Unity in effect did not have a common electoral platform to fight the general elections of March 1973. This was underlined by the fact that its main campaign document concentrated on vague proposals to reform the constitution which had already been turned down by the Congress and which had no bearing on the substantive political issues of the moment.[56] The Socialist Party's refusal to take advantage of the presence of the military in the cabinet effectively killed the last coherent political initiative put forward by the government. From then on, government policy lacked any sense of direction.

Prelude to the Military Coup

The results of the March general elections did not substantially change the composition of the Congress. The Popular Unity did surprisingly well, despite the absence of a coherent electoral platform and the open conflict between Communists and Socialists. It obtained 43.4 per cent of the vote, an increase of 7 per cent over its performance of September 1970. It gained six new seats in the Chamber of Deputies and two in the Senate. The Socialists did better than any other member, thus consolidating their position as the largest party within the coalition.[57] Within CODE, the National party did marginally better than the CDP. However, CODE naturally claimed the results as a victory since it obtained 54.7 per cent of the vote.

After the elections, the military's participation in the cabinet was no longer justified. The Communist Party and Allende wanted to keep them in the cabinet, but could not persuade either the military or the Socialists of this. The military believed that, having fulfilled their task of seeing the government through the March elections, their participation could only inflict irrevocable damage to the unity of their institution.[58] The Socialists, for their part, believed that their continuing presence would have involved an abdication of the political objectives of the Popular Unity. Thus, late in March, Allende appointed a new civilian cabinet in which all the Popular Unity parties were represented.

The electoral results were disappointing to the CODE, particularly to the CDP, which was hoping that a major defeat of the government would give the opposition the required two-thirds majority in the Congress to either impeach the President or to force the government to change its policy. Since this did not happen, the CODE, through former President Frei, called upon all Chileans to organise themselves against the totalitarian threat posed by the government.[59] This call was complemented by a plea to the military to enforce the recently approved Arms Control Act against left-wing organisations, mainly trade unions, which were allegedly preparing for the armed struggle.[60] Given the political vacuum existing at the time, the CODE's attitude amounted to a call for a military coup. However, the CDP still had to be cautious. For while its right-wing faction was now in control of the party, many of its supporters did not wish to be involved in military conspiracies with the National Party and Patria y Libertad and anyway did not believe that a military coup would resolve the fundamental political problems affecting the country. Indeed, while the CDP leaders were adopting an increasingly tougher line towards the government, its youth section passed a resolution calling upon the party to break away from the CODE and to form an alliance with any political party, or group, willing to work for socialism in a democratic framework.[61]

The CDP's reluctance to be seen working with right-wing politicians who were openly calling upon the military to intervene was not an obstacle to effective action by the opposition. In this respect, the opposition was greatly helped by the fact that the government had all but lost its sense of political direction, bringing out into the open differences between the Communists and the Socialists, and by the fact that both inflation and the black market were out of control. The differences within the Popular Unity were brought into sharp focus by a major proposal on educational reform made by the government in early 1973. This was a sensible proposal, but was presented as a major revolutionary breakthrough designed to achieve marxian egalitarian objectives in the educational system. In brief, its aim was to integrate classroom work with practical experience, thus removing the sharp differences among various educational institutions and providing greater equality of opportunity.[62] Because it was presented as a revolutionary measure – which was clearly not the case – and because the government tried to implement it by decree, the opposition's response was sharp and strident. They not only argued that such a major reform should be implemented through legislation, but claimed that it was yet another illustration of the totalitarian objectives of the government.[63]

The proposed educational reform provided the opposition with a powerful issue for mobilising public opinion against the government. A major campaign against the proposal was launched through the opposition-controlled media, and parents' associations throughout the country alerted their members to the dangerous marxist influence to which their children were soon to be exposed. The campaign culminated in street demostrations, which, in turn, led to violent confrontations with government supporters. In the event, the opposition succeeded in persuading the hierarchy of the Catholic Church, as well as senior military officers, to express their concern about the government's proposal.[64] The growing opposition against the proposed reform forced the government to withdraw it. Moreover, the debate on this reform had shown that not all the parties of the Popular Unity supported it.

According to the Communist Party, the reform introduced by the Department of Education was different from the proposals actually approved by the Popular Unity. It therefore publicly disassociated itself from the proposed reform, thus greatly annoying the Socialist Party, whose members had drafted and campaigned vigorously in favour of the government's proposal.[65]

While the debate over educational reform was going on, the government was confronting a more serious crisis involving the powerful unions at the El Teniente copper mines. The conflict was based on a disagreement between unions and management in the recently-nationalised El Teniente mine over the level of wage re-adjustments for 1973. The matter was referred to an arbitration panel, in which government officials were in the majority. The arbitrators found against the unions, but the unions refused to comply with the award and instead declared an indefinite strike from the beginning of April. Aware of the serious implications of this strike, the government tried desperately to find a solution acceptable to the union. In the event, the government made an offer, but unfortunately it divided the copper workers. Some accepted it and called for a return to work, while others rejected it and vowed to continue their strike.[66]

As some workers began to return to work, violent confrontations developed with those still on strike, who erected road blocks and attacked buses carrying non-striking workers. The opposition parties were quick to take advantage of the embarrassing position in which the government found itself. They attempted, unsuccessfully, to broaden the conflict to include copper workers in other parts of the country. They impeached the Ministers of Mining and Labour on the ground that they had acted illegally during the conflict, and they lent financial and logistical support to the striking miners in order to prolong the conflict artificially.

The conflict lasted seventy days, causing immense economic and political damage to the government. At the height of the conflict, striking workers marched into Santiago under the sponsorship of the ultra right-wing Student Union Federation of the Catholic University. President Allende met a delegation of striking workers in an attempt to put an end to the conflict. But this meeting was strongly condemned by the Communist and Socialist parties, which, in an unusual joint statement, declared that they regarded it as imprudent since those on strike did not represent the majority of the El Teniente workforce. Allende replied that the objective of his meeting had been to explain to striking workers the government's position. In a separate letter addressed to all copper workers, Allende pointed out that, as President, it was his obligation to make every effort possible to persuade striking workers to change their mind, as he believed that they were acting against their own class interests.[67] The strike was eventually resolved, but it had seriously weakened the government for it had exposed the President's isolation from his own coalition, even from his hitherto staunchest supporters, the Communist Party. Needless to say, the conflict did not bring the Communists and Socialists closer together, despite the joint letter they addressed to the President.

Meanwhile, the confrontation between the Congress and the President over the constitutional amendment had reached its height. In April, the Chamber of Deputies rejected the government's veto, and the opposition argued that the President was then bound to enact the text of the amendment as approved by the Congress and that he only had sixty days to do so. The President disagreed and in May referred the matter to the Constitutional Tribunal. The opposition parties rejected this move, claiming that the Tribunal did not have jurisdiction over the matter and that, accordingly, its decision would not be binding on the Congress.

In the event, at the end of May, the Constitutional Tribunal found that it did not have jurisdiction and thus the matter, still unresolved, was referred back to the government. As the Supreme Court declared that the government had repeatedly violated the rule of law, the opposition parties demanded that Allende should either immediately promulgate the text approved by the Congress or call for a plebiscite.[68] But the government, aware of the risk of losing the plebiscite, and afraid of the political consequences of enacting the text approved by the Congress, continued to delay its decision, thus creating the impression, albeit false, that it was preparing the ground for a dramatic political gesture.

According to his own account, General Prats was asked by Allende in June to try to achieve some form of political truce with the opposition. The objective was to put forward a national emergency programme acceptable to all political parties, which the government would then implement with the help of the armed forces.[69] However, at this late stage, a compromise was beyond the reach of all the parties involved in the political game. While the opposition no longer trusted the Popular Unity, or even Allende, the left wing of the Popular Unity, mainly the Socialists, dismissed the idea of a truce as unrealistic and unacceptable.[70] For their part, the military agreed to the idea only if the government allowed them more power.[71]

The idea of a political truce was soon forgotten when, late in June, rebel troops seized control of downtown Santiago, attacking the presidential palace and the Ministry of Defence. Troops loyal to the government, led by General Prats and General Augusto Pinochet, surrounded them and forced them to surrender. The government immediately declared a state of emergency and sent a bill to the Congress requesting the imposition of a ninety-day state-of-seige. The opposition in the Congress rejected Allende's request, claiming that the government already had adequate powers to maintain order and, instead, called upon the military to disarm left-wing groups which, according to them, were preparing an armed confrontation with the forces of law and order.[72]

After the attempted coup the government again tried unsuccessfully to persuade the military to participate in the cabinet. According to Prats, they refused because, in the absence of a truce and given the serious breach of discipline which had occurred in June, their priority was to restore discipline within their own tanks.[73] By the end of July, popular mobilisation against the government increased as lorry drivers once again went on strike, claiming that the government had not respected the agreement they had reached with General Prats in November. This time the strike by the lorry drivers and by other *gremios* was combined with an outbreak of right-wing terrorism directed at disrupting essential services. In the week from 27 July to 3 August the government reported 180 different acts of terrorism, one of which included the assassination of the President's naval aide-de-camp.[74]

At the suggestion of the head of the Catholic Church, Cardinal Raúl Silva, Allende met the chairman of the CDP in a bid to establish a minimum democratic consensus. The talks collapsed as neither the government nor the CDP was in a position to compromise.[75] However, as the opposition's offensive intensified, the government finally convinced the military to participate in a new cabinet, which was described as a Cabinet of National Security. It included the three chiefs of the armed forces and the head of the national police. By 18 August, eight days after taking office, the air force chief resigned from the cabinet, claiming that he had not been given sufficient powers to end the lorry strike. Four days later, the Chamber of Deputies adopted a resolution calling upon the military members in the cabinet to force the government to act within the law, otherwise they would be held responsible for violating the constitution. The following day, 23 August, General Prats, under strong pressure from the military, resigned from the cabinet as well as from his post as Commander-in-Chief of the army. With Prats and a handful of loyal generals out of the way, the military were ready for the final move against the government. This came on the morning of 11 September, the day in which

Allende was supposed to have announced a plebiscite on the controversial constitutional amendment.

IV   THE ECONOMIC POLICY: AN ASSESSMENT

The failure of the government to change its economic policy in the early part of 1972 had a decisive impact on the developments leading up to the military coup. In this section, I provide general information about some key economic indicators during the last eighteen months of the government. I also briefly discuss general issues relating to the government's agricultural and industrial policies.

Fiscal Deficit

In the middle of 1973 the government's economic policy was still plagued by the same problems which had remained unresolved since the end of 1971. The fiscal deficit was still larger than expected, the import bill continued to rise, the deficit in the balance of payments remained at the same level and the government's incomes policy continued to be disregarded in wage negotiations. In addition to these by now chronic problems, the government had to face an inflationary explosion which was nearly out of control, as well as a serious breakdown in the distribution system, which allowed the black market to flourish. In 1972 the fiscal deficit remained at record levels. However, while in 1971 the deficit had been largely attributable to the imbalances caused by the economic re-activation policy and to the unexpected fall in export revenues, in 1972 the cause of the deficit was more clearly political. On the one hand, the opposition in the Congress made more effective use of its power by refusing to provide adequate financing to the annual re-adjustment bill. Thus, 72 per cent of the re-adjustment law of 1972 was not financed by the Congress, and over 90 per cent of the supplementary re-adjustment law of that year was not financed. On the other hand, the deficit of the newly-nationalised enterprises was five times greater than expected.[76] As explained in Section II above, this was largely attributable to the fact that, in August 1972, the government did not re-adjust the prices of the products manufactured by nationalised enterprises as it had originally planned, because it feared that inflation would get out of control. This decision also constituted a hidden subsidy to firms in the private sector which used as inputs intermediate goods produced by state-sector firms.

From 1972 to 1973 as demand for foodstuffs continued to expand without a corresponding increase in domestic production, the import of foodstuffs continued its upward trend. By 1972, foodstuffs and food-industry imports represented 31 per cent of all imports, and by 1973 they had reached 37 per cent.[77] These figures are impressive not only because, in 1970, these items represented only 14 per cent of all imports, but because nearly 75 per cent of them could have been produced domestically.[78] In any event, the higher import bill of 1973 together with the continuing fall in export revenue, had the effect of increasing the trade deficit from 88 to 438 million dollars.[79]

Throughout 1972, the government made great efforts to improve the balance of payments, which, in 1971, had shown a deficit of 300 million dollars. To achieve its objective, it entered into negotiations to re-schedule interest payments on the foreign debt and began to reconstitute its links with foreign lenders. In the re-negotiation of the foreign debt, the government managed to postpone payment of a substantial proportion of the interest due to be paid in 1972. Likewise, it managed to obtain new credits to replace the loans from United States banks and from multi-lateral development banks, mainly the World Bank and the Inter-American Development Bank, which had dried up. Indeed, in 1972 the net resource flow between Chile and foreign lenders was 160 million dollars, that is, almost exactly what Chile had received in the year Allende took office.[80] However, despite these efforts, the balance of payments continued to show a deficit of 310 million dollars.

The growing deficit, together with a huge increase of money held by the private sector, led in 1972 to an inflationary explosion which reached unprecedented levels. As conditions keeping inflation within manageable bounds in 1971 – mainly financial reserves and spare capacity in industry – did not obtain in 1972, the inflationary pressure became uncontrollable. The government's effort in August 1972 to restore the balance between supply and demand by authorising price increases led, in a single month, to a 22 per cent rise in the consumer price index; in other words, inflation for the month of August was equal to the rate of inflation during the whole of 1971. Also, money held by the private sector was diverted away from productive investments and into speculative ventures, thus generating a black market in basic consumer goods, which caused incalculable political damage to the government. The strike of October 1972 had in fact almost completely disrupted the government's control of wholesale and retail trade.

In 1971 the annual inflation rate stood at 20 per cent. By 1972 it had increased to 78 per cent, and in 1973 it reached 353 per cent.[81] The spectacular increase in the rate of inflation eventually eroded the income gains of both white- and blue-collar workers. However, not all workers were affected in the same way, or at the same time. Blue-collar workers, on average, did better than white-collar workers, while organised blue-collar workers did, on average, better than the lowest paid blue-collar workers. However, what is interesting is that, despite the onslaught of inflation, the income gains achieved by most workers in 1971 were not completely eroded until the middle of 1973.[82]

It should be noted that the impact which inflation had on income gains was not reflected in the electoral results. Indeed, the impressive gains the government achieved in the general election of March 1973 show that, by that stage, the political struggle had been clearly defined along class lines so that its electoral strength could not be significantly damaged by the impact of inflation on income gains. It is also necessary to bear in mind that government measures in education, health and housing had an effect on the redistribution of income. Thus, for example, in primary education places were offered to practically all children between the ages of six and fourteen years of age, while in tertiary education there was an 88 per cent increase in the number of new entrants.[83] Health was also a priority of government policy. Infant mortality was reduced from 88 to 71 per 1,000, milk was made available free to the poorest sections of the population and emergency health services aimed at the poorest groups was significantly increased.[84] In housing there were 20,000 new units built in 1971 alone, representing a four-fold increase on the preceding year.[85]

Agricultural Policy

Together with the financial problems created by the short-term economic policy, the government also confronted difficulties in the agricultural and industrial sectors. In agriculture, it had set out to expropriate during its six years in office all holdings of more than eighty basic irrigated hectares, representing 35 per cent of all agricultural land. This target was reached by the end of the government's second year in office. The speed of the expropriation process stemmed partly from pressure by peasants and partly from the government's fear that, otherwise, the landowners would have time to organise themselves and disrupt agricultural production. However, the rapid pace at which land was expropriated did not make it easier for the government to organise production, as there were important differences within the Popular Unity on this point, and the Department of Agriculture did not have adequate powers to carry out a coherent policy.

The existing agrarian reform legislation had important limitations. On the one hand, it provided for the expropriation of the land only, excluding farm machinery and other equipment. On the other hand, it introduced a transitional cooperative arrangement for exploiting the land – the *asentamiento* – but membership was restricted to individuals who had previously worked on the same land. This meant that only 10 per cent of the agricultural workforce would directly benefit from the land reform process and that the state had to provide massive financial and technical assistance to keep production going in the holdings that had been expropriated.

The issue of how to organise production in the expropriated land was one which divided the Popular Unity and eventually brought it into conflict with the CDP. The Communist Party advocated a system which would follow as closely as possible the *asentamiento* introduced by the previous CDP administration. They advocated this, believing that it was the best way to ensure that agricultural production would not be disrupted. They also did not want to annoy the CDP and thus endanger the chances of securing their cooperation on other policies. The Socialist Party, for its part, believed that the scope of the agrarian reform process had to be broadened so as to include the majority of agricultural workers. They therefore advocated the establishment of large state farms as a more effective vehicle for assisting production in expropriated land, which would also incorporate more workers into the land-reform process.

To resolve the differences between Communists and Socialists the government proposed a compromise solution, the Centres of Agrarian Reform. The CERAS were constituted by grouping together land expropriated from several holdings and including all workers in the region. The CDP, which controlled 30 per cent of the organised agricultural workforce, strongly opposed their creation on the grounds that they were illegal, that they were state farms in disguise and that they would undermine the *asentamientos* established during the Frei administration.[86] Apart from the political problems they caused, the government was unable to introduce them as the dominant form of organising production in the reformed sector. Indeed, alongside them, new *asentamientos* continued to be established. Moreover, new organisations developed, the Peasants' Committees, created by agricultural workers themselves, which resembled more the old *asentamientos* than the new CERAS. The variety of forms through which the reformed sector was administered made it extremely difficult for the government to carry out the complicated task of re-structuring production.[87] But the government had to accept this heterogeneous mix since it could not be rid of the *asentamientos*, and the compromise on the CERAS had not resolved the differences concerning agricultural policy within the Popular Unity.

Considering the constraints under which the government was operating, it is hardly surprising that production in the reformed sector was inefficient. It has been estimated that, in 1972, the amount of money which state agencies transferred to the reformed sector in the form of unrecoverable production subsidies was almost as much as the amount it contributed to agricultural production.[88] The high cost of running the reformed sector was aggravated by the fact 80 per cent of its produce was marketed through private channels. This not only reinforced the role of capital in the agricultural sector, but also provided the basis for a black market of agricultural products.[89] The government made great efforts to increase state control over distribution of agricultural produce, mainly through import control. However, despite these efforts, distribution of more than 70 per cent of agricultural products was outside the government's control.

The most difficult issue in the long run facing the government was the stratification which was developing as a consequence of the limited scope of the agrarian reform. Since under the existing law landowners were entitled to all their machinery and up to eighty hectares of land, the agrarian reform in fact created a new private sector consisting of holdings between twenty and eighty hectares, which comprised 40 per cent of all the agricultural land, employed 25 per cent of the agricultural workforce and accounted for 45 per cent of total production. On the other hand, there was the heterogeneous reformed sector which comprised 35 per cent of agricultural land, employed 18 per cent of the agricultural workforce and accounted for 30 per cent of production. In between these two main sectors, there was a group of small property owners, who controlled 23 per cent of the land, employed 55 per cent of agriculture workers and accounted for just over 25 per cent of production.[90] These figures show that the reformed sector was not the dominant force in agricultural production and explain why the Socialist Party and other radical groups in the Popular Unity were so keen to broaden the scope of agrarian reform, even at the cost of ignoring the provisions of the Agrarian Reform Act.

Industrial Policy

The government's *de facto* nationalisation policy in the industrial sector was also plagued by political differences within the Popular Unity and by the inherent limitations of the method used to carry it out. Indeed, the reason for the government's delay in introducing its nationalisation bill was because the Popular Unity could not agree on two issues: whether to define in advance the firms that would be nationalised, and what the actual size of the 'commanding heights of the economy' was. Again, characteristically, the Communist Party and the Socialist Party had different opinions. The Communist Party advocated indentifying as early as possible the industrial firms to be nationalised so as not to alienate the non-monopolistic sectors of the industrial bourgeoisie. The Socialists were opposed to identifying the firms in advance as this would artificially limit the natural development of the class struggle.[91] Hence their reluctance to agree to a precise definition of the national-isation programme. In the event, when the government was forced to make its plans explicit – under pressure from the CDP – the Popular Unity parties could not agree on the size of the state sector in industry.[92] By October 1971, the Popular Unity finally agreed to nationalise all firms with assets valued at 14 million escudos or more, which was then roughly equivalent to 1.5 million dollars. Applying this criterion, there were about 250 firms that would have been nationalised out of a total of 13,000 which employed more than five workers.[93] However, less than five months after making this announcement, the govern-ment – again under pressure from the opposition – was forced to abandon its original plan and to identify precisely the companies it intended nationalising. This is how the list of ninety enterprises origi-nated. The publication of the list turned out to be little more than an academic exercise. In practice, the government took over the com-manding heights of industry, relying largely on administrative mea-sures. However, this method, apart from annoying the opposition, had severe limitations. Firstly, because the effect of these measures was to transfer to the government only the administration of the firm and not its property. This meant that the power of state-appointed managers was limited: they could not introduce major changes in pro-duction processes or merge their firms with other 'nationalised' firms operating in the same branch of industry. Besides, the owners of the firms obtained injunctions from the courts re-affirming the limited powers of state-appointed managers. The second important limitation was that the government could not plan in advance the take-over of specific firms. By applying this method the government ended up with the control of firms that it did not want, but it was unable to requisi-tion all the firms on the list of ninety. Indeed, many of the firms on the list were not requisitioned because considerations of a general political nature, such as trying not to antagonise European investors, did not make it feasible.[94] By 1973, although the government had taken over the administration of 300 firms, there were still some thirty from the list of ninety which remained safely in the private sector.[95] Thus, while the State was supposed to control 40 per cent of industrial production according to the government's plan, by 1973 it only controlled 20 per cent.[96] These figures underline the limitations of the government's methods for bringing industrial firms under state control.

According to technical studies prepared by Popular Unity economists, the government's political problems would not have ended had it nationalised all the firms on the list. Had this happened, the state sector in manufacturing would have represented 70 per cent of the value of assets, but only 44 per cent of production and 22 per cent of employment.[97] But participation of the state in production was relatively low because, in some branches of manufacturing – mainly in basic consumer goods and food – the level of concentration of capital was not high. Hence here, private capital would have been predominant, controlling up to 70 per cent of production, while the state would have controlled over 60 per cent of production in those branches producing intermediate goods, consumer durables and capital goods.[98] This type of mixed economy probably raised doubts as to whether the state sector would have been capable of effectively playing a dominant role as expected by the Popular Unity strategists. However, a more obvious flaw of the government's plan was that it excluded nearly 80 per cent of workers in the manufacturing sector from direct participation in the nationalisation process. It is therefore not surprising that the radical view of the Socialists Party, which advocated a more comprehensive nationalisation policy, should have been so popular among left-wing supporters.

CHAPTER 14

Power to the People

THE Popular Unity Programme stated that the objective of the Allende government was to destroy the power base of monopoly capitalism in order to initiate the construction of socialism. To this effect, the new government would take control of the commanding heights of the economy and would immediately establish new institutional mechanisms to facilitate the transfer of power to the popular masses. The distinctive feature of this road to socialism was the assumption that these tasks could be fulfilled by making use of the procedures and mechanisms of the prevailing political system.

The question of whether the Popular Unity's road to socialism was viable has been the subject of extensive debate in political and academic circles. This chapter concentrates on two issues which have a direct bearing on this debate: the mechanisms of participation introduced by the government; and the organs of popular representation which sprang up during this period. The study of these two issues provides insights into the Popular Unity's views about the nature of state power and its conception about the role of the popular masses during the transition. Section I examines the question of participation. It provides basic information on popular mobilisation and levels of unionisation during the period and discusses in detail the mechanisms of participation proposed by the government for workers in the agricultural and manufacturing sectors. Section II deals with the various issues arising from the emergence of new forms of political representation at the grassroots level. It explains the factors which led to the emergence of these organisations, it traces the political background of the 'popular power' debate in the Popular Unity and concludes with some brief comments on the revolutionary potential of the new organs of popular representation.

I WORKERS' PARTICIPATION

One of the main objectives of the Popular Unity was to introduce new forms of popular participation, thus involving the popular masses fully in the revolutionary process. To fulfil this objective, the government established several organs of participation in various areas of state activity, such as health, education and distribution. On the whole, these organs were conceived as mere consultative structures, through which people would liaise with the authorities at the local level. In many respects, the Popular Unity's approach to participation was not altogether different from the CDP's notion of 'popular promotion'. Therefore it is not surprising that, apart from the case of the JAPs, created by the government to assist in the distribution of essential consumer goods, the opposition was not greatly concerned with these new structures of participation. However, this was not the case with those created in the productive sectors, mainly agriculture and manufacturing industry. For here, although government policy was far from revolutionary or even novel, the process of participation acquired its own momentum, which the opposition rightly identified as potentially capable of challenging the prevailing power structure.

The workers' participation schemes in the agricultural and manufacturing sectors were plagued by conflict. For they were not only a major target of criticism by the opposition, but also provided a concrete issue around which Communists and Socialists fought out their different conceptions about the nature of the revolution. Yet, the problems the government confronted here were not merely caused by narrow ideological divisions between marxists, but were a reflection and a symptom of more general problems arising from the nature of the Popular Unity's political strategy. Thus, to assess the participation schemes it is necessary to provide some information on their immediate context; that is, the development of the process of unionisation and political mobilisation during this period.

Growth of the Union Movement

When the CUT was established in 1953 there were some three hundred thousand unionised workers, representing just over 12 per cent of the labour force. Twelve years later, in 1965, union membership in absolute terms remained the same, but the rate of unionisation had dropped to 10.9 per cent. However, from 1965 onwards the union movement began to grow at an unprecedented rate. Between 1965 and 1970, union membership increased by nearly 80 per cent to five hundred and fifty thousand, representing 19.4 per cent of the workforce.[1]

This trend continued unabated so that by the end of 1972 the number of workers in unions stood at six hundred thousand and the rate of unionisation had reached 22 per cent of the workforce.[2] Also between 1965 and 1972 the number of unions doubled, reaching four thousand.

The expansion in the number of workers belonging to unions was remarkable not only because it was fast, but also because it was so uneven. Indeed, more than 60 per cent of the newly-unionised contingent were agricultural workers, while only 14 per cent came from manufacturing. Thus, between 1965 and 1972 the rate of unionisation among agricultural workers had increased from less than 1 per cent to 35 per cent. This figure is all the more impressive if compared with the 38 per cent rate of unionisation among the traditionally influential and politically-aware workers in manufacturing. The sectors in which the rate of unionisation was below average included construction (12 per cent), commerce (14 per cent) and services (6 per cent).[3]

The form in which the membership expanded in the seven years up to 1972 brought about an interesting change in the relative size of the various groups within organised labour. Thus, while up to the mid-sixties workers in manufacturing and in mining accounted for 60 per cent of unionised workers (44 per cent in manufacturing and 16 per cent in mining), by 1972 these two groups accounted for only 38 per cent (30 per cent in manufacturing and 8 per cent in mining). The largest group was now made up of those in agriculture and manufacturing, which now accounted for 64 per cent of unionised workers.[4]

The Wave of Strikes

As the union movement expanded, so did the number of strikes and the number of workers involved in strikes. While in 1960 there were 257 strikes involving 88,000 workers, by the end of the decade the number of strikes per year stood at 1,000, involving nearly 300,000 workers; that is one half of the total number of unionised workers. During the Popular Unity government the number of strikes continued to increase, reaching 2,709 in 1971 and 3,289 in 1972. However, in 1971 the increase in the number of strikes did not bring about a corresponding increase in the number of workers involved in strikes. Indeed, in 1971 the number of workers on strike was 300,000; that is, the same as during the last two years of the Frei administration. However, in 1972 the number increased by 30 per cent, reaching the 400,000 mark.[5]

The interpretation of the statistics on rates of unionisation and strike activity during this period has generated some controversy among specialists.[6] For the purpose of this chapter I shall note only

255

two points which are relevant to this debate: one concerns the identity of strikes in the years immediately preceding Allende's electoral victory; and the other concerns the changing nature of strikes during the Popular Unity period.

The increase in the number of strikes which occurred towards the end of the sixties was accompanied by an interesting change regarding those involved. In the past, the main protagonists had been workers in manufacturing and mining. Now, the main groups were agricultural workers and the relatively unorganised workers in the building industry. The decline in the level of strike activity by workers in manufacturing and mining has been attributed to the fact that these workers were closely identified with the CUT, which at the time – a pre-electoral period – was engaged in containing popular mobilisation.[7] Likewise, the spectacular increase in mobilisation among the newly-organised groups should be regarded as an indication that the CUT was not yet capable of exercising full control over the mass of newly-organised workers. This is why in 1971 the President of the CUT described the new members of the labour movement as a heterogeneous group, which urgently needed political education so as to channel their energies towards the revolutionary process.[8]

During the Popular Unity government the number of strikes continued to rise, reaching 2,709 in 1971 and 3,526 in 1972. However, as already pointed out, in 1971 the total number on strike remained at around 300,000 which was roughly the same figure as during the last two years of the Frei administration. Consequently, the average number of workers per strike dropped from around 270 in 1968–9 to 108 in 1971.[9] Likewise, the average length of strikes during the Popular Unity government dropped from seven days in 1971 to 3.7 days in the first semester of 1972. This trend towards shorter strikes had already appeared during the Frei administration, and it was as much a reflection of the government's sympathetic response as it was evidence of the union movement's strength.[10]

Strike statistics during the Popular Unity government have to be interpreted with considerable caution for three reasons. In the first place, as explained in Chapter 13, in some sectors of the economy, mainly manufacturing and to some extent agriculture, strikes were instigated by party activists or by workers themselves in order to put pressure on the government to issue intervention or requisition decrees. Secondly because, during this period, strikes became an important weapon in the strategy of the opposition, particularly from the middle of 1972 up to the military coup, and therefore the increase in their number was to some extent an indication of divisions which were beginning to appear within the labour movement. And thirdly, during this period the strike began to lose ground to other forms of struggle, mainly land seizures and factory occupations. As explained in the preceding chapters, in 1971 alone there were some 1,200 cases of land seizure, of which more than one-third was resolved by the expropriation of the respective holding.[11]

Workers' Participation in Agriculture

To understand the difficulties which the government encountered in the implementation of its participation scheme in the agricultural sector, it is necessary to bear in mind that, despite the rapid growth of agricultural unions, by 1972 more than half of all agricultural workers (65 per cent) were not unionised. Most of these non-union-ised workers were seasonal (*afuerinos*), part-time (*minifundistas*), and volunteers (non-remunerated) workers. These workers, who laboured side-by-side with unionised workers, did not belong to unions largely because of procedural requirements imposed by the law. This artifical division among workers labouring in the same locality, and often on the same property, was further compounded by the fact that agri-cultural unions were aligned into two major blocs: one supporting the CDP and the other supporting the Popular Unity parties. In 1970, nearly 50 per cent of agricultural unions were affiliated to El Triunfo Campesino, a CDP-controlled confederation of unions. However, the change of government altered the balance in favour of the Popular Unity. Thus, by 1972 nearly 65 per cent of unionised workers belonged to the two Popular Unity-controlled confederations, Ranquil and Unidad Obrero Campesina.[12] By December 1971, the political division among organised agricultural workers was institutionalised when the CDP established the Central Unica Campesina. This organisation was a supra-confederation, which coordinated the activities of all anti-government unions and organisations in agriculture.[13] But the Popular Unity was itself divided in the countryside. Ranquil, the largest confederation, was jointly controlled by Communists and Socialists, who, as explained below, had conflicting views about the government's participation schemes. The other pro-government con-federation was Unidad Obrero Campesina which represented 15 per cent of unionised workers and was controlled by the MAPU, a party which on agricultural issues was often on the side of the Socialist Party and MIR.

The participation scheme introduced by the government in January 1971 consisted of three different organs: a Peasants' Council at the commune level, a Provincial Council and a National Council.[14] These organs were similar insofar as all three were mere consultative bodies with no decision-making power. They were conceived as organs through which government officials and representatives of peasants would exchange views about all matters relating to agriculture. Unorganised workers were excluded from this scheme as membership of all three organs was restricted to legally recognised unions and confederations of unions.

The question of representation in the Peasants' Councils became an instant source of conflict between government officials and peasants in regions where Socialist and MIR influence was dominant. In some communes, union leaders and party activists refused to accept the guidelines issued by the government for the establishment of the Councils. Instead of restricting membership to union representatives, they expanded it by allowing all agricultural workers in the commune – whether or not they belonged to unions – to elect representatives to the Council. The government agreed to recognise these newly-formed councils, aware of the risks they would be taking if they restricted them, but did not substantially change their functions. Because this decision was taken when the majority of Councils had already been established there co-existed two different Councils: the majority – nearly 65 per cent of all Councils – established in accordance with the government's original proposals; and the rest, made up of fourteen representatives nominated by local unions and fifteen representatives elected directly by agricultural workers in the area.[15]

The two types of councils reflected conflicting ideas within the Popular Unity about the nature and limits of popular mobilisation in the countryside.[16] On the one hand, the original scheme proposed by the government, and strongly backed by the Communist Party, assigned the principal role to existing unions and sought to achieve a balance between them and government officials in charge of formulating agricultural policy. Hence the conception of the Peasants' Councils as organs in which union representatives would exchange views and assist government officials in the design and implementation of policy. On the other hand, some regional leaders of the Socialist Party and of the MIR saw them as the basic structure through which peasants would begin to exercise effective power. In the immediate political context, they regarded them as indispensable tools for organising and coordinating the day-to-day struggle against the agricultural bourgeoisie and for pressing for a more radical agrarian reform. It was therefore necessary to include in the Councils representatives from all agricultural workers to achieve these goals. It must be noted that the CERAs – the structures created by the government to organise production in land expropriated under agrarian reform – were in fact more in line with the Socialists Party's conception of Peasants' Councils than with the government's original proposal on participation.[17]

According to official reports, Peasants' Councils were established in all the 275 rural communes in the country.[18] Although there are no comprehensive studies on the work of the Councils, most specialists agree that at least one-third of them never actually functioned and those that were active had a very limited influence.[19] Instead of becoming organs of power reflecting the views of peasants at the grass-roots level they became little more than pressure groups.[20] Yet their efficacy even in this limited role often depended on just how far the political views of the majority of their representatives coincided with those of government officials working in the same area.[21] These sectarian practices not only deepened divisions within the Popular Unity, but also interfered with the government's production targets for the sector.

The National Council of Peasants, the organ which stood at the pinnacle of the government's participation scheme, was an even greater failure than the Peasants' Councils. It met only six times during the period 1970–3, and the meetings were simply formal occasions in which government officials informed the Council members about developments in the sector. The government's lack of enthusiasm in promoting the National Council is explained by the fact that opposition-controlled confederations held the majority of the seats. Ironically, this was a consequence of the government's own misconceived participation scheme, which allocated an equal number of seats to each confederation, irrespective of the size of their membership. This method favoured the opposition-controlled confederations in the Council, leaving the pro-government forces in the minority.[22]

Workers' Participation in Industry

Shortly after taking office, the government established, jointly with the CUT, a committee to consider ways in which workers could participate in the management of industrial firms. The committee's proposals were then circulated to and discussed by all unions affiliated to the CUT. Eventually in June 1971, after six months of consultation, the government issued a document entitled *Basic Norms of Participation*, containing the structure for a new system of management. The government assumed in this document that only a small proportion of firms would be nationalised and that the vast majority would remain in the private sector. Accordingly, the government proposed two different systems of participation. In the private sector it proposed that unions should establish vigilance committees to monitor the productive process. However, very few vigilance committees were in fact established since the system proposed by the government did not give workers any real say in management and was little more than a gesture towards the majority of workers who would, according to the government's plans, remain in the private sector.[23] In the nationalised sector, the government opted for a system in which management responsibilities were, at least on paper, shared by workers and state-appointed representatives. The Yugoslavian system of self-management was considered, but rejected because it was felt that the prevailing monopolistic economic conditions would give a disproportionately large amount of power to a tiny minority of workers.[24] The government system also sought to keep intact the union's independence by providing that representatives on the organs of participation were to be directly elected by workers in the enterprise and that union leaders could not stand as candidates in those elections.

The system of management participation for industrial firms in the state sector was an elaborate tiered structure, consisting of the General Assembly of Workers, an Administrative Council and various Production Committees corresponding to specific sections of the enterprise.[25] The main function of the General Assembly of Workers was to elect representatives to the Administrative Council, and to oversee the activities of the Council and of other organs of representation in the enterprise. The Assembly met once a month, and its meetings were chaired by union representatives.

The Administrative Council was the highest decision-making body in the enterprise. It had a membership of eleven: five workers elected by the General Assembly, five representatives of the state appointed by the government, plus an administrator, also appointed by the government. Production workers elected three of the five workers' representatives to the Council, while administrative and professional workers each elected one. Workers' representatives to the Council were elected for a two-year term, but could be removed from office by a majority vote by the Assembly.

Workers in each production section of the enterprise formed a Sectional Assembly, which in turn elected representatives to form a Production Committee. These Committees, together with union representatives and the workers' representatives to the Administrative Council, formed the Workers' Coordinating Committee. This

Committee acted as a channel for communicating information to the Administrative Council and as a mechanism for harmonising the work of the various organs of representation within the enterprise.

Implementation of the *Basic Norms of Participation* proceeded at a slow pace. To some extent, the complexity of the system and the fact that several elections had to be called, account for the difficulties in launching the system. However, some union officials regarded this new system with suspicion and accordingly, delayed as long as possible convening the first General Assembly meeting. Moreover, since the *Basic Norms* were mere guidelines, their implementation was delayed in some cases by workers negotiating minor amendments to the system with government authorities. In any event, by June 1972 the system of management participation was in operation in 75 per cent of state-controlled enterprises.[26]

Some critics of the government's participation scheme have pointed out that it was simply a co-management system, in which the final say on important decisions remained in the hands of state officials.[27] From a purely formal point of view, this is a valid criticism since the composition of the Administrative Council – the supreme decision-making body – gave a majority of one to the state-appointed members. However, in practice, labour generally had a working majority in the Council, either because state-appointed representatives did not always attend meetings, or because the government would often select its representatives from among the workforce.[28] Nonetheless, the government could always exercise control over management decisions at the enterprise level since state representatives were only accountable to the government and could be removed from office without the General Assembly of Workers being consulted. Besides, the government provided Administrative Councils with technical advice, which usually had a decisive influence on the policies adopted by the enterprise.[29]

It is not easy to assess the impact of management participation schemes on discipline and on productivity. There are only three studies available on this topic and their findings are inconsistent. Two of them, analysing the experience of participation in individual enterprises, found that, on the whole, discipline had relaxed.[30] One of the case studies, comparing data of July 1970 with that of July 1972, found that the number of days lost by absenteeism and sick-leaves doubled, while days lost by industrial accidents nearly trebled.[31] These findings are in contrast with the third study, which analyses the impact of participation in thirty-five enterprises in the manufacturing sector. According to this study discipline was actually strengthened

261

in those enterprises in which workers were active in running the newly-established organs of participation.[32] This study also found a positive correlation between intensity of participation and productivity. In fifteen of the thirty-five enterprises, productivity increased slightly or remained the same, while in fourteen productivity increased by as much as 6 per cent. The higher rates of productivity were found in enterprises where participation was more intense and better organised.[33]

The results of efficiency tests applied to assess the management of state-controlled enterprises should be interpreted with caution. Most of the firms in the so-called Area of Social Property were still formally in the private sector for although they were the object of temporary measures of requisition or intervention, they had not been nationalised. Accordingly, the state-appointed administrators were in fact simply caretakers with restricted powers. Their capacity to run their respective enterprises efficiently was therefore severely limited. The scant evidence available makes it difficult to arrive at a general assessment of the government's participation scheme. However, most observers agree that the main obstacles to the implementation of the *Basic Norms* were derived from difficulties in reconciling the role of the existing union structure with that of the new organs of participation. The government's decision to maintain the one separate from the other not only created confusion among workers, but also gave rise to suspicion among some union leaders. The confusion stemmed from the fact that there were now at least three organs claiming to represent their interests: the union, the Administrative Council and the Co-ordinating Committee.[34] Union leaders, mainly from the Communist Party and CDP, were naturally reluctant to support fully a new power structure which – regardless of the government's assurances to the contrary – was perceived as encroaching upon their own jurisdiction.[35] This suspicion was not groundless, as the implementation of the participation schemes often brought about changes within the union in favour of the Socialist Party, at the expense of the Communist Party and CDP.[36]

Tension between the unions and the new organs of popular participation stemmed largely from the different views which Communists and Socialists held about the role of the new organs of participation. The Socialists regarded wrokers' participation in management as essential to the Popular Unity's objective of transferring power to the working class. Accordingly, they advocated more power to workers in the management of nationalised enterprises. The Communists, for their part, believed that one of the primary aims of state intervention was to increase production in nationalised industries and this justified restricting workers' initiative.

Underlying this disagreement between Communists and Socialists was an immediate political issue. Indeed, the parallel existence of two power structures representing different interests of the same working-class constituency led, inevitably, towards increasing the traditional competition between the two marxist parties for control over the unions. Since most unions in the manufacturing sector were controlled by the Communists, and they, following the government line, were campaigning for moderate wage settlements and for increases in production, it is not surprising that the Socialists, who were putting forward more radical demands for workers' participation should have increased their popularity and managed to gain control over many of the new organs of participation and, at the same time, to undermine the strength of the Communists within the union structure. Aware of the political implications of these developments, the Communists began demanding an amendment to the *Basic Norms of Participation*. They argued that it had been a mistake not to assign a greater role to the unions in the system of participation. Accordingly, they proposed an amendment which would recognise the central political role of unions as organs of representation of working-class interests.[37] The Communist Party's call to strengthen the role of the unions was also prompted by their fear that CDP workers in state-controlled enterprises were becoming increasingly alienated from the Popular Unity parties, thus making it highly unlikely that the government and the CDP would ever reach an agreement. The changes advocated by the Communist Party were discussed by the CUT, but no decision to amend the *Basic Norms* had been taken by the time of the military coup.

II   POPULAR POWER

Government Policy on Popular Mobilisation

In section I above I discussed the extent to which popular mobilisation had increased during the last years of the Christian Democratic administration. The electoral victory of the Popular Unity not only failed to stop this process, but intensified it. Because of this the new government was confronted with a characteristic dilemma: because of its commitment to taking the first steps towards a socialist revolution, it could not simply contain popular mobilisation by using the coercive powers of the state; however, because of its commitment to act within the boundaries of the political system, it could not afford to be seen either as an instigator or as an accomplice of actions which, under the prevailing system, were patently illegal.

During its first weeks in office, the Allende administration attempted to use persuasion as a means of controlling popular mobilisation. But this policy was unsuccessful, partly because it was impractical and partly because the government itself did not apply it consistently. Indeed, as explained in Chapter 13, the intervention and requisition decrees used by the government to take over the commanding heights of the economy were generally preceded by land seizures and factory occupations instigated by government officials purporting to carry out Popular Unity policy. On the whole however, the Popular Unity was aware of the urgent need to chanel this immense social energy in a constructive direction. Hence the CUT's attempt to assume leadership over the newly-unionised workers, as well as the government's efforts to set up organs of participation – such as the Supply and Prices Committees (JAPs) – to create a meaningful political link between government departments and the daily life of the popular masses.

The Popular Unity's efforts to channel popular mobilisation effectively were hindered by several factors. In the first place, there was the fact that individual members of the coalition assigned a higher priority to recruiting new sympathizers than to strengthening political support for the government. As a consequence, a highly competitive atmosphere developed, in which sectarian practices flourished and popularity was measured exclusively by electoral success. In the second place, the government's efforts to deal effectively with popular mobilisation were also hindered by the political constraints within which it was operating. Each time a new organ of participation was set up or even considered by the government, the opposition would criticise it, describing it as illegal and as the beginning of totalitarianism. The practical effects of these attacks were significant since the opposition had a majority in the Congress, had firm control over the leading employees' organisations, and exercised predominant influence over members of the judiciary. As a consequence, the work of the Supply and Prices Committees was effectively disrupted by boycotts organised by shopkeepers, while the government was forced to withdraw from the Congress the bill on Neighbourhood Tribunals. Likewise, in the area of health care, the work of Local Health Committees, established by the government, received practically no support from the medical profession.[38]

The third factor to hinder the success of the measures for dealing

264

with the growing popular mobilisation was that the Popular Unity's own approach to this area of policy was ambiguous. As explained already, the government's nationalisation policy relied largely for its success on the militancy of workers. Factory and land occupations would often provide the government with the necessary excuse to issue an intervention decree and thus incorporate the respective enterprise into the Area of Social Property. But this tactic was double-edged. Since the scope of the Popular Unity's nationalisation policy was not defined until nearly a year after Allende took office, the government had no guidelines for refusing to issue intervention decrees when demanded by workers. There thus began a spiral; factory occupations were followed by intervention decrees, which led to the incorporation into the state sector of many enterprises which could hardly be regarded as belonging to the commanding heights of the economy. When in October 1971 the Popular Unity finally named the enterprises on its nationalisation list, government officials found it extremely difficult to turn down requests for intervention decrees from workers in firms not included on the list, as the spiral of occupation and intervention had developed a momentum of its own and could not be easily controlled.

The government's attempt to apply technical criteria in deciding which firms should become social property was bound to create conflict with those members of the Popular Unity who worked in close contact with supporters at the grassroots level. This conflict became more acute as the government's initial economic policy began to lose dynamism and the opposition started to adopt more aggressive tactics. The first indication of a major discrepancy between the government and a significant group within the Popular Unity came during the by-election campaign in December 1971. On that occasion, all the regional branches of the Popular Unity parties in the province of Linares, plus the MIR, issued a statement calling for the immediate expropriation without compensation of all large farms in the region, including farm machinery. The demands put forward in the Linares manifesto clearly went beyond the limits set by the agrarian reform legislation and accepted by the government. Accordingly, the Popular Unity in Santiago promptly disavowed the Linares manifesto, while the Communist Party denied, despite evidence to the contrary, that its regional branch had participated in drafting the Manifesto.[39] It claimed instead that the whole episode had been engineered by ultra-left agitators.[40]

The row over the Linares manifesto was symptomatic of tensions that were beginning to develop within the Popular Unity. These tensions intensified in the first half of 1972 as the government, attempting to secure an agreement with the CDP on the issue of nationalisation, began to put the brakes on popular mobilisation. But this policy of containment failed not only because it was implemented half-heartedly, but because the prevailing economic and political conditions were unfavourable. Indeed, as inflation began to erode income gains, and the CDP started to abandon all pretence of behaving as a loyal opposition, the government's containment policy met with considerable resistance.

In May 1972 there took place in Concepción an incident which illustrates well the type of problem confronted by the Popular Unity coalition and by the government. The Intendant of the province, a member of the Communist Party, had authorised a march and a rally by the opposition parties. Shortly thereafter, the Popular Unity parties in the province requested permission to stage another demonstration on the same day in response to the opposition. The Intendant authorised this counter-demonstration, but later on, following orders from the Minister of the Interior in Santiago, rescinded it while confirming the permission granted to the opposition. Most of the Popular Unity parties in Concepción, with the exception of the Communist and Radical parties, regarded this sudden change of mind as unacceptable. Accordingly, they decided to defy the Intendant's order and to go ahead with their demonstration. This led to clashes with the police in which one student was killed and several injured.[41]

Shortly after the May events in Concepción, the Popular Unity met in Lo Curro to approve major changes of economic policy. This new economic policy was formally introduced by Allende in a speech in which he called for sacrifices from all sectors of the population.[42] Allende's speech, however, was not welcomed by most Popular Unity supporters. In fact, only three days after the speech, once again in Concepción, all the local branches of the Popular Unity, with the exception of the Communists, plus several unions and other grassroots organisations, held a meeting which they described as the People's Assembly. The meeting, apart from calling for the immediate dissolution of the Congress and the removal of reactionary judges to create true people's power, strongly rejected the new economic policy. Aware of the implications of this meeting. Allende reacted by sending a strongly-worded letter to the leaders of all the Popular Unity parties. In this letter he described the People's Assembly of Concepción as a divisive manoeuvre and called upon the Popular Unity parties to reject it.[43] All the Popular Unity parties with the exception of the Socialist Party, distanced themselves from the events in Concepción and rallied around the government. The Socialists, for their part, though reaffirming their loyalty to the government, were cautious in their assessment of the People's Assembly because their local branch in Concepción claimed that their action had been based on directives issued by the Party's Central Committee in Santiago.[44]

Cordones and Comandos

Opposition to the government's new economic policy was neither confined to Concepción nor restricted to mere rhetoric. In various industrial areas of Santiago, workers began to establish direct contact with each other in order to oppose specific aspects of government policy or to resolve concrete problems affecting their areas, such as public transport and water supplies. This process led to the creation of the *cordones industriales* (industrial belts). The *cordones* purported to represent the interest of industrial workers in a given location.

Decisions of the *cordón* were taken by a committee of workers which represented all the enterprises in the area. The first *cordón* to acquire public notoriety was the *cordón Cerrillos* created in mid-1972. Later on, *cordones* were established in all the main industrial areas of Santiago and in some provinces, mainly Concepción and Valparaíso. By August 1973 almost 50 per cent of workers in manufacturing were members of a local *cordón*.[45] Together with the *cordones*, there emerged another organ of popular representation: the *comandos comunales* (communal councils). These were also territorially-based organs, but with a broad membership which included not only representatives of workers from the area, but also representatives of other grassroots organisations, such as neighbourhood committees, mothers' associations, student unions, Supply and Prices Committees, etc. The *comandos* were actively promoted by the MIR, which regarded them as a means for providing the urban poor and other members of the popular masses, together with unionised workers, with a political organ to prepare themselves for the exercise of power. The MIR regarded the *comandos* as political organs already exercising real power, albeit in embryonic form, parallel to the government.

By comparison with the *cordones*, the importance of the *comandos* was negligible. Few *comandos* were established, and those that existed functioned irregularly. However, because they posed the question of power and purported to offer a solution to it, they acquired enormous importance in the debate over popular power which took place during the last twelve months of the Allende government.[46]

Development of the Cordones

Initially the *cordones* sprung up in response to changes in government policy which workers regarded as unacceptable. This was the case of the *cordón Cerrillos*, the first to acquire public notoriety. The creation of this *cordón* was prompted by the fact that the government, following the new policy agreed at the Lo Curro meeting, refused to intervene in favour of workers of a small firm in the Cerrillos area, who were involved in a long-standing industrial conflict. These workers were actively supported by colleagues from other firms in the area, who, acting in solidarity, joined together to form a *cordón*. Eventually, after an embarrassing conflict in which the workers of the *cordón* organised road blocks in protest against the government, the Minister of Labour gave in and resolved the conflict in favour of the workers.[47]

After the experience of the *cordón Cerrillos* and the People's Assembly of Concepción, it was natural for the government, as well as for the established union movement, to view the *cordones* with suspicion. However, things changed dramatically during the opposition-led strike of October 1972. On that occasion, as the political struggle intensified and the government was forced to take over firms to prevent lock-outs and industrial sabotage, the *cordones* and other popular organisations became the mainstay of government support. The government relied on these newly-established popular organisations to keep production going and to secure the regular supply of basic goods to the market. However, since the strike was resolved only after the government agreed to allow the military to participate in the cabinet, it is not surprising that, by the end of 1972, relations between the government and the *cordones* once again began to deteriorate.

In January 1973, the government introduced a bill to the Congress reducing from ninety to forty the number of firms which they proposed to nationalise and providing that all the firms already subject to intervention or requisition measures would be returned to their owners. As explained in Chapter 13, this bill caused a major row between the Socialist Party on the one hand, and the Communist Party and the government on the other. It was also strongly rejected by the *cordones* as a shameful abdication of the Popular Unity's revolutionary objectives.[48] At the time, the serious political implications of this row were obscured by the electoral campaign for the March general elections as it was in everybody's interest to rally in support of the government. However, since the elections failed to resolve the political deadlock between the Congress and the executive the government was confronted with the dilemma of either giving in to the demands of the opposition by accepting the CDP's constitutional amendment on nationalisation, or to press ahead with its programme, relying on the political strength of the working class and other popular organisations.

In the circumstances, the *cordones* and *comandos* began to play a crucial role. But the government did not seem to recognise the full implications of the dilemma that it was facing. Instead, it tried, through the CUT, to take over the leadership of the *cordones* while maintaining a dialogue with the CDP in a vain attempt to stay in office. In the remaining paragraphs of this chapter, I outline the main issues and identify the leading actors in the debate over popular power which took place during the last twelve months of the Popular Unity administration.

Official Response

The government's response to the new organs of popular power was initially one of total rejection, but slowly changed towards a position of qualified acceptance. When Popular Unity supporters in Concepción called for the immediate establishment of a People's Assembly, Allende immediately rejected it, describing the meeting as a divisive manoeuvre. According to him, the notion of dual power implicit in the proposal was misplaced and irresponsible. Historically, he argued, the notion of dual power had emerged as a challenge to reactionary governments. This was not the case here since the Popular Unity was a legitimate government truly representing the interests of the working class. Allende further argued that his government was not confronting a fundamental power struggle, but a mere constitutional conflict with the Congress. The Popular Unity had to concentrate its efforts on winning the general elections of March 1973 rather than wasting its energies on the romantic and illusory notion of forming a People's Assembly.[49]

The importance acquired by the *cordones* after the October strike, combined with the fact that they were becoming a major source of opposition to the government, brought about a change in policy. Instead of rejecting the notion of popular power, the government began publicly to accept the need to create it but defined it as a process involving mainly the strengthening and consolidation of existing organs of popular representation. The stated objective was now to give these organs a degree of autonomy from the state bureaucracy while keeping them firmly within the framework of existing political structures.[50]

The government's intention of absorbing the new organs of popular representation into the existing political system was spelled out in some detail by Allende in his annual message to the Congress in May 1973. On that solemn occasion, he told the Congress that his government supported the idea of creating *comandos comunales* as vehicles for facilitating direct participation of the people. However, he went on to describe them as mere consultative organs which would act as a channel to pass on to existing municipal authorities information about the problems and aspiration of people living in the area.[51] This conception of popular power was not altogether different from the CDP notion of popular promotion (see Chapter 9), and was consistent with the often-stated official view that popular power should not be regarded as a structure parallel or antagonistic to the existing government.[52] In view of this narrow conception of the functions of the new organs of popular representation, it is not surprising that the *cordones* should have offered, in return, only conditional support to the government.

Cordones: Socialists vs Communists

The government's attempt at enlisting the support of the new organs of popular power while confining their activities to the limits set by the political system was strongly supported by the Communist leadership of the CUT. From the early days of the Allende administration, the Communist Party had assigned the highest priority to the task of incorporating the large contingent of newly-unionised workers into the structure of the CUT. From the Communist Party's perspective such priority was justified not only on ideological grounds, but also because of the unique role played by the CUT in the labour movement – and by the Communist Party within the CUT. Since its creation in 1953, the CUT had succeeded in establishing itself as the unchallenged leader and representative of organised workers. As explained in Chapter 10, the CUT's unique position had been achieved at the cost of sacrificing the unions' independence from the political parties, an objective which the founding members of the CUT regarded as essential. As the CUT's influence within the labour movement and the political system increased, so did the Communist Party's influence within it. By the late fifties the Communist Party had overtaken the Socialists as the single largest party within it, and from the early sixties, the presidency and other key posts in the organisation were filled by Communists. Towards the end of the Frei administration, CUT policy came to be closely identified with the political line of the Communist Party. This was deeply resented by the Socialists, who considered that the Communist Party was mistakenly containing popular mobilisation to prepare the ground for an electoral victory which, at the time, they regarded as impossible.[53]

During the first months of the Allende administration there were clear signs that the CUT was beginning to lose ground as leader of the popular masses. On the one hand, it had practically no influence among the recently-unionised peasants, one of the groups leading the mobilisation at the time. On the other hand, it was unable to maintain discipline among its own long-standing members, as shown by the proliferation of factory occupations, which were contrary to both CUT and government policy. Perhaps the clearest indication that it no longer represented the whole of organised labour and that its influence was declining was the fate of the government's income policy. As explained in Chapter 13, in 1971 and again in 1972 the government and the CUT agreed to keep wage increases within clearly-defined limits. However, in practice wage increases far exceeded those limits, thus showing that CUT's influence among the working class could no longer be taken for granted.

When the *cordones* came into existence in mid-1972, the CUT had good reasons to regard them with great suspicion. On the one hand, the very existence of the *cordones* signified a rejection of its policies. For they had been established in opposition to the government's new economic policy, one which was strongly supported by the Communist Party and the CUT. On the other hand, the form in which they were organised was also a challenge to the CUT's supremacy. For the executive organs of the *cordones* were directly elected by the workforce and not made up of union representatives. While this made it possible for non-unionised workers to be represented, it also by-passed the unions.

The *cordones* were neither a spontaneous outcome of the sharpening of the class struggle, nor were they merely a creature of the Socialist Party. They were an expression of the growing opposition among workers, mainly in the manufacturing sector, to some aspects of government policy. However, their growth and further development were achieved largely through Socialist support. They in fact provided the Socialists with a solid base from which to organise and coordinate workers' opposition against what were regarded as unacceptable transgressions of the Popular Unity's Programme. Yet as they began to assume a more prominent role, their demands and activities were almost identical to those of the Socialist Party. Their successful mobilisation against the government's nationalisation bill in January 1973 was an indication of the Socialist Party's enormous influence over them.

The Socialist Party's influence on the *cordones* is apparent in the way they presented their general aims and conceived of their concrete tasks. In a statement issued in July 1973 by seven of the leading

271

cordones based in Santiago, they defined their principal aim as the struggle to achieve real proletarian democracy. This concept entailed a rejection of decisions made by the government behind the back of the masses.[54] The decisions to which this statement referred were those which the government was taking in order to pave the way for an agreement with the CDP on the scope of the state-owned sector of the economy. They were the same decisions which, as explained above, the Socialist Party had always opposed from within the Popular Unity.

The specific tasks to which the *cordones* assigned top priority confirm the close link between them and the Socialist Party. Most of these tasks were taken directly from the Popular Unity Programme and did not greatly depart from actual government policy. Thus, for example, in a statement issued in July 1973, four of the largest *cordones* in Santiago reaffirmed that the Area of Social Property was to be dominant in the economy, that workers ought to participate more actively in the system of national planning, that workers' organisations should be decentralised and that workers should be more involved in the process of drafting and implementing the rules governing their participation in the management of nationalised enterprises.[55] These demands were based on the false assumption that the government had the power to secure these objectives. Hence the role of the *cordones* was conceived as that of a pressure group within a political system in which the question of power was not at issue. This unrealistic reliance on the capacity of the government to bring about political results reveals the close links existing between *cordones* and the Socialist Party. For the position of the Socialists was also based on the mistaken assumption that the government indeed had the power to implement its programme; hence their rejection of any form of compromise with the CDP and their insistence that the government should accelerate the process of expropriations. Seen from this perspective, the *cordones* were undoubtedly an important development in the process of popular mobilisation, but were not alternative or parallel organs of power to the government.

The *cordones'* approach to the question of power puts them clearly within the framework of the Popular Unity's road to socialism, since their demands were based on the assumption that the government would continue to function normally. Yet this fact did not make it any easier for the government to control them as their radicalism was as much a sign of the intense socialist commitment prevailing among their membership as it was a symptom of the rapid disintegration of the Popular Unity. The *cordones* acted as a catalyst for all the political groups within the Popular Unity which rejected the government's attempt to change its economic policy. Since this change of policy was fully supported by the Communists, they naturally rejected the idea of forming *cordones* and refused to participate in them. Apart from rejecting them on the ground that they were controlled by the ultra-left, they believed that their very existence undermined the rightful place which unions had as representatives of working-class interests.[56] Underlying this criticism was the knowledge that the Socialist Party was beginning to use them not only to oppose communist policies within the Popular Unity, but to enhance its influence among the working class, at the expense of the Communist Party.

Cordones Recognised by the Communist Party and CUT

After the general elections of March 1973 the Communist Party agreed to participate in the *cordones*. But this decision did nothing to further the unity between the two marxist parties; instead, it brought out into the open their conflicting views about the nature of the *cordones*. According to the Communists, their main function was to defend the government without reservations. To ensure that the *cordones* would behave in a politically responsible manner, the Communists proposed that they should be led by union representatives in the given area, not by individuals directly elected by the workforce. Moreover, the Communists opposed the establishment of a coordinating committee of *cordones* as they regarded this to be an unacceptable challenge to the authority of the CUT and to their own influence within the labour movement.[57]

According to the Socialists, the selection of representatives to the *cordones* by direct elections was fair and equitable since it ensured that all workers in a given area would be represented by the *cordones*, even those who did not belong to unions. Undoubtedly, the Socialists also preferred this method because it favoured the election of the more radical candidates, thus off-setting the moderating influence of Communist-controlled unions. However, Socialist policy in the *cordones* should not be interpreted as a mere reflection of anti-Communist or anti-CUT views within the Popular Unity. The Socialists had good reasons to complain about the shortcomings of the CUT. In their view, the *cordones* had been created to fulfil the important function of enabling workers to develop a broader, more class-based perspective by providing an institutional framework that would link all workers in a particular area, beyond the limited confines of individual enterprises. The CUT initially did not identify this as an important function. Later on, when it did recognise this as an important function, it tried to change the nature of the *cordones* by defining them as a loose association of local unions. The objective of the CUT was naturally to ensure that it would influence the activity of the *cordones* through its control over the unions. Thus, it is not surprising that the CUT should have regarded the creation of a confederation of *cordones* in mid-1973 as unacceptable parallel unionism and as a serious threat to the unity of the working class.[58]

Comandos Communales: Socialists vs MIR

The argument between Socialists and Communists about the nature and composition of the *cordones* was carried out at the same time as the argument between the Socialists and the MIR over the *comandos communales*. The MIR supported the work of the *cordones*, but believed that the Socialists were wrong in assigning top priority to the task of creating *cordones*. For the *cordones* merely strengthened the organisational capacity of workers already belonging to unions, thus further isolating organised workers from the rest of the exploited masses.[59] What was needed, according to the MIR, was the immediate creation of alternative organs of power: the *comandos comunales*. The *comandos*, operating in the same territorial unit of the existing municipalities, would link up all existing grassroots organisations to form a solid alliance between organised workers and the rest of the exploited masses, represented mainly by the urban poor, the peasants, the self-employed, the unemployed and the lower strata of the petty bourgeoisie. This strategic alliance would make it possible for the working class to assume effectively its vanguard role in the unfolding revolutionary process.[60]

The Socialists supported the work of the *comandos*, but disagreed with the MIR about their nature and role. The MIR regarded them as organs of power – albeit in embryonic form – acting independently of the government and the state bureaucracy.[61] The Socialists on the other hand regarded them simply as vehicles to coordinate the work of popular organisations in a given locality.[62] The Socialists therefore rejected the notion of dual power implicit in the MIR's conception on the ground that the government was already controlled by parties representing the working class. Hence, according to the Socialists, the *comandos* were not the people's power in embryo, although they did not rule out the possibility that they might perform such a function in the future.[63]

The position of the Socialists regarding the nature of the *comandos* is, interestingly enough, quite similar to the official view of the government as explained above. Yet this policy was based, not on a principled rejected of the possibility of using the executive branch of a bourgeois state to bring about a revolution, but on the fact that the government was not implementing its programme fast enough and that this process could not be accelerated by forming an alliance with the CDP. The objective of the Socialist Party was therefore to become the main force within existing government so as to rectify this error. But to achieve this objective the Socialists not only had to maintain their electoral superiority over the rest of the members of the coalition, but had to assume leadership over working-class organisations. Hence their interest in creating *cordones* and their reluctance to accept the MIR's conception about the *comandos*.

It must be noted that despite its apparent radicalism the MIR's notion about the *comandos* and popular power generally was slightly ambiguous. For, it argued, although the organs of popular power were independent from the government, they were not necessarily opposed to or in contradiction with it. The notion of an independent and non-contradictory relationship between these two forms of power stemmed from a curious idea about the nature of state power, which regarded it not as a whole, but as divided between the power of the Popular Unity government on the one hand and the rest of the state apparatus on the other. Hence, the notion of parallel power in fact entailed a conception of triple power: the government, the rest of the state and popular power.

The ambiguity of the MIR's views on popular power stemmed from its peculiar political predicament. In the late sixties the MIR, together with several other urban guerrilla movements in Latin America, had opted for the armed struggle. Although Allende's electoral victory did not invalidate the theoretical assumptions on which it was based, it all but destroyed its political appeal. It reacted to the Popular Unity's victory, reaffirming its conviction that the confrontation between the working class and the bourgeoisie was inevitable, but announcing also that it was prepared to support the government in the implementation of measures which would benefit the exploited masses and further political mobilisation. Shortly after the MIR made this announcement, Allende granted a general amnesty to its members convicted for offences against the Internal Security Act during the previous administration. This decision was strongly criticised by the opposition, but Allende defended it on the ground that his government had made the armed struggle redundant, and hence political groups on the left would no longer need to resort to violence.[64]

During the Popular Unity government, the MIR gave up its

commando-style operations – consisting mainly of spectacularly-staged bank- and supermarket-robberies – to become an active participant in the political process. Having abandoned its military activities, it concentrated on the difficult task of building a base of popular support. In this respect, its success was limited. In the countryside it managed to establish a solid foothold in only one or two provinces around its home-base of Concepción; while in Santiago, its main support came from scattered groups in shanty-town areas. Its strength within the union movement in agriculture and industry was insignificant and was unlikely ever to become a threat to the established marxist parties.[65] It participated actively in many of the land and factory occupations which took place during the period. However, only in a tiny fraction of these events was it the leading force as the wave of occupations was part of the policy of several Popular Unity parties and was tolerated by the government.

The MIR's influence during the Popular Unity administration was blown up out of all proportion by the opposition press – which had an interest in depicting the government as dominated by former guerrilla fighters – and by the Communist Party, which mistakenly attributed the proliferation of occupations and land seizures to the activities of the ultra-Left. Undoubtedly, it played an important role during the Popular Unity period, but it was mainly as a participant in the debate within the Left since its ideological position was a constant reminder to the Popular Unity about the inevitability of violent confrotation with the real wielders of state power. However, in practice, the MIR moved close to the position of the Socialist Party. Indeed, once it had abandoned its military activities to concentrate on broadening its popular appeal its demands became almost identical with those of the Socialist Party. For they were based on the same assumption: that the government had the power to fulfil its programme and that once this was achieved the question of power would be easily resolved in favour of the exploited masses. In this respect, the notion of parallel power was an attempt to provide a theoretical basis for its political practice. The Socialists, for their part, did not agree with the parallel power thesis since they expected to become the leading force in the government that was to bring about the revolution.

An Alternative Road to Power?

By mid-1973, the *cordones* and other organs of popular power had become the main focus of attacks by the opposition and the first targets of repression by the military. While the opposition portrayed them as key tools in the government's plan to bring about civil war, the military – acting under the powers granted to them by the recently-enacted Arms Control Act – began to search for weapons in factories and other places where these new organs of popular power held their meetings.[66] A few small defensive weapons were found in these raids, but neither their quantity nor their nature justified the allegations that these organs were to be the vanguard in a civil war. These military operations were in fact mainly designed to intimidate workers and to prepare rank-and-file soldiers for the forthcoming repression. Yet because of the hopeless situation in which the government found itself after the October strike, it is not surprising that these new organs of popular power were regarded by many left-wing supporters as foundations for an alternative road to socialism.

The *cordones* and other organs of popular power were a genuine working-class response to the shortcomings of the Popular Unity. Their practice demonstrates that the absence of adequate political leadership is not an obstacle to the development of class consciousness. Although they were implacable opponents of some aspects of government policy, at the end of the day their loyalty to the government was never in any doubt. From an ideological perspective, and contrary to what happened to the relatively isolated workers in the copper mines, the *cordones* proved to be unconquerable by the opposition's propaganda machinery. Nonetheless, as the materials in this chapter have shown, their potential as an alternative road to power was limited. For they merely reproduced the ideological conflicts within the Popular Unity, but were unable to resolve them. Consequently, they could not provide independent leadership and their fate was inextricably linked to that of the government.

Concluding Remarks

BETWEEN 1932 and 1973 the Communist and Socialist parties were intensely involved in Chilean politics. They played a prominent role in the country's political development despite the fact that their electoral base was relatively small and that relations between them were less than amicable. Their exclusive control over organised labour from 1932 to 1952 made them acceptable partners in government coalitions led by the Radical Party. Although initially participation in government enhanced their own political influence, by the late 1940s they were in disarray: the Socialist Party was fragmented, the Communist Party had been banned and the labour movement was divided.

By the mid-1950s the marxist parties found themselves under very different conditions. They were now in opposition to governments no longer interested in forming coalitions with them, and in competition with a new political force, the Christian Democratic Party, which was rapidly winning over the support of sections of the population hitherto within their constituency. These new developments did not, however, diminish their political importance. On the contrary, and largely as a consequence of the re-alignment of political forces, by the late 1950s they emerged as the single largest electoral bloc in the country, despite the fact that they still controlled only a plurality of the vote. These bright electoral prospects contributed towards consolidiating the partnership between them and led them to concentrate on winning the Presidency.

In 1970, at their fourth attempt, they finally won the Presidency with a candidate of their own. Indeed, it could well be argued that from the mid-1950s onwards, the main concern of the other parties in the political system – as well as that of the United States government – was to prevent them from ever winning at the polls.

278

The foregoing suggests that throughout this period the behaviour of the marxist parties was purely pragmatic, as it seems to have been largely shaped by the demands of the electoral system rather than by adherence to marxism as a revolutionary ideology. Although it is undeniable that short-term considerations were important, marxist ideology provided the general terms of reference. Indeed, the Communists' ever-cautious and moderate political line and the Socialists' characteristic impatience can both be traced to the way in which they each sought to interpret and apply the main tenets of marxist ideology.

Both parties agreed that the revolution was not on their immediate agenda and that, instead, it was necessary to carry out certain tasks – generally described as anti-oligarchical and anti-imperialist – to prepare the ground for the revolution. However there was disagreement between them on the nature of these tasks and the type of alliances needed to fulfil them. The Communist Party regarded these tasks as part of the first stage of the revolution, which could be carried out in alliance with progressive forces of the bourgeoisie. Since, according to the Communist Party, these progressive forces were represented by some political parties, the Communists advocated forming alliances with them. The Socialists, for their part, did not believe that in a backward country such as Chile there were such progressive forces, mainly because of the overriding influence of imperialism. Accordingly, they were opposed to forming alliances with non-marxist parties.

In so far as the Socialist Party rejected alliances, it was consistently more radical than the Communist Party. But this radicalism was misleading. For its refusal to enter into alliances with bourgeois parties was not combined with an alternative strategy for popular mobilisation, and it continued to rely exclusively on electoral results to evaluate performance. Thus, paradoxically, its radicalism had the effect of intensifying its electoral orientation. The short-comings of its strategy probably explain why its leaders were constantly searching for new models and were as easily attracted to Ibañism as they were to Castro's experience in Cuba.

By contrast, the Communists were consistent advocates of forming broad alliances with non-marxist parties. Yet they were not particularly successful in this. Their political links with the Radicals in the 1940s were short-lived and plagued by conflict. Their expectations that the CDP would follow a left-wing course and join the Left in a broad alliance were never realistic. It is true that the Popular Unity can be regarded as being the broad alliance they had envisaged. Yet

279

the members of the Popular Unity represented only a small fraction of the centrist forces, which were largely controlled by the CDP.

The Communist Party's failure to form a broad centre-left alliance could well be attributed to the Socialists' persistent opposition to it. This was undoubtedly an important factor. But it must also be noted that the Communist Party had never reálly been regarded by the other parties as a reliable partner. To some extent this was because of anti-communist ideology, spread initially by the Catholic church and later by Cold War propaganda; but it was not solely a matter of anti-communist ideology. For, over the years, the Communist Party had shown that its loyalty to the international communist movement took precedence over domestic politics.

The conflicting views which Communists and Socialists held about the party system and its role in bringing about the socialist revolution were not resolved by the establishment of the FRAP in the mid-1950s. For the FRAP was a mere electoral alliance, acceptable to them precisely because each regarded it as the embodiment of its own political strategy. Allende's electoral victory in 1970 did not bring the two parties any closer. On the contrary, during the three years of Popular Unity government, the conflict was exacerbated. The Communists regarded the Popular Unity as yet another step in the process of forging a broad alliance of all progressive forces. In their view, such an alliance was essential to the Popular Unity's commitment to initiating the transition to socialism. According, they concentrated on persuading the Popular Unity to act with moderation so as to win over the Christian Democrats to the government's Programme.

By contrast, the Socialists did not believe that the government would be strengthened by making concessions to the CDP. In their view, the CDP was a reactionary party committed to capitalism and as such could never sincerely share the government's revolutionary objectives. Accordingly, they called for the speedy implementation of the Popular Unity's Programme as the only way of winning over from the CDP the popular sectors which still supported it.

The Popular Unity government did nothing to resolve the differences between Socialists and Communists. Indeed, instead of trying to resolve these differences, it circumvented them, expecting, mistakenly as it turned out, that they would be superseded by the political struggle. This unresolved conflict led in practice to innumerable policy deadlocks and to contradictory policies. All this contributed, in turn, to reinforcing the opposition's perception of the government as both ruthless and aimless; and the ultra-Left's view of it as both hesitant and revolutionary.

With hindsight, it seems that perhaps the most important mistake of both Communists and Socialists was their failure to combine political practice with a systematic analysis of the context in which they were operating. Their ideological controversy about the nature of the revolution took place at such a high level of generality that, even if it had been resolved, it would not have provided useful answers to the problems before them. For this controversy neglected fundamental issues such as the nature of the prevailing political system and its relationship to state power as it had evolved in Chile. The Communists took it for granted that an alliance with specific parties representing the interests of the progressive wing of the bourgeoisie would eventually usher in the national democratic stage of the revolution. The Socialists, for their part, refused, without further analysis, to take the system of political representation seriously. Yet, because their separate views stemmed more from conflicting interpretations of marxism than from alternative interpretations of Chilean reality they found it possible, in practice, to reconcile their continuing ideological conflict with the establishment of a durable alliance which was as pragmatic as that of any other grouping of parliamentary parties.

The Popular Unity provided Communists and Socialists with the ideal opportunity of giving concrete expression to their views about the nature of the socialist revolution. For the Popular Unity indeed proposed a novel way of achieving socialism. However, they accepted the notion of a transition to socialism through the existing democratic framework, without fully assessing its political implications. This oversight could be attributed to the fact that when the popular Unity was established, the chance of a left-wing victory at the polls was seen as so remote that its Programme was regarded only as a campaigning platform. However, it may have been due to the fact that the Communists, on the one hand, did not actually believe that the tasks of the Popular Unity government could be properly described as socialist, while, on the other hand, the Socialists believed that the collapse of bourgeois democracy was inevitable and imminent.

Had the Communists and Socialists carefully considered the possibilities of a peaceful transition, they would perhaps have adopted a less sanguine view about the virtues of the existing political system, as well as a more flexible attitude towards the CDP. For some of the weaknesses of the political system, which were to become so obvious during the Allende administration, were already beginning to show during the CDP administration. Indeed, during the Frei administration the locus of political power was beginning to shift – albeit slowly – from the democratically-generated organs of the political system to

281

other parts of the state apparatus, such as business associations, the judiciary and the army. Had the marxist parties reflected upon the implications of these developments they would perhaps have been capable of regarding the CDP not as an arch-rival committed to neo-capitalism, irrevocably on the side of United States imperialism, but as a necessary ally in their own struggle to achieve socialism.

The Communists' and Socialists' failure to foresee what the implications were for the proposed road to socialism deprived them of a viewpoint from which to determine and assess the pace and scope of government policy. In the absence of such a framework, neither the moderation of the Communists nor the radicalism of the Socialists was convincing. For while, on the one hand, Communist moderation could be easily interpreted as political abdication, Socialist radicalism could be seen as irresponsible petty-bourgeois leftism.

The Popular Unity's policy towards its opponents and supporters alike reveals the absence of a well-thought-out strategy. For government policy appears to have been based on the assumption that political opponents could easily be neutralised by manipulating a few economic variables and, likewise, that support for the government could be increased simply by redistributing income in favour of the poor. As it turned out, however, this policy did not shield the government from right-wing and foreign-induced subversion, nor did it transform those benefiting from its policy into committed revolutionaries. Thus, government policies appeared to have been based on a conception of state power alien even to the most eclectic strands of marxism.

The response of the Communist and Socialist parties to the *cordones industriales* and *comandos comunales* again illustrates the shortcomings of their approach to revolutionary politics. Despite their different policies, they both ultimately rejected them, perceiving them as a threat to their longstanding hegemony among organised workers. Yet, these organs of popular power pose the crucially important issue concerning whether and how parliamentary democracy can be reconciled with an effective transfer of power to grassroots organisations. For the experience of the *cordones* and *comandos* shows that unless civil and political rights already acquired by the popular masses are preserved and further developed, truly democratic socialism will never be achieved.

Notes

Chapter 2

1 Markos J. Mamalakis, 'The Role of Government in the Resource Transfer and Resource Allocation Processes: The Chilean Nitrate Sector, 1880–1930', in Gustav Ranis (ed.), *Government and Economic Development* (New Heaven, Conn., 1971), p. 182.
2 Ibid.
3 Markos J. Mamalakis, *The Growth and Structure of the Chilean Economy: From Independence to Allende* (New Haven, Conn., 1976), p. 38.
4 Karen L. Remmer, *Party Competition in Argentina and Chile: Political Recruitment and Public Policy* (Lincoln, Nebraska 1984), p. 40.
5 Maurice Zeitlin, *The Civil Wars in Chile* (Princeton, N.J., 1984), p. 144.
6 Harold Blakemore, 'Chile From the War of the Pacific to the World Depression, 1880–1930', in *The Cambridge History of Latin America, Vol. V* (Cambridge, 1986), p. 510.
7 Remmer, *Party Competition*, p. 144.
8 Ibid.
9 Ibid., p. 43.
10 Ibid., p. 84.
11 Zeitlin, *The Civil Wars*, p. 219.
12 Frederick B. Pike, *Chile and the United States, 1880–1962* (Notre Dame. 1963), p. 37.
13 Carmen Cariola and Osvaldo Sunkel, 'Chile', in Roberto Cortés Conde and Stanley J. Stein (eds.), *Latin America: A Guide to Economic History 1830–1930* (Berkeley, Ca., 1977), p. 290.
14 Jay Kinsbruner, *Chile: A Historical Interpretation* (New York 1973), p. 110.

15 Julio Heisse, *La Constitución de 1925 y las Nuevas Tendencias Político Sociales* (Santiago, 1951), pp. 120–21.
16 See Hernán Ramírez, *Historia del Imperialismo en Chile* (Santiago, 1960), *passim.*
17 Remmer, *Party Competition*, p. 148.
18 Mamalakis, *The Growth and Structure of the Chilean Economy*, p. 39.
19 See Hernán Ramírez, *Balmaceda y la Contrarrevolución de 1891*, 2nd. ed. (Santiago, 1969), p. 216; Heisse, *La Constitución de 1925*, pp. 46–60 and Andre Gunder Frank, *Capitalism and Underdevelopment in Latin America* (Harmondsworth, Middlesex, 1971), pp. 92–99.
20 See Blakemore, 'Chile From the War of the Pacific' in *The Cambridge History of Latin America*, p. 521, and Pike, *Chile and the United States*, pp. 40–46.
21 Pike, *Chile and the United States*, p. 86.
22 Mario Vera, *Una Política Definitiva para Nuestras Riquezas Básicas* (Santiago, 1964), pp. 219–20.
23 Gabriel Palma, 'Chile 1914–1935: De Economía Exportadora a Sustitutiva de Importaciones', *Nueva Historia*, 2 (1983), p. 167.
24 Michael Monteon, *Chile in the Nitrate Era* (Madison, Wisconsin, 1982), p. 16.
25 See René Millar, *Las Elecciones Presidenciales de 1920* (Santiago, 1981).
26 Atilio Borón, La Evolución del Régimen Electoral y sus Efectos en la Representación de los Intereses Populares: El Caso de Chile', *Revista Latinoamericana de Ciencia Política*, 2 (1971), p. 432.
27 See Sol Serrano, "Arturo Alessandri y la Campaña Electoral de 1920", in Claudio Orrego (ed.), *Siete Ensayos Sobre Arturo*

Alessandri Palma (Santiago, 1979), pp. 55–118.

28 Frederick M. Nunn, *Chilean Politics 1920–1931* (New Mexico, 1970), p. 81.

29 ECLA, *Economic Survey of Latin America, 1949* (New York, 1951), p. 378.

30 Palma, 'Chile 1914–1935', p. 171.

31 Oscar Muñoz, *Crecimiento Industrial de Chile 1914–1965* (Santiago, 1968), p. 24.

32 For a summary of the main features of the 1925 Constitutión see Federico G. Gil, *The Political System of Chile* (Boston Mass., 1966), pp. 88–122.

33 Albert Hirschman, *Journeys Toward Progress* (New York 1963), p. 175.

34 See Heisse, *La Constitución de 1925*, pp. 120–21.

35 See *Código del Trabajo* (Santiago, 1964), Articles 384 and 414.

36 P. T. Ellsworth, *Chile an Economy in Transition* (New York, 1945), p. 9.

37 World Bank, *Chile: An Economy in Transition* (Washington, D.C., 1980), p. 25.

38 Ellsworth, *Chile an Economy in Transition*, pp. 11–12.

39 Vera, *Una Política Definitiva*, p. 219.

40 Ibid., p. 220.

41 Ibid., pp. 210, 212.

42 Ibid., p. 217.

43 Department of Overseas Trade, *Report (No. 646) on Economic and Commercial Conditions in Chile* (London, 1936), p. 36.

44 Dirección General de Estadística, *Sinopsis Geográfico Estadística de la República de Chile, 1933* (Santiago, 1933), p. 236.

45 Ellsworth, *Chile an Economy in Transition*, p. 14.

46 ECLA, *Economic Survey of Latin America, 1954* (New York, 1955), p. 27.

Chapter 3

1 Alan Angell, *Politics and the Labour Movement in Chile* (London, 1972), p. 12.

2 Ibid., p. 18.

3 Ibid., p. 36.

4 Brian Loveman, *Chile: The Legacy of Hispanic Capitalism* (New York, 1979), p. 227.

5 Peter De Shazo, *Urban Workers and Labour Unions in Chile, 1902–1927* (Madison, Wisconsin, 1983), pp. 195–6.

6 Julio Samuel Valenzuela, 'Labour Movement Formation and Politics: The Chilean and French Cases in Comparative Perspective. 1850–1950' (Columbia University PhD thesis, 1979), p. 567.

7 Angell, *Politics and the Labour Movement*, p. 37.

8 Valenzuela, *Labour Movement Formation*, p. 565.

9 James O. Morris, *Elites, Intellectuals and Consensus: A Study of the Social Question and the Industrial Relations System in Chile* (Ithaca, 1966), p. 255.

10 Jorge Barría, *El Movimiento Obrero en Chile* (Santiago, 1971), p. 62.

11 Ibid., p. 63.

12 Ibid.

13 Valenzuela, *Labour Movement Formation*, p. 567.

14 Hernán Ramírez, *Origen y Formación del Partido Comunista de Chile* (Santiago, 1965), p. 195.

15 Luis Emilio Recabarren, *Obras Escogidas, Vol. I* (Santiago, 1965), p. 47.

16 De Shazo, *Urban Workers and Labour Unions in Chile*, p. 235.

17 Ramírez, *Origen y Formación del Partido Comunista*, pp. 259–63.

18 Paul W. Drake, *Socialism and Populism in Chile, 1932–1952* (Urbana, Illinois, 1978), pp. 139–50.

19 Ibid., pp. 150–64. See also Miriam Ruth Hochwald, 'Imagery in Politics: A Study of the Ideology of the Chilean Socialist Party' (University of California, Los Angeles PhD thesis, 1971), pp. 50–61.

20 Ramírez, *Origen y Formación del Partido Comunista*, p. 210.

21 Drake, *Socialism*, Chapter 6.

22 See Angell, *Politics and the Labour Movement*, pp. 102–33 and 131–36.

23 Dirección General de Estadística, *Sinopsis Geográfico Estadística de la República de Chile, 1933* (Santiago, 1933), p. 240.

24 Morris, *Elites, Intellectuals and Consensus*, p. 260.

25 See generally Julio Heisse, *La Constitución de 1925 y las Nuevas Tendencias Político Sociales* (Santiago, 1951), pp. 50–60.

26 See Atilio Borón, 'La Evolución del Régimen Electoral y sus Efectos en la Representación de los Intereses Populares: El Caso de Chile', *Revista Latinoamericana de Ciencia Política*, 2 (1971), pp. 428, 432.

27 Michael Potashnik, 'Nacismo: National Socialism in Chile. 1932–1938' (University of California, Los Angeles. PhD thesis, 1974), pp. 156 and 183.

28 Ibid., p. 258.

29 Maurice Zeitlin and Richard E. Ratcliff, 'Research Methods for the Analysis of the Internal Structure of Dominant Classes: The Case of Landlords and Capitalists in

Chile', *Latin American Research Review*, 10:3 (1975), p. 54.

30 P. T. Ellsworth, *Chile an Economy in Transition* (New York, 1945), pp. 25 and 45.

31 Ibid., p. 161.

32 Oscar Muñoz, *Crecimiento Industrial de Chile 1914–1965* (Santiago, 1968), p. 68.

33 Ellsworth, *Chile an Economy in Transition*, pp. 23, 32 and 63.

34 Jere R. Behrman, *Macroeconomic Policy in a Developing Country: The Chilean Experience* (Amsterdam, 1977), p. 23.

35 Muñoz, *Crecimiento Industrial de Chile*, p. 9.

36 Loveman, *Chile*, p. 266.

37 See Frederick M. Nunn, *The Military in Chilean History* (New Mexico, 1976), pp. 222–28.

38 On the Republican Militia see Ibid., pp. 228–30.

39 Richard R. Super, 'The Chilean Popular Front Presidency of Pedro Aguirre Cerda: 1938–1941' (Arizona State University PhD thesis, 1975), p. 24.

40 Germán Urzúa, *Los Partidos Políticos Chilenos* (Santiago, 1968), p. 78.

Chapter 4

1 Luis Palma, *Historia del Partido Radical* (Santiago, 1967), p. 175.

2 Ibid., p. 179.

3 John R. Stevenson, *The Chilean Popular Front* (Philadelphia, Pa., 1942), p. 73.

4 See Elías Laferte, *Vida de un Comunista* (Santiago, 1957), p. 123 and Richard R. Super, 'The Chilean Popular Front Presidency of Pedro Aguirre Cerda: 1938–1941' (Arizona State University PhD thesis, 1975), p. 55.

5 Stevenson, *The Chilean Popular Front*, p. 68.

6 Alan Angell, *Politics and the Labour Movement in Chile* (London, 1972), p. 108.

7 Palma, *Historia del Partido Radical*, p. 180.

8 Stevenson, *The Chilean Popular Front*, pp. 82–85.

9 Super, 'The Chilean Popular Front Presidency', p. 116.

10 Oscar Muñoz, *Crecimiento Industrial de Chile 1914–1965* (Santiago, 1968), p. 38.

11 ECLA, *Economic Survey of Latin America, 1949* (New York, 1951), p. 264.

12 On Corfo see Markos Mamalakis, 'An Analysis of the Financial and Investment Activities of the Chilean Development Corporation: 1939–1964', *Journal of Development Studies*, 5 (1969), pp. 118–37.

13 P. T. Ellsworth, *Chile an Economy in Transition* (New York, 1954), pp. 95–96.

14 Oscar Muñoz and Ana María Arriagada, *Orígenes Políticos y Económicos del Estado Empresarial en Chile* (Santiago. 1977), p. 16.

15 Ibid., pp. 18–19.

16 Ibid., pp. 15–16. See also Marcelo José Cavarozzi, 'The Government and the Industrial Bourgeoisie in Chile: 1930–1964' (University of California, Berkeley PhD thesis, 1975), p. 120.

17 Ellsworth, *Chile an Economy in Transition*, p. 88.

18 Muñoz and Arriagada, *Orígenes Políticos*, pp. 33, 34.

19 Brian Loveman, *Struggle in the Countryside: Politics and Rural Labor in Chile, 1919–1973* (Bloomington, Indiana, 1976), pp. 118–19.

20 Muñoz and Arriagada, *Orígenes Políticos*, p. 47.

21 Paul W. Drake, *Socialism and Populism in Chile, 1932–1952* (Urbana, Illinois, 1978), pp. 78 and 218.

22 Cavarozzi, *The Government and the Industrial Bourgeoisie*, pp. 136, 140.

23 Muñoz and Arriagada, *Orígenes Políticos*, p. 40.

24 Ibid., pp. 49–51.

25 Ibid., p. 47.

26 Cavarozzi, 'The Government and the Industrial Bourgeoisie', pp. 75 and 147.

27 ECLA, *Economic Survey of Latin America, 1949*, p. 264.

28 Max Nolff, 'Industria Manufacturera', in *Geografía Económica* (Santiago, 1965), p. 517.

29 Cavarozzi, 'The Government and the Industrial Bourgeoisie', pp. 145–48.

30 See David Felix, 'Structural Imbalances, Social Conflict, and Inflation: An Analysis of Chile's Recent Anti-Inflationary Effort,' *Economic Development and Cultural Change*, 8:2 (1960), p. 118.

31 Anibal Pinto, *Chile un Caso de Desarrollo Frustrado*, 3rd. edition (Santiago, 1973), pp. 155, 177.

32 ECLA, *Economic Survey of Latin America, 1949*, p. 378.

33 Instituto de Economía, *Desarrollo Económico de Chile 1940–1956* (Santiago, 1956), p. 69.

34 Ibid., p. 179.

35 Ibid., p. 186.

36 Pinto, *Chile un Caso de Desarrollo Frustrado*, p. 179.
37 Mario Vera, *La Política Económica del Cobre en Chile* (Santiago, 1961), p. 55.
38 Michael J. Francis, 'The United States and Chile during the Second World War: the Diplomacy of Misunderstanding', *Journal of Latin American Studies*, 9 (1977), pp. 94–96.
39 A. Cohen, *Economic Change in Chile, 1929–1959* (Gainsville, Florida, 1960), p. 15.
40 Mario Vera, *Una Política Definitiva para Nuestras Riquezas Básicas* (Santiago, 1964), pp. 211–12.
41 Andrew Barnard, 'Chilean Communists, Radical Presidents and Chilean Relations with the United States, 1940–1947', *Journal of Latin American Studies*, 13 (1981), p. 368.
42 Roger S. Abbott. 'The Role of Contemporary Political Parties in Chile', *American Political Science Review*, 45 (1951), p. 454.
43 Vera, *La Política Económica del Cobre*, p. 59.
44 Ricardo French-Davis, *Políticas Económicas en Chile 1952–1970* (Santiago, 1973), p. 282.
45 Vera, *La Política Económica del Cobre*, p. 59.
46 Felix, 'Structural Imbalances, Social Conflict and Inflation', p. 119.
47 Instituto de Economía, *Desarrollo Económico de Chile 1940–1956*, p. 200.
48 Jere R. Behrman, *Macroeconomic Policy in a Developing Country: The Chilean Experience* (Amsterdam, 1977), p. 27.
49 Solon Barraclough, 'Reforma Agraria: Historia y Perspectivas', *Cuadernos de la Realidad Nacional*, 9 (1971), pp. 52–53.
50 ODEPLAN, *Antecedentes sobre el Desarrollo Chileno 1960–1970* (Santiago, 1971), p. 104.
51 Solon Barraclough (ed.), *Agrarian Structure in Latin America* (Lexington, 1973), pp. 137–38.
52 Serigo Aranda and Alberto Martínez, *La Industria y la Agricultura en el Desarrollo Económico Chileno* (Santiago, n.d.), pp. 74–76.
53 Pinto, *Chile un Caso de Desarrollo Frustrado*, p. 236.
54 Ricardo Lagos, *La Tributación Agrícola* (Santiago, 1965), p. 85.
55 Ernest Feder, 'Feudalism and Agricultural Development: The Role of Controlled Credit in Chile's Agriculture', *Land Economics*, 36 (1960), p. 99.

56 Maurice Zeitlin and Richard E. Ratcliff, 'Research Methods for the Analysis of the Internal Structure of the Dominant Classes: The Case of Landlords and Capitalists in Chile', *Latin American Research Review*, 10 (1975), p. 54.
57 Markos J. Mamalakis, *The Growth and Structure of the Chilean Economy: From Independence to Allende* (New Haven' Conn., 1976), p. 181.
58 Albert Hirschman, *Journeys Toward Progress* (New York, 1963), p. 160.
59 Ibid., p. 183.
60 Instituto de Economía, *Desarrollo Económico de Chile 1940–1956*, p. 4.
61 ECLA, *Economic Survey of Latin America, 1949*, p. 270.
62 Ricardo Lagos, *La Industria en Chile: Antecedentes Estructurales* (Santiago, 1966), p. 146.
63 Mamalakis, *The Growth and Structure of the Chilean Economy*, p. 212.
64 Pinto, *Chile un Caso de Desarrollo Frustrado*, p. 273.
65 Mamalakis, *The Growth and Structure of the Chilean Economy*, p. 219.
66 ECLA, *Economic Survey of Latin America, 1954* (New York, 1955), p. 32.
67 Felix, 'Structural Imbalances, Social Conflict and Inflation', p. 121.
68 Hirschman, *Journeys Toward Progress*, p. 160.
69 Mamalakis, *The Growth and Structure of the Chilean Economy*, p. 163.

Chapter 5

1 Richard R. Super, 'The Chilean Popular Front Presidency of Pedro Aguirre Cerda: 1938–1941' (Arizona State University PhD thesis, 1975), p. 21.
2 Julio S. Valenzuela, 'Labor Movement Formation and Politics: The Chilean and French Cases in Comparative Perspective, 1850–1950' (Columbia University PhD thesis, 1979), p. 575.
3 Brian Loveman, *Chile: The Legacy of Hispanic Capitalism* (New York, 1979), p. 266.
4 Super, 'The Chilean Popular Front', p. 82.
5 On relations between Congress and the executive during the Aguirre administration, see John R. Stevenson, *The Chilean Popular Front* (Philadelphia, Pa., 1942), pp. 94–112.
6 Super, *The Chilean Popular Front*, pp. 196, 200.

7 Ibid., p. 208.
8 Ibid., p. 222.
9 Ibid., p. 250.
10 Stevenson, *The Chilean Popular Front*, p. 106.
11 Luis Palma, *Historia del Partido Radical* (Santiago, 1967), p. 218.
12 Paul W. Drake, *Socialism and Populism in Chile, 1932-1952* (Urbana, Illinois, 1978), p. 259.
13 For Allende's views on health care see his book *La Realidad Médico-Social Chilena* (Santiago, 1939).
14 Stevenson, *The Chilean Popular Front*, p. 109.
15 Super, 'The Chilean Popular Front', p. 259.
16 Alberto Cabero, *Recuerdos de don Pedro Aguirre Cerda* (Santiago, 1948), pp. 253-59.
17 Elías Laferte, *Vida de un Comunista* (Santiago, 1957), p. 322.
18 Stephen G. Rabe, 'Interamerican Military Cooperation, 1944-1951', *World Affairs*, 137 (1974), p. 133.
19 Michael Francis, 'The United States and Chile During the Second World War: the Diplomacy of Misunderstanding', *Journal of Latin American Studies*, 9 (1977), pp. 93-99.
20 Instituto de Economía, *Desarrollo Económico de Chile 1940-1956* (Santiago, 1956), p. 156.
21 Loveman, *Chile*, p. 266.
22 Manuel Barrera, 'Perspectiva Histórica de la Huelga en Chile', *Cuadernos de la Realidad Nacional*, 9 (1971), p. 98.
23 Julio César Jobet, *El Partido Socialista de Chile, Vol. I*, 3rd. edition (Santiago, 1971), p. 188.
24 On ACHA see Arturo Olavarría, *Chile Entre Dos Alessandri*, Vol. II (Santiago, 1962), pp. 41-54.
25 Brian Loveman, *Struggle in the Countryside: Politics and Rural Labor in Chile, 1919-1973* (Bloomington, Indiana, 1976), p. 124.
26 Almino Affonso, 'Esbozo Histórico del Movimiento Campesino Chileno', *Revista Latinoamericana de Ciencias Sociales*, 3 (1972), p. 54.
27 Peter G. Snow, *Radicalismo Chileno* (Buenos Aires, 1972), p. 111.
28 Andrew Barnard, 'The Chilean Communist Party, 1922-1947' (University of London PhD thesis, 1977), p. 357.
29 Affonso, 'Esbozo Histórico', p. 54.
30 Ibid., p. 61.
31 Rabe, 'Interamerican Military Coopera-

tion', p. 136.
32 Bernard, *The Chilean Communist Party*, p. 368.
33 Ibid., p. 367.
34 Ibid., p. 372.
35 Ibid., p. 373.
36 Palma, *Historia del Partido Radical*, pp. 192-93.

Chapter 6

1 Robert J. Alexander, *Labor Relations in Argentina, Brazil and Chile* (New York, 1962), p. 260.
2 See, for example, Ignacio Walker, *Del Populismo al Leninismo y la 'Inevitabilidad del Conflicto': El Partido Socialista de Chile (1933-1973)* (Santiago, 1986), pp. 15-17. For a lucid interpretation of the Socialists' populism see Paul W. Drake, *Socialism and Populism in Chile, 1932-1952* (Urbana, Illinois, 1978), pp. 11-13 and 37-40.
3 On Grove see Jack R. Thomas, 'The Evolution of a Chilean Socialist: Marmaduque Grove', *Hispanic American Historical Review*, 47 (1967), pp. 22-37.
4 Walker, *Del Populismo al Leninismo*, p. 24. See also Tomás Moulián, *Democracia y Socialismo en Chile* (Santiago, 1983), pp. 85-86 and *passim*.
5 See Torcuato Di Tella, 'Populism and Reform in Latin America', in *Claudio Veliz (ed.), Obstacles to Change in Latin America*, (London 1965), pp. 47-74.
6 Drake, *Socialism and Populism*, p. 79.
7 Oscar Schnake, *Chile y la Guerra* (Santiago, 1941), pp. 18-19.
8 Hernán Ramírez, *Origen y Formación del Partido Comunista de Chile* (Santiago, 1965), pp. 207-08.
9 Manuel Caballero, *Latin America and the Comintern 1919-1943* (Cambridge, 1986), p. 62.
10 Alejandro Chelén, *Trayectoria del Socialismo* (Buenos Aires, 1966), p. 92.
11 Julio César Jobet, *El Partido Socialista de Chile, Vol. I* (Santiago, 1971), p. 133.
12 Chelén, *Trayectoria del Socialismo*, p. 99.
13 The case against participation is strongly argued in Humberto Mendoza, *y Ahora?* (Santiago, 1942), pp. 231-34, 299, 307-11.
14 Jobet, *El Partido Socialista, Vol. I*, p. 188.
15 María Soledad Gómez, *Partido Communista de Chile, Factores Nacionales e Internacionales de su Política Internacional, 1922-1952* (Santiago, 1984), p. 14.

16 Germán Urzúa, *Historia Política Electoral de Chile (1931–1973)* (Santiago, 1986), p. 63.
17 The 1947 Programme is reproduced in Jobet, *El Partido Socialista, Vol. II*, pp. 207–28.
18 Caballero, *Latin America and the Comintern*, pp. 18–20.
19 Partido Comunista, *Hacia la Formación de un Verdadero Partido de Clase: Resoluciones de la Conferencia Nacional del Partido Realizada en Julio de 1933* (Santiago, n.d.), pp. 3, 20.
20 Ibid., p. 20.
21 Ibid., pp. 5, 51.
22 Ibid., p. 33.
23 Eudocio Ravines, *The Yenan Way* (Westport, 1972), pp. 164–186.
24 Caballero, *Latin America and the Comintern*, pp. 35, 46, 55, 61–62, 125–27.
25 Fernando Claudín, *The Communist Movement: From Comintern to Cominform* (Harmondsworth, Middlesex, 1975), pp. 302–04.
26 Gómez, *Partido Comunista de Chile*, p. 13.
27 On Browderism in Latin America see Caballero, *Latin America and the Comintern*, pp. 134–148.
28 Claudín, *The Communist Movement*, pp. 381, 395.
29 Andrew Barnard, 'Chilean Communists, Radical Presidents and Chilean Relations with the United States, 1940–1947', *Journal of Latin American Studies*, 13 (1981), p. 357.
30 Gómez, *Partido Comunista de Chile*, p. 44.
31 Ibid., pp. 47–8. On the Reinoso affair see also Carmelo Furci, *The Chilean Communist Party and the Road to Socialism* (London, 1984), pp. 44–52.
32 Claudín, *The Communist Movement*, pp. 465–73.
33 Barnard, 'Chilean Communists', p. 359.
34 See Bernardino Bravo, *Régimen de Gobierno y Partidos Políticos en Chile, 1924–1973* (Santiago, 1978), pp. 139–143 and p. 300, notes 199 and 203. The behaviour of the Communists towards Socialists during this period was later used quite effectively in anti-communist propaganda. See Beipi, 'El Partido Comunista de Chile', *Estudios Sobre el Comunismo*, 30 (1960), p. 52.
35 Germán Urzúa, *Los Partidos Políticos Chilenos* (Santiago, 1968), pp. 151–52.
36 Florencio Durán, *El Partido Radical* (Santiago, 1958), p. 126.
37 Luis Palma, *Historia del Partido Radical* (Santiago, 1967), p. 243.

Chapter 7

1 On Ibáñez' style of leadership see Jean Grugel, 'Populism, Nationalism and Liberalism in Chile: The Second Administration of Carlos Ibáñez, 1952–1958' (University of Liverpool PhD thesis, 1986), pp. 39–40, 80–86.
2 Arturo Olavarría, *Chile Entre Dos Alessandri, Vol. II* (Santiago, 1962), pp. 201–04.
3 Donald W. Bray, 'Peronism in Chile', *Hispanic American Historical Review*, 44 (1967), p. 45.
4 Grugel, *Populism*, pp. 62–70.
5 Marcelo José Cavarozzi, 'The Government and the Industrial Bourgeoisie in Chile: 1930–64' (University of California, Berkeley PhD Thesis, 1975), p. 276.
6 Mario Vera, *Una Política Definitiva para Nuestras Riquezas Básicas* (Santiago, 1964), p. 211.
7 Raymond, F. Mikesell, *Foreign Investment in the Petroleum and Mineral Industries* (Baltimore, 1971), p. 370.
8 Vera, *Una Política Definitiva*, pp. 71–76.
9 Theodore Moran, *Multinational Corporations and the Politics of Dependence* (Princeton, N.J., 1974), p. 97.
10 Enrique Sierra, *Tres Ensayos de Estabilización Económica* (Santiago, 1969), p. 10.
11 Cavarozzi, 'The Government and the Industrial Bourgeoisie', p. 262.
12 Manuel Barrera, *Desarrollo Económico y Sindicalismo en Chile: 1938–70* (Santiago, 1979), pp. 28–29.
13 Sierra, *Tres Ensayos*, p. 59.
14 Ibid., p. 63.
15 Ibid., p. 64.
16 Sandra Powell, 'Political Change in the Chilean Electorate, 1952–64', *Western Political Quarterly*, 23 (1970), p. 381.
17 See Olavarría, *Chile Entre Dos Alessandri* Tomo II, p. 400–01.
18 For an assessment of Alessandri's economic policy see Ricardo Ffrench-Davis, *Políticas Económicas en Chile 1952–70* (Santiago, 1973), pp. 41–50.
19 Barbara Stallings, *Class Conflict and Economic Development in Chile* (Stanford, Ca., 1978), p. 88.
20 ECLA, *Economic Survey of Latin America 1964* (New York, 1966), p. 318.
21 Sierra, *Tres Ensayos*, p. 78.

22 ECLA, *Economic Survey*, p. 320.
23 Ffrench-Davis, *Políticas Económicas*, pp. 47-48.
24 Sierra, *Tres Ensayos*, p. 140.
25 Ibid., p. 180.
26 See ECLA, *Economic Survey*, p. 318 and Lucio O. Geller, Lá Ayuda Externa: el Caso Chileno', *Desarrollo Económico*, 6 (1967), p. 632.
27 ECLA, *Economic Survey*, p. 320.
28 Sierra, *Tres Ensayos*, p. 164.
29 Geller, 'La Ayuda Externa', p. 631.

Chapter 8

1 Alejandro Chelén, *Trayectoria del Socialismo* (Buenos Aires, 1966), p. 130.
2 Instituto de Economía, *Desarrollo Económico de Chile, 1940-1956* (Santiago, 1956), p. 7.
3 Manuel Barrera, *Desarrollo Económico y Sindicalismo en Chile: 1938-1970* (Santiago, 1979), p. 17.
4 Eliana Cea, 'Clotario Blest: 52 Años en la Lucha Sindical', *Punto Final*, 9 November 1971, p. 8.
5 Jorge Barría, *El Movimiento Obrero en Chile* (Santiago, 1971), p. 62.
6 Donald W. Bray, 'Peronism in Chile', *Hispanic American Historical Review*, 47 (1967), p. 44.
7 Germán Urzúa, *Los Partidos Políticos Chilenos* (Santiago 1968), p. 98.
8 Federico G. Gil, *The Political System of Chile* (Boston, Mass., 1966), p. 242.
9 George Grayson, *El Partido Demócrata Cristiano Chileno* (Buenos Aires, 1968), p. 285.
10 See Atilio Borón, 'La Evolución del Régimen Electoral y sus Efectos en la Representación de los Intereses Populares: el Caso de Chile', *Revista Latinoamericana de Ciencia Política*, 2 (1971), p. 430.
11 Ibid., pp. 428-9.
12 See Charles J. Parrish (et al.), 'Electoral Procedures and Political Parties in Chile', *Studies in Comparative International Development*, 6 (1970-71), pp. 255-267 and Ricardo Cruz-Coke, *Geografía Electoral de Chile* (Santiago, 1952), pp. 58-59.
13 Sandra Powell, 'Political Change in the Chilean Electorate', *Western Political Quarterly*, 23 (1970), p. 381.
14 See Maurice Zeitlin and James Petras, The Working-Class Vote in Chile: Christian Democracy versus Marxism', *British Journal of Sociology*, 21 (1970), pp. 16-29.

15 On the Alliance for Progress in Chile see Agency for International Development, 'The United States Assistance Program to Chile', in Paul E. Sigmund (ed.) *Models of Political Change in Latin America*, (New York, 1970), pp. 316-22.
16 See Seymour M. Hersh, 'The Price of Power: Kissinger, Nixon and Chile', *Atlantic Monthly*, December 1982, p. 32.
17 U.S. Senate, *Staff Report of the Select Committee to Study Governmental Operations with Respect to Intelligence Activities: Covert Action in Chile* (Washington D.C., 1975), pp. 16-17.
18 Ibid., p. 15.
19 Aníbal Pinto, *Chile Un Caso de Desarrollo Frustrado* (Santiago, 1973), p. 177.
20 Instituto de Economía, *La Economía Chilena en el Período 1950-1963, Volume II* (Santiago, 1963), Cuadro 2, p. 3.
21 Ibid., p. 11.
22 Markos J. Mamalakis, *The Growth and Structure of the Chilean Economy: From Independence to Allende* (New Haven, Conn., 1976), p. 214.
23 Ibid., pp. 56, 165.
24 Ibid., p. 163.
25 J. W. Wilkie (ed.), *Statistical Abstract of Latin America, Volume 21* (Los Angeles, Ca., 1981), p. 284.
26 Ricardo Lagos, *La Industria en Chile: Antecedentes Estructurales* (Santiago, 1966), p. 146.
27 Max Nolff, 'Industria Manufacturera', in *Geografía Económica de Chile* (Santiago 1965), p. 511.
28 Ibid., pp. 533-34.
29 Lagos, *La Industria en Chile*, p. 89.
30 Sergio Molina, *El Proceso de Cambio en Chile* (Santiago, 1972), p. 202.
31 Wilkie, *Statistical Abstract*, p. 284 and PREALC, *Mercado de Trabajo en Cifras* (Santiago, 1982), p. 50.
32 Mamalakis, *The Growth and Structure of the Chilean Economy*, p. 131.
33 Mario Vera, *Una Política Definitiva para Nuestras Riquezas Básicas* (Santiago, 1964), p. 211.
34 World Bank, *Chile: An Economy in Transition* (Washington D.C., 1980), p. 19.
35 ECLA, *Economic Survey of Latin America 1964* (New York, 1966), p. 317.
36 Lucio O. Geller, 'La Ayuda Externa: el Caso Chileno', *Desarrollo Económico*, 6 (1967), p. 632.
37 Isabel Heskia, *La Distribución del Ingreso en Chile* (Santiago, 1973), pp. 3-6.
38 See ECLA, *Economic Survey of Latin*

America 1964, p. 32; and Molina, *E Proceso de Cambio*, p. 85.
39 World Bank, *Chile*, Table 9.9.

Chapter 9

1 For a discussion of the ideological founda tions of the Christian Democratic Party see Jaime Castillo, *Las Fuentes de la Democracia Cristiana* (Santiago, 1963).
2 For Maritain's political philosophy, see Joseph W. Evans and Leo R. Ward, *The Social and Political Philosophy of Jacques Maritain* (London, 1956), pp. 137-75.
3 For a selection of Frei's speeches and writings, see Oscar Pinochet (ed.), *El Pensamiento de Eduardo Frei* (Santiago, n.d.).
4 Jorge Ahumada, *En Vez de la Miseria* (Santiago, 1958), pp. 13-54.
5 For ECLA's approach to economic devel opment, see Raul Prebisch, 'Toward a Dynamic Development Policy for Latin America', in Paul E. Sigmund (ed.), *The Ideologies of the Developing Nations* (New York, 1967), pp. 368-79.
6 Jorge Ahumada, *La Crisis Integral de Chile* (Santiago, 1966), pp. 21-25.
7 Eduardo Frei, 'The Role of Popular Organizations in the State', in Sigmund (ed.) *The Ideologies of Developing Nations*, p. 390.
8 Ricardo Ffrench-Davis, *Políticas Económicas en Chile 1952-1970* (Santiago, 1973), p. 55.
9 Sergio Molina, *El Proceso de Cambio en Chile* (Santiago, 1972), p. 82.
10 Enrique Sierra, *Tres Ensayos de Estabilización Económica* (Santiago, 1969), p. 122.
11 For Frei's copper policy, see Theodore Moran, *Multinational Corporations and the Politics of Dependence* (Princeton, N.J., 1974), pp. 119-52.
12 Ibid., pp. 129-36.
13 For information on CIPEC, see Dorothea Mezger, *Copper in the World Economy* (London, 1980), pp. 19-55.
14 For the factional struggle within the CDP over agrarian reform, see Robert R. Kaufman, *The Politics of Land Reform in Chile, 1950-1970* (Cambridge, Mass., 1972), pp. 79-113.
15 For a discussion of Frei's agrarian reform, see Brian Loveman, *Struggle in the Countryside: Politics and Rural Labor in Chile, 1919-1973* (Bloomington, Indiana, 1976), pp. 241-78.
16 Barbara Stallings, *Class Conflict and Eco-

nomic Development in Chile* (Stanford, California, 1978), p. 246.
17 Patrick V. Peppe, *The Frei Government and the Chilean Labour Movement* (New York, 1974), p. 10. For a discussion of the factional struggle within the CDP during the Frei government, see Ricardo Yocelevsky, *La Democracia Cristiana Chilena y el Gobierno de Eduardo Frei (1967-1970)* (Mexico, 1987), pp. 279-316.
18 Paul E. Sigmund, *The Overthrow of Allende and the Politics of Chile, 1964-1976* (Pittsburgh, Pa., 1977), p. 65.
19 Julio Silva and Jacques Chonchol, 'Development without Capitalism: Toward a Communitarian World', in Paul E. Sigmund (ed.) *Models of Political Change* (New York, 1970), p. 310.
20 Ibid., p. 311.
21 Jaime Casillo, 'Property and the Communitarian Society', in Sigmund (ed.), *The Ideologies of Developing Nations*, pp. 400-04.
22 Ibid., p. 403.
23 For a discussion of the transition to a communitarian society, see James Petras, *Politics and Social Forces in Chilean Development* (Berkeley, 1969), p. 219.
24 William Thayer, 'Communitarianism and Christian Democracy', in Sigmund (ed.), *Models of Political Change*, p. 315.
25 Ibid., p. 313.
26 Jorge Barría, *El Movimiento Obrero en Chile* (Santiago, 1971), p. 116.
27 For a discussion of CUT/CDP relations, see Alan Angell, *Politics and the Labour Movement in Chile* (London, 1972), pp. 119, 143-47, 194-98.
28 Barría, *El Movimiento Obrero*, p. 127.
29 For a discussion of the *Tacnazo* see Michael Fleet, *The Rise and Fall of Christian Democracy* (Princeton, N.J., 1985), p. 112; and Sigmund, *The Overthrow of Allende*, p. 86.
30 See Sergio Onofre Jarpa, *Creo en Chile* (Santiago, 1973), p. 78.
31 Marcelo José Cavarozzi, 'The Government and the Industrial Bourgeoisie in Chile: 1930-1964' (University of California, Berkeley PhD thesis, 1975), p. 248.
32 For a discussion of the reaction of business associations to Frei's agrarian reform, see David F. Cusack, 'The Politics of Chilean Private Enterprise Under Christian Democracy' (University of Denver PhD thesis, 1970), pp. 249-55.
33 Ibid., pp. 49, 112, 131.
34 Luis Pacheco, 'La Inversión Extranjera y las Corporaciones Internacionales en el

Desarrollo Industrial Chileno', in Oscar Muñoz (ed.), *Proceso a la Industrialización Chilena* (Santiago, 1972), pp. 117–20.

35 Emir Sader, *Movilización de Masas y Sindicalización en el Gobierno de la Unidad Popular* (Santiago, 1973), p. 32.

36 See *Sexto Mensaje del Presidente de la República Eduardo Frei Montalva ante el Congreso Pleno, 21 de Mayo 1970* (Santiago, 1970), pp. 148–9.

37 Stallings, *Class Conflict and Economic Development*, p. 247.

38 Sader, *Movilización de Masas*, pp. 5–6.

39 Joaquín Duque and Ernesto Pastrana, 'La Movilización Reivindicativa Urbana de los Sectores Populares en Chile, 1964–1972', *Revista Latinoamericana de Ciencias Sociales*, 4 (1972), p. 268.

40 Ffrench-Davis, *Políticas Económicas en Chile*, p. 246.

41 Molina, *El Proceso de Cambio*, p. 140.

42 Ibid., p. 84.

43 Between 1964 and 1970 the number of children in primary schools increased from 1.3 million to 2 million. See ODEPLAN, *Antecedentes Sobre el Desarrollo Chileno 1960–1970 (Santiago, 1971), p. 297.* For a discussion of Frei's policies on education, see Kathleen B. Fischer, *Political Ideology and Educational Reform in Chile, 1964–1976* (Los Angeles, Ca., 1979), pp. 30–49.

44 Molina, *El Proceso de Cambio*, p. 82.

45 Stallings, *Class Conflict and Economic Development*, p. 248.

46 Ibid.

47 Molina, *El Proceso de Cambio*, p. 202.

48 Markos J. Mamalakis, *The Growth and Structure of the Chilean Economy: From Independence to Allende* (New Haven, Conn., 1976), p. 163.

49 ODEPLAN, *Antecedentes*, p. 71.

50 Aníbal Pinto, *Chile Un Caso de Desarrollo Frustrado* (Santiago, 1973), p. 133. See also Oscar Muñoz, Crecimiento Industrial, Estructura de Consumo y Distribuición del Ingreso', in Muñoz (ed.), *Proceso a la Industrialización*, p. 20.

51 ODEPLAN, *Antecedentas*, p. 414.

52 Mamalakis, *The Growth and Structure of the Chilean Economy*, p. 169.

53 Molina, *El Proceso de Cambio*, p. 128.

Chapter 10

1 See Galo González, 'Informe a la Comisión Política (Octubre 1957)', in Partido Communista, *El Partido Comunista de Chile y el Movimiento Comunista Internacional* (San-

tiago, 1963), p. 44.

2 *Julio César Jobet, El Socialismo Chileno a Través de sus Congresos* (Santiago. 1965), p. 76.

3 For Blest's letter, see Eliana Cea, 'Clotario Blest: 52 Años en la Lucha Sindical', *Punto Final*, 9 November, 1971, p. 11. On Blest, see also Maximiliano Salinas, *Clotario Blest* (Santiago, 1980).

4 Marcela Noé, 'La Central Unica de Trabajadores: Orientaciones de su Acción Histórica', *Cuadernos de la Realidad Nacional*, 8 (1971), p. 45.

5 Jorge Barría, *El Movimiento Obrero en Chile* (Santiago, 1971), p. 106.

6 Luis Corvalán, *Camino de Victoria* (Santiago, 1971), p. 46. See also Comité Central del Partido Comunista, 'Conclusions del Pleno de Setiembre 1964' *Principios*, 103 (1964), pp. 132–43.

7 Julio César Jobet, *El Partido Socialista de Chile, Vol. II* (Santiago, 1971), p. 129.

8 See 'Declaración del Comite Central del Partido Socialista el Día del Tacnazo', in Fernando Casanueva and Manuel Fernández (eds.), *El Partido Socialista y la Lucha de Classes en Chile* (Santiago, 1973), pp. 230–31.

9 Corvalán, *Camino*, pp. 315–18.

10 Jobet, *El Socialismo Chileno*, p. 76.

11 Ibid., p. 90.

12 Ibid., p. 108.

13 Benny Pollack and Hernan Rosenkranz, *Revolutionary Social Democracy – The Chilean Socialist Party* (London, 1986), p. 42.

14 For a discussion of the influence of the Yugoslav model among Socialists, see Ernst Halperin, *Nationalism and Communism in Chile* (Cambridge, Mass., 1965), pp. 144–58.

15 For a discussion of Almeyda's views, see Ibid., pp. 158–69.

16 Heraldo Muñoz, 'La Inserción Internacional de los Partidos de Izquierda Chilenos: Un Análisis en la Perspectiva de la Redemocratización', *Alternativas*, 3 (1984), pp. 54–55.

17 Ignacio Walker, *Del Populismo al Leninismo y la 'Inevitabilidad del Conflicto': El Partido Socialista de Chile (1933–1973)* (Santiago, 1986), p. 53.

18 Cecil Johnson, *Communist China and Latin America 1959–1967* (New York, 1970), p. 145.

19 For Soviet policy in the Latin American region, see Herbert S. Dinerstein, 'Soviet policy in Latin America', *American Political Science Review*, 61 (1967), pp. 80–90.

20 For the Communists' views on the need to

broaden the FRAP alliance, see Orlando Millas, 'Informe al Comité Central (Mayo 1960)', in *El Partido Comunista y el Movimiento Comunista Internacional*, pp. 117–19.

21 For a good summary of this polemic, see Halperin, *Nationalism and Communism*, pp. 144–58.

22 See Jobet, *El Partido Socialista*, Vol. II, p. 563.

23 Ibid., pp. 96–7.

24 Adonis Sepúlveda, 'El Partido Socialista y la Revolución Chilena', in Julio César Jobet and Alejandro Chelén (eds.) *Pensamiento Teórico y Político del Partido Socialista en Chile* (Santiago, 1972), p. 232.

25 D. Bruce Jackson, *Castro, the Kremlin and Communism in Latin America* (Baltimore, Maryland, 1969), p. 90.

26 Ibid., p. 21.

27 Ernesto 'Ché' Guevara, *Guerilla Warfare* (New York, 1961), p. 16.

28 Jobet, *El Partido Socialista*, Vol. II, p. 151.

29 For a discussion of maoism within the Communist Party, see Halperin, *Nationalism and Communism*, pp. 93–117.

30 Johnson, *Communist China and Latin America*, p. 248.

31 Luis Corvalán, 'Las Discrepancias con los Camaradas Chinos', in *El Partido Comunista y el Movimiento Comunista Internacional*, pp. 253–71.

32 Johnson, *Communist China and Latin America*, p. 153.

33 'Comunicado Conjunto: Partido Comunista de Chile y Partido de la Revolución Socialista de Cuba', in *Principios*, 108 (1965), pp. 134–36.

34 Comité Central del Partido Comunista, 'Conclusiones del Pleno de Setiembre 1964', *Principios*, 103 (1964), p. 135.

35 Comité Central del Partido Comunista, 'Mensaje de saludo enviado por el Comité Central del Partido Comunista al XXI Congreso Nacional del Partido Socialista', *Principios*, 108 (1964), pp. 126–32.

36 Corvalán, *Camino*, pp. 140, 149–53.

37 Jobet, *El Socialismo*, p. 119.

38 Brian H. Smith, *The Church and Politics in Chile* (Princeton, N.J., 1982), pp. 109–11.

39 Orlando Millas, 'New Trends in Catholicism and the Policy of the Chilean Communists', *World Marxist Review*, 7 (1964), pp. 25–40. See also Orlando Millas, *Los Comunistas, los Católicos y la Libertad* (Santiago, 1964), pp. 57–71.

40 Smith, *The Church and Politics*, p. 140.

41 Corvalán, *Camino*, p. 323. See also Luis Corvalán, 'The Peaceful Way-A Form of Revolution', *World Marxist Review*, 6 (1963), pp. 2–9.

42 Partido Comunista de Chile, *Estatutos* (Santiago, 1969), Article 1.

43 Raúl Araya, 'De Donde Viene la Vía no-Capitalista', *Principios*, 133 (1970), pp. 44–45.

Chapter 11

1 Sergio Onofre Jarpa, *Creo en Chile* (Santiago, 1973), p. 75.

2 Seymour M. Hersh, 'The Price of Power', *Atlantic Monthly*, December 1982, p. 37.

3 Nathaniel Davis, *The Last Two Years of Salvador Allende* (London, 1985), pp. 12–13.

4 Carlos Prats, *Memorias: Testimonio de un Soldado* (Santiago, 1985), pp. 148, 152.

5 Ibid., p. 100.

6 For the role of ITT during this period, see Bertrand Russell Foundation, *Subversion in Chile: A Case Study in United States Corporate Intrigue in the Third World* (Nottingham, 1972).

7 See Carlos Fortín, 'Law and Economic Coercion as Instruments of International Control', in Julio Faúndez and Sol Picciotto (eds.), *The Nationalisation of Multinationals in Peripheral Economies*, (London, 1978), pp. 132–60.

8 See Arturo Valenzuela, *The Breakdown of Democratic Regimes: Chile* (Baltimore, Maryland, 1978), note 4, p. 127.

9 United States Senate, *Staff Report of the Select Committee to Study Governmental Operations with Respect to Intelligence Activities: Covert Action in Chile* (Washington DC., 1975), p. 24.

10 Davis, *The Last Two Years*, pp. 336, 342.

11 See speech by Senator Francisco Bulnes (National Party) in Andrés Echeverría and Luis Frei (eds), *La Lucha por la Juridicidad en Chile*, Vol. I (Santiago, 1974), p. 93.

12 Jarpa, *Creo en Chile*, p. 164.

13 Bernardino Bravo, *Régimen de Gobierno y Partidos Políticos en Chile 1924–1973* (Santiago, 1978), p. 134.

14 *El Mercurio*, 20 June 1971, p. 31.

15 José Garrido, 'The Increasing Social Participation in Chile', in Tomás MacHale (ed.), *Chile: A Critical Survey*, (Santiago, 1972), pp. 187–91.

16 Michael Fleet, *The Rise and Fall of Chris-*

tian Democracy (Princeton, N.J., 1985), p. 137.

17 See Senator Patricio Aylwin's (CDP) speech in Echeverría and Frei (eds.), *La Lucha por la Juridicidad, Vol. I*, pp. 71–84.

18 See Senator Bulnes' (National Party) speech in Ibid., p. 93.

19 See Allende's statements in Regis Debray, *Conversations with Allende* (New York, 1971), pp. 77, 119–20.

20 See Fleet, *The Rise and Fall*, pp. 149–54.

21 Senator Aylwin's speech in Echeverría and Frei (eds.), *La Lucha por la Juridicidad, Vol. I*, pp. 54, 72.

22 Radomiro Tomic, 'La Democracia Cristiana y el Gobierno de la Unidad Popular', in Federico G. Gil, Ricardo Lagos and Henry A. Landsberger, *Chile 1970–1973* (Madrid, 1977), pp. 215–43.

23 See Miles D. Wolpin, 'Systemic Constraints and Chilean Socialism in Comparative Perspective', *Politics and Society*, 3 (1973), pp. 363, 367.

24 For the Programme of the Popular Unity, see Salvador Allende, *Chile's Road to Socialism* (Harmondsworth, Middlesex, 1973), pp. 23–51. The phrase quoted in the text is on page 35.

25 Ibid., p. 50.

26 This quotation is taken from Allende's First Annual Message to the Congress. See Ibid., p. 148.

27 Ibid., p. 42.

28 Ibid., p. 147–50.

29 Jorge Insunza, 'Nuevos Problemas Tácticos', *El Siglo*, 11 May 1971, p. 4.

30 Luis Corvalán, *Camino de Victoria* (Santiago, 1971), p. 418.

31 Carlos Altamirano, 'El Partido Socialista y la Revolución Chilena', in Julio César Jobet and Alejandro Chelén (eds.), *Pensamiento Teórico y Político del Partido Socialista de Chile*, (Santiago, 1972), p. 336.

32 Ibid.

33 Secretariado Nacional del Movimiento de Izquierda Revolucionaria, 'El MIR Frente a la Situación Política', *Punto Final*, 29 September, 1970, pp. 24–25.

Chapter 12

1 Joan Garcés, *Allende y la Experiencia Chilena* (Barcelona 1976), p. 216.

2 See Enrique Evans, *Relación de la Constitución Política de la República de Chile* (Santiago, 1970), pp. 172–75.

3 For the composition of the Congress, see Germán Urzúa, *Historia Política Electoral de Chile (1931–1973)* (Santiago, 1986), pp. 133–37.

4 For the background of the programme of action, see Pío García, 'El Area de Propiedad Social: Alcances Políticos', in Federico G. Gil, Ricardo Lagos and Henry A. Landsberger (eds.), *Chile 1970–1973* (Madrid, 1977), pp. 170–77.

5 See Pedro Vuskovic, 'La Experiencia Chilena: Problemas Económicos', in Manuel A. Garretón and Roberto Pizarro (eds.), *Transición al Socialismo y Experiencia Chilena* (Santiago, 1972), pp. 99–114.

6 For an outline of the government's legal strategy see, Eduardo Novoa, 'The Constitutional and Legal Aspects of the Popular Unity Government's Policy', in Anne Zammit (ed.), *The Chilean Road to Socialism*, (Falmer, Sussex, 1973), pp. 26–40.

7 The best critical analysis of Allende's economic policy is Sergio Bitar's *Transición, Socialismo y Democracia: La Experiencia Chilena* (México, 1979). There is an English translation of this book under the title *Chile: Experiment in Democracy* (Philadelphia, Pa., 1986).

8 For a discussion of the budgetary process, see Instituto de Economía, *El Proceso Presupuestario Fiscal Chileno* (Santiago, 1958).

9 See Pedro Vuskovic's speech in Washington before the Committee of the Alliance for Progress, 'La Política Económica de la Transición al Socialismo', *Panorama Económico*, 260 (1971), pp. 11–18.

10 See Pedro Vuskovic, 'The Economic Policy of the Popular Unity', in Zammit (ed.), *The Chilean Road to Socialism*, pp. 49–56. For a more recent restatement of Vuskovic's views, see his article 'Los Problemas Económicos de la Transición', *Trimestre Económico*, 50 (1983), pp. 473–518.

11 For an outline of Allende's foreign policy see Clodomiro Almeyda, 'La Política Exterior del Gobierno de la Unidad Popular en Chile', in Gil et al. (eds.), *Chile 1970–1973*, pp. 88–115.

12 See Norberto García, 'Algunos Aspectos de la Política de Corto Plazo de 1971, in Instituto de Economía (ed.), *La Economía Chilena en 1971* (Santiago, 1972), pp. 250–54.

13 Bitar, *Transición, Socialismo y Democracia*, p. 25.

14 Alejandro Foxley and Oscar Muñoz, *Redistribución del Ingreso, Crecimiento Económico y Estructura Social: El Caso Chileno* (Santiago, 1973), p. 4.
15 For a discussion of the consequences of the government's incomes policy see Arturo León and José Serra, *La Economía Política de la Distribución del Ingreso en Chile Durante el Gobierno de la Unidad Popular* (Río de Janeiro, 1980). See also Fernando Cortés and Ricardo Yocelevsky, 'La Distribución del Ingreso en el Gobierno de la Unidad Popular (1970–1973)' (México, Colegio de México, unpublished paper, 1979).
16 Solon Barraclough and José Antonio Fernández, *Diagnóstico de la Reforma Agraria* (México, 1974), pp. 102–03.
17 Ibid., p. 107.
18 Stephany Griffith-Jones, *The Role of Finance in the Transition to Socialism* (London, 1981), pp. 146–47.
19 See, for example, Paul N. Rosenstein-Rodan, 'Why Allende Failed', *Challenge*, May-June 1974, pp. 7–13, and Alec Nove, 'The Political Economy of the Allende Regime', in Philip O'Brien (ed.), *Allende's Chile*, (New York, 1976), pp. 51–78.
20 Griffith-Jones, *The Role of Finance*, p. 140.
21 World Bank, *Chile: An Economy in Transition* (Washington, 1980), p. 82.
22 Ibid., p. 80.
23 Bitar, *Transición, Socialismo y Democracia*, pp. 106–07.
24 Eduardo Novoa, *La Batalla por el Cobre* (Santiago, 1972), p. 272.
25 Bitar, *Transición, Socialismo y Democracia*, pp. 115–18.
26 Griffith-Jones, *The Role of Finance*, p. 53.
27 García, 'Algunos Aspectos', in *La Economía Chilena en 1971*, p. 196.
28 Bitar, *Transición, Socialismo y Democracia*, p. 189.
29 Barraclough and Fernández, *Diagnóstico*, p. 108.
30 Alexis Guardia, 'Structural Transformations in Chile's Economy and its System of External Relations', in *Chile 1970–73: Economic Development in its International Setting* (The Hague, 1979), p. 96.
31 World Bank, *Chile: An Economy in Transition*, p. 87.
32 Bitar, *Transición, Socialismo y Democracia*, p. 189.
33 See Henry A. Landsberg and Tim McDaniel, 'Hypermobilization in Chile, 1970–1973', *World Politics*, 28 (1976), pp. 502–41.
34 Barraclough and Fernández, *Diagnóstico*, p. 192.
35 Joan Garcés, *El Estado y los Problemas Tácticos en el Gobierno de Allende* (Buenos Aires, 1973), pp. 150–51.
36 For Allende's statement see *El Siglo*, 24 November 1970, p. 9.
37 For the government bill on occupations, see *Diario de Sesiones del Senado*, Sess. 34, 8 February 1971, pp. 2003–4.
38 Adonis Sepúlveda, 'Informe al Pleno del Comite Central', *Aurora de Chile*, April 1973.
39 ODEPLAN, *Informe Económico Anual 1971* (Santiago, 1972), pp. 31–32.
40 Ibid., pp. 13–61. See also Stefan de Vylder, *Allende's Chile: The Political Economy of the Rise and Fall of the Unidad Popular* (Cambridge, 1976), pp. 52–80.
41 Juan G. Espinosa and Andrew S. Zimbalist, *Economic Democracy: Workers' Participation in Chilean Industry 1970–1973* (New York, 1978), pp. 46, 49.
42 ODEPLAN, *Informe Económico 1971*, p. 94.
43 For an outline of the nationalisation of copper, see Novoa, *La Batalla*, pp. 120–31.
44 Brian Loveman, *Struggle in the Countryside: Politics and Rural Labor in Chile, 1919–1973* (Bloomington, Indiana, 1976) pp. 279–301.
45 Instituto de Economía, *La Economía Chilena en 1972* (Santiago, 1973), pp. 116–24.
46 See statement by leaders of the National Party in *El Mercurio*, 20 June 1971, p. 30 and 25 October 1971, p. 25.
47 Novoa, *La Batalla*, pp. 140–45.
48 Rodomiro Tomic, 'Aclaraciones Sobre Ciertos Hechos Históricos', in Gil et al. (eds.), *Chile 1970–1973*, p. 198.
49 See Nathaniel Davis, *The Last Two Years of Salvador Allende* (London, 1985), pp. 21, 308, 312, 334.
50 See speech by Senator Narciso Irureta (CDP) in *El Mercurio*, 20 June 1971, p. 31.
51 For Frei's statements, see *El Mercurio*, 23 September 1971, p. 1.
52 See resolution approved by the youth section of the CDP in *El Mercurio*, 15 October 1971, p. 19.
53 Loveman, *Struggle in the Countryside*, pp. 293–94.
54 For the political debate on the government's proposal, see Jack Spence, *Search for Justice: Neighborhood Courts in Allende's*

Chile (Boulder, Colorado, 1979), pp. 41–52.

55 *El Mercurio*, 28 January, 1971, p. 23.

56 See speech by Senator Benjamín Prado (CDP), *Diario de Sesiones del Senado*, Sess. 23, 19 January 1971, pp. 812–23.

57 See U.P., 'PDC: El Adiós Tiene su Hora', *Ahora*, 3 August 1971, pp. 9–11.

58 Michael Fleet, *The Rise and Fall of Christian Democracy* (Princeton, 1985), p. 147.

59 Alberto Martínez, 'The Industrial Sector: Areas of Social and Mixed Property in Chile', in Sideri (ed.), *Chile 1970–73*, p. 230.

60 For the text of the CDP's constitutional amendment, see Reinhard von Braun, *Chile ¿Con Leyes Tradicionales Hacia una Nueva Economía?* (Santiago, 1972), pp. 86–97.

61 For a good account of the events surrounding the 'empty-pots' march, see *Cámara de Diputados Boletín 932–71–2*, 5 January 1972, pp. 36–41.

62 Garcés, *Allende*, p. 168.

63 For the speech by Senator Renán Fuentealba, President of the CDP, announcing the decision to bring impeachment proceedings against the Minister of the Interior, see Andrés Echeverría and Luis Frei, *La Lucha por la Juridicidad en Chile, Vol. II* (Santiago, 1974), pp. 9, 34.

64 Ibid., p. 24.

65 See speech by Luis Corvalán, Secretary General of the Communist Party, in *El Siglo*, 24 October 1971, p. 6.

66 Luis Corvalán, 'The Popular Government in Chile', *World Marxist Review*, 13 (1970), pp. 2–6.

67 See Luis Alberto Mansilla, 'Volodia Habla de sus Dos Amores, *Ahora*, 7 September 1971, pp. 62–64. See also Eduardo Labarca, *Corvalán 27 Horas* (Santiago, 1972), p. 180.

Chapter 13

1 See for example, the speech by Luis Figueroa of the Communist Party, President of the CUT, in *El Siglo*, 27 June 1971, p. 4; the speech by Carlos Cerda, a prominent Communist Party leader, in *El Siglo*, 29 June 1971, p. 3; and Roberto Pinto, 'The MIR Attack on the Communist Party', in Dale L. Johnson (ed.) *The Chilean Road to Socialism* (New York, 1973), pp. 371–76.

2 *El Mercurio*, 3 February 1972, pp. 1, 8.

3 For the text of the document approved by the Popular Unity at the Arrayán, see *El Mercurio*, 10 February 1972, pp. 1, 8, 16.

4 For the proposed Constitutional Amendment and the government's vetoes, see Reinhard von Braun, *Chile ¿Con Leyes Tradicionales Hecia una Nueva Economía?* (Santiago, 1972), pp. 86–111.

5 *El Siglo*, 13 February 1972, p. 6.

6 *La Prensa*, 10 March 1972, p. 1.

7 Paul E. Sigmund, *The Overthrow of Allende and the Politics of Chile, 1964–1976* (Pittsburgh, Pa., 1977), pp. 168–69.

8 For this statement see *Diario de Sesiones del Senado*, Sess. 7, 6 de julio 1972, pp. 668–81.

9 Ibid., p. 668. For the background material on the Constitutional Court, see Enrique Silva, *El Tribunal Constitucional* (Caracas, 1978), pp. 27–60.

10 For press coverage of this meeting, see *La Prensa*, 6 March 1972, p. 1 and 7 March 1972, p. 1.

11 See Nathaniel Davis, *The Last Two Years of Salvador Allende* (London, 1985), p. 161.

12 See speech by Senator Patricio Aylwin (CDP) in *El Mercurio*, 13 April 1972, pp. 20–21.

13 Instituto de Economía, *La Economía Chilena en 1972* (Santiago, 1973), p. 202.

14 See interview with Senator Renán Fuentealba in *El Mercurio*, 26 March 1972, p. 9.

15 See speech by Senator Aylwin (CDP) in *El Mercurio*, 13 April 1972, pp. 20–21.

16 For a lucid analysis of the Christian Democratic Party's opposition strategy see Richard Parker, 'The Reaction of the Opposition Forces to Allende' (Santiago; Universidad de Chile, Instituto de Estudios Internacionales unpublished paper), pp. 22–25.

17 On wage settlements, see Sergio Bitar, *Transición, Socialismo y Democracia: La Experiencia Chilena* (México, 1979), p. 182.

18 Barbara Stallings, *Class Conflict and Economic Development in Chile* (Stanford, Ca., 1978), p. 246.

19 Alan Angell, 'Political Mobilisation and Class Alliances in Chile, 1970–1973' (Oxford: Latin American Centre, unpublished paper, 1978), p. 21.

20 Orlando Millas, 'La Clase Obrera en las Condiciones del Gobierno Popular', *Principios*, 145 (1972), pp. 34–36.

21 On the opposition's campaign, see Bitar, *Transición, Socialismo y Democracia*, pp. 146–48.

22 See Manuel Antonio Garretón (ed.), *Chile: Cronología del Periodo 1970–1973, Vol. I* (Santiago, 1978), pp. 231–33.

23 On the black market, see Sergio Ramos, 'Inflation in Chile and the Political Economy of the Unidad Popular Government,' in *Chile 1970–73: Economic Development and its International Setting* (The Hague, 1979), pp. 330, 334.

24 On the role of the mass media generally, see Ian Roxborough, Philip O'Brien and Jackie Roddick, *Chile: The State and Revolution* (London, 1977) pp. 105–07.

25 Bitar, *Transición, Socialismo y Democracia*, p. 149.

26 *El Mercurio*, 9 June 1972, p. 32.

27 For details of these negotiations, see Bitar, *Transición, Socialismo y Democracia*, pp. 151–55.

28 See *Diario de Sesiones del Senado*, Sess. 9, 12 June 1972, pp. 854–82.

29 For the text of this new constitutional amendment see *Diario de Sesiones del Senado*, Sess. 17, 20 June 1972, pp. 1104–06.

30 For a brief explanation of the role of Comptroller-General, see Enrique Silva, *El Tribunal Constitucional*, pp. 167–68.

31 On the role of the judiciary during this period, see Eduardo Novoa, *¿Vía Legal Hacia el Socialismo?* (Caracas, 1978), pp. 108–18.

32 *El Mercurio*, 10 July 1972, p. 26.

33 For an interesting perspective on the Popular Assembly, see Jorge Palacios, *Chile: An Attempt at 'Historic Compromise'* (Toronto, 1979), pp. 373–75.

34 *El Siglo*, 1 August 1972, p. 3.

35 *El Siglo*, 31 August 1972, pp. 6–7.

36 For the response of the Socialist Party see *El Mercurio*, 4 August 1972, pp. 1, 10.

37 Bitar, *Transición, Socialismo y Democracia*, p. 158.

38 See speech by Senator Aylwin (CDP) in *Diario de Sesiones del Senado*, Sess. 70, 6 September 1972, pp. 3935–36.

39 See statement by the President of the CDP, Senator Fuentealba in *El Mercurio*, 15 September 1972, p. 1.

40 Jorge Larraín, 'Orientaciones y Actividades de la Confederación Democrática de Partidos Durante la Crisis de Octubre de 1972', *Cuadernos de la Realidad Nacional*, 16 (1973), p. 233.

41 *Diario de Sesiones del Senado*, Sess. 97, 14 September 1972, p. 4571.

42 Larraín, 'Orientaciones', p. 234.

43 Ibid., p. 236.

44 Ibid., pp. 238–39.

45 See United States Senate, *Staff Report of the Select Committee to Study Governmental Operations with Respect to Intelligence Activities: Covert Action in Chile* (Washington, D.C., 1975), pp. 28–30.

46 Larraín, 'Orientaciones', p. 241.

47 Interview with General Carlos Prats, *Chile Hoy*, 22 (1972), p. 29.

48 *Diario de Sesiones del Senado*, Sess. 55, 27 December 1972, p. 2227.

49 Garretón, *Chile*, p. 332.

50 For a description of these economic measures, see Bitar, *Transición, Socialismo y Democracia*, pp. 223–29.

51 For the new nationalisation bill, see *Cámara de Diputados*, Sess. 27, 21 February 1973, pp. 1904–10.

52 On at least two occasions the opposition brought impeachment proceedings against cabinet ministers on the ground that the government-sponsored JAPs were unconstitutional. See *Cámara de Diputados*, Sess. 51, 17 May 1983, pp. 2833–52 and *Diario de Sesiones del Senado*, Sess. 30, 5 July 1973, pp. 1193–95.

53 See *El Mercurio*, 18 January 1973, p. 12, 25 January 1973, p. 25, 19 April 1973, p. 21 and 24 May 1973, p. 9.

54 *El Mercurio*, 30 January 1973, pp. 10, 17.

55 Interview with Carlos Altamirano, *Punto Final*, 13 February 1973, pp. 1–6.

56 See *Plataforma de Gobierno del Partido de la Unidad Popular* (Santiago, n.d.).

57 For details on the results of these elections, see *Chile Hoy*, 39 (1973), p. 7.

58 Carlos Prats, *Memorias: Testimonio de un Soldado* (Santiago, 1985), p. 370.

59 See letter from Eduardo Frei to Senator Fuentealba in *Diario de Sesiones del Senado*, Sess. 90, 24 April 1973, pp. 3612–14.

60 See 'Declaración del Consejo Plenario del PDC', *Política y Espíritu*, 11 April 1973, pp. 70–73.

61 See 'Voto Político de la Junta Nacional de la JDC', *Política y Espíritu*, 11 April 1973, pp. 73–74.

62 On ENU, see Kathleen B. Fischer, *Political Ideology and Educational Reform in Chile, 1964–1976* (Los Angeles, Ca., 1979), pp. 100–17.

63 See speech by Senator Tomás Pablo (CDP) in *Diario de Sesiones del Senado*, See. 84, 3 March 1973, pp. 3261–78.

64 For a discussion of the reaction of the Catholic Church to the ENU project, see Brian H. Smith, *The Church and Politics in*

Chile (Princeton, 1982), pp. 196–99.
65 *El Siglo*, 16 April 1973, p. 12.
66 On the copper strike, see Bitar, *Transición, Socialismo y Democracia*, pp. 229–33.
67 *El Mercurio*, 17 June 1973, pp. 29, 37.
68 For the Supreme Court's Resolution see Andrés Echeverría and Luis Frei, *La Lucha por la Juridicidad en Chile, Vol. 3* (Santiago, 1974), pp. 159–60.
69 Prats, *Memorias*, pp. 395–409.
70 Ibid., p. 396.
71 Ibid., p. 410.
72 *Diario de Sesiones del Senado*, Sess. 28, 3 July 1973, pp. 1120–23, 1135–39.
73 Prats, *Memorias*, p. 425.
74 See *United States and Chile During the Allende Years, 1970–1973*, (Hearings before the Subcommittee on Inter-American Affairs of the Committee on Foreign Affairs House of Representatives) (Washington, D.C., 1976), p. 391.
75 Sigmund, *The Overthrow of Allende*, pp. 223–25.
76 Stephany Griffith-Jones, *The Role of Finance in the Transition to Socialism* (London, 1981), pp. 144, 149.
77 Alexis Guardia, 'Structural Transformations in Chile's Economy and in its System of External Relations', in Sideri (ed.) *Chile 1970–73*, p. 96.
78 Solon Barraclough and José Antonio Fernández, *Diagnóstico de la Reforma Agraria* (México, 1974), p. 107.
79 Bitar, *Transición, Socialismo y Democracia*, p. 189.
80 World Bank, *Chile: An Economy in Transition* (Washington, D.C., 1980), p. 87.
81 Ramos, 'Inflation in Chile', in Sideri (ed.) *Chile 1970–73*, p. 358.
82 World Bank, *Chile*, p. 79.
83 ODEPLAN, *Informe Económico Anual 1971* (Santiago, 1972), pp. 184, 187.
84 Bitar, *Transición, Socialismo y Democracia*, pp. 186–87.
85 ODEPLAN, *Informe*, p. 293.
86 See speech by Senator Rafael Moreno (CDP) in *Diario de Sesiones del Senado*, Sess. 43, 17 July 1973, pp. 1512–14.
87 Barraclough, *Diagnóstico*, p. 55.
88 Ibid., p. 113.
89 Ibid., p. 69.
90 Ibid., p. 255.
91 Interview with Julio Benítez, acting Secretary-General of the Socialist Party, *Chile Hoy*, 35 (1973), pp. 29, 32.
92 Alberto Martínez, 'The Industrial Sector: Areas of Social and Mixed Property in Chile', in Sideri (ed.) *Chile 1970–73*, ed.

Sideri, p. 230.
93 Bitar, *Transición, Socialismo y Democracia*, p. 271.
94 See interview with Fernando Flores, Economic Minister, in *Chile Hoy*, 31 (1973), pp. 29–31.
95 Martínez, 'The Industrial Sector', in Sideri (ed.), *Chile 1970–73*, p. 238.
96 Ibid., p. 245.
97 See Sergio Bitar, 'Efecto de las Areas de Propiedad Social y Mixta en la Industria Chilena', *El Trímestre Económico*, 41 (1974), p. 548.
98 Ibid., p. 549.

Chapter 14

1 See *Tercer Mensaje del Presidente Allende Ante el Congreso Nacional, 21 May, 1973*, p. 793.
2 Official statistics on rates of unionisation actually underestimate the real proportion of the labour force in unions. For they are based on the total active population and not on the number of workers legally allowed to form unions. Also, they do not take into account the 'illegally' organised workers in the public sector. It has been estimated that in 1969 the real rate of unionisation was around 30%. See Alan Angell, *Politics and the Labour Movement in Chile* (London, 1972), pp. 43–5.
3 Emir, Sader, *Movilización de Masas y Sindicalización en el Gobierno U.P.* (Sántiago, 1973), p. 37.
4 Ibid., p. 36.
5 Ibid., pp. 11–12.
6 Compare Arturo Valenzuela, *The Breakdown of Democratic Regimes: Chile* (Baltimore, Maryland, 1978), p. 27, with Henry A. Landsberger and Tim McDaniel, 'Hypermobilization in Chile', *World Politics*, 28 (1976), pp. 502–41.
7 Sader, *Movilización*, pp. 5–6.
8 *El Siglo*, 27 June 1971, p. 4.
9 Sader, *Movilización*, p. 14.
10 Ibid., p. 15. On strikes during the Frei administration see Valenzuela, *Breakdown*, pp. 32–33.
11 Solon Barraclough and José Antonio Fernández, *Diagnóstico de la Reforma Agraria* (México, 1974), pp. 196–98.
12 Ibid., p. 180.
13 Brian Loveman, *Struggle in the Countryside: Politics and Rural Labor in Chile, 1919–1973* (Bloomington, Indiana, 1976), p. 289.

14 For an outline of the government's participation scheme, see ODEPLAN, *Informe Económico Anual 1971* (Santiago, 1972), pp. 66–68.

15 Barraclough, *Diagnóstico*, p. 203.

16 Ibid., pp. 205–12.

17 On CERAS, see Ibid., pp. 193–5.

18 ODEPLAN, *Informe*, pp. 66–8.

19 Cristobal Kay, 'Agrarian Reform and the Transition to Socialism', in Philip O'Brien (ed.), *Allende's Chile*, ed. Philip O'Brien (New York, 1976), pp. 86–89.

20 Barraclough, *Diagnóstico*, p. 207.

21 Loveman, *Struggle in the Countryside*, p. 287.

22 Barraclough, *Diagnóstico*, p. 207.

23 For an outline of the structure of the vigilance committees, see ODEPLAN, *Informe*, pp. 91–92.

24 Alan Angell, *Political Mobilisation and Class Alliances in Chile, 1970–1973* (Oxford, 1978), p. 43.

25 ODEPLAN, *Informe*, pp. 72–92.

26 Juan G. Espinosa and Andrew S. Zimbalist, *Economic Democracy: Workers' Participation in Chilean Industry 1970–1973* (New York, 1978), p. 53.

27 Michael Raptis, *Revolution and Counter-Revolution in Chile: A Dossier on Workers' Participation in the Revolutionary Process* (London, 1974), p. 28.

28 Espinosa, *Economic Democracy*, p. 55.

29 Manuel Barrera, Gustavo Aranda and Jorge Díaz, *El Cambio Social en una Empresa del APS* (Santiago, n.d.), p. 24.

30 See Barrera, *El Cambio Social*, p. 28 and Peter Winn, 'Workers into Managers: Workers Participation in the Chilean Textile Industry', in Jorge Dandler, Nicholas Hopkins and June Nash (eds.), *Popular Participation in Social Change* (The Hague, 1976), p. 599.

31 Barrera, *El Cambio Social*, p. 29.

32 Espinosa, *Economic Democracy*, pp. 141–44.

33 Ibid., pp. 158–162.

34 Winn, 'Workers into Managers' in Dandler et al. (eds.) *Popular Participation*, p. 586.

35 Manuel Barrera, *Participación de Trabajadores en la Gestión de las Empresas de Chile: Una Experiencia Histórica* (Santiago, 1979), p. 19.

36 Barrera, *Cambio Social*, pp. 27, 40–41.

37 Orlando Millas, 'La Clase Obrera en las Condiciones del Gobierno Popular', *Principios*, 145 (1972), pp. 34–36.

38 On Allende's health policies see Peter Hakim and Giorgio Solimano, *Development, Reform and Malnutrition in Chile* (Cambridge, Mass., 1978), *passim*.

39 See Manuel Antonio Garretón, *Chile: Cronología del Periodo 1970–1973, Vol. I* (Santiago, 1978), pp. 172–74.

40 *El Siglo*, 25 December 1971, p. 1.

41 Garretón, *Chile*, pp. 233–34.

42 *El Mercurio*, 25 July 1972, pp. 1, 16, 19.

43 *El Siglo*, 1 August 1972, p. 3.

44 See statement on the Peoples' Assembly by the Concepción branch of the Socialist Party in *Diario El Sur*, 26 July 1972, reprinted in *Diario de Sesiones del Senado*, Sess. 45, 1 August 1972, p. 2248.

45 See Patricia Santa Lucía, 'The Industrial Working Class and the Struggle for Power in Chile', in O'Brien (ed), *Allende's Chile*, pp. 161–5. On the *cordones*, see also Ian Roxborough, Philip O'Brien and Jackie Roddick, *Chile: The State and Revolution* (London, 1977), pp. 161–86.

46 On *commandos comunales*, see Eduardo Santa Cruz, 'Comandos Comunales: Organos de Poder del Pueblo', *Punto Final*, 31 July 1973, supplement.

47 Ernesto Pastrana and Mónica Threlfall, *Pan, Techo y Poder* (Buenos Aires, 1974), pp. 110–13.

48 Santa Lucía, 'The Industrial Working Class', in *Allende's Chile*, O'Brien (ed.), pp. 147–48.

49 *El Siglo*, 1 August, 1972, p. 3.

50 *El Siglo*, 6 February 1973, p. 3.

51 *Tercer Mensaje*, p. XXXI.

52 Speech by Salvador Allende to the National Congress of the Popular Unity, *Chile Hoy*, 55 (1973), p. 7.

53 See Julio Cesar Jobet, *El Partido Socialista de Chile, Vol. 2* (Santiago, 1971), p. 128.

54 See Raptis, *Revolution and Counter-Revolution*, pp. 148–49.

55 Ibid., pp. 144–47.

56 See interview with union leader Galvarino Escorza of the Communist Party, in *Chile Hoy*, 61 (1973), p. 9.

57 *El Siglo*, 14 August 1973, p. 9.

58 *Chile Hoy*, 61 (1973), p. 9.

59 Nelson Gutiérrez, 'El Poder Popular y la Lucha del Proletariado Chileno', *Punto Final*, 14 August 1973, p. 11.

60 Interview with Miguel Enríquez, *Chile Hoy*, 59 (1973), p. 29.

61 See MIR, Les Commandos Communaux: Organes de Pouvoir Organes de Combat des Masses', in *Le MIR et la Lutte de*

Classes (Paris, 1974), p. 31. This document was originally published in Chile in July 1973.

62 Raptis, *Revolution and Counter-Revolution*, p. 107.
63 Ibid., pp. 108–09.
64 For the political debate on Allende's decision to grant amnesty to the MIR, see *Diario de Sesiones del Senado*, Sess. 23, 19 January 1971, pp. 817–18.
65 In the CUT elections held in May 1972, the MIR polled only 1% of the vote. See Barrera, *Participación*, p. 15.
66 See Roxborough (et al.), *Chile*, pp. 216–17.

Index